T0138651

David W. South

THE
COMPUTER AND INFORMATION SCIENCE AND TECHNOLOGY

ABBREVIATIONS AND ACRONYMS DICTIONARY

CRC Press

Boca Raton   Ann Arbor   London   Tokyo

Library of Congress Cataloging-in-Publication Data

Catalog record is available from the Library of Congress.

No claim to original U.S. Government works
International Standard Book Number 0-8493-2444-0
Library of Congress Card Number 00-00000
Printed in the United States of America   1 2 3 4 5 6 7 8 9 0
Printed on acid-free paper

This book is dedicated to my family...

To my father, William W. South, who died on April 29, 1993, at the age of 74, and to my surviving mother, Mary N. South. I believe that when my father died, he knew that I would do just fine throughout the course of my life. He always wanted the best. Dad, I tried my hardest and will keep on trying. I love you and I miss you. If it were not for the help and enduring patience of my parents, my endeavors as a professional writer could never have materialized.

To my son, David, my brother Jim, my sisters Shirley and Judy.

Additionally, I would like to dedicate this book to one of the "pioneers" in abbreviations dictionaries, Mr. Ralph De Sola, author of *Abbreviations Dictionary*, 8th edition. Mr. De Sola (died in 1993) was a humanitarian; I am certain that he will be missed by those who knew him, and by his readers — a great loss to the humanities.

Contents

Preface

An *acronym* is a word derived from the first or most important letters in a multi-word descriptive noun or other expression, often serving as a mnemonic whose letters recall the actual words in the term. Additionally, an acronym is not necessarily the same as an *abbreviation*, which is not, nor cannot be, "pronounced" as a word. Computer terminology is rife with acronyms; three common examples are BASIC (Beginner's All-purpose Symbolic Instruction Code), RAM (Random Access Memory), and DOS (Disk Operating System). Some acronyms, through frequent usage become words in their own right such as "laser" for example. At one time it was written as LASER, for Light Amplification by Stimulated Emission of Radiation.

How important is knowing the definition or meaning of an acronym, or some other type of short form, used in daily communication? It is as important as the time lost searching for or the consequence of not finding it. Acronym agglomeration is an affliction of the technological age. This book will help you cope with acronym addicts who find it impossible to resist using acronyms both in spoken language and in writing. This book offers both professional and layperson, the meanings of important and interesting acronyms in the broad area of computing and information science industry.

The acronyms contained in this book were created to save time and space and eliminate unnecessary repetition and wordage. The complexity of today's projects, systems, and equipment have necessitated descriptive, sentence-length nomenclature that is not only long but burdensome. The use of an acronym can reduce this nomenclature to a few, easy-to-remember letters without loss of its communicative value.

Acronymic appeal and acceptance have been so universal within the industry that the easy-to-remember acronym is becoming difficult to decipher.

In preparing this work, it was necessary to consult many sources, since the choice of clear and concise definitions is always a difficult task. My selection of terms (abbreviations, acronyms, initialisms, codes, designators, symbols, etc.) has been based mainly on the reading of current literature, including some of the foremost engineering and technical journals and periodicals, and information received from various companies and organizations. Many well known but little used terms may be found. However, I have made an honest attempt not to include too many of those terms which may be considered as outdated.

As the computers and information science revolution spreads into increasing numbers of offices, organizations, institutions, factories and homes, an *alphabet soup* language comes with it. This revolution forces contemporary conversation and communication media to be filled with undefined short-forms, and a host of specialized jargon. Anyone from another discipline, industry, profession or occupation can be baffled by such language.

This first edition will be of value to communicators, writers, librarians, media personnel, editors, students, sales representatives, various engineers, scientists and technologists, executives and managers in technical fields, programmers, systems analysts, anyone who owns or is planning to buy a computer and any layperson who is interested in the short forms of communication which has swept the 90s.

David W. South

i

How to Use This Book

To increase the economy of presentation, the author decided to incorporate some stylistic conventions which are worth noting. The completeness of a listing is dependent upon both the nature of the term and the amount of information the author was able to obtain during his research.

Arrangement of Terms

The terms (i.e., acronyms/abbreviations) appear throughout this reference in **bold face type** and are listed in alphabetical order, on a "letter-by-letter" basis, and in numerical order. For entries containing the same letter, lowercase precedes capital; roman precedes italics (rarely used in this reference); unpunctuated precedes punctuated (rarely used).

The following connectives, characters and symbols are ignored and treated as blanks in the alphabetical arrangement; * (asterisk); & (ampersand); @ (at sign); : (colon); $ (dollar sign); / (diagonal or forward slash); = (equal sign); - (hyphen or minus sign); + (plus sign); # (pound sign), etc.

In the case of terms which incorporate parenthetical plural endings (rarely used), the parenthesis will be ignored.

Separation of Entries

Where terms listed throughout this reference involve multiple entries (expanded meanings/phrases), the alternative expansions of that particular term have been separated by a semicolon (;).

Capitalization

The use of capital, lowercase, or the combination of both uppercase and lower case letters for the expanded or spelled-out versions of abbreviations or acronyms essentially has never been "universally" agreed upon. Throughout most instances in this reference, the author has tried to use the preferred or most commonly used forms. This was primarily accomplished by comparing a multitude of different sources, and then deriving at a final conclusion on its expanded form. However, I have tried to include as many variations to the spelled-out forms as possible that was noticed during research. When an abbreviated form involves the use of proper names, then capital letters are the correct choice. Other than that, the selected form of capitalization that has been adopted throughout this work is more a matter of "manuscript style", or "book presentation" than of literary correctness. The author therefore advises the readers of this reference to adhere to standard practices when he or she is using acronyms/abbreviations in ones writing communications---the trend to capitalize only those letters that would normally be capitalized: proper names, companies, persons, institutions, committees, countries, important words in titles and when referring to the name of a commercial product (or trademarks).

Punctuation

Short forms are devised to save time and space and to overcome the necessity of repeating long words and phrases. Punctuation is avoided as much as possible in modern practice unless the form is taken from Latin or there is some conventional use demanding punctuation, as with academic degrees and a few governmental designations.

Italics

Items from non-English languages, as well as titles of books, databases, databanks, journals, newsletters, periodicals, and other such publications, are usually set in italic type.

Symbols

Frequently used special signs and symbols such as the chemical elements and others employed in engineering and technical literature have been included in this reference. All are listed alphabetically throughout this work. These symbols are properly identified in parenthetical form.

Trade names

Also included are numerous corporate and proprietary acronyms/abbreviations that seem to have become rather commonplace terminology in various technical literature. Whenever possible entries that refer to the name of a commercial product, the company responsible for its development, production, or marketing of that product has been given. For the readers' convenience, there are interesting tradenames, which can be found in the Appendix called **Trade names**.

General Format and Arrangement of Entries

Below are hypothetical entries illustrating the format of each term and definition found throughout this reference. A typical entry may provide the following information:

Example

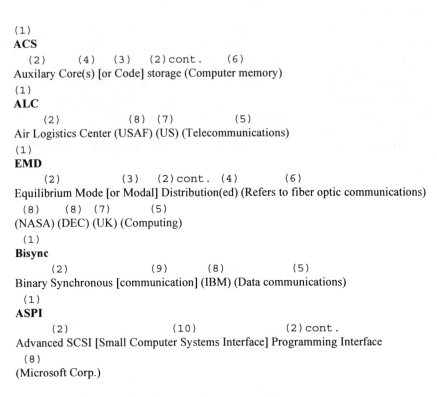

(1)
ACS
   (2)   (4)   (3)   (2) cont.   (6)
Auxilary Core(s) [or Code] storage (Computer memory)
(1)
ALC
    (2)   (8) (7)   (5)
Air Logistics Center (USAF) (US) (Telecommunications)
(1)
EMD
    (2)   (3)   (2) cont. (4)   (6)
Equilibrium Mode [or Modal] Distribution(ed) (Refers to fiber optic communications)
  (8)   (8) (7)   (5)
(NASA) (DEC) (UK) (Computing)
 (1)
Bisync
    (2)   (9)   (8)   (5)
Binary Synchronous [communication] (IBM) (Data communications)
 (1)
ASPI
    (2)   (10)   (2) cont.
Advanced SCSI [Small Computer Systems Interface] Programming Interface
 (8)
(Microsoft Corp.)

(1) Abbreviation/Acronym/Initialism/Symbol, etc. (the "Terms")
(2) Expanded or translation of, meaning/phrase (what the "short form" stands for).
(3) Alternate acceptable word and/or words (occasionally used in an expanded meaning/ phrase).
(4) Alternate acceptable spelling, or plural form of word (which is part of the expanded meaning/phrase).
(5) Subject area or area of application
(6) Definition/explanation/notation, etc.
(7) Location or country (or language) of origin
(8) Source or source code, which is usually in an "all-caps", abbreviated form (decoded at the end of the Appendix under "Key to Source Codes").
(9) Implied and nonrepresented elements (occasionally, a term implies additional wording whose designators do not appear in the term itself, or the description in question contains more clarifying information).
(10) Compounded terms (entries in their expanded forms are sometimes composites of other acronyms/abbreviations, consisting generally of a root or base acronym and a prefix, suffix, or other appropriate modifier [or secondary] acronym. In some cases, the "acronym within the acronym" have been expanded in their full meaning. These expansions have been primarily reserved [for the sake of economy] for those that are more obscure or less common in nature. These, along with many of the more commonly used acronyms can be found in the Key to Source codes, under the heading **Common Abbreviations Within Definitions**. All such acronyms appearing within the expanded meaning/phrase, have been placed within square brackets [...]).

Commonly Used Terms and Prefixes

The following are definitions of frequently encountered terms and prefixes used throughout this reference.

abort. To cancel, or terminate, a program, command, or procedure while it is in progress.

access. To retrieve data or program instructions from a secondary storage device or some other on-line computer device.

adapter. A device that allows compatibility between different equipment.

address. The term most generally used to refer (in some way) to a location within the computer memory.

application. Task to be performed by a computer program or system.

architecture. A general term referring to the structure of all or part of a computer system.

automatic. Pertaining to a process or device that, under specified conditions, functions without intervention by a human operator.

bandwidth. In data communications, the difference between the highest and lowest frequencies of a band. The term is used as a measure of the capacity of a communication channel; measurement, expressed in cycles per second (hertz) or bits per second (bps), of the amount of information that can flow through a channel. In computer networks, greater bandwidth indicates faster data-transfer capability.

batch. A group of records or programs that is considered a single unit for processing on a computer.

baud. A unit for measuring data transmission speed.

bit. Short for "binary digit"; either 1 or 0 in the binary number system. The smallest unit of information recognized by a computer and its associated equipment.

buffer. A memory or CPU area used for temporary storage of data records during input or output operations.

byte. Eight contiguous "bits", the fundamental data unit of personal computers, capable of storing a single alphabetic, numeric or special character of information.

compiler. A computer program that converts or translates a high-level, user-written language into a language that a computer can understand.

database (or data base). A collection of interrelated data values (logically related records or files). In more common usage the word often means any accessible collection of information.

environment. In a computing context, this is more likely to refer to the hardware and/or operating system, or mode of operation for application programs (e.g., Microsoft Windows and the Apple Macintosh operating system are referred to as "windowing environments", another example would be "in a time-sharing environment") than to physical conditions of temperature, humidity, and so forth. But either kind of environment may affect operational efficiency.

Ethernet. One of the architectures for local area networks. A type of network system that allows audio and video information to be carried as well as computer data.

field. A group of characters that is treated as a single unit of information that represents something meaningful.

file. A collection of related records treated as a basic unit of storage.

gain. A general term used to denote an increase in signal power or voltage produced by an amplifier in transmitting a signal from one point to another.

giga. A prefix indicating one billion (10^9). A term common to computer users when referencing a measured capacity of extremely high-density computer media.

hardware. The physical components of a computer system, such as the electronic components, boards, and including any peripheral devices such as keyboards, monitors, printers, modems, etc., and any other type equipment that make up your computer's system—distinguished from the programs (software) that generally tell these components what to do and how to perform.

integrate. The process of putting various components together to form a harmonious computer system.

interactive. Used to describe a system or a mode of working in which there is a response to operator instructions as they are input. Hence, refers to a user's ability to interact (i.e., conversational manner) with the workstation, to create, delete, or modify instructions, questions and commands in real-time (immediate feedback).

interface. The point of meeting between a computer and an external entity, whether an operator, a peripheral device, or a communications medium.

kilo. A prefix indicating one thousand (10^3). A term common to computer users when referencing a measured capacity of computer media and memory.

library. A collection of programs kept with a computer system and made available for processing purposes.

local. In data communications, pertaining to devices that are attached (close at hand; at one's own location) to a controlling unit by cables, rather than by means of a communications line (data links); it is the opposite of "remote".

logical. 1. Involving or used in logic. 2. Conceptual or virtual, or involving conceptual entities, as opposed to physical or actual.

macro. A set or sequence of keyboard keystrokes and computer instructions recorded and saved under a "short-key code". When the key code is typed (generally executable as a single command), the program carries out the instructions of the saved macro. Macros are very useful for automating tedious and often-repeated tasks.

mainframe. A large, centralized computer, or computer facility. A multi-user computer designed to meet the computing needs of larger organizations.

media. The plural form of medium. A collective word for the physical material, such as paper, disk, microfilm, cassettes, and tape. In short, all forms of computer information secondary storage devices (medium).

mega. A prefix indicating one million (10^6). A term common to computer users when referencing a measured capacity of high-density computer media and memory.

micro. A prefix indicating one millionth (10^{-6}).

network. An arrangement of two or more interconnected computer systems to facilitate the exchange of information in order to perform a specific function.

node. A junction of some type. On local area networks, a connection point that can create, receive, or repeat a message.

offline (or off-line). The state in which a device cannot communicate with or be controlled by a computer.

online (or on-line). Connected directly to the computer's CPU so that input, output, data access, and computation can take place without further human intervention.

packet. In general usage, a unit of information transmitted as a whole from one device to another on a network. A block of data for data transmission.

peripheral. Any device, including I/O devices and backing store, that is connected to a computer. Such devices would include: disk drives, printers, modems, plotters, keyboards, joy sticks, mice, graphics tablets, and monitors.

program. A complete sequence of instructions, text and routines that can be executed by a computer to completely perform a desired operation. Hence, the term "program" implies a degree of completeness.

protocol. A set of conventions, rules, or standards (agreements) governing the exchange of information between computer systems.

quantum. The smallest unit of measure employed in a system.

query. To ask for information. The process of extracting data from a database and presenting it for use.

queue. A priority-ranked collection of tasks (i.e., group of items) waiting to be performed or acted upon by the computer.

real-time. The term is descriptive of computer transaction- processing systems that receive and process data quickly enough to produce output to control, direct, or affect the outcome of an ongoing activity or process, such as a point-of-sale register/terminal transaction that would provide instantaneous update of inventory records as retail sales are transacted throughout the coarse of the day, or week.

record. A data structure that is a set or collection of related data fields (elements), each with its own name and type, that a program treats (stores) as a unit.

remote. In its general sense, not in the immediate vicinity; physically distant from a local computer, such as a video display terminal or printer. A term used to describe a computer, process, system, or other device located in another place (room, building, or city) that is accessible through some type of cable or communications link, as in remote job entry, remote sensing, and remote data-access facilities.

sequential access. A method of storing or retrieving information that requires the program to start reading at the beginning and continue until it finds the desired data. Also called serial access.

software. A generic term for those components of a computer system that are intangible rather than physical. In simpler terms, the programs or instructions that tell a computer what to do.

table. In programming, a collection of data in which each item is uniquely identified by a label, its position relative to the other items or by some other means.

terminal. A general name for input/output peripheral devices that have keyboards, video displays, and/or printers, commonly used with multiuser systems.

user. In its general sense, anyone who owns or utilizes a computer for problem solving or data manipulation; anyone who requires the services of a computer system.

virtual. In computing, a term used to describe a device or service that is perceived to be what it is not in actuality. A simulated or conceptual environment, which, as a result, may refer to virtually anything.

wideband. In data communications, a channel wider in bandwidth than a voice-grade channel.

A

a

absolute; accumulator; acceleration; acre; adder; address; alphabetic; ampere; amplitude; analog; analysis; angstrom; area; anode; asynchronous; attribute; automatic; atto (SI prefix denoting 10^{-18})

A

Angstrom (Alternate form is Å); Absolute (Temperature scale); Ampere (SI unit for current); Argon (Symbol); Gain (Symbol for); Area of a plane surface (Symbol);

Å

Ångstrom (Metric unit of length denoting 10^{-8} cm)

A+

A-plus; A-positive (Symbol for positive [side] terminal of an A-battery or positive polarity of other sources of filament-voltage in a vacuum-tube circuit

A-

A-minus; A-negative (Symbol for negative [side] terminal of an A-battery or negative polarity of other sources of filament-voltage in a vacuum-tube circuit)

A/D

Analog/Digital [or Analog to Digital]

A/DC

Analog to Digital Converter

A:drive

A common designation for the first floppy disk drive in DOS and OS/2

A/I

Artificial Intelligence (Factory automation)

A&I

Abstracting and Indexing

A/M

Amperes per Meter

a/n

alphanumeric

A/Q

Amendment/Query

A&R

Analysts and Researchers

A&T

Assemble and Test

A/UX

Apple Computer's version of the UNIX operating system, provided for the Macintosh II and based on the AT&T System V

A/V

Audio/Visual

AA

AA voltaic cell; Arithmetic Average (IEEE); Asset Amount; Author Affiliation (Searchable fields); Auto Answer

AAA

AAA voltaic cell; *Astronomy and Astrophysics Abstracts* (German Database, Astronomisches Rechen-Institut)

AAAB

American Association of Architectural Bibliographers

AAAI

American Association for Artifical Intelligence

AAAS

American Association for the Advancement of Science

AAB

Analytical Abstract (Searchable field)

AAC

Automatic Aperture Control

AACC

American Automatic Control Council

AACOBS

Australian Advisory Council on Bibliographic Services

AACR

Anglo-American Cataloguing Rules

AAcS

Advanced Academic System (IBM)

AACS

Advanced Automatic Compilation System; Asynchronous Address Communications Systems

AADC

All-Application Digital Computer

AADE

American Association of Dental Publishers

AADS

Automatic Applications Development System

AAE

American Association of Engineers

AAEC

Australian Atomic Energy Commission

AAED

Academic American Encyclopedia Database

AAEE
American Association of Electrical Engineers

AAIMS
An Analytical Information Management System

AAL
Absolute Assembly Language (Computer programming language); ATM [Asynchronous Transfer Mode] Adaption Layer

AALL
American Association of Law Librarians

AAM
Air-to-Air Missile

AAME
American Association of Microprocessor Engineers

AAMRS
Automated Ambulatory Medical Record System

A and I
Abstracting and Indexing

AAO
Authorized Acquisition Objective

AAP
Analyst Assistance Program; Associative Array Processor; Attached Applications Processor; Association of American Publishers

AAPL
An Array Processing Language (Computer programming language)

AARLMP
Afro-American Resources and Library Manpower Project (Columbia University)

AARP
AppleTalk Address Resolution Protocol (Apple Computer Inc, US)

AARS
Automatic Address Recognition System [or Subsystem]. (Computers)

AAS
Advanced Administrative System; Annual Authorizations Service; Advanced Automation System; Arithmetic Assignment Statement

AASF
Advanced Address Space Facility (IBM)

AASL
American Association of School Librarians of the *ALA*

AATC
Automatic Air Traffic Control system

AAU
Address Arithmetic Unit (Computers)

AAV
Alternate Access Vendor

AAVD
Automatic Alternate Voice Data

ab
abstract (used to define a searchable field in an online search [OLS])

AB
Address Bus (Computing); Automated Bibliography

ABA
American Banker's Association; American Bookseller's Association; Antiquarian Bookseller's Association; Australian Bookseller's Association

ABAC
Association of Business and Administrative Computing

ABACUS
Agents and Brokers Automated Computer Users System; Association of Bibliographical Agencies in Britain, Australia, Canada and US; AB Atomenergi - Computerized User-oriented Services (Sweden)

ABANK
Annual State Databank, Kentucky (Databank)

ABB
Array of Building Blocks

ABBS
Apple-Based Bulletin Board Service

ABC
Atanasoff-Berry Computer (First digital calculating machine that used vacuum tubes); Approach By Concept; Adaptable Board Computer (Signetics, US); American Broadcasting Company; Australian Broadcasting Commission; Automatic Bandwidth Control (IEEE); Automatic Brightness Control (IEEE); Automatic Block Controller; Accounting By Computer

ABC-Clio
American Bibliographical Center - Clio Inc. (Database originator)

ABCA
American Business Communication Association

ABCD
Association of Better Computer Dealers

ABCS
Automatic Base Communication Systems

ABD
Association Belge de Documentation (Also BVD)

ABDL
Automatic Binary Data Link

ABE
Arithmetic Building Element (Computing)

ABEL
Acid/Base Electrolyte Disorders

ABEND
Abnormal End(ing), of task (Computing)

ABEP
Advanced Burst Error Processor

ABES
Association for Broadcast Engineering Standards (US)

ABF
Association des Bibliothécaires Francais (Association of French librarians)

ABFD
Affordable Basic Floppy Disk

ABI
Application Binary Interface (AT&T); *Association des Bibliothèques Internationales*

ABI/INFORM
Abstracted Business Information/Information needs (Database on business management and administration)

ABIPC
Abstract Bulletin of the Institute of Paper Chemistry (US)

ABIX
Australian Business Index (Database on AUSINET)

ABL
Architectural Block diagram Language; Atlantic Basic Language; *Atlas* Basic Language (computer programming languages, See also *ATLAS*); Automatic Bootstrap Loader (Computing)

ABL
Accepted Batch Listing; Architectural Blockdiagram Language; Automatic Bootstrap Loader

ABLISS
Association of British Library and Information Science Schools

ABM
Asynchronous Balance(d) Mode (IBM);

Automated Batch Mixing; Accunet Bandwidth Manager (AT&T): Anti-Ballistic Missile (DOD)

ABMPS
Automated Business Mail Processing System

ABMS
Automated Batch Manufacturing System

ABN
Australian Bibliographic Network (National Library of Australia's shared centralized cataloguing facility)

ABNO
All But Not Only (Information retrieval system mode)

ABOA
Australian Bibliography On Agriculture (Database on AUSINET)

ABOL
Adviser Business Oriented Language (Computer programming language)

ABP
Actual Block Processor (IBM); Advanced Business Processor (Datapoint Corp., US)

ABPA
Australian Book Publisher's Association

ABPS
Automated Bill Payment System

ABR
Automatic Backup Restore

ABRD
Auto Baud Rate Detector

abs
absolute

Abs key
In Lotus 1-2-3, the F4 function key (Lotus 1-2-3 is a full-powered spreadsheet program)

ABS
Abstract; Air Baring Surface (Computing, Part of *R/W* head in a magnetic disc unit); Automatic Bibliographic Services

ABSLDR
Absolute Loader

ABSTI
Advisory Board on Scientific and Technical Information (Canada)

ABSW
Association of British Science Writers

ABT
Australian Broadcasting Tribunal; Automatic Bench Test

ABU
Asia-Pacific Broadcasting Union

ABW
Advise By Wire

Ac
Actinium (Symbol)

AC
Access Control (IEEE); Acoustic Coupler; Actual Count; Adaptive Control; Address Counter (Computing); Alternating Current; Automatic Configuration; Automatic Control; Accession Number (Searchable field); Accumulator; Activity Code (Searchable field); Analog Computer; Area Code; Assignee Code; Authority Code (Searchable field); Automatic Checkout; Automatic Computer

ac (AC)
accumulator

AC/DC
Alternating Current to Direct Current

AC&WS
Air Control and Warning System

ACA
American Communications Association; Asynchronous Communications Adapter; Adjacent Channel Attenuation (IEEE); Alternating Current Amperes; Application Control Architecture

ACAC
Associate Committee on Automatic Control (National Research Council, Canada)

ACAM
Augmented Content-Addressed Memory

ACAMI
Alternate Channel/Alternate Mark Inversion

ACAMPS
Automated Communications And Message Processing System

ACAP
Advanced Computer for Array Processing; Automatic Circuit Analysis Program

ACAPS
Automated Cost And Planning System

ACARD
Advisory Council for Applied Research and Development (Advisory body to government, UK)

ACAS
Airborne Collision-Avoidance System; American Computer Appraisal Service

ACB
Access Control Block (IBM); Adapter Control Block; Asynchronous Communications Base

ACBGEN
Application Control Block Generation

ACBR
Accumulator Buffer Register

acc
accept; accumulate; accumulator

ACC
Accumulator; Amateur Computer Club (UK); Association of Computer Clubs (UK); Asynchronous Communications Control; Asynchronous Communications Controller; Automatic Color Control

ACCA
Asynchronous Communications Control Attachment

ACCAP
Autocoder-to-COBOL [Common Business-Oriented Language] Conversion-Aid Program (IBM)

ACCAT
Advanced Command and Control Architectural Testbed

ACCC
Ad hoc Committee for Competitive Communication (US)

acce
acceptance

ACCEL
Automated Circuit Card Etching Layout (IEEE)

ACCESS
Aircraft Communication Electronic Signalling System (IEEE); Architect's Central Constructional Engineering Surveying Service (Greater London Council, UK); Architecture, Construction and Consulting Engineers Special Services (Information service, Stanton Municipal Library, Australia); Access Characteristics Estimation System; Argonne Code Center Exchange and Storage System (US Atomic Energy Commission); *Automated Catalog of Computer Equipment and Software Systems* (US Army); Automatic Computer-Controlled Electronic Scanning System (IEEE)

ACCI
Apportionment of Close Companies' Income (Expert system for tax specialism)

ACCIS
Advisory Committee for Coordination of Information Systems (UN)

ACCLAIM
Automated Circuit Card Layout and Implementation

ACCT
Ad Hoc Committee for Competitive Telecommunications

accum
accumulator

ACCWP
Acquisition, Cataloguing and Circulation Working Party, of the Aslib Computer Applications Group (UK)

ACD
Automatic Call Distribution (AT&T, switching system); Automatic Call Distribution System (IBM/Rolm); Automatic Call Director (AT&T); Automatic Call Distributor (Datapoint, US); Authorized Computer Distributors

ACDMS
Automated Control of a Document Management System

ACE
Adaptive Computer Experiment; Asynchronous Communication Element; Animated Computer Education; Automatic Computing Engine; Automated Computing Engine; Automatic Calculating Engine; Automatic Computer Evaluation (IEEE); Automatic Checkout Equipment; Adapter Communication Executive (TI); Advanced Computing Environment; Application Construction Environment; Application Control Environment

ACEA
Association of Computing in Engineering and Architecture

ACEC
American Consulting Engineers Council; *Ateliers de Constructions Electriques de Charleroi* (Belgium telecommunications equipment manufacturers)

ACES
Automated Code Evaluation System; Automated Circulation and Enquiry System (University of Aberdeen, UK)

ACF
Access Control Field; Advanced Communication(s) Function (IBM); *Les arrêts de la Cour Fédérale* (Canadian Department of Justice legal database); Authorization Control Facility (Computer access security software)

ACF/Vtam
Advanced Control Function/Virtual telecommunications access method (IBM)

ACFNAT
Advanced Communication Function Network (IBM)

ACG
Automatic Code Generator; Addressed Command Group (IEEE)

ACH
Association for Computers and the Humanities (International organization); Attempts per Circuit per Hour; Automated Clearing House(s)

ACI
Adjacent Channel Interference; Advanced Chip Interconnect; Alternating Current Inputs; Automatic Card Identification (IEEE)

ACIA
Asynchronous Communications Interface Adapter (Provides data formatting and control for data communications)

ACIC
Aeronautical Chart and Information Center (US Air Force)

ACID
Acceleration, Cruising, Idling, Deceleration; Automatic Cross-Referencing and Indexing Document Generator; Automated Classification and Interpretation of Data (Computer programming language); Automatic Classification and Identification of Data (IEEE)

ACITS
Advisory Committee on Information Technology Standardization (Commission of the European Communities [CEC])

a c k
acknowledge; acknowledgment (Control character)

ACK
Acknowledge (CCITT)

ACK1
Acknowledgement (i.e., message received OK—send next message)

ACKI
Acknowledge Input

ACKO
Acknowledge Output

ackt
acknowledgment

ACL

Access Control Language (IBM); Access Control List; Advanced CMOS [Complementary Metal-Oxide Semiconductor] Logic; Application Control Language (IEEE); Association for Computational Linguistics (US); *Atlas* Commercial Language; Audit Command Language (Computer programming languages); Automatic Cartridge Loader

ACLR

Access Control-Logging and Reporting

ACLS

American Council of Learned Societies

ACM

Advanced Composite Materials; Alterable Control Memory; Association for Computing Machinery; Associative Communications Multiplexer; Asynchronous Communication Control Module; Authorized Controlled Material; Address Calculation Machine (Honeywell-Bull, France); Analog Command Module

ACMAC

ACM [Association for Computing Machinery] Accreditation Committee

ACMS

Advance Configuration Management System; Application Control and Management System (DEC, a software product for the VAX)

ACMSC

ACM [Association for Computing Machinery] Standards Committee

ACN

Accession Number; *Alternative Catalog Newsletter* (John Hopkins University, US)

ACNS

Advanced Communications Network Service

ACO

Alternating Current Outputs; Automatic Call Originate [or Origination] (IBM)

ACOL

Application Control Language

ACOMPLIS

A Computerized London Information Service (Greater London Council, UK)

ACOPP

Abbreviated COBOL Preprocessor

ACORN

Associative Content Retrieval Network

(A.D. Little Inc. information system, US); Automatic Conversion and Test Score Analysis Package; Computer manufacturer (UK, not an acronym)

ACOS

Application Control Operating System

ACOUSTINT

Acoustical Intelligence

ACP

Accomplishment/Cost Procedure; Advanced Computational Processor; Airline Control Program (IBM); Ancillary Control Processor; Ancillary Control Process (DEC); Arithmetic and Control Processor (Computing); Associate Compute Professional

ACP/TF

Airline Control Program/ Transaction-processing Facility (IBM)

ACP/TPF

Airline Control Program/Transaction Processing Facility (Developed jointly in the 1950s by IBM and American Airlines)

ACPA

Association of Computer Programmers and Analysts (US)

ACPS

Attitude Control Propulsion System (NASA)

acpt

accept; acceptance

ACQM

Automatic Circuit Quality Monitoring

ACQS

Association of Consultant Quantity Surveyors

ACR

Access Control Register; Address Control Register; Alternate Recovery, or Alternate *CPU* Recovery; *American Computer Referal* (US databank)

ACRE

Automatic Call Recording Equipment

ACRIS

Aperture Card Raster Image Scanner (Versatec Company)

ACRIT

Advisory Committee for Research on Information Transfer (Committee reporting to Netherlands government)

ACRL

Association of College and Research Libraries of the *ALA*

ACRODABA

Acronym Data Base (Cancelled in 1973, US)

ACRTC

Advanced *CRT* Controller (Hitachi graphics chip)

ACS

Access Control Set; Advanced Communications Service (AT&T); Advanced Computer Series (Honeywell); Advanced Concepts Simulator (NASA); Advanced Computer System (IBM); Altos Computer Systems (US); American Chemical Society; *Les arrêts de la Cour Suprême* (Canadian Department of Justice legal database); Associated Computer System; Australian Computer Society; Automatic Call Sequencer; Automatic Checkout System; Automatic Control System; Auxiliary Core [or Code] Storage (Computer memory); Aberdeen Cable Services (UK cable TV network); Automated Communications Set; Advanced Control System (IBM); Alternating Current Synchronous (IEEE); Assembly Control System (IBM); Attitude Control System (IEEE); Automated Cartridge System; Asynchronous Communications Server

ACSAP

Automated Cross-Section Analysis Program

ACSE

Application Common Service Element; Association Control Service Element

ACSES

Automated Computer Science Education System

ACSI

Association Canadienne des Sciences de l'Information (Also known as *CAIS*)

ACSL

Advanced Continuous Simulation Language

ACSM

Assemblies, Components, Spare Parts and Materials

ACSTI

Advisory Committee for Scientific and Technical Information

ACSU

Advanced Channel Service Unit

ACSYS

Accounting Computer System (Burroughs Corp., US)

ACT

Active Control Technology (British Aerospace); Actuarial Programming Language; Acoustic Charge Transport; Advanced Composites Technology; Advanced Computing Technology; Advanced Communications Technology; Algebraic Compiler and Translator; Alternative Community Telephone (Sydney, Australia); Applied Computerized Telephony (H-P); Applied Computer Techniques (Computer manufacturer, UK); Analogical Circuit Technique; Automated Contingency Translator; Automatic Code Translator [or Translation] (IEEE); Adaptive Control of Thought (Theory of cognition, applied to some computer instruction systems)

ACTA

Automatic Computerized Transverse Axial

ACTD

Automatic Telephone Call Distribution

ACTEL

Alternating Current Thin-Film Electroluminescence

ACTIS

Auckland Commercial and Technical Information Service (New Zealand)

ACTO

Automatic Computing Transfer Oscillator (IEEE)

ACTOR

An object-oriented language for PCs from the Whitewater Group, Inc.

ACTRAN

Audocoder-to-COBOL [Common Business-Oriented Language] Translator [or Translation]

ACTS

Advanced Communications Technology Satellite (NASA); Application Control and Teleprocessing System; Automatic Computer Telex Services

ACTSU

Association of Computer Time-Sharing Users (US)

ACU

Address Control Unit; Arithmetic and Control Unit (IEEE); Association of Computer Users (US); Automatic Calling Unit

(Telecommunications device)

ACUA
Automatic Calling Unit Adapter

ACUG
Association of Computer Users Groups

ACUTA
Association of College and University Telecommunications Administrators

ACUTE
Accountants Computer Users Technical Exchange

ACV
Alternating Current Volts; Analysis of Covariance

ACVS
Automatic Computer Voltage Stabilizer

ACW
Access Control Word

ACWS
All-Canada Weekly Summaries (Canadian Law Book Ltd. legal database)

ad
address

AD
Analog to Digital; Applications Development (IBM)

AD/CYCLE
Applications Development/Cycle (IBM)

Ada (ADA)
Ada (Not an acronym, computer programming language, preferred form is Ada, **Note:** for purposes of this dictionary, upper-case lettering shall be used)

ADA
Ada (Not an acronym, computer programming language); Automatic Data Acquisition (IEEE)

ADABAS
Adaptable Data Base System (Software, DBMS)

ADAC
Analog to Digital/Digital to Analog Converter; Automatic Direct Analog Computer

ADACS
Automated Data Acquisition and Control System

ADAEX
Automatic Data Acquisition and Computer Complex

ADAL
Action Data Automation Language

ADAM
A Data Management system; Adaptive

Dynamic Analysis and Maintenance; Advanced Data Access Method; Advanced Data Management (Mitre Corp., US); Automatic Direct Access Management; Automatic Document Abstracting Method; Automatic Distance and Angle Measurement (IEEE)

ADAMS
Automated(ic) Dynamic Analysis of Mechanical Systems (Mechanical Dynamics Inc [MDI])

ADANET
ADABAS-Network (Software)

ADAPS
Automatic Display And Plotting System (IEEE); Automated Design and Packaging Service

ADaPSO
Association of Data-Processing Service Organizations (Canada and US)

ADAPSO
Association of Data-Processing Service Organizations (Canada and US)

ADAPT
Automatic Density Analysis Profile Technique

ADAPTICOM
Adaptive Communication

ADAPTS
Analog/Digital/Analog Process and Test System

ADAR
Advanced Design Array Radar (IEEE)

ADARTS
Ada-based Design Approach for Real-Time Systems; Automated Data Retrieval Technical System

ADAS
Automatic Disk Allocation System; Automatic Data Acquisition System (IEEE); Architecture Design and Assessment System

ADAT
Automatic Data Accumulation(or) and Transfer; Artificially Intelligent Devices and Techniques (UK company)

ADATE
Automatic Digital Assembly Test Equipment

ADAU
Auxiliary Data Acquisition Unit

ADB
Adjusted Debit Balance; book teleordering

system (Denmark); *Angendatenbank* (Steel making databank); Apple Desktop Bus (Apple Computer Inc, US)

ADBS
Advanced Data Base System; *Association des Documentalistes et des Bibliothécaires Spécialisé* (Also known as *AFDBS*, France)

ADBT
Access Decision Binding Time

ADC
Analog-to-Digital Converter(sion) (Computing); Area Distribution Center; Advise Duration and Charge (UK Telephone operator service); Airborne Digital Computer; Air Data Computer; Automatic Data Collection (IEEE)

ADCAD
Airways Data Collection and Distribution

ADCC
Asynchronous Data Communications Channel

ADCCP
Advanced Data Communications Control Procedure(s) (ANSI)

ADCIS
Association for the Development of Computer-based Instruction(al) Systems (US)

ADCOM
Association of Data Center Owners and Managers

ADCON
Analog-to-Digital Converter

ADCP
Advanced Data Communication Protocol

ADCR
Alternate Destination Call Redirection (AT&T)

ADCU
Advanced Data Communications Utility (IBM); Association of Data Communications Users (US)

ADCVR
Analog-Digital Converter

add
addition

ADD
Address (Location in computer memory); Automatic Document Distribution

ADDA
Australian Database Development Association

ADDAM
Adaptive Dynamic Decision Aiding Methodology

ADDAR
Automatic Digital Data Acquisition and Recording (IEEE)

ADDAS
Automatic Digital Data Assembly System

ADDDS
Automatic Direct Distance Dialing System (AT&T)

ADDF
Address Field

addit
additional

ADDM
Automated Drafting and Digitizing Machine

addr
adder; address; addressing

ADDR
Address Register

ADDS
Advanced Data Display System; Applied Digital Data Systems (NCR)

ADDSB
Address Disable

ADDSRTS
Automated Digitized Document Storage, Retrieval and Transmission System

ADE
Address Error; Advanced Data Entry; Applications Development Engineering; Applications Development Environment (IBM); Automated Debugging Environment (Applied Data Research [ADR], US); Automated Design Engineering (IEEE); Automated Drafting Equipment (IEEE); Automated Design Equipment; Automatic Data Entry

ADECAP
Automated Engineering Design Circuit Analysis Program

ADEM
Automatic Data Equalized Modem

ADEPS
Automated Engineering Documentation Preparation System

ADEPT
Advanced Development Prototype; Automated Direct Entry Packaging Technique; *ADA* Development Environment Portable

Tools (Computer project by Commission of the European Communities [CEC], Defense Documentation Center [DDC], US and International Computers Ltd [ICL], UK)

ADES
Automated Data Entry System; *Association de la Documentation Economique et Sociale* (Association for Economic and Social Documentation, France); Automatic Digital Encoding System (US Naval Ordnance language)

ADEX
Advanced Data Entry Executive

ADF
Application Development Facility (IBM); Automatic Direction Finder (IEEE); Automatic Document Feed(er)

ADI
Alternating Direction Implicit; Alternating Direction Iterative; American Documentation Institute (Know called *ASIS*); Automatic Direction Indicator; Attitude Director Indicator (IEEE); Analog Devices Inc. (US company)

ADIC
Analog to Digital Conversion

ADIF
Analog Data Information Format

ADIO
Analog-Digital Input-Output

ADIOS
Analog-Digital Input-Output System; Automatic Diagnosis Input-Output System; Automatic Digital Input-Output System (IEEE)

ADIP
Automated Data Interchange Systems Panel

ADIS
Air Defense Integrated System; Association for the Development of Instructional Systems (US); Automatic Data Interchange System (Teletype Corp., US)

ADIT
Analog-Digital Integration Translator; Automatic Detection and Integrated Tracking

adj
adjustment

ADJ
Adjacent (Term used in text search)

ADL
Automatic Data Link (IEEE); Automatic Data Logger; Arthur D. Little (US-based [European offices also] major information technology consultancy, also originates databases); Applications Development Language; Automated Disk Library

ADLC
Advanced Data Link Control(ler) (Link protocol)

ADLIB
Adaptive Library management system (Library automation software)

ADLIBUG
ADLIB Users Group

ADLIPS
Automatic Data Link Plotting System

ADLM
Account Data List Management

ADM3A
A terminal developed by Lear Siegler and used in the late 1970s and early 1980s

ADM
Activity Data Method; Adaptive Data Base Manager; Adaptable Data Manager (Hitachi Corp.); Add-Drop Multiplexer; Adaptive Delta Modulation; Advanced Development Models; Advanced Microdevices Inc. (US company)

ADMA
Advanced Direct Memory Access (Siemens)

ADMD
Administrative Management Domain

admin
administration; administrative; administrator

ADMIN
Automated Document Management Information Network

ADMINID
Administrative Identification

ADMIRE
Adaptive Decision Maker in an Information Retrieval Environment (Stanford University, US); Automated Diagnostic Maintenance Information Retrieval system (IEEE)

ADMIS
Automated Data Management Information System

admn
administration

admr
administrator

ADMS
Advanced Data Management System; Automated Document Management System; Automatic Data Message Switching (IEEE); Automatic Digital Message Switching

ADMSC
Automatic Digital Message Switching Center(s)

ADN
Advanced Digital Network (Bell)

ADO
Automatic Dial-Out; Address Only transfer

ADOC
Air Defense Operation Center(s) (USAF)

ADONIS
Automated Document Delivery Over Networked Information Service; Automatic Digital On-Line Instrumentation System; Automatic Document Online Information System (Document delivery system, Association of European Publishers)

ADOPT
Approach to Distributed Processing Transaction

ADOS
Advanced Diskette Operating System

ADP/TM
Office of Automatic Data Processing and Telecommunications Management

ADP
Airborne Data Processor; Acoustic Data Processor; Association of Database Producers (UK); Automatic Data Processing; Advanced Data Processing

ADP (Network Services)
Advanced Data processing Network Services (UK host)

ADPACS
Automated Data Processing and Communications Service

ADPC
Automatic Data Processing Center

ADPCM
Adaptive Differential Pulse Code Modulation; Association for Data Processing and Computer Management (US)

ADPE/S
Automatic Data Interchange System; Automatic Data Processing Equipment and

Software

ADPE
Automatic Data Processing Equipment; Auxiliary Data Processing Equipment

ADPP
Automatic Data Processing Program

ADPREP
Automatic Data Processing Resource Estimating Procedures

ADPS
Automatic Data Processing System

ADPSO
Automatic Data Processing Selection Office

adr
address; addressing

ADR
Alternate Data Retry; Analog-Digital Recorder; Automatical Digital Relay; Applied Data Research (Software house)

ADRA
Automatic Dynamic Response Analyzer

ADRAC
Automatic Digital Recording And Control (IEEE)

ADREN
Address Enable

ADRES
Army Data Retrieval System (US)

ADRMP
AutoDialed [or Automatic Dialer] Recorded Message Player(s)

ADROIT
Automated Data Retrieval and Operations Involving Timeseries

ADRS
A Departmental Reporting System (A report writer from IBM that runs on IBM mainframes); Adaptive Data Reporting System; Analog-to-Digital Data Recording System; Automatic Document Request Service

ADRT
Analog Data Recording Transcriber

ADS
Accurately Defined Systems; Activity Data Sheet; Advanced Debugging System; Analog Digital Subsystem; Autographed Document Signed; Automated Design System (Microsoft Corp, US); Advanced Digital Systems (US computer peripheral manufacturer); Agency Data System; Anker

Data Systems (Library automation system producer); Automatic Dependent Surveillance (FAA); Automatic Duplicating System (Itek Corp., US); Application Development System (Supports expert system development on IBM PC)

ADSATIS
Australian Defence Science and Technology Information System

ADSC
Automatic Digital Switching Center (IEEE)

ADSE
Alternative Delivery Schedule Evaluator

ADSEL
Address Selective

ADSG
Alternative Delivery Schedule Generator

ADSOL
Analysis of Dynamical Systems On-Line

ADSP
Advanced Digital Signal Processor

ADSS
Accelerated Data Storage Subsystem; Advanced Software System

ADSTAR
Automatic Document Storage And Retrieval

ADSUP
Automatic Data Systems Uniform Practices (Computer programming language)

ADT
Active Disk Table; Asynchronous Data Transceiver; Attribute Distributed Tree; Automatic Detection and Tracking; Autonomous Data Transfer; Application(s) Dedicated Terminal; Automatic Data Translator

ADTD
Association of Data Terminal Distributors (US)

ADTS
Automated Data and Telecommunications Service; Automatic Data Test System; Automated Driver's License Testing System

ADU
Asynchronous Data Unit (AT&T); Automatic Data Unit; Automatic Dialing Unit (IBM)

adv
advice; advise

ADVAST
Advanced Station

ADW
Application Development Workbench

ADX
Asymmetric Data Exchange; Automatic Data Exchange; Automatic Digital Exchange

AE
Application Entity; Arithmetic Element

AEA
Aircraft Electronics Association (US); American Electronics Association

AEBIG
Aslib Economics and Business Information Group

AEC
Automatic Energy Control; Automatic Exposure Control (Image Technology); Atomic Energy Commission (Defunct in 1975, now the Nuclear Regulatory Commission [NRC], US)

AECT
Association of [or for] Educational Communications and Technology (US)

AED
ALGOL Extended for Design; Association of Equipment Distributors; Automated Engineering Design (A form of CAD); Advanced Electronics Design (UK terminal manufacturer)

AED
Automated Engineering Design

AEDP
Association for Educational Data Processing (US)

AEDS
Advanced Electric Distribution System; Association for Educational Data Systems (US)

AEG
Active Element Group (In IC, storage call or logic gate); *Allgemeine Elektriziäts Gesellschaft* (German manufacturer)

AEGIS
Agricultural Ecological and Geographical Information System

AEI
Associated Electrical Industries (UK); *Australian Educational Index* (Database, Australian Council for Educational Research)

AEIMS
Administrative Engineering Information Management System

AEL
Accessible Emission Limit (Lasers); Audit Entry Language (Burroughs Corp., US)

AEM
Association of Electronic Manufacturers (US)

AEMS
American Engineering Model Society

AEN
Asynchronous Event Notification (ANSI)

AEON
Advanced Electronics Network (UK)

AEPS
Advanced Electronic Publishing System (British Printing and Communication Corp [BPCC] system)

AERIS
Automatic Electronic Ranging Information System

AEROS
Aerometric and Emissions Reporting System (EPA, databank)

AES
Audio Engineering Society (US); Atomic Emission Spectroscopy; Automatic Extraction System

AESA
Active Electronically Scanned Array

AESC
Aerospace and Electronic Systems Society (US); Automatic Electronic Switching Center

AESI
Australian Earth Sciences Information system (Database on AUSINET)

AESOP
Automated Engineering and Scientific Optimization Programming

AESS
Aerospace and Electronics Systems Society

AET
Acoustic Emission Testing; Automatic Exchange Tester

AETMS
Airborne Electronic Terrain Map System (USAF digital mapping system)

AEVS
Automatic Electronic Voice Switch

AEW
Airborne Early Warning

AEWIS
Army Electronic Warfare Information System (US)

AEWM
Acoustic Emission Weld Monitor

AEWS
Advanced Early Warning System

AF
Advanced Function (IBM); Arithmetic Flag; Aspect Factor; Audio Frequency (20 Hz to 20 kHz band); Affiliation of First author (A term used to define a searchable field)

AFAM
Automatic Frequency Assignment Model

AFC
Automatic Field Control; Automatic Frequency Control

AFCAC
Air Force Computer Acquisition Center (USAF)

AFCAD
Automatic File Control And Documentation

AFCAL
Association Francaise de Calcul (French computing association)

AFCC
Air Force Communications Command (USAF); Association of Federal Communications Consulting Engineers (US)

AFCEA
Armed Forces Communications and Electronics Association (US)

AFCET
Association Francaise pour la Cybernétique Economique et Technique

AFCS
Attitude Flight Control System

AFD
Automatic Fire Detection

AFDAC
Association Francaise pour la Documentation Automatique en Chimie (French information broker)

AFDBS
Association Francaise des Documentation et des Bibliothécaires Spécialisés (Also known as *ADBS*, French association of documentalists and special librarians)

AFDEC
Association of Franchised Distributors of Electronic Components (UK)

AFE
Apple File Exchange (A Macintosh utility)

AFES
Automatic Feature Extraction System

AFF
Automatic Fast Feed; Automatic Frequency Follower

affil
affiliated

AFG
Analog Function Generator

AFI
Automatic Fault Isolation

AFIP
American Federation of Information Processing (Formerly, AFIPS)

AFIPS
American Federation of Information Processing Societies (Pronounced "ay-fips")

afirm
affirmative

AFIS
Automated Financial Information System

AFL
Abstract Family of Languages

AFM
Application Functions Module; Automated Flexible Manufacturing (Factory automation)

AFMDC
Air Force Machinability Data Center (Metcut Research Association for the US Air Force)

AFN
Advanced Fractional Networking (AT&T)

AFNOR
Association Francaise de Normalisation (French Society for Standards)

AFO
Advanced File Organization

AFOS
Advanced Field Operating System; Automation of Field Operations and Services

AFP/SME
Association for Finishing Processes of the Society of Manufacturing Engineers

AFP
Advanced Function Printing (Intel Corp, US); Agency France Press (French news agency, supplies full text databases); Attached FORTRAN Processor (Burroughs Corp., US); Associative File Processors; AppleTalk Filing Protocol (Apple Computer Inc, US)

AFPA
Automatic Flow Process Analysis

AFPDS
Advanced Function Printing DataStream (IBM)

AFR
Advanced Fault Resolution; Automatic Field/Format Recognition

AFRC
Automatic Frequency Ratio Controller

AFRE
Australian Financial Review (Database on AUSINET)

AFRTS
American Forces Radio and Television Service

AFSARI
Automation For Storage And Retrieval of Information (Information retrieval term)

AFSCC
Air Force Super Computer Center (USAF)

AFSK
Audio Frequency Shift Keying

AFSM
Association of Field Service Managers (Electronics, computing association, US)

AFT
Analog Facility Terminal; Automated Funds Transfer; Automatic Fund Transfers

AFTN
Aeronautical Fixed Telecommunications Network

AFTS
Automated Funds Transfer System

AFU
Autonomous Functional Unit

Ag
Argentum [or Silver] (Symbol)

AG
Address Generator; Association Graph; Attribute Grammar; Assets Greater than (Searchable field); Audiographic

AGC
Automatic Gain Control (Electronics); Automatic Generation Control

AGDEX
Agricultural Index (Database and current

awareness service, Edinburgh School of Agriculture, UK)

AGE
American Bibliography of Agricultural Economics (Database originator, US); Asian Center for Geotechnical Engineering (Taiwan)

AGLINE
Agriculture Online (Database, Doane Western Inc., US)

AGLINET
Agricultural Libraries Information Network (UN)

Agricola
Agricultural Research Projects (Database, US Department of Agriculture)

AGS
Alternating Gradient Synchrotron

AGT
Arithmetic Greater Than

AGT
Alberta Government Telephones (Canada); Audiographic Teleconference

AGU
Address Generation Unit

AGV
Automated [or Automatically] Guided Vehicle (Factory automation)

AGW
Advanced Graphics Workstation (Autotrol Technology Corp.)

Ah
Ampere-hour(s)

AH
Ampere-Hour(s); Acceptor Handshake (Telecommunications); Analog Hybrid (Computing)

AHAM
Association of Home Appliance Manufacturers (US)

AHB
Austrian Historical Bibliography (Database)

AHCS
Advanced Hybrid Computer(ing) System

AHIP
ARPANET [Advanced Research Projects Agency Network] Host Interface Protocol (DOD)

AHONDA
Ad Hoc Committee on New Directions of the Research and Technical Services of the ALA

AI
Artificial Intelligence (Factory automation); Automatic Input

AI-TSL
Artificial Intelligence-Transaction Security Ltd (UK)

AIA
Accident/Incident Analysis; Automation One Association

AIAA
American Institute of Aeronautics and Astronautics (Pioneered information systems in the 1960s and 1970s)

AIB
Analog Input/output Board

AIC
Analog Interface Circuit (TI); Automatic Intercept Center

AICA
International Association for Analog Computing

AICRO
Association of Independent Contract Research Organizations (UK)

AICS
Association of Independent Computer Specialists (UK); Automated Industrial Control System

AID
Algebraic Interpretive Dialogue (Computing); Analog Interface Device; Automated Industrial Drilling; Automatic Information Distribution (Term used in information retrieval); Automatic Interaction Detection; Adaptive Intelligent Dialogue; *Augmented Index and Digest* (Information Retrieval Ltd., UK)

AIDA
Analysis of Interconnected Decision Areas (Term used in management); Advanced Integrated circuit Design Aids

AIDAPS
Automatic Inspection, Diagnostic And Prognostic Systems

AIDAS
Advanced Instrumentation and Data Analysis System

AIDC
Automatic Image Density Control (Toning technique used in some photocopiers)

AIDE
Accountability In Data Entry; Automated

Integrated Design and Engineering; Automated Integrative Design Engineering

AIDE/TPS
Advanced Interactive Data Entry/Transaction Processing System

AIDES
Automated Image Data Extraction System

AIDS
Acoustic Intelligence Data System; Advanced Impact Drilling System; Advanced Interactive Debugging System; Advanced Interactive Display System; Advanced Interconnection Development System; American Institute for Decision Science; Automatic Illustrated Document(ation) System; Automatic Interactive Debugging System; Automatic Inventory Dispatching System; Amdahl Internally Developed Software (Amdahl Corporation, US); Automated Information Dissemination System; Automatic Integrated Debugging System; Automation Instrument Data Service (Indata Ltd., UK); *Aerospace Intelligence Data System* (IBM)

AIEE
American Institute of Electrical Engineers (Merged with Institute of Radio Engineers [IRE] to form IEEE)

AIET
Average Instruction Execution Time (Computing, a parameter)

AIFF
Audio Interchange File Format (Apple Computer file format standard for storing digitized sound data)

AIFU
Automated Instruction Fetch Unit

AIG
Address Indicating Group

AIGA
American Institute of Graphical Arts

AIIE
American Institute of Industrial Engineers

AIIM
Association for Information and Image Management (Formerly, National Micrographics Association, US)

AIKR
Artificial Intelligence Knowledge Representation

AIL
Arithmetic Input Left; Array Interconnection Logic (Computing)

AIM
Abridged Index Medicus (Database on medical sciences, National Library of Medicine, US); Access Isolation Mechanism (Computing); Advanced Informatics and Medicine; Advanced Information in Medicine; Associative Index Method; Asynchronous Interface Module (AT&T); Adaptive Inference Machine; Automated Inventory Management; Advanced Information Manager (Fujitsu, Japan); Association for Information Management; Association of Information Managers (US); Analog Input Multiplexer; Automation of Interlending by Microcomputer; Accunet Information Manager (AT&T)

AIM/ARM
Abstracts of Instructional Material/Abstract of Research Materials in vocational and technical information (Database, Center for Vocational Education, Ohio State University, US)

AIM-TWX
Abridged Index Medicus-Teletypewriter Exchange network (Information network, US)

AIMC
Academic Information Management Center (US)

AIMIS
Advanced Integrated Modular Instrumentation System

AIMLO
Auto-Instructional Media for Library Orientation (Reader education device, Colorado University Library, US)

AIMS
Annual Improvement Maintenance and Support; Automated Industrial Management System; Automated Information and Management Systems

AIN
Advanced Intelligent Network (Bell)

AIO
Analog Input/Output board

AIOD
Automatic Identification of Outward Dialing

AIOP
Analog Input/Output Package; Automatic Identification of Outward Dialling (Tele-

communications)

AIOPI
Association of Information Officers in the Pharmaceutical Industry (UK)

AIP
Alphanumeric Impact Printer; Automated Imagery Processing; American Institute of Physics

AIPC
Army Information Processing Center (US Army)

AIPR
Applied Imagery Pattern Recognition

AIPU
Associative Information Processing Unit

AIR
Acoustic Intercept Receiver; Arithmetic Input Right; Automatic Interrogation Routine

AIRES
Automated Information Resource System; Automated Information Retrieval and Expert System (US Army)

AIRHPER
Alberta Information Retrieval for Health, Physical Education and Recreation (Information retrieval system, University of Alberta, Canada)

AIRS
Alliance of Information and Referral Services; American Information Retrieval Service (Document delivery service for US government and other US organizations); Automatic Image Retrieval System; Automatic Information Retrieval System

AIS
Accounting Information System; Advanced Information Systems; Analog Input System; Automated Information System; Automatic Intercept System (Telecommunications); Aeronautical Information Service (Civil Aviation Authority, UK); Acctex Information Systems (US); Acorn Interactive System (Videodisc control system); Adaptive Imaging System; Alarm Indication Signal

AISB
Society for the Study of Artificial Intelligence and the Simulation of the Brain

AISC
Association of Independent Software Companies

AISP
Association of Information Systems Professionals

AIST
Agency of Industrial Science and Technology (Japan)

AIT
Advanced Information Technology

AIU
Abstract Information Unit

AIX
Advanced Interactive Executive (IBM)

AJ
Anderson Jacobson (Terminal manufacturer)

AJAD
Automated Joint Application Development

AJG
Automatic Job Stream Generator

ak
acknowledge

AKM
Automatic Key Management

AKO
A Kind Of

AKR
Address Key Register

AKS
Associated Knowledge Systems (UK)

AKWIC
Author and Keyword In Context (Indexing system)

al
alphabet; alphabetic

Al
Aluminum (Symbol)

AL
Assembler Language; Assembly Language; Assets Less than (Searchable field); Analog Loop

ALA
American Library Association

ALA/ISAD
American Library Association Information Science and Automation Division

ALABOL
Algorithmic And Business-Oriented Language

ALADIN
Algebraic Automated Digital Iterative Network

ALAP
Associative Linear Array Processor (Computing)

ALARM
Anaesthesia Literature Abstracting Retrieval Method (American Society of Anesthesiologists)

ALAS
Automated Literature Alerting System (Current awareness system)

ALB
Arithmetic and Logic Box; Assembly Line Balancing

ALBIS
Australian Library-Based Information System (National Library of Australia)

ALBO
Automatic Line Build-Out

ALC
Air Logistics Center (USAF); Adaptive Logic Circuit; Assembly Language Coding (Computing); Amplitude Limiting Circuit; Audio Level Control; Automatic Light Control (Image Technology); Automatic Level Control

ALCAPP
Automatic, or Automotive List Classification And Profile Production

ALCC
Association of London Computer Clubs (UK)

ALCOM
Algebraic Compiler

ALCS
Author's Lending and Copyright Society (UK)

ALCU
Arithmetic Logic and Control Unit (Computing); Asynchronous Line Control Unit (Telecommunications)

ALD
Advanced Logic Design; Asynchronous Limited Distance; Automated Logic Diagram (IBM); Analog Line Driver; Asynchronous Line Driver

ALDEP
Automated Layout Design Program

ALDP
Automatic Language-Data Processing

ALDS
Analysis of Large Data Sets

ALE
Address Latch Enable; Automatic Line Equalization

ALE
Adaptive Line Enhancer(ment) (Telecommunications)

ALEC
Analysis of Linear Electronic Circuits

ALEM
Association of Loading Equipment Manufacturers

ALEPH
Automatic Library Expendable Program Hebrew University (Online library system, Hebrew University, Israel)

ALERT
Automatic Linguistic Extractor and Retrieval Technique

ALF
Application Library File (Computing); Automatic Line Feed

ALFA
Automatic Line Fault Analysis

ALFC
Automatic Load-Frequency Control

ALFTRAN
ALGOL to FORTRAN translator

ALG
Asynchronous Line Interface

ALGEC
Algorithmic Language for Economic Problems

ALGO
Algebraic compiler (Based on ALGOL)

ALGOL
Algorithmic Language (Computer programming language)

ALI
Asynchronous Line Interface (Telecommunications); Automated Logic Implementation (Computing); Automatic Link Intelligence; Automatic Location Identification

ALICE
Application Language Interface Conversion and Extension; Applicative Language Idealised Computing Engine (Imperial College, London, UK)

ALIS
Advanced Life Information System; Automated Library Information System

ALIT
Automatic Line Insulation Test; *Australian Literature* (Database)

ALL
Application Language Liberator (A fourth

generation programming language from Microdata)

ALLC
Association for Literary and Linguistic Computing (US)

Allied AIMS
Allied Advanced Information and Management Systems (UK)

alloc
allocation

ALM
Alarm Master; Asynchronous Line Module; Assembler Language for MULTICS [Multiplexed Information and Computing Service]; Asynchronous Line Multiplexer (Telecommunications)

ALMA
Alphanumeric-code for Music Analysis

ALMS
Automated Logic Mapping System; Analytic Language Manipulation System

ALMSA
Automated Logistics Management Systems Activity

ALN
Attribute Level Number

ALOFT
Airborn Light Optical Fiber Network (US)

ALP
Arithmetic and Logic Processor; Assembly Language Program; Automated Learning Process; Assembly Language Processing; Automated Language Processing (Computing); Automated Learning Process

ALPAC
Automated Language Processing Advisory Committee of the National Academy of Sciences (US)

ALPES
Advanced Logical Programming Environments Support

alph
alphabet; alphabetic

ALPHA
Automated Literature Processing Handling and Analysis (US Army)

alphanum
alphanumeric

ALPROS
ALGOL Process Control System

ALPS
Advanced Linear Programming System;

Assembly Line Planning System; Associative Logic Parallel System (Computing); Automated Library Processing Services; Automated Language Processing Systems (US company)

ALPSP
Association of Learned and Professional Society Publishers (UK)

ALQ
Almost Letter Quality (Printers)

ALRS
Arithmetic Logic Register Stack

ALS
Advanced Logistics System; Arithmetic Logic Section (Computing); Advanced Low-Power Schottky; Automated Library Systems Ltd. (UK)

ALSA(s)
Area Library Service Authority/authorities (US)

ALSC
Automatic Level and Slope Control

ALSI
Analog Large Scale Integration

ALSPEC
Automated Laser Seeker Performance Evaluation System

alt
alternate

ALT
Accelerated Life Test; Average Logistic Time

ALTA
Automatic Line Test and Administrative system

ALTAPE
Automatic Line Tracing And Processing Equipment

ALTINSAR
Alternate Instruction Address Register

ALTRAN
Algebra Translator (FORTRAN extension); Assembly Language Translator (Xerox Corp.)

ALTS
Automated Library Technical Services (Los Angeles Public Library, US)

ALU
Advanced Logical Unit; Arithmetic and Logic Unit (Computing); Asynchronous Line Unit (Telecommunications)

ALV
Autonomous Land Vehicle (NASA)
ALWIN
Algorithmic Wiswesser Notation
Am
Americium (Symbol)
AM
Access Manager; Address Marker; Address(ing) Mode (Computing); Address Modifier; Addressing Mode; Algorithm Model; Amplitude Modulation (Telecommunications); Associative Memory (Computing); Asynchronous Modem (Telecommunications); Auxiliary Memory (Computing)
AM/FM
Automated Mapping for Facilities Management; Amplitude Modulation/Frequency Modulation (Telecommunications)
Am386
A 32-bit microprocessor developed by Advanced Micro Devices
AMA
Associative Memory Address; Associative Memory Array (Computing); Automatic Message Accounting (Telecommunications); Asynchronous Multiplexer Adapter; American Medical Association
AMA/MTR
Automatic Message Accounting—Magnetic Tape Recording
AMA/NET
American Medical Association Network
AMANet
American Medical Association Network
AMAPS
Advanced Manufacturing, Accounting, and Production System
AMARC
Automatic Message Accounting Recording Center
AMAVU
Advanced Modular Audio Visual Unit
AMBER
Acquisition of Monographs and Bibliographical Enquiry Remotely (Acquisitions software)
AMC
Autonomous Multiplexer Channel (Telecommunications); Automatic Modulation Control; Automatic Message Counting; Advanced Medical Communications (UK company)
AMCAP
Advanced Microwave Circuit Analysis Program
AMCAT
Addressograph Multigraph Computer Access Terminal
AMD
Associative Memory Data; Advanced Micro Devices (US manufacturer)
AMDAC
Amdahl Diagnostic Resistance Center (US)
AMDF
Absolute Magnitude Difference Function
AMDS
Advanced Microcomputer Development System
AMDT
ASCII Message Definition Table
AME
Angle Measuring Equipment; Automatic Microfiche Editor; Automatic Monitoring Equipment; Average Magnitude of Error
AMEDA
Automatic Microscope Electronic Data Accumulator
AMEDS
Automated Measurement Evaluator and Director System
AMEME
Association of Mining, Electrical and Mechanical Engineers
AMERITECH
American Information Technologies Corp.
AMES
Automatic Message Entry System
AMEX
American Stock Exchange
AMFIS
Automatic Microfilm Information System
AMH
Automated Materials Handling
AMHS
American Material Handling Society; Automated Message Handling System
AMI
Association of Multi-Image; Average Mutual Information; Alternative Mark Inversion signal (Telecommunications); American Microsystems Inc.; Access Methods Inc. (US consultancy); Austria Microsystems International (IC manufacturer)

AMIGAS II
Advanced Meteorological Image and Graphics Analysis (A meteorological software package) Whitewater Group, Incorporated

AMIS
Acquisition Management Information System (Center for Information and Documentation, European Economic Community [EEC]); Automated Management Information System; Audio Massaging Interchange Specification

AML
Advanced Math Library; A Manufacturing Language (IBM robotics programming language); Amplitude Modulated Link; Application Module Library; Application Macro Language; Array Machine Language (Computing)

AMLC
Asynchronous Multiline Controller (Telecommunications)

AMLCC
Asynchronous Multiline Communications Coupler (Telecommunications)

AMLCD
Active-Matrix Liquid Crystal Display

AMM
Additional Memory Module; Advanced Manufacturing Methods; Alternative Method of Management; Analog Measurement Module; Analog Monitor Module (Computing)

AMMA
Automated Media Management System

AMME
Automated Multi-Media Exchange

AMMINET
Automated Mortgage Management Information Network

AMMS
Automated Multi-Media Switch

AMMSS
Automatic Message and Mail Sorting Systems

AMNIP
Adaptive Man-machine Non-arithmetical Information Processing (IBM)

AMNIPS
Adaptive Man-machine Non-numeric Information Processing System (IBM)

AMO
Area Maintenance Office

AMOS
Adjustable Multi-Class Organizing System; Alpha Microsystems Operating System (Alpha Microsystems, US); Associative Memory Organization Systems (Compiler)

AMOSS
Adaptive Mission-Oriented Software System

amp
ampere; amplifier

AMP
Associative Memory Processor (Computing); Asymmetrical Multiprocessor(ing) (DEC)

AMPA
American Medical Publishers Association

AMPCR
Alternate Microprogram Count Register

AMPL
Advanced Microprocessor Programming Language; Advanced Microprocessor Prototyping Laboratory (Texas Instruments, US)

AMPP
Advanced Microprogrammable Processor

AMPS
Automatic Message Processing System (Telecommunications); Advanced Mobile Phone Service (AT&T); Assembly Manufacturing Payroll System; Assignment Management Planning System; Automatic Message Processing System

AMR
Arithmetic Mask Register; Automatic Meter Reading; Automatic Message Registering; Automatic Message Routing (Telecommunications)

AMRA
American Medical Record Association

AMRF
Automated Manufacturing Research Facility (NIST)

AMRPD
Applied Manufacturing Research and Process Development

AMS
Access Method Services (IBM); Account Management System; Administrative Management Society; Application Management System; Asymmetric Multiprocessing System (IBM); Automated Main-

tenance System; Advanced Memory Systems Inc (US); Advanced Monitor System (DEC); American Mathematical Society

AMSAT
Radio Amateur Satellite Corp.

AMSCO
Access Method Services Cryptographic Option

AMSDL
Acquisition Management System and Data Requirements Control List

AMSEC
Analytical Method for System Evaluation and Control

AMSO
Automated Microform Storage and Retrieval

AMSP
Array Machine Simulation Program

AMST
Automated Maintenance Support Tool

AMT
Advanced Manufacturing Technique(s); Advanced Manufacturing Technology; Automated Microfiche Terminal

AMTC
Association for Mechanical Translation and Computation Linguistics (US); Advanced Manufacturing Technology Center (University of Manchester Institute for Science and Technology [UMIST], UK)

AMTD
Automatic Magnetic Tape Dissemination (Dissemination service, Defense Documentation Center, US)

AMTRAN
Automatic Mathematical Translator

amu
atomic mass unit

AMU
Association of Minicomputer Users (US)

AMVER
Atlantic Merchant Vessel Alert (Computer-based disaster alert system)

AMWA
American Medical Writer's Association

AN
Abstract Number (Searchable field); Accession Number (Searchable field); Agency Name (Searchable field); Alphanumeric; Assignee Name (Searchable field)

an (AN)
alphanumeric

ANA
Automatic Number Analysis; Automated Network Analyzer; Article Numbering Association (UK)

ANACOM
Analog Computer

ANACONDA
Ad hoc Committee to Work with Activities Committee On New Directions for ALA Activities (US); Analytical Control and Data

anal
analysis; analyst

ANALIT
Analysis of Automatic Line Insulation Tests

ANAPAC
Analysis Package

ANATRAN
Analog Translator

ANAYTAN
Analog Translator

ANB
Australian National Bibliography (Database)

ANC
All-Numbers Calling

ANCE
Automated News Clipping Indexing and Retrieval System (Image Systems, UK)

ANCHOR
Alpha-Numeric Character Generator

ANCOVA
Analysis of Covariance

ANCOVA
Analysis of Co-Variance

ANCS
American Numerical Control Society

AND
Alpha-Numeric Display; AND (Circuit or logic gate)

ANDMS
Advanced Network Design and Management System

ANDVT
Advanced Narrow-band Digital Voice Terminal

ANI
Advanced Network Integration; Automatic Number Identification (Telecommunica-

tions)

ANIRC
Annual National Information Retrieval Colloquium

ANL
Automatic New Line; Automatic Noise Limiter

ANLES
Analog Switch (Computing)

ANLP
Alpha-Numeric Logic Package

anlyst
analyst

ANN
Airports National Network (British Airports Authority)

ANOM
Analysis Of Means

ANOVA
Analysis Of Variance

ANPA
American Newspaper Publisher's Association

ANRF
Area Normalization with Response Factors

ANRIC
Annual National Information Retrieval Colloquium (US)

ANS
American National Standard(s)

ANSA
Advanced Network System Architecture

ANSC
American National Standards Committee

ANSCR
Alpha-Numeric System for Classification of Recordings

ANSC X3
American National Standards Committee for Computers and Information Processing

ANSC X4
American National Standards Committee for Office Machines and Supplies

ANSI
American National Standards Institute (Pronounced "ann-see", formerly, American Standards Association [ASA])

ANSIM
Analog Simulator

ANSLICS
Aberdeen and North Scotland Library and Information Cooperative Services (UK)

ANSR
Add-on Non-Stop Reliability

ANSTI
African Network for Scientific and Technological Institutions

ANSWER
Algorithm for Non-Synchronized Waveform Error Reduction

ANSYS
Analysis System

ANT
Alternate Number Translation (AT&T)

ANTC
Advanced Networking Test Center

ANTS
ARPA Network Terminal System

AO
Abort Output; Acousto-Optic(al)

AOA
Angle of Arrival (Radar)

AOC
Automatic Output Control; Advanced Office Computer (Northern Telecom)

AOCE
Attitude and Orbit Control Electronics (Telecommunications)

AOCR
Advanced Optical Character Reader; Advanced Optical Character Recognition

AOCU
Arithmetic Output Control Unit; Associative Output Control Unit (Computing)

AOD
Arithmetic Output Data (Computing)

AOE
Application Operating Environment (AT&T); Auditing Order Error

AOEF
Automated Operations Extension Facility (IBM)

AOF
Advanced Operating Facility(ies) (Computer Technology Inc., US)

AOG
AND/OR Graph

AOH
Add-on Header

AOI
Acousto-Optical Imaging; ADD-OR INVERT [or Inverter] (TI); Automated Operator Interface (IBM); Automated Opti-

cal Inspection

AOIPS
Atmospheric and Oceanic, or Oceanographic Information Processing System (Satellite image enhancing system)

AOL
Application Oriented Language (Computing)

AOM
Acoustic-Optic Modulator

AON
All Or None, order

AOQ
Average Outgoing Quality

AOQL
Average Outgoing Quality Limit

AORS
Abnormal Occurrence Reporting System

AOS
Advanced Operating System (Data General Corp, US); Alternate Operator Service (Third-party service firms); Algebraic Operating System (Texas Instruments, US); Author Organization Source (Searchable field); Automated Operating System

AOS/VS
Advanced Operating System/Virtual Storage (Data General Corp, US)

AOSP
Automatic Operating and Scheduling Program

AOTF
Acousto-Optical Tunable Filter

AOU
Arithmetic Output Unit; Associative Output Unit (Computing)

AOV
Analysis Of Variance; Attribute Object = Value

AP
Application Profile; Applications Protocol; Application Program (Computing); Approach (Searchable field); Argument Pointer; Arithmetic Processor; Array Processor (Computing); Associative Processor; Attached Processor (Computing); Audio Processing; Associated Press (News agency and wire service, US); Advanced Processor

APA
All Points Addressable; American Psychological Association

APACE
Aldermaston Project for the Application of Computers to Engineering

APACHE
Analog Programming And Checking

APAL
Array Processor Assembly Language (Computing)

APAM
Array Processor Access Method (Computing)

APAR
Authorized Program Analysis Report (IBM); Automatic Processing, or Programming and Recording

APAS
Adaptable-Programmable Assembly System

APB
Application Program Block

APC
Adaptive Predictive Coding; Advanced Personal Computer; Area Positive Control; Associative Processor Control (Computing); Automatic Peripheral Control; Automatic Phase Control; Automatic Potential Control; Automated Production Control (Factory automation)

APCC
Association of Professional Computer Consultants (UK)

APCHE
Automatic Programmed Checkout Equipment

APCM
Adaptive Pulse Code Modulator(ion); Authorized Protective Connecting Module

APCS
Associative Processor Computer System; Attitude and Pointing Control System

APD
Approach Progress Display; Automated Payment and Deposit; Avalanche Photodiode

APDL
Algorithmic Processor Description Language

APDM
Associative Push Down Memory

APDU
Application Protocol Data Unit

APE
Application Program Evaluation

APE(x)C
All-Purpose Electronic x Computer (An early computer, Birkbeck College, UK)
APET
Application Program Evaluator Tool
APEX
Assembler and Process Executive; Automated Planning and Execution, Control System
APF
Authorized Program Facility (IBM)
APG
Application Program Generator; Automatic Priority Group (Fujitsu, Japan)
API
American Petroleum Institute; Auerbach Power Index (Benchmark); All Purpose Interface; Application Program Interface (IBM); Automatic Priority Interrupt
APIA
Application Program Interface Association (A group of computer and communication product vendors, US)
APICS
American Production and Inventory Control Society
APILIT
American Petroleum Institute Literature (Database)
APIPAT
American Petroleum Institute Patents (Database)
APIS
Array Processing Instruction Set
APK
Amplitude Phase Keyed (Telecommunications)
APL
Algorithmic Programming Language; A Programming Language; Automatic Program Load; Automatic Program Loading; Average Picture Level (Image technology); Associative Programming Language
APLL
Analog Phased-Locked Loop; Automatic Phased-Locked Loop
APM
Automatic Predictive Maintenance
APMS
Automatic Performance Management System
APO
Automatic Power Off

APOLLO
Article Procurement with On-Line Local Ordering (Document delivery system)
APOMA
American Precision Optics Manufacturers Association
APP
Advance Procurement Plan; Associative Parallel Processor (Computing); Application Portability Profile
APPC
Advanced Program-to-Program Communication (IBM); Application Program-to-Program Connectivity
APPECS
Adaptive Pattern Perceiving Electronic Computer System
APPI
Advanced Planning Procurement Information
APPLE
Analog Phased Processing Loop Equipment; Associative Processor(ing) Programming Language Evaluation
APPN
Advanced Peer-to-Peer Networking (IBM)
appr
approximate; approximately; approximation
approx
approximate; approximately
APPU
Application Program Preparation Utility
APR
Active Page Register; Automatic programming and Recording; Alternate Path Reentry (Fujitsu, Japan); Alternate Path Retry (IBM)
APRICOT
Automatic Printed Circuit Board Routing with Intermediate Control of the Tracking
APRIL
Accounts Payable, Receivable, Inventory Library; Automatically Programmed Remote Indication Logging; Application Rational Interface Logic (A logic from IBM)
APRIS
Alcoa Picturephone Remote Information System (AT&T telecommunications device, US)
APRS
Automatic Position Reference System

APRST
Averaged Probability Ratio Sequential Test

APS
Assembly Programming System; Auxiliary Power System; Array Processor Software (Data General Corp, US); Attached Processor for Speech (IBM); Augustan Prose Sample; Application Productivity System; Automatic Page Search (Document retrieval aid); Auxiliary Program Storage; Automated Patent System; Automatic Protection Switch

APSE
ADA Programming Support Environment (Software)

APSK
Amplitude and Phase Shift Keying

APSL
Access Path Specification Language

APSM
Auxiliary Power Supply Module

APSP
Array Processor Subroutine Package

APSS
Automated Program Support System

APT
A Programmer' Tool; Automatic Picture Transmission; Automatic Programming Tool; Automatic Pattern Translator; Automatically Programmed Tool(s) (Factory automation, CNC software); Asia Pacific Telecommunications (Telecommunications union)

APTE
Automatic Production Test Equipment

APTF
Automated Program Testing Facility

APTI
Automatic Print Transfer Instrument

APTIC
Air Pollution Technical Information Center (Database, US)

APTIF
Average Process Time Inverted File

APTP
Arithmetic Proficiency Training Program

APTR
Association Printer

APU
Adaptive Peripheral Unit; Analog Processing Unit; Arithmetic Processing Unit; Assessment of Performance Unit; Asynchronous Processing Unit; Auxiliary Power Unit; Auxiliary Processing Unit

AQD
Analysis of Quantitative

AQL
Acceptable Quality Level (Term used in engineering)

Ar
Argon (Symbol)

AR
Access Register (IBM); Accumulator Register; Address Register; Arithmetic Register; Aspect Ratio; Associative Register (Computing); Automated Register; Automatic Restart; Authority Record (Searchable field)

ARA
Attitude Reference Assembly; Automatic Route Advance

ARABSAT
Arab Satellite Communications Organization

ARAC
Array Reduction Analysis Circuit

ARAL
Automatic Record Analysis Language

ARAMIS
Automation Robotics and Machine Intelligence System

ARAP
AppleTalk Remote Access Protocol (Apple Computer Inc, US)

ARASEM
Artificially Random Self-Motivated

ARAT
Automatic Random Access Transport

arb
arbitrary; arbitration

ARC
Applications Research Center; Attached Resource Computer (Datapoint, US); Automatic Revenue Collection; Atlantic Research Corp (US); Attended Resource Computer (Datapoint, US); Automatic Relay Calculator (An early computer, Birkbeck College, UK); Applied Research of Cambridge (UK)

ARCADE
Automatic Radar Control And Data Equipment;

ARCAIC
Archives and Record Catologing And In-

dexing by Computer

ARCHEDDA
Architectures for Heterogenous European Distributed Databases (European database study)

ARCnet
Attached Resource(s) Computer Network

ARCNET
Attached Resource(s) Computer Network (LAN, Datapoint, US)

ARCS
Advanced Reconfigurable Computer System; Automated Reproduction and Collating System; Automated Revenue Collection system; Automated Ring Code Search, or System (Chemical structures information retrieval method)

ARD
Answering, Recording and Dialing

ARDA
Analog Recording Dynamic Analyzers

ARDI
Analysis, Requirements Determination, Design and Development, and Implementation and Evaluation

Ardis
Advanced National Radio Data Information Service (A joint venture of IBM and Motorola)

ARDIS
Advanced Radio Data Information Service (IBM); Army Research and Development Information System (US)

ARDS
Accunet Reserved Digital Service (AT&T); Advance Remote Display System

AREOSAT
Aeronautical Satellite, for air traffic control

ARF
Automatic Report Feature

arg
argument

ARGS
Advanced Raster-Graphics System

ARGUS
Automatic Routine Generating and Updating System (Compiler)

ARI
Applications Reference Index; Automobile drivers Radio Information

ARIES
Alvey Research for Insurance Expert Sys-

tems; Automated Reliability Interactive Estimation System

ARIMA
Autoregressive Integrated Moving Average

ARIS
Activity reporting Information System; Automated Reactor Inspection System; Agricultural Information System (International information system)

ARISTOLE
Annual Review of Information and Symposium on the Technology of Training and Learning and Education (Annually held symposium, US)

arith
arithmetic

ARL
Average Run Length; Association of Research Libraries (US)

ARLAN
Advanced Radio Local Area Network

ARLL
Advanced Run-Length Limited (Hard disk storage and retrieval method)

ARM
Asynchronous Response Mode (IBM, Computing); Autoregressive Moving Average; Automated Route Management (Business management system); Availability, Reliability and Maintainability (Term used in computer performance); Acorn RISC [Reduced Instruction Set Computer] Machine (Acorn Computing)

ARMA
American Records Management Association; Autoregressive Moving Average

ARMAN
Artificial Methods Analyst

ARMM
Automatic Reliability Mathematical Model

ARMMS
Automated Reliability and Maintainability Measurement System

ARMS
Automated Record Management System (Tyne & Wear County Council, UK); Automated Records Management System (Tera Corporation, US)

ARO
After Receipt of Order; Automatic Recov-

ery Option

AROM

Alterable Read-Only Memory

AROS

Alterable Read-Only Operating System

ARP

Advanced [or Automatic] Routing Protocol; Analogous Random Process

ARPA

Advanced Research Projects Agency (DOD, now called Defense Advanced Research Projects Administration [DARPA], Also sometimes refers to ARPANET)

ARPANET

Advanced Research Projects Agency Network (DOD, US computer network)

ARPAT

Advanced Research Projects Agency Terminal (DOD)

ARPS

Advanced Real-Time Processing System

ARQ

Answer-Return Query; Automatic Repeat Request; Automatic Request for correction, or repetition

ARR

Address Recall [or Record] Register; Associated Recovery Routines (IBM)

ARRL

American Radio Relay League (Organization)

ARS

Advanced Record System (of General Services Administration [GSA], US); Automatic Route Selection; Audio Response System; Automatic Route Setting

ARSC

Automatic Resolution Selection Control

ARSTEC

Adaptive Random Search Technique

ART

Access Register Translation (IBM); Actual Retention Time; Authorization and Resource Table; Automated Request Transmission; Average Run Time; Automatic Reporting Telephone; Automated Reasoning Tool (Factory automation, expert system)

ARTEMIS

Automatic Retrieval of Text through European Multipurpose Information Services

(Document delivery system); Advanced Relay Technological Mission Satellite

ARTIC

A Real-Time Interface Processor (IBM)

ARTS

Audio Response Time-Shared System; Automated Radar Terminal System

ARTS/DB

Analysis of Real-Time Systems/Data Base-Oriented Systems

ARU

Address Recognition Unit; Application Resource Unit; Audio Response Unit (Telecommunications); Auxiliary Read-Out Unit; Arithmetical Unit (Computing)

ARX

Automatic Retransmission Exchange

As

Arsenic (Symbol)

AS

Address Space; Auxiliary Storage (Computing); Advanced Systems; Application System; Advanced Schottky

AS/RS

Automated Storage and Retrieval System

ASA

Acoustical Society of America; American Standards Association (Former name of the American National Standards Institute [ANSI]); American Statistical Association; Analog Sampling Array; Asynchronous Adapter; Asynchronous/Synchronous Adapter; Automatic Separation System; Automatic Spectrum Analyzer; Advanced Software Architecture

ASAI

Adjunct/Switch Application Interface (AT&T)

ASAP

Advanced Scientific Array Processor; Automated Statistical Analysis Program; Automatic Spooling with Asynchronous Processing; "As Soon As Possible"

ASB

Analog Source Board

asbl

assemble; assembler

ASBU

Arab States Broadcasting Union

ASC

Adaptive Speed Control; Address Space Control (IBM); Advanced Scientific Computer (TI); Associative Structure Computer; Automatic System Controller; American Satellite Corp; American Society for Cybernetics; American Standards Committee

ASCA
Automatic Subject Citation Alert (Current awareness service)

ASCB
Address Space Control Block

ASCC
Aeronautical Satellite Communications Center (US); Automatic Sequence Controlled Calculator

ASCE
American Society of Civil Engineers; Annual Schedule of Circuit Estimates (Telecommunications)

ASCENT
Assembly System for Central processor

ASCII
American Standard Code for Information Interchange (Pronounced "as-kee" or "askee")

ASCOM
Association of Telecommunication Services

ASCON
Automated Switched Communications Network

ASCP
Automatic System(s) Checkout Program

ASCR
Asymmetrical Silicon-Controlled Rectifier

ASCT
Address Space Control Task (Fujitsu, Japan)

ASCU
Association of Small Computer Users (US)

ASCUE
Association of Small Computer Users in Education (US)

ASDA
Accelerate-Stop Distance Available

ASDI
Automatic(ed) Selective Dissemination of Information

ASDIC
Association of Information and Dissemination Centers

ASDL
Aeronautical Satellite Datalink system

(Mitre Corp); Asymmetric Digital Subscriber Line

ASDM
Automated Systems Design Methodology

ASDS
Accunet Spectrum of Digital Services (AT&T)

ASE
Application Support Environment; Automatic Stabilization Equipment

ASEE
American Society for Engineering Education

ASES
Automated Software Evaluation System

ASET
ADA and Software Engineering Technology

ASF
Active Segment Field; Automatic Sheet Feeder (For printer)

ASFIR
Active Swept Frequency Interferometer Radar

ASFIS
Aquatic Sciences and Fisheries Information System

ASFM
Association of Field Service Managers

ASI
American Standards Institute; *American Statistical Index* (Congressional Information Service databank, US); Addressing Systems International (UK mailing list systems manufacturer); Articulated Subject Index; Asynchronous Serial Interface

ASIC
Analog Semi-Custom Integrated Circuit; Application-Specific Integrated Circuit

ASID
Address Space Identifier (IBM, computers)

ASIDIC
Association of Scientific Information and Dissemination Centers (US)

ASIDP
American Society of Information and Data Processing

ASII
American Science Information Institute

ASIN
Agricultural Service Information Network

(National Agricultural Library, US)

ASIP
Application-Specific Image Processor

ASIS
American Society for Industrial Security; American Society for Information Science

ASIST
Advanced Scientific Instruments Symbolic Translator (Assembly program)

ASIT
Adaptable Surface Interface Terminal

ASK
Amplitude Shift Keying (Telecommunications); Anomalous State of Knowledge (Term used in artificial intelligence); Applied Systems Knowledge Ltd (UK software publisher)

ASKS
Automatic Station Keeping System

ASL
Association for Symbolic Logic (US)

ASLO
Assembly Layout

aslr
assembler

ASLT
Advanced Solid Logic Technology

asm
assembler

ASM
Algorithmic State Machine; Association for Systems Management (US); Asynchronous Sequential Machine; American Society for Materials (respectively, ASM International); Address Space Manager (Software code); Area Stores Module; Automated Storage Management; Auxiliary Storage Manager (IBM)

ASM/GEN
Assembler Generating System

ASME
American Society of Mechanical Engineers

ASN
Average Sample Number; Abstract Syntax Notation

ASN.1
Abstract Syntax Notation.1 (A method of describing the form of data in an OSI communication)

ASP
Acoustic Signal Processor; Adaptive Sig-

nal Processing; Association-Storing Processor; Associative Storing Processor; Attached Support Processor; Automated Spooling Priority; Associative Structures Package; Automatic Schedule Procedures (Computing)

ASPC
Application-Specific Power Conditioning

ASPER
Assembly Program for Peripheral processes (Assembly program)

ASPEX
Automated Surface Perspectives

ASPI
Advanced SCSI [Small Computer Systems Interface] Programming Interface; Asynchronous Synchronous Programmable Interface (Computing)

ASPIC
Author's Standard Pre-press Interface Code (Electronic typesetting 'mark-up code')

ASQ
Analytic Solution to Queues

ASQC
American Society for Quality Control

ASR
Active Status Register; Address Shift Register (Computing); Analog Shift Register; Assigned Slot Release; Automatic Send/Receive (Telecommunications); Available Supply Rate; Automatic Speech Recognition

ASRF
Automation Sciences Research Facility (NASA)

ASRL
Average Sample Run Length

ASRS
Automatic Storage and Retrieval System

ASS
Analog Switching Subsystem (Telecommunications)

ASSASSIN
Agricultural System for Storage And Subsequent Selection of Information (Information retrieval system, UK)

ASSET
Advanced Systems Synthesis and Evaluation Technique

ASSISTENT
Automated Information System for Sci-

ence and Technology (Russia)

assm
assembler

ASSM
Associative Memory

assmt
assessment

assn
association

assoc
associated; associative

ASSORT
Automatic System of Selection Of Receiver and Transmitter

ASSP
Application Specific Standard Part

ASSR
Automated Systems Service Request

AST
Abstract Syntax Tree; Address Synchronizing Track; Asynchronous to synchronous Transmission Adapter; Automatic Scan Tracking; Anti-Sidetone (Telecommunications)

ASTA
Association of Short-Circuit Testing Authorities; Automatic System Trouble Analysis

ASTAP
Advanced Statistical Analysis Program

ASTC
Australian Science and Technology Council

ASTI
Automated System for Transport Intelligence

ASTIA
Armed Services Technical Information Agency (Now called Defense Documentation Center [DDC], US)

ASTINFO
Scientific and Technical Information in Asia (Regional network for information exchange)

ASTM
American Society for Testing of Materials

ASTME
American Society of Tool and Manufacturing Engineers (Now called, Society of Manufacturing Engineers [SME])

ASTMS
Association of Scientific, Technical and

Managerial Staff (UK)

ASTOVL
Advanced Short Take-Off and Vertical Landing

ASTRA
Advanced Structural Analyzer; Automatic Scheduling and time-dependent Resource Allocation; Automatic Scheduling and time-integrated Resource Allocation

ASTRAIL
Analog Schematic Translator to Algebraic Language; Assurance and Stabilization Trends for Reliability by Analysis of Lots

ASTRAM
Advanced Self-Timed Random Access Memory

ASTROS
Advanced Systematic Techniques for Reliable Operational Software

ASTS
Air to Surface Transport System

ASTTL
Advanced Schottky Transistor-Transistor Logic

ASTUTE
Association of System 2000 Users for Technical Exchange

ASU
Add/Subtract Unit; Apparatus Slide-in Unit; Automatic Switching Unit (Telecommunications); Autonomous Switch Unit

ASV
Automatic Self-Verification (Computing)

ASVIP
American Standard Vocabulary for Information Processing

ASVS
Automatic Signature Verification System

ASW
Accumaster Services Workstation (AT&T); Applications Software

ASYLCU
Asynchronous Line Control Unit

async
asynchronous

asynch
asynchronous

At
Astatine (Symbol)

AT
Absolute Title; Address Translation [or Translator] (Computing); Anomalous

Transmission; Advanced Technology (e.g., the IBM PC/AT); Appropriate Technology; Automatic Transmission; Article Type; Asset Type (Searchable fields)

AT&T
American Telephone and Telegraph Company

ATA
Asynchronous Terminal Adapter (Telecommunications); American Translators Association; Alternative Type Acceptance (Model for interference measurement)

ATAE
Associated Telephone Answering Exchanges

ATAP
Automated Time and Attendance Procedures

ATARS
Automated Travel Agents Reservation Systems

ATAS
Automated Telephone Answering System

ATB
Access Type Bits (Computing); All-Trunks Busy (Telecommunications)

ATBM
Average Time Between Maintenance

ATC
Advanced Technology Components; Address Translation Cache; Automated Technical Control; Automatic Tool Changer; Air Traffic Control

ATCCS
Army Tactical Command and Control System (US Army)

ATCD
Automatic Telephone Call Distribution

ATCRBS
Air Traffic Control Radar Beacon System

ATD
Actual To Date

ATDE
Advanced Technology Demonstrator Engine

ATDG
Automated Test Data Generator

ATDM
Analog Time-Division Multiplexer; Asynchronous Time-Division Multiplexing(er) (Telecommunications)

ATDRSS
Advanced Tracking and Data Relay Satellite System (NASA)

ATDT
Attention Dial Tone (On Hayes and compatible modems, the ATDT command initiates touch-tone [as opposed to pulse] dialing)

ATE
Artificial Traffic Equipment (Telecommunications); Automatic Test Equipment; Automatic Telephone Exchange

ATEA
Automatic Test Equipment Association

ATEC
Automated Technical Control; Automated Test Equipment Complex

ATEMIS
Automatic Traffic Engineering and Management Information System

ATES
Advanced Techniques integration into Efficient Scientific application software

ATEV
Approximate Theoretical Error Variance

ATEX
Automatic Test Equipment Conference and Exposition

ATF
Advanced Tactical Fighter (USAF); Automatic Track Finding

ATF
Automatic Text Formatter

ATFA
Association of Technicians in Financing and Accounting

ATFC
Automatic Traffic-Flow Control

ATG
Advanced Technology Groups (Groups established within larger companies); Assistive Technology Group (DEC); Automatic Test Generation; Automatic Test Generator

ATGF
Automatic Test Generation Facility

ATI
Automatic Track Initiation; Average Total Inspection

ATIR
Autotransaction Industry Report

ATIS
Automatic Terminal Information Service; Automatic Transmitter Identification System

ATL
Active Task List; Analog-Threshold Logic; Applications Terminal Language; Automated(ic) Tape Library

ATLA
American Theological Library Association (Database originator)

ATLAS
Abbreviated Test Language for Avionics Systems; Automated Testing and Load Analysis System; Automatic Tabulating, Listing And Sorting System

ATM
Adobe Type Manager (A font generator and utility program for Macintosh computers from Adobe Systems Inc, US); Asynchronous Time Multiplexing; Automated(ic) Teller Machine (Electronic on-line banking service or system); Advanced Technology Maintenance (UK computer maintenance company); Asynchronous Transfer Method; Asynchronous Transfer Mode

ATMAC
Advanced Technology Microelectronic Array Computer

ATMS
Advanced Terminal Management System; Advanced Text Management System (IBM); Automatic Transmission Measuring System

ATMSS
Automatic Telegraph Message Switching System

atn
attention

ATN
Attention (IEEE); Aeronautical Telecommunications Network (FAA)

A to D
Analog to Digital

ATOLS
Automatic Testing On-Line System

ATOM
Automatic Transmission Of Mail (Early US electronic mail system)

ATOMS
Automated Technical Order Maintenance Sequence(s)

ATOS
Automated Technical Order System

ATP
Air Transportable

atr
attribute

ATR
Angle, Time, Range; Automatic Traffic Recorder (Telecommunications); Anti-Transmit-Receive tube; Automatic Target Recognition

ATRAC
Angle Tracking Computer

ATRJ
Advanced Technology Radar Jammer

ATRVAL
Attribute Value

ATS
Administrative Terminal System (IBM, early text handling system); Analytic Trouble-Shooting; Applications Technology Satellite (Communications satellite); Automated Test System; Automatic Test System; Automatic Transfer Service; Audio Test Set

ATSC
Advanced Television Systems Committee (US)

ATSF
Alert Transport Service Facility (IBM)

ATSS
Automatic Telecommunications, or Telephone Switching System; Automatic Test Support Systems

ATSS-D
Automatic Telecommunications Switching System - Data Services

ATSU
Association of Time-Sharing Users (US)

att
attribute

ATT
Address Translation Table; Average Total Time

attach
attachment

ATTIS
AT&T Information Systems (US)

attn
attention

attr
attribute

ATU
Address Translation Unit; Analysis and Transformation Unit; Autonomous Transfer Unit (Computing); Arab Telecommu-

nications Union

ATVG
Automatic Test Vector Generation

au
audio

Au
Aurum [or Gold] (Symbol)

AU
Adder Unit; Arithmetic Unit (Computing); Author (Searchable field); Astronomical Unit

AUCBE
Advisory Unit for Computer Based Education (UK)

AUD
Asynchronous Unit Delay

AUDACIOUS
Automatic Direct Access to Information with Online UDC [Universal Decimal Classification] System (Information retrieval system, American Institute of Physics)

AUDDIT
Automatic Dynamic Digital Test System

AUDICS
Auditable Internal Control Systems

AUDREY
Audio Reply

audvis
audiovisual

AUI
Access Unit Interface; Attachment Unit Interface (Computing)

AUNT
Automatic Universal Translator

AURP
AppleTalk Update Routing Protocol (Apple Computer Inc, US)

AUSINET
Australian Information Network

AUSMARC
Australian MARC [Machine-Readable Catalog(ing)]

AUSSAT
Australian Satellite

AUSTPAC
Australian Packet switching service (Telecommunications)

AUT
Author (Searchable field); American United Telecom

AUT
Advanced User Terminal; Assembly Un-

der Test; Automated Unit Test

AUTODIN
Automatic Digital Network (DOD)

AUTODOC
Automated Documentation

AUTOFACT
Automated, Integrated Factory of Tomorrow Conference and Exposition (Held annually)

AUTOFLOW
Automatic Flowcharting

AUTOMAP
Automatic Machining Program

AUTOMAST
Automatic Mathematical Analysis and Symbolic Translation

AUTOMAT
Automatic Methods And Times

AUTOMEX
Automatic Message Exchange service

automtn
automation

AUTONET
Automatic Network Display Program

AUTOPIC
Automatic Personal Identification Code (IBM)

AUTOPROMPT
Automatic Programming of Machine Tools (IBM)

AUTOPROS
Automated Process Planning System

AUTOPSY
Automatic Operating System

AUTOSATE
Automated Data Systems Analysis Technique

AUTOSEVOCOM
Automatic Secure Voice Communications, system

AUTOSPOT
Automatic System for Positioning Tools

AUTOVON
Automatic Voice Network (US Department of Defence)

AUTRAN
Automatic Translation; Automatic Utility Translator

AUTRAX
Automatic Traffic Recording and Analysis Complex

AUW
All-Up-Weight

aux
auxiliary
AUXRC
Auxiliary Recording Control Circuit
av
audiovisual; available; availability (searchable field); average
AV
Analysis of Variance; Array/Vector; Attribute Value; Audiovisual [or Audio-Visual]
AVA
Absolute Virtual Address (Computing)
avail
available
AVC
Audio-Visual Connection (IBM); Automatic Volume Control; Auxiliary Video Connector (IBM)
AVD
Alternate Voice and Data (Telecommunications)
ave
average
avg
average
AVHRR
Advanced Very High Resolution Radiometer
AVIP
Association of Viewdata Information Providers (UK)
AVISAM
Average Index Sequential Access Method; Average Indexed Sequential Access Method
AVLC
Adaptive Variable Length Coder
AVLINE
Audiovisual Online (Database, National Library of Medicine, US)
AVLSI
Advanced Very-Large-Scale Integration
AVM
Automatic Voltage Margin
AVMARC
Audiovisual Machine Readable Catalogue (Database)
AVNL
Automatic Video Noise Limiter
AVOCON
Automated Vocabulary Control

AVOS
Acoustic Value Operating System; Advisor Virtual memory Operating System
AVP
Attached Virtual Processor
AVR
Automatic Voice Recognition; Automatic Volume Recognition (IBM)
AVS
Automated Verification System; Automatic Volume Sensing; Application Visualization System (DEC)
AVT
Automatic Vision Testing; Attribute Value Time
AVTR
Analog Video Tape Recorder
AW
Awardee (Searchable field); Acoustic Wave
AWACS
Advanced Warning and Control System; Amalgamated Wireless Australasia Computers Division Services; Airborne Warning and Control System (DOD)
AWAR
Area Weighted Average Resolution
AWC
Association for Women in Computing
AWDS
Automated Weather Distribution System
AWF
Acceptable Work-Load Factor
AWGN
Additive White Gaussian Noise (Telecommunications)
AWIPS
Advanced Weather Interactive Processing System
AWJM
Abrasive Water Jet Machining (Factory automation)
AWK
Aho Weinberger Kernigham (A UNIX programming utility)
AWRE
Atomic Weapons Research Establishment (UK)
AWS
American Wire Guage; Active Work Space
AX
Authorization Index (IBM)

AXP
Associative Crosspoint Processor

AY
Accession number Year (Searchable field)

AYT
Are You There?

AZ
Azimuth

AZAS
Adjustable Zero Adjustable Span

B

b

base; batch; bel; binary; bit; blank; block; boolean; buffer; bus; byte; bass; barn (Symbol); susceptance (Symbol for); base of a transistor (Symbol)

B

Susceptance (Symbol for); Flux density [or Magnetic flux] (Symbol for); Boron (Symbol); Battery; Bass; Base of a transistor (Symbol); Photometric brightness; Bel; Bearer channel

B+

B-plus [or B-positive] (Positive terminal [side] of a B-battery or the positive polarity of other sources of anode voltage)

B-

B-minus [or B-negative] (Negative terminal [side] of a B-battery or the negative polarity of other sources of anode voltage)

B+tree

Balanced+tree (A version of the *B-tree* indexing method)

B-DCS

Broadband Digital Cross-Connect System

B:drive

A common designation for the second floppy disk drive in DOS and OS/2

B/F

Background/Foreground (Monitors)

B-ISDN

Broadband ISDN [Integrated Services Digital Network]

B-LINK

Birmingham Library and Information Network (Library cooperative scheme, UK)

B&S

Brown and Sharpe gauge (The standard American method of designating the various wire sizes)

b/s

bits per second

B/S/Hz

Bits per Second per Hertz

B-tree

Balanced-tree (An organization technique for indexes)

B/W

Black and White

B8ZS

Binary Eight Zero Substitution [or Suppression] (AT&T)

Ba

Barium (Symbol)

BA

Binary Add (Computing); *Biological Abstracts* (Database, US); Bus Available; Bus Arbiter

BA/BASIC

Business Applications written in BASIC

BABS

Batch Automated Balancing System

BABT

British Approval Board for Telecommunications

BAC

Bus Adaptor Control

BACE

Basic Automatic Checkout Equipment

BACIS

Budget Accounting Information System

BACS

Banks Automated Clearing System (UK); Bibliographic Access and Control System (Washington University School of Medicine, St Louis, MO, US)

BACT

Best Available Control Technology

BAG

Bibliographic And Grouping system (US)

BAIS

Bulletin Articles Information Subsystem

BAK

Backup

BAK file

Backup file [or an auxiliary file] (In DOS and OS/2, a commonly used file extension for backup files)

bal

balance

BAL

Basic Assembly Language (Sperry Univac, US); Business Application Language

BALGOL

Burroughs Algebraic Compiler

BALLOTS

Bibliographic Automation of Large Library Operations using a Time-Sharing System (Stanford University, US)

BALM
Block And List Manipulator
BALSA
Brown Algorithm Simulator and Animator (Brown Univents, US)
balun (BALUN)
balanced to unbalanced
BALUN
Balanced Unbalanced (A communications device)
BAM
Basic Access Method; Block Access Method (Computing); Block Allocation Map
BAMP
Basic Analysis and Mapping Program
BAMS
Bell Atlantic Mobile Systems (US)
BAP
Basic Assembly Program; Bus Available Pulse
BAPTA
Bearing and Power Transfer Assembly
BAR
Bar Address Register; Base Address Register; Buffer Address Register (Computing)
BARON
Business/Accounts Reporting Operating Network
BARS
Bell Audit Relate System (Telephone Laboratories)
BART
Basic Aerodynamic Research Tunnel (NASA)
BAS
Bell Audit System (Telephone Laboratories); Block Automation System; Business Accounting System
BASBOL
Basic Business Oriented Language
BASE
Basic Semantic Element
base 2
binary
base 8
octal
base 10
decimal
base 16
hexadecimal

BASH
Bookseller's Association Service House (UK)
BASIC
Basel Information Center for Chemistry; Basic Algebraic Symbolic Interpretive Compiler; Basic Automatic Stored Instruction Computer; Battle Area Surveillance and Integrated Communications; Biological Abstracts Subjects In Context; Beginner's All-Purpose Symbolic Interaction [or Instruction] Code
BASICA
An interpreter for the Microsoft BASIC programming language
BASIS
Bank Automated Service Information System; Battelle Automatic Search Information System (Battelle Memorial Institute, US); *Bulletin of the American Society for Information Science*
BASS
Basic Analog Simulation System
BASYS
Basic System
bat
batch
BAT
Best Available Technology
BATAB
Baker and Taylor Automated Buying (Teleordering system, US)
BATEA
Best Available Technology Economically Achievable
BATS
Basic Additional Teleprocessing Support (Computing)
BAUD
Baudot Code (Pronounced "bawd")
BAVIP
British Association of Viewdata Information Providers
BAW
Bulk Acoustic Wave
BB
Begin Bracket; Base Band; Broadband; Building Block; Bulletin Board
bb (BB)
broadband
BBAC
Bus-to-Bus Access Circuit

BBC
British Broadcasting Corp; Broadband Coaxial Cable; Broadband Control

BBL
Basic Business Language; Branch Back and Load

BBP
British Business Press (Trade association, UK)

BBR
Bad Block Replacement (DEC)

BBRAM
Battery Backup Random Access Memory

BBS
Bulletin Board Service [or System] (PC message network system); Business Batch System; Bulletin Board Software

BBSP
Building Block Signal Processor

BBU
Battery Backup; BIT Buffer Unit

BC
Basic Control; Binary Code; Binary Counter; Bulk Core; Business Computer; Bibliographic Classification (Library classification system); Biosystematic Code (Searchable field); Branch City (Searchable field); Bus Controller

BCA
Bisynchronous Communications Adapter; Bit Count Appendage

BCAM
Basic Communication Access Method

BCAVM
British Catalogue of Audiovisual Materials (British Library)

BCB
Bit Control Block (IBM); Buffer Control Block (IBM)

BCC
Block-Check Character (Telecommunications); Blocked Calls (Telecommunications); Business Computer Center; Business Card Computer (Motorola Inc, US)

BCCL
Birkbeck College Computation Laboratory (UK)

BCD
Binary-Coded Decimal

BCDC
Binary-Coded Decimal Counters

BCDIC
Binary-Coded Decimal Interchange Code

(Extended character)

BCDNAF
Binary Coded Decimal Nonadjacent Form

BCE
Basic Comparison Element; Before Common Era

BCF
Background Communications Facility (IBM)

BCH
Bids per Circuit per Hour; Block Control Header (IBM); Blocked Calls Held (Telecommunications); Bose-Chaudhuri-Hocquenghem (Code)

BCI
Basic Command Interpreter; Binary-Coded Information

BCIA
Bounded Carry Inspection Adder

BCIP
Belgian Center for Information Processing

BCIS
Bank Credit Information System

BCIU
Bus Control Interface Unit

BCJS
Buffer Control Junction Switch

BCL
Bar Coded Label; Burroughs Common Language (Burroughs Corp, US); Business Computers Ltd (UK); Base-Coupled Logic

BCLN
British Columbia Library Network

BCM
Basic Control Memory; Basic Control Monitor (Xerox Corp, US); *British Catalogue of Music*; Bit Compression Multiplexer (AT&T); Buried Coarctate Mesa (Laser diode technology)

BCML
Burroughs Current Mode Logic (Burroughs Corp, US)

BCN
Biomedical Communication Network (US)

BCO
Binary Coded Octal

BCP
Batch Communications Program; BIT Control Panel; Budget Change Proposal; Byte Control Protocol; Bisynchronous Communications Processor (H-P);

Burroughs Control Program (Burroughs Corp, US); Biphase Communications Processor (National Semiconductor Inc, US)

BCPA
British Copyright Protection Association

BCPL
Basic Combined Programming Language

BCPS
Basic Call Processing System (Telecommunications)

BCR
Badge Card Reader; Byte Count Register; Bibliographic Center for Research (Denver, CO, US); Buffer Control Register

BCRT
Bus Controller/Remote Terminal

BCS
Basic Catalog Structure (IBM); Basic Communications Support; Basic Control System (H-P); Block Check Sequence; British Computer Society; Business Computer System; Binary Communications Synchronous; Biomedical Computing Society (US); Bridge Control System (Telecommunications); British Cable Services; The Boston Computer Society (US)

BCSI
Biometric Computer Service, Incorporated

BCT
Bandwidth Compression Technique; Between Commands Testing (Computing)

BCU
Basic Counter Unit; Binary Counting Unit; Block Control Unit (IBM); Buffer Control Unit

BCUA
Business Computers Users Association

BCUG
Bilateral Closed User Group (CCITT)

BCUGO
Bilateral Closed User Group with Outgoing access (CCITT)

BCW
Buffer Control Word

bd (BD)
baud

BD
Baud; Binary Decoder; Binary Divide; Binary-to-Decimal; Blank Display

BDAM
Basic Direct Access Method (IBM)

BDBE
Basic Data Base Environment

BDC
Binary Decimal Counter; Binary-Differential Computer

BDCB
Buffered Data and Control Bus

BDD
Binary-to-Decimal Decoder

BDDF
Bidirectional Diffraction Distribution Function

BDE
Basic Data Exchange

BDES
Basic Data Exchange Services (IBM); Boeing Data Entry System (Boeing Computer Services, US)

BDF
Backwards Differentiation Formulas; Basic Display File; Building Distribution Frame (Telecommunications)

BDFS
Basic Disk Filing System

BDIC
Binary-coded Decimal Interchange Code

BDL
Build Definition Language; Building Description Language

BDLC
Burroughs Data Link Control (Burroughs Corp, US)

BDM
Basic Data Management

BDN
Bell Data Network

BDOS
Basic Disk Operating System; Batch Disk Operating System

BDP
Business Data Processing

BDR
Bi-Duplexed Redundancy (Telecommunications); Binary Dump Routine

bdry
boundary

BDS
Bulk Data Switching; Business Definition System

BDT
Binary Deck-to-Tape

BDTS
Buffered Data Transmission Simulator

BDU
Basic Device Unit (IBM); Basic Display Unit
BDX
Bar Double-X
Be
Beryllium (Symbol)
BE
Back End; Beam Expander; Bus Enable
BEAB
British Electrotechnical Approvals Board
BEAMA
British Electrical and Allied Manufacturers Association
BEAMOS
Beam Accessed [or Addressed] Metal-Oxide Semiconductor (Memory technology)
BEAMS
Base Engineer Automated Management System
BEAR
Berkeley Elites Automated Retrieval (Information retrieval system, University of California at Berkeley, US)
BEAST
Basic Experimental Automatic Syntactic Translator
BEC
Bit Error Correction
BECS
Basic Error Control System
BECTIS
Bell College Technical Information Service (Hamilton, UK)
BED
Business Equipment Digest (UK)
BEEBUG
BBC [British Broadcasting Corp] Computer User Group (UK)
BEEC
Binary Error-Erasure Channel
BEEF
Business and Engineering Enriched FORTRAN (Computer programming language)
BEFAP
Bell Laboratories FORTRAN Assembly Program
BEI
British Education Index (Database, The British Library [BL])

bel
bel (ASCII control character)
BELINDIS
Belgian Information Dissemination Service
Bell
Bell System (American Telephone and Telegraph [AT&T], before 1984 divestiture)
Bell 103
An AT&T standard (family) for asynchronous 300 bps full-duplex modems using frequency-shift keying (FSK)
Bell 113
Same as Bell 103
Bell 201
An AT&T standard (family) for synchronous 2,000 or 2,400 bps full-duplex modems differential phase-shift keying (DPSK)
Bell 202
An AT&T standard (family) for asynchronous 1,800 bps full-duplex modems using DPSK
Bell 208
An AT&T standard (family) for synchronous 4,800 bps modems
Bell 209
An AT&T standard (family) for synchronous 9,600 bps full-duplex modems using quadrature amplitude modulation (QAM)
Bell 212
An AT&T standard (family) for asynchronous 1,200 bps full-duplex modems using DPSK modulation
Bellcore
Bell Communications Research Inc (Bell Laboratories, an R&D consortium, US)
BELLCORE
Bell Communication Research Inc (Bell Laboratories, an R&D consortium, US)
BELLREL
Bell Laboratories Library Real-time Loan (Library loan system, Bell Telephone Laboratories, US)
bells and whistles
A slang used to describe an application program's or computer system's advanced features, i.e., attractive features added to hardware or software beyond basic functionality
BELLTIP
library on-line acquisitions and cataloguing system (Bell Telephone Laboratories,

US)

BEM
Basic Editor Monitor (Sperry-Univac)

BEMA
Business Equipment Manufacturers' Association (US)

BEN
Bus Enable

BER
Basic Encoding Rules (One method for encoding information in the OSI environment); Bit Error Rate (Data communications)

BERM
Bit Error Rate Monitor

BERNET
Berliner Rechner Netz (German computer network)

BERT
Bit Error Rate Test(er)

BES
Basic Executive System (Honeywell, US)

BESSY
Bestell System (German teleordering system)

BEST
Basic Executive Scheduler and Timekeeper; Business EDP [Educational Data Processing] System Technique (NCR, US)

BET
Black Entertainment Television (Cable TV, US)

BETA
Business Equipment Trade Association (US)

BETRS
Basic Exchange Telecommunications Radio Service

BEU
Basic Encoding Unit

BeV
Billion electron Volts

BEX
Broadband Exchange (Telecommunications system, Western Union, US)

BF
Base File; Blocking Factor; Boundary Function

B factor
penalty factor (Refers to Via Net Loss [VNL])

BFAP
Binary Fault Analysis Program

BFAS
Basic File Access System

BFD
Basic Floppy Disk (Computing)

BFF
Buffered Flip-Flop

BFI
Batch Freeform Input

BFIC
Binary Fault Isolation Chart

BFICC
British Facsimile Industry Consultative Committee (Telecommunications)

BFL
Back Focal Length; Busy Flash (Telecommunications); Buffered FET [Field-Effect Transistor] Logic

BFN
Beam-Forming Network (Telecommunications)

BFO
Beat Frequency Oscillator

BFPDDA
Binary Floating Point Digital Differential Analyzer

BFPR
Binary Floating Point Resistor

BFS
Balanced File organization Scheme

BFT
Binary File Transfer; Binary File Transmission; Bulk Function Transfer

bg
background

BGP
Border Gateway Protocol (DEC)

BGRAF
Basis Graphics software (Magnavox, US)

BGS
Basic Graphic System

BH
Binary-to-Hexadecimal; Buried Heterostructure (Laser diode technology)

BHLF
ASCII Subset

BHSI
Beyond very High Speed Integration

Bi
Bismuth (Symbol)

BI
Basic Index (Searchable field); Batch Input; Buffer Index; Bus Interface;

Backplane Interconnect (DEC)

BIAS
Broadcast Industry Automation System (US); Biomedical Instrumentation Advisory Service (Clinical Research Center, UK)

BIB
Balanced Incomplete Block

BIBDES
Bibliographic Data Entry System

BIBLIOFILE
small library automation system (Information Planning Associates Inc, US)

BIBLIOS
Book Inventory Building Library Information Oriented System (Orange County Public Library, California, US)

BIBO
Bounded-Input Bounded-Output

BIC
Buffer Interlace Controller; Byte Input Control; Bus Interface Controller; Biodeterioration Information Center (University of Aston in Birmingham, UK)

BICARSA
Billing, Inventory Control, Accounts Receivable, Sales Analysis

BICEPS
Basic Industrial Control Engineering Programming System

BICEPT
Book Indexing with Context and Entry Point from Text (Indexing method)

BiCMOS
Bi-polar Complementary Metal-Oxide Semiconductor

BIDAP
Bibliographic Data-processing Program (Information retrieval software package)

BIDFET
Bipolar DMOS FET [Double-diffused Metal-Oxide Semiconductor Field-Effect Transistor]; Bipolar Diffused Field-Effect Transistor

BIDS
Burroughs Information Display Systems (Burroughs Corp, US)

BIE
Boundary-Integral Equation

BIF
Benchmark Interchange Format; Bus Interface

BIFET
Bipolar combined with JFET [Junction Field-Effect Transistor]

BIFF
Binary Interchange File Format

BiFIFO
Bidirectional First-In, First-Out

Big Blue
Nickname for International Business Machines Corp (IBM), which uses blue as its corporate color (i.e., because of IBM's blue covers on most of its earlier mainframes)

BIGFON
Broadband Integrated Glass Fibre Optical Network (Germany)

BIIT
Bureau International d'Information sur les Télécommunications (Switzerland)

BIL
Block Input Length

BILBO
Built-In Logic Block Observer (Logic element for self-testing)

BIM
Beginning of Information Marker; BIT Image Memory; Bus Interface Module; Branch If Multiplexer

BiMOS
Bipolar MOS [Metal-Oxide Semiconductor]

BIMS
Business Information Management System

bin
binary

BINAC
Binary Automatic Computer

BIO
Buffered Input-Output

BIO-L
Bi-phase Level

BIO-M
Bi-phase Mark

BIO-S
Bi-phase Space

BIOI
Block Input-Output Input

BIONIC
Biological and Electronic

BIOO
Block Input-Output Output

BIOP
Buffer Input-Output Processor
BIOR
Business Input-Output Return (Univac system)
BIOS
Basic Input-Output System (Pronounced "bye-ose")
BIOSIS
Biosciences Information Service (Database, US)
BIP
BASIC Interpreter Package (For BASIC language); Binary Image Processor (Computing); *Books In Print* (Publication, R.R. Bowker, US)
BIPAC
Bibliographic Procedures and Control Committee of RLG [Research Libraries Group] (US)
BIPS
Billions of Instructions per Second (Measure of computing power)
BIR
Bus Interface Register
BIRS
Basic Indexing and Retrieval System; Basic Information Retrieval System (Cataloguing and indexing package, Information Systems Laboratory, Michigan State University, US)
BIS
Bureau of Information Science (US); Business Information System; *Blood Information Service* (Database, US); *Brain Information Service* (Database, University of California, US); British Imperial System (Weights and measures system); Bowne Information Systems (Host, US); Business Information Service
BISA
Bibliographic Information on South-east Asia (Database, University of Sydney, Australia)
BISAC
Book Industry Systems Advisory Committee (Sub-committee of BISG)
BISAD
Business Information Systems Analysis and Design
BISAM
Basic Indexed Sequential Access Method

(IBM)
BISDN
Broadband Integrated Services Digital Network (AT&T)
BISFA
British Industrial and Scientific Film Association
BISG
Book Industry Study Group (US)
BISITS
British Iron and Steel Institute Translation Service
BISL
British Informatics Society Ltd
BISNET
Bank Information System Network (US)
BISNY
Binary Synchronous communication (Also known as BSC)
BIST
Built-In Self-Test(ing)
Bisync
Binary synchronous communication
BiSync
Binary Synchronous communication
BISYNC
Binary Synchronous communication (Pronounced "bye-sink")
BIT/s
Bits per second
bit
binary digit
BIT
Binary Digit; Built-In-Test; Bipolar Integrated Technology
BITBLT
Bit Block Transfer
BITE
Built-In Test and Evaluation
BITnet
Because It's Time network (A wide-area network that links well over 1,000 colleges and universities in the U.S., Canada, and Europe)
BITNET
Because It's Time Network
BIU
Basic Information Unit (IBM); Buffer Image Unit; Bus Interface Unit
BIVA
British Interactive Video Association
BIW
Business Information Wire (Canadian

Press database)

BIX
Binary Information Exchange; Byte Information Exchange (Byte Magazine)

BIZMAC
Business Machine Computer

BJF
Batch Job Foreground (Computing)

BJM
Between Job Monitor (Computing)

BJT
Bipolar Junction Transistor

Bk
Berkelium (Symbol)

BKER
Block Error Rate

bkg
bookkeeping

bkgrd
background

bksp
backspace

bl
blank; blanking

BL
BLAISE [British Library Automated Information Service] number; Block Length (Computing); The British Library

BLA
Binary Logical Association; Blocking Acknowledgment signal (Telecommunications)

BLADES
Bell Laboratories Automatic Design System (US)

BLAISE
British Library Automated Information Service (Host for bibliographic databases, See (BL)

BLAST
Blocked Asynchronous Transmission

BLBSD
The British Library Bibliographic Services Division

BLC
Board Level Computer

BLD
Binary Load Dump

BLERT
Block Error Rate Test

BLF
Branch Loss Factor

BLINK
Backward Linkage

BLIS
Bell Laboratories Interpretive System; Biblio-techniques Library and Information System

BLISS
Basic Language for the Implementation of System Software; Basic List-Oriented Information Structures System

blk
black; block

BLL
Base Locator Linkage; Below Lower Limit

BLLD
The British Library Lending Division

BLM
Basic Language Machine (Type of computer)

BLMPX
Block Multiplexer

BLMUX
Block Multiplexer

BLO
Blocking signal (Telecommunications)

BLOC
Booth Library Online Circulation (Library circulation system, Eastern Illinois State University, US)

BLP
Bypass Label Processing (IBM)

BLR&DD
The British Library Research and Development Department

BLRD
The British Library Reference Division

BLSL
British Leyland Systems Ltd

BLT
Basic Language Translator (For BASIC language); Block Transfer

BLU
Bipolar Line Unit (Telecommunications); Basic Link Unit (IBM)

BLUE
Best Linear Unbiased Estimate

bm
benchmark

BM
Base Machine; Basic Material; Bill of Materials; Buffer Module; Business Machine; Binary Multiply

BMC
Block Multiplexer Channel; Buffer Management Chip; Bubble Memory Controller; Bulk Media Conversion; Burst Multiplexer Channel (Telecommunications)

BMD
Benchmark Monitor Display system (Sperry Univac, US); Bubble Memory Device

BMDP
Biomedical Data Processing

BMDS
British Medical Data Systems

BMEDSS
Biomedical Engineering Decision Support Services (Database and electronic mail service, Akron City Hospital, US)

BMG
Business Machine Group (Burroughs Corp, US)

BMI
Bibliography Master Index (Database, Gale Research, US)

BMIC
Bus-Master Interface Controller (Intel Corp, US)

BMIS
Bank Management Information System

BML
Basic Machine Language

BMLC
Basic Multiline Controller

BMMC
Basic Monthly Maintenance Charge

BMMG
British Microcomputer Manufacturers' Group

BMOM
Base Maintenance and Operational Model

BMP
Batch Message Processing (IBM); Benchmark Program; Bill of Materials Processor

BMS
Basic Mapping Support (IBM); Basic Monitor System (DEC); Building Management Systems; Bandwidth Management Service (AT&T)

BMT
Block Mode Terminal interface

BMTI
Block Mode Terminal Interface (Computing)

BMTT
Buffered Magnetic Tape Transfer

BN
Binary Number; Block Number; Biosystematic code Name (Searchable field); Branch Name; Bureau Number (Searchable fields); diminutive of ISBN

BNA
Bureau of National Affairs Inc (US); Burroughs Network Architecture (Burroughs Corp, US)

BNB
British National Bibliography (Database, BLBSD)

BNC
Bayonette Connector (Electronics, for co-axial cable)

BNCOD
British National Conference On Databases

BNF
Backus Naur [Normal] Form (ALGOL)

BNF ABS
British Non-Ferrous Abstracts (Database, British Non-Ferrous Metals Technology Center)

BNG
Branch No Group

BNIST
Bureau National de l'Information Scientifique et Technique (Coordinating body, France)

BNPF
Beginning Negative Positive Finish (Subset of ASCII)

BNZS
Bipolar with N Zeros Substitution (Used in PCM terminology)

BO
Binary-to-Octal; Byte Out

BOA
Basic Ordering Agreement

BOB
Brains On Board (Personal robot, Androbot, US); Break-Out Box

BOC
Back Office Crunch; Block-Oriented Computer; Breach Of Contract; Byte Output Control; Bell Operating Company (AT&T)

BOCI
Business Organization Climate Index

BOCOL
Basic Operating Consumer Oriented Language

BOD
Board Of Directors

BOFADS
Business Office Forms Administration Data System

BOG
Board of Governors

BOI
Beginning Of Information (Computing); Branch Output Interrupt

BOLD
Bibliographic Online Library Display

BOM
Bill of Materials; Bureau Of Mines (US)

BOMP
Bill Of Material(s) Processor (IBM)

BOMS
Base Operations Maintenance Simulator

BOOG
British Osborne Owners Group (User group)

BOOGIE
BOOG [British Osborne Owners Group] Information Exchange

Bool
Boolean

boot
bootstrap

BOP
Balance Of Payments (Databank, IMF [International Monetary Fund]); Basic Operating Program; Bit-Oriented Protocol (Computing); Binary Output Program

BOPA
Basic Operating Programming Aid

BOR
Bureau of Operating Rights; Bus Out Register (Computing)

BORAM
Block Oriented [or Organized] Random Access Memory

BORIS
Book Order Register and Invoicing System (Microcomputer based bookshop system, UK)

BORSCHT
Battery-feed Overvoltage-protection, Ringing, Supervision, Codec, Hybrid and Testing (AT&T, interface circuitry, digital communications)

BORSHT
Battery, Overvoltage, Ring, Supervision, Hybrid Test

BOS
Background Operating System; Basic Op-

erating System; Batch Operating System (Computing); Book Order System (Automated system, University of Massachusetts, US); Business Operating Software

BOSFET
Bidirectional Output Switch (FET) Field Effect Transistor

BOSR
Base Of Stack Register

BOSS
Basic Operating Software System (or, System Software) (Basic Four, US); Basic Operating System (Toshiba, Japan); Batch Operating Software System; Business Oriented Software System (DEC); Backup Optical Storage System (Aquidneck Data Corp)

BOT
Beginning Of Tape (Computing)

BOTMA
British Office Technology Manufacturers Alliance

BP
Batch Processing; Bit Processor; Buffered Printing

BPA
Bandpass Amplifier

BPAM
Basic Partitioned Access Method (IBM)

BPC
Basic Peripheral Channel; Binding Post Chamber (Telecommunications)

BPCC
British Printing and Communication Corp

BPDA
Bibliographic Pattern Discovery Algorithm

BPE
Basic Programming Extensions

BPF
Bandpass Filter

BPI
Bits Per Inch; Bytes Per Inch (Computing, storage density); British Phonographic Industry

bpi (BPI)
bits per inch

BPIF
British Printing Industries Federation

BPL
Binary Program Loader; Business Planning Language; Business Programming

Language; Burroughs Program Loader (Burroughs Corp, US)

BPM
Ballistic Particle Machining (Factory automation); Balanced Processing Monitor (Mitsubishi Corp, Japan); Batch Processing Monitor (Xerox Corp, US)

BPMM
Bits Per Millimeter (Computing, storage density)

BPPF
Base Program Preparation Facility

BPR
By-Pass Ratio

BPRA
British Pattern Recognition Association

BPS
Basic Programming Support (IBM); BASIC Programming System; Batch Processing System; Binary Program Space; Bits Per Second (Computing, transmission rate); Bytes Per Second (Computing)

BPSA
Business Products Standards Association (US)

BPSI
Bits Per Square Inch (Computing)

BPSK
Binary Phase Shift Keying [or Keyed] (Telecommunications)

BPSS
Basic Packet Switching System (AT&T)

BPV
Bipolar Violation

BQL
Basic Query Language; Batch Query Language (Computer programming languages)

br
break

Br
Bromine (Symbol)

BR
Base Register; Break Request (Telecommunications); Bus Request

BRA
Basic Rate Access; British Robot Association

BRASTACS
Bradford Science Technology and Commercial Services (Information service, UK)

BRC
Bit Reversion Circuit; Bounded Right

Context

BRD
Binary Rate Divider

BRDF
Bidirectional Reflectance Distribution Function

BREMA
British Radio Equipment Manufacturers Association

BRF
Benchmark Reporting Format

BRG
Baud Rate Generator

BRI
Book Review Index (Database, Gale Research, US); Basic Rate Interface (AT&T)

BRICMICS
British Committee for Map Information and Catalogue Systems (UK)

brk
break

BRL
Ballistic Research Laboratory (US Army)

BRM
Binary Rate Multiplier; Bit Rate Multiplier; Binary Relationship Model (Computing)

BRMC
Business Research Management Center

BROM
Bipolar Read-Only Memory

BROWSER
Browsing Online With Selective Retrieval (Information retrieval searching system)

BRS
Bibliographic Retrieval Services (US); Break Request Signal (Telecommunications); Business Recovery Service (IBM)

BRSL
British Robotics Systems Ltd

BRT
Binary Run Tape

BRTM
Basic Real-Time Monitor

BRU
Basic Resolution Unit

BRUCE
Buffer Register Under Computer Edit

BS
Back Space; Backspace Character; Back Spread; Beam Splitter; Bits per Second; Block Sale; British Standard; Bureau of

Ships; Bureau of Standards; Business System; Binary Subtract; Branch State (Searchable field)
BSA
Binary Synchronous Adapter
BSAL
Block Structured Assembly Language
BSAM
Basic Sequential Access Method (IBM, system procedure)
BSC
Basic message Switching Center (Telecommunications); Binary Symmetric Channel; Binary Synchronous Communication(s) (IBM, transmission protocol)
BSC/SS
Binary Synchronous Communications/ Start-Stop
BSCA
Binary Synchronous [or BiSynchronous] Communication Adapter
BSCC
Binary Synchronous [or BiSynchronous] Communications Controller
BSCFL
Binary Synchronous [or BiSynchronous] Frame Level (NCR)
BSCM
Binary Synchronous [or BiSynchronous] Communications Macro
BSCS
Binary Synchronous [or BiSynchronous] Communication System
BSD
Bibliographic Services Division (The British Library); Bulk Storage Device; Boundary Scan Diagnosis
BSDL
Boundary Scan Description(ive) Language (H-P)
BSDP
Bibliographic Service Development Program (CLR [Council on Library Resources Inc], US)
BSD UNIX
Berkeley Software Distribution UNIX (Versions of the UNIX system that were developed at the University of California at Berkeley, US)
BSE
Basic Service Element; Broadcast Satellite Experiment (Communications satel-

lite, Japan)
BSELCH
Buffered Selector Channel
BSF
Back Space File; Bandwidth Shape Factor; British Software Factory (UK)
BSI
British Standard Interface; British Standards Institution; Boundary Scan Input
BSIE
Banking Systems Information Exchange (US)
BSL
Bit Serial Link
BSM
Basic Storage Module; Batch Spool Monitor
BSO
Bismuth Silicon Oxide (Laser crystal); Boundary Scan Output
BSP
Business Systems Planning (IBM); Burroughs Scientific Processor (Burroughs Corp, US)
BSQI
Basic Schedule of Quantified Items
BSR
Back Space Record; Buffered Send/Receive; Blip Scan Ratio; Boundary Scan Register
BSS
Bulk Storage System; Broadcasting Satellite Service
BST
Business Systems Technology (US); British School Technology (Government initiative to promote technology in schools); Boundary Scan Test
BSTAT
Basic Status register (IBM)
BSY
Binary Synchronous
bt
between
BT
Barred Trunk (Telecommunications); British Telecom (Common carrier, UK); Busy Tone; Block Terminal (Telecommunications); Burst Trapping
BTADC
British Telecom Action for Disabled Customers

BTAM
Basic Tape Access Method (Computing);
Basic Telecommunications Access Method
(IBM); Basic Terminal Access Method
(Computing); Basic Teleprocessing Access
Method

BTBS
British Telecom Business Systems

BTC
Batch Terminal Controller; Block Trans-
fer Controller (Computing); Business and
Technology Center

BTD
Binary-To-Decimal

BTDF
Bidirectional Transmittance Distribution
Function

BTE
Bi-directional Transceiver Element (Tele-
communications); Business Terminal
Equipment; British Telecom Enterprises

BTE/Vass
British Telecom Enterprises' Value added
systems and services

BTF
Bulk Transfer Facility

BTG
British Technology Group

BTI
British Telecom International (International division of BT [British Telecom])

BTL
Business Translation Language; Beginning of Tape Level; Bell Telephone Laboratories (US); Backplane Transistor Logic
(IEEE)

BTLZ
British Telecom Lempel Ziv (A data compression algorithm)

BTM
Basic Transport Mechanism; Batch Time-
sharing Monitor (Xerox Corp, US); Bell
Telephone Manufacturing Co; Benchmark
Timing Methodology

BTMA
Busy Tone Multiple-Access

BTMF
Block Type Manipulation Facility

BTNS
Basic Terminal Network Support

BTOS
Burroughs version of the CTOS [Conver-
gent Technologies {now part of Unisys}

Operation System] operating system;
Burroughs Time-Share Operating System
(Burroughs Corp, US)

BTP
Batch Transfer Program

BTRL
British Telecom Research Laboratories

B TRON
Business TRON [The Real-time Operating system Nucleus]

BTS
British Telecommunications Systems;
Business Telecommunications Services
(Satellite communications network, Aus-
tralia); Batch Terminal Simulator(ion)
(Systems testing software)

BTSS
Basic Time Sharing System; Braille Time
Sharing System

BTT
Bank Teller Terminal

Btu
British thermal unit

BTU
Basic Transmission Unit (IBM); British
Thermal Unit

BTV
Broadcast Television

BU
Base Unit; Bottom Up

BUC
Bus Control

BUDS
Building Utility Design System

BUDWSR
Brown University Display for Working Set
References

BUE
Built-Up-Edge

buf
buffer

BUFVC
British Universities Film and Video Council

BUG
Basic Update Generator

BUGS
Brown University Graphic System

BUIC
Back-Up Interceptor Control

Bull HN
Bull HN Information Systems Inc (A computer manufacturer that is the outgrowth

of Honeywell Bull Inc)

BUMP
Bottom-Up Modular Programming

BUNCH
Burroughs, Univac, NCR, Control Data and Honeywell (The "BUNCH" were IBM's competitors after RCA and GE got out of the computer business)

BUR
Backup Register

BURISA
British Urban and Regional Information Systems Association

bus
business

BUS
Basic Utility System

BUSREQ
Bus Request

BVA
British Videogram Association; Best Vision Antenna Services (Australia)

BVGA
British Videogram Association

BVR
Balanced Visual Response

BW
Band Width; Bits per Word

BWC
Buffer Word Counter (Computing)

BWD
Basic Work Data

BWG
Beam Waveguide

BWR
Bandwidth Radio; Bandwidth Ratio

BWT
Backward Wave Tube; Bandwidth Ratio

BX
Base Indexed; Branch Exchange (Telecommunications)

BXB
British Crossbar (Telephone exchange)

BYMUX
Byte Multiplexer channel

BYP
By Pass

bypro(s)
by-product(s)

BYSINC
Binary Communications Synchronous (Protocol)

BZ
Branch Zip code (Searchable field)

C

c

capacitance (Symbol); capacitor; carry; cents; centi (SI prefix denoting 10^{-2}); clear; clock; computer; constant; control; controller; counter; speed of light [in a vacuum] (Symbol for)

C

Capacitance; Carbon (Symbol); Calorie; Celsius [or Centigrade] Collector [of a transistor] (Symbol); Character; Constant (Mathematics); Coulomb (Symbol, electricity); Computer language (A low-level general purpose programming language associated with the UNIX operating system, Bell Laboratories); Cycle; Roman numeral designation for "100"; C-cell (Voltaic cell)

C&A

Classification and Audit

C-ARMS

Commercial-Accounts Routing and Design System

C & B

Concurrency and control Bus (Computing)

C-BASIC

Commercial BASIC (High level computer language)

C & C

Computer and Communications

C/CDSB

Command/Control Disable

C/CSI

Commercial/Computer Systems Integration

C/R

Carriage Return; Command/Response

c/s

cycles per second

C/S

Certificate of Service

C/SP

Communications/Symbiont Processor

C&T

Classification and Testing

C/TP

Control/Test Panel

C & W

Cable and Wireless (UK telecommunications company)

C+

C-plus [or C-positive] (The positive [side] terminal of a C-battery, or the positive polarity of other sources of grid-bias voltage)

C-

C-minus [or C-negative] (The negative [side] terminal of a C-battery, or the negative polarity of other sources of grid-bias voltage)

C^2

Command and Control

C^2I

Command, Control, and Intelligence

C^3

Command, Control, and Communications; Command and Control Center

C^3I

Command, Control, Communications and Intelligence

C3

Command, Control, and Communications

C3I

Command, Control, Communications and Intelligence

C^4

Command, Control, Communications, and Computer Systems

C^4I^2

Command, Control, Communications, Computing/Information and Intelligence

C4

Controlled Collapse Chip Connection

Ca

Calcium (Symbol)

CA

Call Number (Searchable field); Card Alert (Searchable field); Channel Adapter; Common Applications (IBM); Communications Adapter; Connecting Arrangement; Control Area; *Chemical Abstracts* (Database, CAS [Chemical Abstracts Service]); Cited Authors (Searchable field); Construction Analysis; Computer Automation Inc (US); Collision Avoidance

CA CON

Chemical Abstracts Condensates (Database, CAS [Chemical Abstracts Service])

CA/D

Character Assemble/Disassemble

CAAD

Computer-Aided Architectural Design;

Computer-Aided Art and Design; Computer-Aided Analysis and Design

CAAIS
Computer-Assisted Action Information System

CAAS
Computer-Aided Approach Sequencing; Computer-Assisted Acquisition System

CAAT
Computer-Assisted Audit Techniques

CAB
Civil Aeronautics Board (Originator of air transport databanks, US); Communications Adaptor Board (Computing); Cabletelevision Advertising Bureau (US)

CABD
Computer-Aided Building Design

CABLIS
Current Awareness Bulletin for Librarians and Information Scientists (Publication, BL [The British Library)

CABP
Campaign Against Book Piracy (Publishers' association, UK)

CABS
Computer-Aided Batch Scheduling; Computer-Aided Batch Searching; Computer Augmented Block System; Computerized Annotated Bibliographic System (Alberta University, Canada); *Current Awareness in Biological Sciences* (Database, Pergamon)

CAC
Computer Acceleration Control; Computer-Aided Classification

CACA
Computer-Aided Circuit Analysis

CACD
Computer-Aided Circuit Design

CACE
Computer-Aided Control Engineering

CACM
Communications of the Association for Computing Machinery (Journal, US)

CACR
Cache Control Register

CACS
Computer-Assisted Communication System; Computer-Aided Communications System; Content Addressable Comput(er)ing System

CACSD
Computer-Aided Control System Design

CAD
Computer-Aided Design; Computer-Aided

Drafting; Computer-Aided Detection; Computer-Aided Dispatching; *Computer Applications Digest;* Character Assemble Disassemble

CAD/CAM
Computer-Aided Design/Computer-Aided Manufacturing; Computer-Aided Design and Manufacture (Less preferred form)

CADA
Computer-Assisted Distribution and Assignment; Computer-Aided Design Analysis

CADAM
Computer-Graphics Augmented Design and Manufacturing

CADAPSO
Canadian Association of Data Processing Service Organizations

CADAR
Computer-Aided Design, Analysis and Reliability; Computer-Aided Design And Reliability

CADAS
Computer Automatic Data Acquisition System

CADAVRS
Computer-Assisted Dial Access Video Retrieval System

CADC
Central Air Data Computer; Computer-Aided Design Centre

CADCOM
Computer-Aided Design for Communications

CADD
Computer-Aided Design and Drafting; Computer-Aided Design and Draughting (UK); Computer-Aided Design and Development

CADDIA
Cooperation in the Automation of Data Documentation for Import/Export and Agriculture (EC)

CADE
Computer-Aided Design and Engineering; Computer-Aided Design Evaluation; Computer-Assisted Data Entry; Computer-Assisted Data Evaluation

CADEP
Computer-Aided Design of Electronic Products

CADES
Computer-Aided Development and Evalu-

ation System

CADI
Call Diverter (NSEM [*Nederlandsche Standard Electric Maatschappij*], ITT subsidiary, the Netherlands)

CADIC
Computer-Aided Design of Integrated Circuits

CADICS
Computer-Aided Design of Industrial Cabling Systems

CADIG
Coventry and District Information Group (Library cooperative, UK)

CADIN
Canadian Integration North (Radar system)

CADIS
Computer-Aided Design of Information Systems

CADLIC
Computer-Aided Design of Linear Integrated Circuits

CADMAC
Computer Assisted Drawing Management and Control

CADMAT
Computer-Aided Design Manufacture and Testing; Computer-Aided Design, Manufacture and Test

CADO
Computer-Aided Document Origination

CADOCR
Computer-Aided Design of Optical Character Recognition

CADPIN
Customs Automated Data Processing Intelligence Network

CADS
Computer-Aided Design System; Computer-Aided Digitizing System; Computer-Analysis and Design System; Content Addressable File Store

CADSS
Combined Analog-Digital Systems Simulator

CADSYS
Computer-Aided Design System

CADTES
Computer-Aided Design and Test

CAE
Computer-Aided Engineering; Computer-Assisted Estimating; Computer-Aided

Education; Computer-Assisted Electrocardiography

CAEDS
Computer-Aided Engineering Design System (IBM)

CAEPS
Computer-Aided Estimating and Planning System

CAESO
Computer-Aided Engineering Support Office (Naval Weapons Center, US)

CAF
Computer-Aided, or Assisted Fraud

CAFC
Computed Automated Frequency Control

CAFE
Computer-Aided Facilities Engineering

CAFRS
Client Accounting and Financial Reporting System

CAFS
Content-Addressable File Store

CAG
Computer Applications Group, of Aslib; Computer-Assisted Guidance; Cooperative Automation Group (UK)

CAGD
Computer-Aided Geometric Design

CAGE
Compiler and Assembler by General Electric

CAHT
Computer Aids for Human Translation (Translation system)

CAI
Computer-Administered Instruction; Computer-Aided Instruction; Computer-Assisted Instruction (Teaching methods); Computer-Aided Industry; Computer Automation Inc (US); Confederation of Ariel Industries

CAIC
Computer-Assisted Indexing and Classification

CAIN
Cataloging And Indexing System (Database on agriculture, National Agricultural Library, US)

CAINS
Computer-Aided Instruction System

CAIOP
Computer-Analog Input-Output

CAIP
Computer-Assisted Indexing Program (CAIC [Computer-Assisted Indexing and Classification] system, UN)

CAIRS
Computer-Assisted Information Retrieval System

CAIS
Canadian Association for Information Science; Computer-Aided Insurance System; Communication And Information Systems division of MEP [Micro-Electronics Education Programme] (UK)

CAISF
Chemical Abstracts Integrated Subject File (Database, CAS [Chemical Abstracts Service])

CAIVR
Computer-Assisted Instruction with Voice Response

CAK
Command Access Keys; Command Acknowledge

CAL
Common Assembler Language; Common Assembly Language; Computer-Aided Learning; Computer-Assisted Learning; Conversational Algebraic Language (High level language); Computer Animation Language; Cray Assemble Language (Cray Research, (US); Copyright Agency Ltd (Australia)

CAL/SAP
Computer Adaptive Language for development of Structural Analysis Programs (University of California at Berkeley, US)

CALA
Computer-Aided Loads Analysis

CALB
Computer-Aided Line Balancing

calc
calculate

CALCOMP
California Computer Products Inc (US)

CALDIS
Calderdale Information Service (Library cooperative scheme, UK)

CALL
Library of Congress call number (Searchable field)

CALLS
California Academic Libraries List of Se-

rials

CALM
Computer Archive of Language Materials (Stanford University, US); Computer-Assisted Library Mechanization

CALMS
Credit And Loan Management System (System for monitoring and measuring electricity usage using signals over telephone system, UK)

CALR
Computer-Assisted Legal Retrieval

CALRS
Centralized Automated Loop Reporting System

CALS
Computer-Aided Acquisition and Logistics Support

CALSSP
Common Assembly Language Scientific Subroutine Package

CAM
Calculated Access Method; Communications Access Manager; Communications Access Method; Computer-Aided Manufacturing; Content Addressable Memory; Content Addressable Memory; Content Addressed Memory; Cascade Access Method (NCR); Computer Access Matrix; Computer Addressed Memory; Computer-Automated Machining; Contact Angle Measurement

CAMA-ONI
Centralized Automatic Message Accounting-Operator Number Identification operator

CAMA
Centralized Automatic Message Accounting; Control and Automation Manufacturers Association

CAMAC
Computer-Aided Measurement and Control; Computer-Automated Measurement and Control (IEEE)

CAMEL
Computer-Aided Manufacturing Network

CAMELOT
Computerization and Mechanization of Local Office Tasks

CAMERA 72
Legal information retrieval project (Camera de Deputati, Italy)

CAMET
Computer Archive of Modern English Texts (University of Oslo, Norway)

CAMIS
Computer-Assisted Make-up and Imaging System

CAMMU
Cache And Memory Management Unit

CAMP
Central Access Monitor Program; Compiler for Automatic Machine Programming; Controls And Monitoring Processor; Cooperative African Microform Project

CAMPRAD
Computer-Assisted Message Preparation Relay and Distribution

CAMPS
Computer-Assisted Message Processing System

CAMS
Computerized Automotive Maintenance System (IBM and General Motors, US)

can
cancel; cancellation

CAN
Cancel (CCITT); Controller Area Network

can (CAN)
cancel (CCITT, control character)

CAN/MARC
Canadian Machine-Readable Cataloguing (Database, NLC [National Library of Canada)

CAN/SDI
Canadian Selective Dissemination of Information (Information dissemination service, CISTI [Canada Institute for Scientific and Technical Information])

canc
cancel; cancellation

CANCERLINE
Cancer Information Online (Database, National Cancer Institute, US)

CANCERLIT
Cancer Literature (CANCERLINE database, US)

CANCERPROJ
Cancer Projects (CANCERLINE database, US)

CANCOM
Canadian Satellite Communications Inc

CANDE
Command and Edit language (Burroughs Corp, US); Culvert Analysis and Design

CANDO
Computer Analysis of Networks with Design Orientation; Classification Alpha-Numérique de la Documentation (Classification for scientific papers [with emphasis on medical], France)

CANDOC
Canadian Documentation (Document ordering system)

CANSIM
Canadian Socio-economic Information Management System (Databank, Canada)

CANTAT
Canadian Transatlantic (Cable system between Canada and UK)

CANTRAN
Cancel Transmission

CANUNET
Canadian University Computer Network

CANYOLE
Canadian On-Line Enquiry (Host, National Research Council, Canada)

CAO
Computer-Aided [or Automated] Office

CAOCI
Commercially Available Organic Chemicals Index (Databank, Chemical Notation Association, UK)

CAOS
Computer-Augmented Oscilloscope System

cap
capacity

CAP
Computer-Aided Planning; Computer-Aided Programming; Card Assembly Program; Cataloguing in Advance of Publication (BLBSD [The British Library Bibliographic Services Division]); Computer-Aided Production; Computer Analysts and Programmers (UK consultancy); Cellular Array Processor; Communications Applications Processor; Compiler Assembly Program; Computer-Aided Publishing

CAPABLE
Controls And Panel Arrangement By Logical Evaluation

CAPARS
Computer-Aided Placement and Routing System

CAPC
Computer-Aided Production Control

CAPDAC
Computer-Aided Piping Design And Construction

CAPE
Computer-Aided Planning and Estimating; Communications Automatic Processing Equipment

CAPER
Computer-Aided Pattern Evaluation and Recognition

CAPERTSIM
Computer-Assisted Program Evaluation Review Technique Simulation

CAPITAL
Computer-Assisted Placing In The Areas of London (Employment Services Agency, Department of Employment, UK)

CAPM
Computer-Aided Production Management

CAPOSS
Capacity Planning and Operation Sequencing System

CAPP
Computer-Aided Part Planning; Computer-Aided Process Planning; Content-Addressable Parallel Processor

CAPR
Catalog of Programs

CAPRI
Card and Printer Remote Interface; Computerized Analysis for Programming Investments; Computer-Aided Personal Reference Index system (Atomic Energy Authority, UK)

CAPS
Computer-Aided Planning System; Computer-Aided Problem Solving; *Current Advances In Plant Science* (Database, Pergamon, UK); Computer-Aided Product Selection

CAPTAIN
Character And Pattern Telephone Access Information Network

CAPTAINS
Character And Pattern Telephone Access Information Network System

CAPUR
Computer-Assisted Programming User Remotes

CAQA
Computer-Aided Quality Assurance

CAR
Carry Register; Channel Address register; Computer-Aided Retrieval; Current Ad-

dress Register; Computer-Assisted Retrieval; Check Authorization Record

CARAD
Computer-Aided Reliability and Design

CARD
Compact Automatic Retrieval Display; Compact Automatic Retrieval Device (MIT [Massachusetts Institute of Technology], US); Computer-Aided Remote Driving (NASA)

CARDA
Computer-Aided Reliability Data Analysis

CARDS
Computer-Aided Reliability Data System

CARESS
Career Retrieval Search System (Pittsburgh University, US)

CARIS
Computerized Agricultural Search Information System (Information system, UN Food and Agriculture Organization)

CARL
Chemical Algorithm for Reticulation Linearization

CAROL
Computer Oriented Language (Olivetti Corp, Italy); Circulation And Retrieval On-Line (Library circulation system, James Cook University, Australia)

CARP
Computer Air-Released Point

carr
carrier

CARS
Computer-Aided Routing System; Computer-Audit Retrieval System; Computerized Audit and Reporting System; Community Antenna Relay Service; Computer-Assisted Referee Selection (System to aid journal editors); Computer-Assisted Reference Service (University of Arizona, US)

cart
cartridge

CARTS
Capacitor And Resistor Technology Symposium

CAS/CPA
Computer Accounting System/Computer Performance Analysis

CAS
Chemical Abstracts Service (Database

compiler, part of ACS [American Chemical Society]); Circuits And Systems; Client Accounting System; Channel-Associated Signalling (CCITT); Column Address Select; Column Address Strobe; Customer Accounting System; Computer Aid System; Computer Acquisition System; Computerized Acquisition System (R.R. Bowker Company, US); Control Automation System (IBM); Current Awareness Service; Column Address Strobe (Computing, RAM refresh method); Cartridge Access Station; Communications Applications Specification (Intel Corp, US); Computer Access Site

CASA
Computer and Automated Systems Association (US)

CASAG
Computer Assisted Synthetic Analysis Group (Chemical analysis aids, US)

CASCADE
Centralized Administrative Systems Control and Design

CASD
Computer-Aided System Design

CASDAC
Computer-Aided Ship Design And Construction

CASE
Computer-Aided Software Engineering; Computer-Aided Systems Engineering; Computer-Aided Systems Evaluation; Computers And Systems Engineering (UK information technology manufacturer); Common Application Service Elements (ANSI, MAP)

CAsearch
Chemical Abstracts Search (Database on chemical science, ACS [American Chemical Society])

CASES
Computer-Assisted Simulation and Education System (Simulation of doctor's decision making, Netherlands)

CAS files
Chemical Abstracts Service files

CASH
Computer-Aided Stock Holdings; Computer-Aided System Hardware; Computer-Assisted Subject Headings Program (Cataloguing project, University of California

at San Diego, US)

CASIA
Chemical Abstracts Subject Index Alert (Database on chemical science, ACS [American Chemical Society])

CASL
Crosstalk Application Script Language

CASLIS
Canadian Association of Special Libraries and Information Services

CASNET
Casual-Associative Network

CASO
Computer-Assisted System Operation

CASOE
Computer Accounting System for Office Expenditure

CASP
Computer-Aided Space Planning

CASS
Computer Automatic Scheduling System; Computer Access Security System

CASSI
Chemical Abstracts Source Index (Database, ACS [American Chemical Society])

CASSM
Context Addressed Segment Sequential Memory

CAST
Computer Applications and Systems Technology; Computer-Assisted Scanning Techniques; Chemical Abstract Searching Terminal (Computer Corp of America); Computerized Automatic System Tester; Cable And Satellite Television; Center for Advanced Studies in Telecommunications; Computer-Aided Software Translation

CASTI
Centers for the Analysis of Science and Technical Information (US)

CASW
Council for the Advancement of Science Writing

CAT
Computer-Aided Test(ing) (H-P); Computer Axial Tomography; Computer-Aided Tomography (Aids to medical diagnosis); Computer-Aided Translation; Computer-Assisted Translation; Computer-Aided Typesetting; Computer-Assisted Teleconferencing; Computer-Assisted Testing; Credit Authorization Telephones; Credit

Authorization Terminal; Capacity Activated Transducer (Electronics); Computer-Aided Teaching; Computer-Assisted Teaching; Computer-Aided Training; Computer-Assisted Training; Computer Average Transients; Computer Assisted Televideo (Company in the Netherlands); Control and Analysis Tool

CATC
Computer-Assisted Test Construction

CATCALL
Completely Automated Technique for Cataloguing and Acquisition of Literature for Libraries

CATCH
Computer Analysis of Thermo Chemical Data (University of Sussex, UK)

CATD
Computer-Aided Test Development

CATE
Computer-Aided Test Engineering; Computer Automated Translation and Editing

CATI
Computer-Automated Testing and Implementation; Computer-Assisted Telephone Interviewing (US)

catl
catalog

catlg
catalog

CATLINE
Catalog(ing) On-Line (National Library of Medicine, US)

CATNIP
Computer-Assisted Technique for Numerical Index Preparation

CATS
Centre for Advanced Television Studies (UK); Computer-Aided Teaching System; Computer-Assisted Trading System (Toronto and Paris stock exchange systems)

CATS
Centralized Automatic Test System; Computer-Aided Trouble-Shooting

CATSS
Catalogue Support System

CATT
Center for Advanced Technology in Telecommunications

CATV
Cable Antenna Television; Cable Telecom-

munications and Video; Cable Television; Community Antenna Television; Cable Television

CATVA
Computer-Assisted Total Value Assessment

CATVCMA
CATV Cable Makers Association (UK)

CAU
Crypto Auxiliary Unit; CPU Access Unit; Command/Arithmetic Unit; Controller Adaptor Unit; Coaxial Access Unit; Control Access Unit

CAV
Constant Angular Velocity (Videodisc operation)

CAVE
Computer Augmented Video Education (US Naval Academy)

CAW
Cable And Wireless Company (UK); Channel Address Word (Data communications)

CAX
Community Automatic Exchange

CB
Citizen's Band, radio; Communications Buffer; Communications Bus (Computing); Condition BIT; Congestion Backward

CBA
Computer-Based Automation

CBAC
Chemical-Biological Activities (Database, CAS [Chemical Abstracts Service)

CBBS
Computerized Bulletin Board Service

CBC
Chain Block Controller; Chain Block Character; Cipher Block Chaining (Encryption method); Computer Based Conferencing

CBCC CODE 22
Chemical-Biological Coordination Center Code 22 (Used for searching by means of chemical structure)

CBCT
Customer-Bank(ing) Communication Terminal

CBDB
Conference Board DataBase (Economics database, US)

CBDS
Circuit Board Design System (IBM)

CBE
Computer-Based Education; Council of Biology Editors (US); Computer Brokers Exchange

CBEMA
Canadian Business Equipment Manufacturers Association; Computer and Business Equipment Manufacturers Association (US)

CBFM
Constant Bandwidth Frequency Modulation

CBI
Charles Babbage Institute; Compound Batch Identification; Computer-Based Instruction; Confederation of British Industry; Computer-Based Instrumentation

CBIC
Complementary Bipolar Integrated Circuit

CBIE
Computer-Based Information Exchange

CBIS
Computer-Based Information System

CBL
Computer-Based Learning

CBLAN
Centralized Bus Local Area Network (AT&T)

CBM
Confidence Building Measure; Commodore Business Machines (US computer manufacturer)

CBMIS
Comprehensive Budget and Management Information System; Computer-Based Management Information System

CBMS
Computer-Based Message(ing) Service; Computer-Based Message(ing) System; Computer-Based Message Service/system

CBN
Christian Broadcasting Network (Cable TV, US)

CBNB
Chemical Business News Base (Database, RSC [Royal Society of Chemistry], UK)

CBOSS
Count, Back Order, and Sample Select (Computing)

CBPI
Canadian Business Periodicals Index (Database on Canadian business, industry, finance, etc., by Micromedia, Canada)

CBR
Constant Bit Rate

CBS
Columbia Broadcasting System (US); City Business System (British Telecom, UK)

CBT
Computer-Based Terminal; Computer-Based Training

CBTA
Canadian Business Telecomm Alliance

CBTS
Computer-Based Training System; Computerized Business Telephone System

CBWF
Call Back When Free

CBX
Centralized Branch Exchange; Centrex service; Computerized Branch Exchange (Telecommunications)

CBX
Campus Branch Exchange

CC
Call Check; Carriage Control; Category Code (Searchable field); Category Code name (Searchable field); Central Computer; Channel Coordinator; Channel Controller; Charge-Coupled; Cluster Controller; Class Code (Searchable field); Classification Code; Colon Classification (Library classification scheme); Command Chain; Communications Computer; Communications Control; Communications Controller; Computer Center; Computer(ized) Conferencing; Condition Code (IBM); Control Computer; Control Counter; Cursor Control; Contractor Company code; Country Code (Searchable field); Concept Code (Searchable field); Constant Current

CC&A
Computer Control and Auditing

CC&S
Central Computer and Sequencer

CCA
Circuit Card Assembly; Channel to Channel Adapter; Common Communication Adapter; Common Cryptographic Architecture (IBM); Central Computer Agency (Civil Service Department, UK); Computer Corporation of America; *Computer and Control Abstracts* (Database, inspection); Comtec Cable Accessories Ltd (UK)

CCAID
Charge-Coupled Area Imaging Device
CCAM
Conversational Communication Access Method
CCAP
Communications Control Application Program
CCAR
Channel Command Address Register
CCAS
Communication Control Aid System
CCB
Character Control Block; Command Control Block; Communications Control Batches; Communications Control Block (Computing); Configuration Control Board; Channel Control Block (DEC)
CCBS
Call Completion to Busy Subscriber (CCITT)
CCC
Canadian Computer Complex; *Canadian Criminal Cases* (Databank, Canadian Law Book Limited); Central Communications Controller; Central Computer Center; Central Computer Complex; Central Computational Computer; Computer Communication Console; Computer Control Complex; Copyright Clearance Center (US); Clear Channel Capability (AT&T); Command Control and Communications (DOD)
CCCC
Computerized Conferencing and Communications Center (NJIT [New Jersey Institute of Technology], US)
CCCI
Command, Control, Communications, and Intelligence (DOD)
CCCL
CMOS Compact Cell Logic
CCCS
Current-Controlled Current Source
CCD
Charge-Coupled Device (Computing); Computer Controlled Display; Council for Computer Development (UK)
CCE
Call Command Exit (IBM); Communication Control Equipment; Cooperative Computing Environment

CCDS
Center for Commercial Development of Space (NASA)
CCEB
Combined Communications Electronics Boards
CCETT
Centre Commun d'Etudes de Télévision et de Télécommunications (Research center active in development of videotex, France)
CCF
Central Computing Facility; Communications Control Field; Complex Coherence Function; Compressed Citation File; Common Communications Format (ISO); Controller Configuration Facility (IBM)
CCG
Computer Communications Group (Trans-Canada Telephone System)
CCH
Channel Check Handler; Commerce Clearing House (Taxation/law reporting service available on Eurolex); Connections per Circuit per Hour
CCHS
Cylinder-Cylinder-Head Sector
CCI
Co-Channel Interface; Computer Communications Inc (US); Computer Composition International (US); Common Communication Interface
CCIA
Computer and Communications Industry Association (US)
CCIP
Command and Control Information Processing
CCIR
Comité Consultatif International des Radiocommunications (International Radio Consultative Committee, radio communications standards body)
CCIS
Common Channel Interoffice Signaling (AT&T); Computer-Controlled Interconnect System
CCITT
Comité Consultatif International Télégraphique et Téléphonique (International Telegraph and Telephone Consultation Committee, telephone and telegraph standards body, French)
CCIU
Command Channel Interface Unit

CCL
Common Command Language; Common Control Language (Computer language for searching across several computers, e.g., in network); Communications Control Language; Concise Command Language; CYBER Control Language; Capacitor Coupled Logic; Composite Cell Logic

CCLN
Council for Computerized Library Networks (US)

CCM
Call Count Meter (Telecommunications); Communications Control Module; Communication Control Multichannel (Data communications); Counter-Countermeasures; Computer Coupled Machines (Term used in numerical control [NC]); Close Confinement Mesa (Laser diode technology)

CCMB
Completion of Calls Meeting Busy (Telecommunications)

CCMD
Continuous Current Monitoring Device

CCMS
Computer Center Management System

CCMSS
Computer Controlled Microform Search System

CCMT
Computer Controlled Machine Tool; Computer-Controlled Microwave Tuner

CCN
Common-Carrier Network

CCO
Computer Controller Operation; Current Controlled Oscillator

CCP
Certificate in Computer Programming; Certified Computer Programmer; Certified Computer Professional; Communications Control Processor; Communications Control Package; Communications Control Program (Sperry Univac, US); Cooperative Computing Platform; Conditional Command Processor; Coordinated Commentary Programming; Channel Control Processor; Console Control Package; Cross Connection Point; Command Control Program (IBM)

CCPD
Charge-Coupled Photodiode

CCR
Catalog Control Record (IBM); Centre for Catalogue Research (Bath University, UK); Channel Command Register; Channel Control Reconfiguration; Computer Character Recognition; Computer Controlled Retrieval; Condition Code Register; Customized Communications Routine; Customer Controlled Reconfiguration (AT&T)

CCRH
Center for Computer Research in Humanities (University of Colorado at Boulder, US)

CCROS
Card Capacity Read-Only Storage

CCS
Common-Channel Signalling (CCITT, telecommunications); Command Set; Common Communications Support (IBM); Communications Control System; Hundred Call Seconds [or C (100) Call Seconds] (AT&T, telecommunications); Canadian Computer Show; Central Computer Station; Conversational Compiling System (Xerox Corp, US); Central Computer Services (Greater London Council, UK)

CCSA
Common Carrier Special Application; Common-Control(ed) Switching Arrangement (AT&T); Common Channel Signalling Arrangement; Customer Controlled Switching Arrangement

CCSB
Computer and Communications Standards Board

CCSC
Coordinating Committee for Satellite Communication (Switzerland)

CCSE
Corporate Communications Switching Equipment

CCSI
Commercial Communications Systems Integration

CCSP
Communications Concentrator Software Package

CCSS
Common Channel Signalling System (AT&T)

CCS7
Common Channel Signalling System Seven (AT&T)

CCST
Center for Computer Sciences and Technology

CCT
Computer Compatible Tape

CCTV
Closed-circuit Cable Television; Closed Circuit Television

CCTV/LSD
Closed Circuit Television/Large Screen Display

CCU
Central Control Unit; Command Chain Unit; Communications Control Unit; Computer Control Unit; Correlation Control Unit; Common Control Unit; Concurrency Control Unit (Computing)

CCV
Common Control Vector; Control Configured Vehicle

CCVS
COBOL Compiler Validation System; Current-Controlled Voltage Source

CCW
Channel Command Word; Channel Control Word; Counterclockwise [or Counter Clockwise]; Continuous Composite Write

cd
card

Cd
Cadmium (Symbol)

CD
Carrier Detect; Chain Data; Compact Disk

CDA
Command and Data Acquisition; Computer Dealers Association; Combined Digital Aggregate; Compound Document Architecture (DEC); Customer-Defined Array (Motorola Inc, US)

CDAC
Communications Dual Access Controller

CDAS
Conceptual Design Analysis and Simulation

CDB
Common Data Bus; Command Descriptor Block (ANSI); Current Data Bit; Communications Data Base

CDC
Call Directing Code; Code Directing Character; Computer Display Channel; Compression/Decompression

CDD
Common Data Dictionary (DEC)

CDE
Contents Directory Entry

CDEC
Central Data Conversion Equipment

CDF
Combined Distribution Frame; Contiguous-Disk File

CDHS
Comprehensive Data Handling System

CDI
Compact Disk-Interactive (Preferred form is CD-I); Collector Diffused Isolation

CDIN
Continental Defense Integrated Network (DOD)

CDIP
Ceramic Dual In-Line Package

CDL
Compiler Description Language; Computer Description Language; Computer Design Language; Computer Development Laboratory

CDLA
Computer Dealers and Lessors Association

CDLC
Cellular Data Link Control

CDM
Cash Dispensing Machine; Code-Division Multiplexing; Charged Device Model

CDMA
Cartridge Direct Memory Access; Code-Division Multiple Access

CDMC
Configurable Dynamic Memory Controller

CDMP
Compound Document Management Program (DEC)

CDMS
Commercial Data Management System

CDN
Corporate Data Network

CDO
Community Dial Office

CDP
Centralized Data Processing; Certificate in Data Processing; Communications Data Processor; Certified Data Professional; Certified Data Programmer

CDPA
Certified Data Processing Auditor
CDPS
Computing and Data Processing Society
CDR
Call Detail Recording; Card Reader; Critical Design Review; Clock and Data Recovery; Compact Disk Recordable; Constant Density Recording
CDRM
Cross-Domain Resource Manager (IBM)
CDRS
Computer Disaster Recovery System
CD-ROM
Compact Disk Read-Only Memory; Computer Disk Read-Only Memory
CD-I
Compact Disk-Interactive
CDS
Case Data System; Central Dynamic System; Comprehensive Display System; Control Data Set; Control Display System
CDSS
Customer Digital Switching System
CDTL
Common Data Translation Language
CDU
Cartridge Disk Unit; Control and Display Unit; Color Difference Unit
CDV
Compact Disk Video
CE
Chip Enable; Concurrent Engineering; Critical Examination; Customer Engineer; Computational Element
Ce
Cerium (Symbol)
CEA
Central Electricity Authority; Communications-Electronics Agency
CEBA
Continuous Electron Beam Accelerator
CEC
Computers, Electronics and Control Symposium
CECUA
Confederation of European Computer User Association
CED
Computer Entry Device
CEDA
Communications Equipment Distributors Association

CEDAC
Computer Energy Distribution and Automated Control
CEDAR
Computer-Aided Environmental Design Analysis and Realization
CEECS
Computer Environment Energy Control System
CEG
Continuous Edge Graphics
CEGL
Cause Effect Graph Language
CEI
Chip Enable Input; Contract End Item; Comparably Efficient Interconnection
CELEX
European Community legal database (EC)
CEM
Central Enhancement and Maintenance; Command Execution Module
CEMAST
Control of Engineering Material, Acquisition, Storage and Transport
CENEL
Comite Europeen de Coordination des Normes Electriques (European Electrical Standards Coordinating Committee, French, EC)
CENELEC
Comite Europeen de Normalisation Electrotechnique (European Community for Electrotechnical Standardization, French, EC)
CEO
Chip Enable Output; Comprehensive Electronics Office; Chief Executive Officer
CEPA
Society for the Advancement of Computers in Engineering, Planning and Architecture
CEPT
Conference Europeenne des administration des Postes et des Telecommunications (European Conference of Postal and Telecommunications Administrations, French)
CERDIP
Ceramic Dual In-Line Package
CER
Civil Engineering Report
CERC
Computer Entry and Read-out Control

CERDEC
Center for Research and Documentation in the (EC) European Community
CERE
Computer Entry and Read-out Equipment
CERT
Character Error Rate Test; Character Error Rate Tester; Constant Extension Rate Test
CESD
Composite External Symbol Dictionary (IBM)
CESO
Council of Engineers and Scientists Organizations
CESSE
Council of engineering and Scientific Society
CET
Console Electric Typewriter
CETI
Continuously Executing Transfer Interface (IBM)
CETIA
Control, Electronics, Telecommunications, Instrument Automation
CEU
Channel Extension Unit
CF
Carried Forward; Commercial FORTRAN; Context Free; Count Forward; Congestion Forward; Continuous Feed; Cryptographic Facility (IBM)
Cf
Californium (Symbol)
CFA
Component Flow Analysis; Crossed-Field Amplifier; Computer Family Architecture
CFB
Cipher Feed Back
CFC
Channel Flow Control
CFCF
Central Flow Control Facility
CFE
Contractor Furnished Equipment
CFF
Continuous Forms Feed(er)
CFG
Context Free Grammar
CFIA
Component Failure Impact Analysis

CFL
Context Free Language
cfm (CFM)
cubic feet per minute
CFMS
Chained File Management System
CFO
Cancel Form Order; Consolidated Functions Ordinary; Chief Financial Officer
CFO+
Consolidated Functions Ordinary Support System
CFP
Creation Facilities Program (IBM)
CFS
Combined File Search; Corporate Financial System; Common File System; Concurrent Filing System; Continuous Forms Stacker
CFSS
Combined File Search System
CFTG
Context Free Transduction Grammar
CG
Color Graphics; Computer Graphics
CGA
Color Graphics Adapter (IBM)
CGI
Computer-Generated Image; Computer Graphics Interface
CGL
Computer Generated Letter
CGM
Color Graphics Metafile; Computer Graphics Metafile
CGOS
Computervision Graphics Operating System
CGP
Color Graphics Printer; Computervision Graphics Processor
CGPC
Cellular General Purpose Computer
cgs
centimeter-gram-second system (The now-little-used system of units)
CGSA
Computer Graphics Structural Analysis
ch
change; channel; character
CHAMP
Character Manipulation Procedures; Com-

munications Handler for Automatic Multiple Programs

chan
channel

char
character

CHAT
Cheap Access Terminal

CHC
Channel Control; Color Hard Copy

CHCAT
Clearing House Catalogue (DEC)

CHCU
Channel Control Unit

CHDL
Computer Hardware Definition Language; Computer Hardware Description Language

CHE
Chip Enable

CHECS
Check Handling Executive Control System

chg
charge

CHI
Computer Human Interaction

CHIF
Channel Interface

CHIL
Current Hogging Injection Logic

CHIPS
Clearing House Interbank Payments System

CHIRP
Confidential Human Factors Incident Report

CHIO
Channel Input/Output (IBM)

CHITO
Container Handling In Terminal Operations

chk
check

chkpt
checkpoint

chnl
channel

CHOL
Common High Order Language

CHP
Channel Processor

chr
character

CHR
Channel Reconfiguration Hardware

CHRT
Coordinated Human Resource Technology

CHS
Corporate Hub Station (AT&T)

CHT
Collection, Holding, and Transfer

CI
Carry In; Communications Interface; Computer Industry; Calling Indicator; Computer Interconnect (DEC); Configuration Item; Current-awareness Information

CIA
Computer Industry Association

CIB
Channel Interface Base; Command Input Buffer

CIC
Corporate Information Center; Custom-Integrated Circuit

CICC
Custom Integrated Circuits Conference

CICA
Construction Industry Computing Association

CICI
Confederation of Information Communication Industries (EC)

CICP
Communication Interrupt Control Program

CICS
Customer Information Control System (IBM); Computerized Information Control System

CICS/VS
Customer Information Control System/ Vertical Storage

CID
Charge-Injection Imaging Device; Communication Identifier; Component Identification Number

CIDA
Channel Indirect Data Addressing

CIDF
Control Interval Definition Field (IBM)

CIDS
Customer-Integrated Development System; Comprehensive Industry Distribution System

CIE
Computer Interrupt Equipment
CIF
Central Information File; Computer-Integrated Factory; customer Information File; Common Intermediate Format (CCITT)
CIK
Cryptographic Ignition Key (AT&T)
CIL
Computer Interpreter Language; Current Injection Logic
CILA
Casualty Insurance Logistics Automated
CILOP
Conversion In Lieu Of Procurement
CIM
Communications Interface Monitor; Computer Input Microfilm; Computer-Integrated Manufacturing; Console Interface Module; Corporate Information Management
CIMC
Communications Intelligent Matrix Control
CIMS
Computer Installation Management System; Computer Integrated Manufacturing System; Countermeasures Internal Management System
CINIT
Control Initiate (IBM)
CINV
Control Interval
CIO
Central Input-Output; Chief Information Officer
CIOCS
Communications Input-Output Control System
CIOU
Central Input-Output Unit
CIOUT
Cache Inhibit Out
CIP
Communications Interrupt Program; Complex Information Processing; Connectionless Internet Protocol
CIPS
Canadian Information Processing Society
CIR
Color Infrared; Current Instruction Register; Committed Information Rate; Connect Initiate Received (DEC)

CIRC
Centralized Information Reference and Control
CIRCA
Computerized Information Retrieval and Current Awareness
CIRCAL
Circuit Analysis
CIRCUS
Circuit Simulator
CIRT
Conference on Industrial Robot Technology
CIS
Central Information System; Commercial Instruction Set; Control Indicator Set; Current Information Selection; Custom Integrated System; Customer Information System; Connect Initiate Sent (DEC)
CISAM
Compressed Index Sequential Access Method
CISC
Complex Instruction Set Computer(ing)
CISD
Corporate Information Service Department
CISS
Conference on Information Science and Systems; Consolidated Information Storage System
CIT
Computer-Integrated Telephony (DEC)
CITA
Commercial Industrial Type Activities
CITCA
Committee of Inquiry into Technological Change in Australia
CITS
Central Integrated Test System Multiplex
CIU
Central Interface Unit; Channel Interface Unit; Computer Interface Unit
CJB
Cold Junction Box
CJS
Chained Job Scheduling (IBM)
ck
clock
CKD
Count-Key-Data Device
CKDS
Cryptographic Key Data Sets (IBM)

ckt
circuit
Cl
Chlorine (Symbol)
cl
centiliter
CL
Command Language; Compiler Language; Control Leader; Control Line
CLA
Carry Lookahead; Communications Line Adapter; Computer Law Association
CLAD
Cover Layer Automated Design
CLAIMS
Class Codes, Assigned, Index, Method, Search
CLAIMS/CLASS
Class Codes, Assigned, Index, Method, Search/Classification
CLAIMS/GEM
Class Codes, Assigned, Index, Method, Search/General, Electrical, Mechanical
CLAMP
Computer Listing and Analysis of Maintenance Programs
CLASP
Circuit Layout, Automated Scheduling and Production
CLASS
Custom Local Area Signalling Services; Capacity Loading and Scheduling System; Closed Loop Accounting for Stores Sales
CLAT
Communications Line Adapter for Teletype
CLB
Central Logic Bus; Clear Both; Configurable Logic Block
CLC
Communication Line Control; Communications Line Controller; Communications Link Controller; Current Leading Components; Color Laser Copier (Canon, US)
CLCC
Ceramic Leaded Chip Carrier
CLCM
Communication Line Concentrator Module
cld
cancelled; cleared
CLD
Current-Limiting Device
CLE
Conservative Logic Element

CLEAR
Closed Loop Evaluation And Reporting
CLEAT
Computer Language for Engineers and Technologists
CLEO
Clear Language for Expressing Orders
CLEOS
Conference on Laser and Electro-Optical Systems
CLG
Compile, Link-Edit, Go (IBM)
CLI
Command Language Interpreter
CLIC
Command Language for Interrogating Computers; Computer Layout of Integrated Circuits; Conversational Language for Interactive Computing
CLIMATE
Computer and Language Independent Modules for Automatic Test Equipment
CLIO
Conversational Language for Input-Output
CLIP
Cellular Logic Image Processor; Computer Layout Installation Planner; Coded Language Information Processing
CLIRA
Closed Loop In-Reactor Assembly
CLISP
Conversational LISP
CLIST
Command List
clk
clock
CLKIN
Clock In
CLKOUT
Clock Out
CLM
Clinical Library Master; Communications Line Multiplexer
CLOB
Core Load Overlay Builder
CLODS
Computerized Logic-Oriented Design System
CLOG
Computer Logic Graphics
CLOS
Common LISP [List Processor] Object System (DEC)

CLP
Communication Line Processor; Current Line Point
clr
clear
CLR
Combined Line and Recording; Clear Screen (MS-DOS)
CLS
Communications Line Switch
CLT
Communications Line Terminals
CLUE
Compiler Language Utility Extension
CLUT
Color Look-Up Table
CLUSAN
Cluster Analysis
CLV
Constant Linear Velocity
CM/CCM
Countermeasures/Counter Countermeasures
Cm
Curium (Symbol)
cm
centimeter (Metric unit of length denoting 10^{-2} meter
CM
Central Memory; Communications Multiplexer; Control Memory; Control Module; Core memory; Corrective Maintenance; Common Mode
CMA
Communications Managers Association; Computer Management Association; Computer Monitor Adapter; Computerized Management Account; Concert Multithread Architecture (DEC)
CMAP
Central Memory Access Priority
CMAR
Control Memory Address Register
CMARS
Cable Monitoring and Rating System
CMAS
Construction Management Accounting System
CMB
Corrective Maintenance Burden
CMC
Communications Management Configuration (IBM); Communications Mode Control; Comparison Measuring Circuit

CMCA
Character Mode Communications Adapter
cmd
command
CMDIS
Computer Management Distributed Information Software
CMDR
Command Reject (CCITT)
CME
Central Memory Extension; Computer Measurement and Evaluation
CMF
Comprehensive Management Facility; Constant Magnetic Field
CMG
Computer Measurement Group
CMI
Computer-Managed Instruction; Computer Memory Interconnect (DEC)
CMIP
Common Management Information Protocol
CMIS
Common Manufacturing Information System; Common Management Information Service; Computer-oriented Management Information System; Corporate Management Information System
CML
Common Mode Logic; Current Mode Logic; Computer-Managed Learning (DEC)
CMM
Communications Multiplexer Module; Coordinate Measuring Machine
CMMS
Computer Maintenance Management System
CMMU
Cache/Memory Management Unit
cmnd
command
CMOS
Complementary Metal-Oxide Semiconductor
CMP
Console Message Processor; Cooperative Marketing Program (DEC)
CMPM
Computer-Managed Parts Manufacture
CMR
Code Matrix Reader; Common Mode

69

Rejection; Cellular Mobile Radio; Commercial Mail Relay

CMRR
Common Mode Rejection Ratio

CMS
Circuit Maintenance System; Conversational Monitor System (IBM); Compiler Monitor System; Computer Management System (Burroughs Corp, US); Code Management System (DEC); Communications Management Series

CMT
Cassette Magnetic Tape; Change Management Tracking; Computer-Managed Training; Computer Mediated Teleconferencing; Construction Materials Testing; Connection Management

CMU
Control Maintenance Unit

CMX
Character Multiplexer; Customer Multiplexer

CMY
Cyan-Magenta-Yellow

CN
Communications Network; Contract Number; Coordination Number; Customer Node

CNA
Communications Network Architecture

CNAR
Computer Network Augmented Research

CNC
Computer Numerical Control (Factory Automation)

cncl
cancel

cncld
canceled

CNDP
Communication Network Design Program

CNE
Communications Network Emulator

CNEP
Cable Network Engineering Program

CNET
Centre National d'Etudes et de Recherches de Telecommunications (Communications Network, French)

cnl
Cancel; cancellation

CNM
Communication Network Manager(ment)

(IBM)

CNMI
Communications Network Management Interface

CNMS
Common Network Management System

CNOP
Conditional NonOperation

CNP
Communications Network Processor

CNR
Carrier-to-Noise Ratio

CNS
Communications Network Simulator; Communications Network(ing) System

cnt
count

cntl
control

cntr
counter

cntrl
control

Co
Cobalt (Symbol); Company

CO
Carry Out; Console Output; Company; Central Office

COADS
Conference on Application Development Systems

COAM
Customer Owned and Maintained

COAMP
Computer Analysis of Maintenance Policies

COAX
Coaxial Cable

COB
Chip-On-Board

COBIT
Control-Office Based Intelligence

COBLOS
Computer Based Loans System

COBOL
Common Business-Oriented Language (IBM)

COC
Character Oriented Communications Controller; Central Office Connection

COCOT
Customer-Owned Coin-Operated Telephone

COCOL
COBOL Compiler-Oriented Language
CO-LAN
Central Office Local Area Network
COCR
Cylinder Overflow Control Record
COCS
Container Operating Control System
CODAP
Comprehensive Occupational Data Analysis Program
CODAS
Customer Oriented Data System
CODASYL
Conference on Data Systems Language(s) (EC)
CODEC
Coder-Decoder; Coding-Decoding Device
codec (CODEC)
code(r)-decode(r)
CODEM
Coded Modulator-Demodulator
CODEST
European Development of Science and Technology (EC)
CODIL
Content Dependent Information Language
CODILS
Commodity Oriented Digital Input Label System
COFAD
Computerized Facilities Design
COGAP
Computer Graphics Arrangement Program
COGENT
Compiler and Generalized Translator
COGO
Coordinate Geometry
COIN
Corporate Office Interconnectivity Network
COLAN
Central Office Local Area Network
COINS
Computer and Information Sciences; Coordinated Inventory Control System
col
column
COL
Communications Oriented Language; Computer Oriented Language
coll
collator

Collat
collateral
COM
Cassette Operating Monitor; Center Of Mass; Computer Output Microform; Computer Output Microfiche; Computer Output Microfilm; Computer Output Microfilmer; Computer Output Microfilming; Computer Output Micrographics
COMAC
Continuous Multiple Access Collator
COMAT
Computer-Assisted Training
comb
combination
COMC
Communications Controller (IBM)
COMCAL
Computerized Calendar (DEC)
COMET
Computer Message Transmission
COMFOR
International Computer Forum and Exposition
COMFORT
Commercial FORTRAN
COMICS
Computer-Oriented Managed Inventory Control System
COMM-STOR
Communications Storage Unit
COMMANDS
Computer Operated Marketing, Mailing and News Distribution System
COMMEND
Computer-aided Mechanical Engineering Design
ComNet
Communications Network Conference
Comp
compatible; composite; computer; computerization; computerize; computerized
COMPARE
Computer Oriented Method of Program Analysis, Review and Evaluation
COMPAS
Computer Acquisition System
COMPASS
Central Office Maintenance Printout Analysis and Suggestion System; Computer Assisted Classification and Assignment System

COMPCON
Computer Conference
COMPEC
Computer Peripherals and Small Computer Systems Trade Exhibition
COMPENDEX
Computerized Engineering Index
COMPETA
Computer and Peripherals Equipment Trade Association
COMPROC
Command Processor
COMPSAC
Computer Software and Applications Conference
compu
computable; computability; computer; computerized
COMRADE
Computer Aided Design Environment
COMS
Computer-based Operations Management System
COMSAT
Communications Satellite Corporation
COMSYL
Communications Systems Language
COMTEC
Computer Micrographics Technology
COMTEX
Communications Oriented Multiple Terminal Executive
COMX
Communications Executive
con
concentrator
cond
condition
conf
conference
CONIO
Console Input-Output
CONIT
Connector for Networked Information Transfer
CONMAN
Console Manager
const
constant
CONS
Connection-Oriented Network Service
cont
controller

conv
conversion; convertible
COP
Common On-Chip Processor (IBM); Communication Output Printer
COPE
Cassette Operating Executive
COPICS
Communications Oriented Production Information and Control System
COPS
Calculator Oriented Processor System
COR
Class of Restriction (AT&T)
CORDIC
Coordinate Rotation Digital Computer
CORREGATE
Correctable Gate
CORS
Canadian Operational Research Society
cos
cosine
COS
Cassette Operating System; Class of Service (AT&T); Commercial Operating System; Communications Operating System; Communications Oriented Software; Concurrent Operating System (Sperry-Univac); Corporation for Open Systems
cos^{-1}
inverse [or arc] cosine
cosh
hyperbolic cosine
cosh^{-1}
inverse hyperbolic cosine
COSINE
Cooperation for OSI [Open Systems Interconnection] Networking (CCITT)
COSAM
COBOL Shared Access Method
COSATI
Committee on Scientific and Technical Information
COSCL
Common Operating System Control Language
COSMIC
Computer Software Management and Information Center (NASA)
COSNAME
Class of Service Name (IBM)
COSTAB
Class of Service Table (IBM)

COSTI
Committee on Scientific and Technical Information

COSY
Compressed Symbolic; Compact Synchrotron

COT
Customer Oriented Terminal

cot
cotangent

cot⁻¹
inverse [or arc] cotangent

coth
hyperbolic cotangent

coth⁻¹
inverse hyperbolic cotangent

COUPLE
Communications Oriented User Programming Language

cp
centipoise

CP
Call Processor; Card Punch; Central Processor; Character Printer; Command Processor; Communications Processor; Condition Precedent; Control Part; Control Program [or Point] (IBM); Correspondence Printer; Critical Path; Check Point; Co-Processor; Connection Processor

CP/M
Control Program Microcomputer

CP-R
Control Program -- Real-time

CP-V
Control Program - Five

CP&R
Card Punch and Reader

CPA
Critical Path Analysis

CPB
Channel Program Block; Critical Path Bar [or chart]

CPC
Card-Programmed Calculator (IBM); Computer Power Center; Computer Production Control; Computerized Production Control

CPCEI
Computer Program Contract End Item

CPCI
Computer Program Configuration Item; CPU Power Calibration Instrument

CPCS
Check Processing Control System; Comprehensive Planning and Control System

CPDAMS
Computer Program Development and Management System

CPDP
Computer Program Development Plan

CPDS
Computer Program Design Specification

CPE
Central Processing Element; Computer Performance Evaluation; Customer Premises Equipment (AT&T)

CPEM
Conference on Precision Electromagnetic Measurements

CPEUG
Computer Performance Evaluation Users Group

CPF
CICS [Customer Information Control System] Print Facility; Control Program Facility; Common Purpose Field (IBM); Cryptographic Programmed Facility (IBM)

CPFSK
Continuous Phase Frequency Shift Keying

CPG
COBOL Program Generator

CPH
Characters Per Hour

CPI
Common Programming Interface (IBM); Characters Per Inch; Computer-to-PBX [Private Branch Exchange] Interface; Cycles Per Instruction; Conference Papers Index

cpi
characters per inch

CPI-C
Common Programming Interface for Communications (IBM)

CPIN
Computer Program Identification Number

CPIS
Computerized Personnel Information System

CPL
Common Program Library; Computer Program Library; Conversational Programming Language

CPL1
Checkout PL/1

CPM
Cards Per Minute; Cards Processed per Minute; Computer Performance Manage-

ment; Computer Performance Monitor; Continuous Processing Machine; Control Program for Microcomputers [or Control Program Micro]; Critical Path Method; Current Processor Mode; Charged Plate Monitor;

CPMA
Central Processor Memory Address; Computer Peripherals Manufacturers Association

CPMS
Control Point Management Services (IBM)

CPN
Computer Product News (Publication); Control Packet Network

CPO
Commodity Pool Operator; Concurrent Peripheral Operations; Catalog Performance Optimizer

CPODA
Contention Priority-Oriented Demand Assignment

CPOL
Communications Procedure-Oriented Language

CPP
Critical Path Plan; Current Purchasing Power

CPPS
Critical Path Planning and Scheduling

CPR
Constant Percentage Resolution; Cost Performance Report

cps
characters per second; cycles per second

CPS
Cards Per Second; Central Processor Subsystem; Characters Per Second; COBOL Programming System; Computerized Publishing System; Control Program Support; Controlled Path System; Conversational Programming System (IBM); Cycles Per Second

CPSK
Coherent Phase-Shift Keying

CPSR
Computer Professionals for Social Responsibility

CPSS
Computer Power Support System

CPT
Chief Programmer Team; Continuous Performance Test

CPT&E
Computer Program Test and Evaluation

CPTO
Chief Programmer Team Organization

CPU
Central Processing Unit; Communications Processing Unit

CPUAX
Central Processing Unit Arithmetic Extended

CQA
Computer-aided Question Answering

CQFP
Ceramic Quad Flat Pack

CQMS
Circuit Quality Monitoring System

CR-LO
Channel Request-Low Priority

CR-MED
Channel Request Medium Priority

CR-HI
Channel Request-High Priority

CR/P
Card Reader/Punch

CR
Card Reader; Carriage Return; Carry Register; Command Register; Communications Register; Control Register; Critical Ratio; Condition Register (IBM); Compressive Receiver

Cr
Chromium (Symbol)

CRA
Catalog Recovery Area (IBM); Computer Retailers Association

CRAM
Card RAM [Random Access Memory] (NCR); Computerized Reliability Allocation Method

CRAMM
Coupon Reading and Marking Machine

CRAR
Control ROM Address Register

CRB
Cache Reload Buffer (IBM); Channel Request Block (DEC); Complementary Return to Bias

CRBE
Conversational Remote Batch Entry

CRC
CRC [Chemical Rubber Company] Press Inc (Publisher); Carrier Return Character; Cyclic Redundancy Check

CRCC
Cyclic Redundancy Check Character

CRD
Computer Read-out Device

CRE
Certified Reliability Engineer

CREDIT
Cost Reduction Early Decision Information Techniques

CREF
Cross Reference(s)

CREN
Corporation for Research and Educational Networking

CREST
Comite de Recherche Scientifique et Technique (Committee of Scientific and Technological Research, French, EC)

CRF
Context Roll File; Cross Reference File

CRIS
Current Research Information System

CRISP
Computer Resources Integrated Support Plan

CRJE
Conversational Remote Job Entry (IBM)

CRLF
Carriage Return, Line Feed

CRM
Computer Resources Management

CRMA
Cyclic Reservation Multiple Access (IBM)

CRMS
Communications Resource Management System

CRO
Cathode Ray Oscilloscope

CROM
Control (ROM) Read-Only Memory

CRONOS
Community Statistical Office computerized economic data bank (EC)

CROS
Capacitor Read Only Storage

CRP
Channel Request Priority (IBM); Combined Refining Process; Counter-Rotation Platform

CRQ
Console Reply Queueing

CRS
Color Recognition Sensor; Computerized Reservation System; Configuration Report Server (IBM)

CRT
Cathode Ray Tube; Computer Remote Terminal

CRTC
Cathode Ray Tube Controller

CRU
Card Reader Unit; Communications Register Unit; Control and Reporting Unit

CRV
Code Rule Violation (IEEE)

CS
Chip Select; Communications Server; Continue Specific mode; Communications System; Computer Science; Condition Subsequent; Constructor Syntax; Control Store; Control Signal

Cs
Caesium (Symbol)

CSA
Canadian Standards Association; Carrier-Serving Area; Common Service Area; COBOL Structuring Aid; Computer Services Association; Common Storage [or System] Area (IBM); Communication Subsystem Architecture (IBM)

CSAM
Circular Sequential Access Memory

CSAR
Communication Satellite Advanced Research; Control Store Address Register

CSB
Communication Scanner Base

csc
cosecant

csc^{-1}
inverse [or arc] cosecant

CSCC
Cumulative Sum Control Chart

csch
hyperbolic cosecant

csch^{-1}
inverse hyperbolic cosecant

CSCS
Cost, Schedule, and Control System

CSD
Circuit Switched Data; Closed System Delivery; Computerized Standard Data

CSDB
Common Source Data Base

CSDC
Circuit-Switched Digital Capability (AT&T)

CSDD
Computer Subprogram Design Document

CSDF
Computer System Development Facility

CSDL
Conceptual Schema Definition Language

CSDM
Continuous Slope Delta Modulation

CSDR
Control Store Data Register

CSE
Computer Science and Engineering

CSECT
Control Section (IBM)

CSERB
Computer, Systems, and Electronics Requirements Board (UK)

CSF
Critical Success Factor

CSG
Context Sensitive Grammar; Constructive Solids Geometry (Computer-aided design [CAD])

CSH
Complementary Software House (DEC)

CSI
Client-Server Interface; Command String Interpreter; Computer Systems Integration; Cosmic Scale Integration

CSIC
Customer Specified Integrated Circuit (Motorola Inc, US)

CSL
Context-Sensitive Language; Control and Simulation Language; Current Switch Logic; Computer Security Laboratory (NIST)

CSM
Central System Manager; Computer System Manual; Communications Server Module

CSMA
Carrier Sense Multiple Access; Communications Systems Management Association

CSMA/CA
Carrier Sense Multiple Access with Collision Avoidance

CSMA/CD
Carrier Sense Multiple Access with Collision Detect(ion)

CSMC
Communications Services Management Council

CSMP
Continuous System(s) Modeling Program

(IBM)

CSMS
Computerized Specification Management System

CSN
Card Security Number

CSNET
Computer Science Network

CSO
Central Statistical Office

CSOS
Complementary Silicon On Sapphire

CSP
Certified Systems Professional; Commercial Subroutine Package; Communicating Sequential Process; Cross-System Product (IBM)

CSPC
Cost and Schedule Planning and Control

CSR
Control Status Register (DEC); Customer Service Representative

CSROEPM
Communication, System, Results, Objectives, Exception, Participation, Motivation

CSS
Character Start-Stop; Computer Scheduling System; Computer Systems Simulator; Continuous System Simulation; Center for Seismic Studies (US)

CSSF
Customer Software Support Facility (IBM)

CSSL
Continuous System Simulation Language

CST
Central Standard Time; Code Segment Table; Consolidated Schedule Technique

CSTR
Current Status Register

CSTS
Computer Sciences Teleprocessing System

CSU
Cartridge Storage Unit (Memorex Corp, US); Channel Service Unit; Circuit Switching Unit; Communications System User; Customer Set Up

CSV
Circuit Switched Voice

CSVR
Common Signal-to-Voltage Ratio

CSW
Channel Status Word (IBM)

ct

count; counter

CT

Cable Transfer; Cassette Tape; Change Ticker; Communications Terminal; Computerized Tomography; Cellular Telephone; Current Transformer; Cordless Telephone

CTAB

Commerce Technical Advisory Board

CTB

Code Table Buffer; Concentrator Terminal Buffer

CTC

Centralized Traffic Control; Channel-To-Channel adapter (IBM); Counter Timer Circuit; Coaxial Token-Ring Connector

CTCA

Canadian Telecommunications Carrier Association; Channel-To-Channel Adapter (IBM)

CTCC

Central Terminal Computer Controller

CTCM

Computer Timing and Costing Model

CTCS

Component Time Control System

CTD

Charge Transfer Device

CTE

Computer Telex Exchange; Customer Terminal Equipment; Charge Transfer Efficiency; Coefficient of Thermal Expansion

CTFC

Central Time and Frequency Control

CTI

Charge Transfer Inefficiency

CTIA

Cellular Telecommunications Industry Association

ctl

control

CTL

Cassette Tape Loader; Compiler Target Language; Complementary Transistor Logic

CTLR

Control Register

CTM

Communications Terminal Module; Composite-Tape Memory

CTMC

Communications Terminal Multiplex

Cabinet

CTN

Compensated Twisted Nematic display

CTOS

Cassette Tape Operating System; Convergent Technologies Operating System (Originally developed by Convergent Technologies, now part of Unisys); Concurrent Technologies Operating System (Concurrent Technologies Inc, US)

ctr

counter

CTR

Current Transfer Ratio; Count Register (IBM)

ctrl

control

CTRS

Computerized Test-result Reporting System

CTS

Carpal Tunnel Syndrome; Clear To Send; Coaxial Terminal Switch; Commercial Transaction System; Communications Technology Satellite; Communications Terminal Synchronous; Computer Technical Specialist; Computer Telegram System; Conversational Time Sharing; Conversational Terminal System (IBM)

CTSS

Compatible Time Sharing System; Computer Time Sharing Service

CTV

Cable Television

CTVPT

Color Television Picture Telephone

CTX

Cosine Transform Exchange [or Extended]

cu

cubic

Cu

Cuprum [or Copper] (Symbol)

CU

Control Unit; Correlation Unit; Customer Use

CUA

Circuit Unit Assembly; Common User Access (IBM); Computer Users Association

CUAG

Computer Users Associations Group

CUDN

Common User Data Network

CUE

Computer Updating Equipment; Correction-Update-Extension

CUESTA
Communications User Emulated System for Traffic Analysis
CUFT
Center for the Utilization of Federal Technology
CUG
Closed User Group (CCITT)
CUI
Character-Based User Interface; Common User Interface (IBM)
CUM
Central-Unit Memory
CUP
Communications User Program
CUPID
Create, Update, Interrogate and Display
CUPS
Connection Updates per Second
CUT
Control Unit Terminal
CUTS
Cassette User Tape System; Computer Users Tape System
CUV
Current Use Value
CV
Constant Velocity
CVG
Constructive Variational Geometry
CVGA
Color Video Graphics Adapter
CVC
Carrier Virtual Circuit
CVD
Chemical Vapor Deposition
CVIS
Computerized Vocational Information System
CVM
COBOL Virtual Machine
CVR
Computer Voice Response; Continuous Video Recorder; Crystal Video Receiver
CVS
Constant Volume Sampling; Conversa-tional System
CVSD
Continuously Variable Slope Delta modulation
CVSDM
Continuously Variable Slope Delta Modulation
CVT
Communications Vector Table; Constant Voltage Transformer
CVTS
Compressed Video Transmission Service
cw
clockwise
CW
Command Word; Carrier Wave; Continuous Wave; Control Word; Clockwise [or Clock Wise]
CWA
Control Word Address
CWD
Clerical Work Data
CWM
Clerical Work Measurement
CWP
Communicating Word Processor; Current Word Pointer
CWPS
Communicating Word Processing System
CWS
Compiler Writing System
CXA
Central Exchange Area
CXI
Common X Interface (H-P)
CXR
Carrier Detector
cxy
carrier
cy
carry; currency; cycle
cyl
cylinder

D

d
data; datum; deci (SI prefix denoting 10^{-1}); decimal; density; destination; digit; digital; double; decimal; domain

D/A
Digital to Analog [converter, or conversion]

D
D channel; Delta channel; Density; D Cell (Voltaic cell)

d (D)
density

D-RAM
Dynamic Random-Access Memory

da
deka (SI prefix denoting 10)

DA
Data Administrator; Data Available; Demand Assignment; Design Automation; Destination Address (IEEE); Direct Action; Directory Assistance; Disk Action; Display Adapter

DAA
Data Access Arrangement; Distributed Application Architecture (Data General Corp)

DAB
Digital Audio Broadcasting

DABS
Discrete Address Beacon System

DAC
Design Automation Conference; Digital-to-Analog Converter; Data Acquisition Controller; Data Acquisition and Control; Data Analysis and Control; Discretionary Access Control

DACBU
Data Acquisition Control and Buffer Unit

DACE
Data Acquisition and Control Executive

DACOR
Data Correction

DACS
Data Access Control System; Data Acquisition and Conversion System

DADS
Data Acquisition and Display System

DAF
Data Acquisition Facility; Destination Address Field (IBM); Dedicated Access Facility

DAFC
Digital Automatic Frequency Control

DAI
Data Acquisition Instrument; Direct Access Information

DAL
Data Access Language; Data/Address Line; Digital Authoring Language (DEC)

DAM
Data Addressed Memory; Direct Access Method

DAM/QAM
Dynamically Allocated Multicarrier/Quadrature Amplitude Modulation

DAMA
Demand [or Dynamic] Assigned (ment) Multiple Access

DAP
Data Access Protocol (DEC); Data Acquisition Processor; Distributed Array Processor

DAPA
Demand-Assigned Packet Access

DAR
Digital Acquire RAM; Data Access Register; Digital Audio Recording

DARPA
Defense Advanced Research Projects Administration (DOD)

DARS
Document Archival Retrieval System

DAS
Data Acquisition System; Data Access Security; Direct Analog Storage

DASD
Direct Access Storage Device (IBM)

DASF
Direct Access Storage Facility

DASM
Direct Access Storage Media

DASS
Design Automation Standards Subcommittee (IEEE)

DAT
Date [of status] (IBM); Digital Audio Tape; Disk Allocation Table (IBM); Dynamic Address Translation (IBM)

DATACOM
Data Communication
DATACOR
Data Correction
DATEL
Data Telecommunication
DaTran
Data Transmission
DAU
Data Access Unit; Data Adapter Unit; Data Acquisition Unit
DAV
Data Valid (IEEE); Data Available
DAVID
Data Above Video system; Distributed Access View Integrated Database (NASA)
DAX
Digital Access Cross-Connect
db
decibel
dB
decibel (Preferred form)
DB
Data Bank; Data Base; Data Bus
DB2
DataBase 2 (IBM)
DB2PM
DataBase 2 Performance Monitor (IBM)
DBA
Data Base Administration(or)
DBAM
Data Base Access Method
DBC
Data Base Computer
DBCCP
Data Base Command and Control Processor
DBCL
Data Base Command Language
DBCS
Data Base Control System; Double-Byte Character Set (IBM)
DBD
Data Base Definition; Data Base Description; Data Base Design; Data Base Directory
DBDD
Data Base Design Document
DBDL
Data Base Definition Language
DBE
Data Bus Enable

DBF
Data Base Facility; Data Base Format
DBG
Data Bus Generator
DBIOC
Data Base Input/Output Control
dbl
double
DBL
Data Base Language
Dbm
decibels [reference, or referred to one] milliwatt
DBM
Data Buffer Memory; Data Base Management; Data Base Manager; Decibels [referenced, or referred to one] Milliwatt
DBML
Data Base Management Language
DBMS
Data Base Management Software; Data Base Management System
DBMS-10
Data Base Management System-10 (For DEC system)
DBMS-20
Data Base Management System-20 (For DEC system)
DBOMP
Data Base Organization and Maintenance Processor (IBM)
DBOS
Disk Based Operating System
DBP
Data Base Processor
dBr
decibels relative
DBR
Data Base Retrieval; Disaster Backup and Recovery; Descriptor Base Register; Distributed Bragg Reflector (Refers to semiconductor laser technology)
DBRAD
Data Base Relational Application Dictionary (IBM)
dBrn
decibels [above] reference noise (In audio circuit literature, a reference level commonly used)
DBRN
Decibels [above] Reference Noise (In audio circuit literature, a reference level

commonly used)

dBRNC

Decibels [above] Reference Noise, C-Message Weighted (IEEE)

DBRNC

Decibels away from the Reference Noise when measured with a C-message filter (Variation of dBRNC)

DBRT

Delay Before Repeat Time (Computing)

DBS

Data Base Service; Data Base System; Direct Broadcast System; Direct Broadcast Satellite

DBSM

Decibels per Square Meter

dBV

decibels [referenced, or referred to one] Volt (In audio circuit literature, a reference level commonly used)

dBW

decibels [referenced, or referred to one] Watt (In audio circuit literature, a reference level commonly used)

DBX

Digital Branch Exchange

DC

Data Cartridge; Data Channel; Double Channel (Refers to laser construction); Data Code; Data Communication; Data Counter; Direct Current; Digital Computer; Disk Controller; Device Control

DC-AC

Direct Current to Alternating Current

DC&AS

Digital Control and Automation System

DC-PBH

Double-Channel-Planar Buried Heterostructure (NEC)

DCA

Data Center Administration (Computer Associates, US); Data Communication Administrator; Digital Computer Association (US); Defense Communications Agency Systems (Obsolete, now DISA, DOD); Direct Current Amperes; Distributed Communications Architecture; Document Content Architecture (IBM)

DCAA

Defense Contract Audit Agency (DARPA)

DCAM

Data Collection Access Method

DCB

Data and Control Bus; Data Control Block

(IBM); Device Control Block (IBM); Disk Co-processor Board

DCC

Double-Coax Conversion (CCITT); Data Collection Center; Data Communications Controller; Direct Control Channel

DCCS

Distributed Capability Computing System

DCCU

Data Communications Control Unit

DCD

Data Carrier Detect; Digital Clock Distributor; Data Correlation and Documentation System (IBM)

DCDS

Digital Control Design System

DCE

Data Circuit Equipment; Data Circuit-terminating Equipment; Data Communications Equipment; Distributed Computing Environment

DCEA

Distributed Computing Environment Architecture

DCF

Disk Controller/Formatter; Document Composition Facility (IBM); Data Communication Facility (IBM); Data Count Field (IBM)

DCH

Data Channel

DCI

Direct Channel Interface

DCIA

Digital Card Inverting Amplifier

DCIU

Data Channel Interface Unit

DCL

Digital Command Language (DEC); Digital Control Logic; Devices Clear (IEEE)

dcl

declaration

DCLZ

Data Compression Lempel Ziv (H-P)

DCM

Device Communications Manager (Cabletron Systems, Inc, US); Data Communications Multiplexer; Digital Circuit Multiplexing; Distributed Computing Model; Display Control Module

DCME

Digital Circuit Multiplication Equipment

(ANSI)

DCMF

Distribution Change Management Facility (IBM)

DCMP

Distributed Cooperative Marketing Program (DEC)

DCMS

Dedicated Computer Message Switching; Device Control Management System (Electronic Data Systems Corp [EDS], US)

DCN

Distributed Computer Network

DCNA

Data Communication Network Architecture

DCO

Digitally Controlled Oscillator

DCOM

Data Center Operations Manager

DCOS

Data Collection Operating System

DCP

Data Collection Program; Data Communications Program; Digital Communications Protocol (AT&T); Distributed Communications Processor

DCPCM

Differentially Coherent Pulse-Code Modulation

DCPP

Data Communications Pre-processor

DCPSK

Differentially Coherent Phase-Shift Keyed(ing)

DCPTF

Digitally Controlled Programmable Transversal Filter (TI)

DCR

Data Collection Routine; Design Change Request; Digital Cassette Recorder; Diffraction-Coupled Resonator

DCRABS

Disk Copy Restore And Backup System

DCS

Data Center Scheduler; Data Communication Standard; Data Collection System; Data Communication System; Digital Cross-Connect Switch; Digital Classified Software (DEC); Digitizing Camera System (Tektronix Inc); Distributed Communications System (AT&T); Distributed Com-

puting System; Distributed Control System; Document Control System

DCSP

Defense Communications Satellite Program (DOD)

DCSS

Digital Conferencing and Switching System (AT&T); Discontinuous Shared Segment (IBM)

DCT

Data Communications Terminal; Destination Control Table (IBM); Device Characteristics Table (IBM); Dispatcher Control Table (IBM); Digital Communications Terminal

DCTL

Direct Coupled Transistor Logic

DCTN

Defense Commercial Telecommunications Network (DOD)

DCU

Data Cache Unit (IBM); Data Control Unit; Data Communications Unit; Device Control Unit; Disk Control Unit

DCV

Direct Current Volts

DCVG

Display Control Vector Generator

DCW

Data Control Word

DCWS

Debris Collision Warning Sensor (NASA)

DD

Data Definition (IBM); Data Dictionary; Data Division; Double Deck; Direct Detection

DD/D

Data Dictionary/Directory

DDA

Digital Differential Analyzer

DDAM

Dynamic Design-Analysis Method

DDAS

Digital Data Acquisition System

DDB

Device Data Block; Device Descriptor Block (IBM); Digital Data Bank

DDBM

Distributed Data Base Manager

DDBMS

Distributed Data Base Management Systems

DDC
Direct Digital Control
DDCMP
Digital Data Communication Message Protocol (DEC)
DDD
Direct Distance Dialing (AT&T)
DDE
Dynamic Data Exchange (Microsoft Corp, US)
DDF
Dump Display Facility
DDI
Device Driver Interface (AT&T)
DDIF
Digital Document Interchange Format (DEC)
DDL
Data Definition [or Description] Language; Digital Data Link; Device Descriptor Language (IBM)
DDM
Device Descriptor Module (IBM); Distributed Data Management (IBM)
DDN
Defense Data Network (DOD)
DDName
Data Definition Name (IBM)
DDNAME
Data Definition Name (IBM)
DDP
Distributed Data Processing
DDR
Dynamic Device Reconfiguration (IBM); DASD [Direct Access Storage Device] Dump Restore (IBM)
DDRS
Defense Data Repository System (DOD)
DDS
Data Description Specification (IBM); Dataphone Digital Service (AT&T); Digital Data System (ANSI); Data Dictionary System; Digital Data Service (AT&T); Digital Data Storage; Direct Digital Synthesis; Digital-Distributed Software (DEC)
DDSA
Digital Data Service Adapter
DDS-SC
Dataphone Digital Service--Secondary Channel (AT&T)
DDSN
Digital Derived Services Network

DDT
Driver Dispatch Table (DEC); Dynamic Debugging Technique (DEC)
DDT&E
Design, Development, Test, and Evaluation
DE
Data Entry; Discard Eligibility (ANSI)
DEA
Data Encryption Algorithm
DEB
Data Extent Block (IBM)
dec
decimal; decoder
DECmcc
Digital Equipment Corporation Management Control Center (DEC)
DECnet
Digital Equipment Corporation Network (DEC)
DECUS
Digital Equipment Computer Users' Society (DEC)
DEDB
Data Entry Data Base (IBM)
DEE
Digital Evaluation Equipment
def
definition
DEF
Data Encryption Facility; Destination Element Field (IBM)
deg
degree
Del
Delete (Key on computer keyboard)
del
delete
DEL
Delete (Key on computer keyboard); Direct Exchange Line
DELNI
Digital Ethernet Local Network Interface (DEC)
dem
demand
DEMA
Data Entry Management Association (US)
DEMPR
Digital Ethernet Multi-Portable Repeater (DEC)
DEMS
Digital Electronic Message Service

DES
Data Encryption Standard (NIST); Digital Encryption Standard; Design and Evaluation System; Document Exchange System

DESC
Defense Electronics Supply Center (DOD)

DeTab
Decision Table

DEU
Data Exchange Unit

DevHlp
Device Driver Helper (IBM)

DF
Data Field; Destination Field

DFA
Design For Assembly

DFC
Data Flow Control (IBM)

DFD
Data Flow Diagram

DFDSS
Data Facility Data Set Services (IBM)

DFHSM
Data Facility Hierarchical Storage Manager (IBM)

DFLD
Device Field (IBM)

DFM
Design For Manufacturability

DFP
Data Facility Product (IBM)

DFR
Dynamic Flexible Routing (AT&T)

DFS
Distributed File Server(ice) [or System] (DEC); Distributed Function Support (IBM)

DFSMS
Data Facility System-Managed Storage (IBM)

DFT
Design For Testability; Diagnostic Function Test (IBM); Distributed Function Terminal (IBM); Discrete Fourier Transform

DFU
Data File Utility (IBM)

DG
Datagram (Service, AT&T)

DH
Design Handbook

DHCF
Distributed Host Command Facility (IBM)

DHS
Data Handling System

DI/DO
Data Input/Data Output

DI
Device Independence; Device Interconnect (DEC); Discrete Input

DIA
Document Interchange Architecture (IBM)

DIAG
Diagnostic

DIAN
Digital Analog

DIB
Data Integrity Block (IBM)

DIBOL
Digital Business-Oriented Language (DEC)

DIC
Digital Incremental Computer; Digital Integrating Computer

dict
dictionary

DID
Direct Inward Dialing (AT&T)

DIDS
Digital Information Display System

DIF
Data Interchange Format; Device Input Format (IBM)

dig
digit; digital

DIN
Data Identification Number; *Deutches Institut für Normung* (The German national standards organization. Standards which are commonly encountered in electronic devices)

DIOCB
Device Input/Output Control Block (IBM)

DIOP
Disk Input/Output Processor (Cray Research Corp, US); Distributed Input/Output Processor

DIOS
Distributed Input/Output System

DIP
Digital Image Printer; Dual In-line Package (IC)

dir
directory

DIRAC
Direct Access

DIRMAINT
Directory Maintenance (IBM)
DIS
Data Interpretation System (IBM); Draft International Standard (Standards defined by ISO); Disconnect Initiate Sent (DEC)
DISA
Direct Inward System Access (AT&T)
DISASM
Disassembler (IBM)
disc
disconnect
DISCO
Distributed Switching with Centralized Optics (AT&T)
DISLAN
Display Language
DISN
Defense Information Systems Network (DOD)
DISNET
Defense Integrated Secure Network (DOD)
DISOSS
Distributed Office Support System (IBM)
DITTO
Data Interfile Transfer Testing and Options utility (IBM)
DIU
Display Interface Unit
DIV
Data In Voice
DKI
Driver Kernel Interface (AT&T)
dkm
dekameter (or decameter)
DL/1
Data Language I (IBM)
DL
Data Language; Data Link; Data List; Diode Laser
DLA
Data Link Adapter (IBM); Defense Logistics Agency network (DOD)
DLC
Data Link Connection; Data Link Control (Character)
DLCI
Data Link Connection (or Circuit) Identifier
DLD
Deadline Date
DLE
Data Link Escape (Character)

DLL
Data Link Layer
DLM
Data Link Mapping; Data Link Monitor; Distributed Lock Manager (DEC)
DLN
Digital Lightwave Network (DEC)
DLR
DOS LAN Requester (IBM)
DLT
Data Loop Transceiver (IBM); Decision Logic Table
dm
decimeter
DM
Data Mark (DOD); Data Management; Data Manager; Design Manual; Distribution Manager (IBM); Disconnect Mode
DMA
Defense Mapping Agency (US Dept of Defense [DOD]); Direct Memory Access; Distributed Management Architecture (IBM)
DMAC
Direct Memory Access Controller
DMERT
Duplex Multi-Environment Real-Time (AT&T)
DMF
Dual Tone Multifrequency (AT&T)
DMH
Device Message Handler (IBM)
DML
Data Manipulation Language (DEC); Database Management Language
DMM
Digital Multi-Meter
DMO
Data Management Officer
DMOS
Double-Diffused Metal-Oxide Semiconductor
DMOSFET
Diffused Metal-Oxide Semiconductor Field-Effect Transistor
dmp
dump
DMR
Data Management Routines
DMS
Data Management System (Sperry-Univac); Database Management System

85

(Burroughs Corp, US); Defense Message System (DOD); Display Management System (IBM)

DMT
Development Management Tool

DMU
Data Management Unit

DN
Data Name

DNA
Digital Network Architecture (DEC); Distributed Network Architecture (Sperry Computer)

DNC
Direct Numerical Control

DNCMS
Distributed Network Control and Management System (NEC)

DNI
Dialed Number Identification

DNIC
Data Network Identification Code

DNL
Do Not Load

DNS
Distributed Name Service (DEC)

DOC
Department of Commerce (US Dept of Commerce); Department of Communications (Canada); Direct Operating Costs

DoD
Department of Defense (US Dept of Defense)

DOD
Department of Defense (US Dept of Defense)

DOF
Degree Of Freedom; Device Output Format (IBM)

DOJ
Department of Justice (US Dept of Justice)

DOMINA
Distribution-Oriented Management Information Analyzer

DOMSAT
Domestic Satellite (NASA)

DOS
Disk Operating System (Pronounced "doss', a generic term for operating system)

DOS/VS
Disk Operating System with Virtual Storage

DOSES
Development of Statistical Expert Systems

DOT
Designated Order Turn-around

DOTS
Digital Optical Tape System

DOV
Data Over Voice

DP
Data Processing; Data Processor; Distribution Point; Display Processor; Dynamic Programming

DPA
Destructive Physical Analysis

DPAGE
Device Page (IBM)

DPC
Data Processing Center

DPCM
Differential Pulse Code Modulation

DPCX
Data Processing Control Executive (IBM)

DPDT
Double-Pole, Double-Throw switch

DPE
Data Processing Equipment

dpi
dots per [linear] inch (Measure of printer resolution); dots per [square] inch (Measure of photographic resolution)

DPL
Distributed Program Link (IBM); Diode-Pumped Laser

DPLL
Digital Phase Locked Loop

DPLS
Digital Private Line Service (MCI)

DPM
Distributed Plant Management (DEC); Distributed Presentation Management (IBM)

DPMA
Data Processing Management Association (US)

DPMI
DOS Protected Mode Interface (Intel Corp)

DPP
Disposable Plotter Pen

DPPX
Distributed Processing Programming Executive (IBM)

DPS
Data Processing Station; Distributed Pre-

sentation Services (IBM); Document Processing System

DPSK
Differential Phase-Shift Keying

DPSS
Diode-Pumped Solid-State laser

DPT
Driver Prolog Table (DEC)

DPU
Data Processing Unit; Data Path Unit (TI)

DQCB
Disk Queue Control Block (IBM)

DQS
Distributed Queuing Services [or System] (DEC)

dr
divisor

DR
Data Report

DRAM
Dynamic Random Access Memory [RAM] (Chip)

DRAW
Direct Read After Write

DRC
Data Recording Control (IBM); Design Rule Check

DRCS
Dynamically Redifinable Character Set(s)

DRD
Data Recording Device (IBM)

DRDA
Distributed Relational Database Architecture (IBM)

DRDS
Dynamic Reconfiguration Data Set (IBM)

DRI
Defense Research Internet (DOD)

DRO
Digital Read-Out; Digital Recording Oscilloscope

DRP
Distributed Resource Planning

DRQ
Data Ready Queue (IBM)

DRS
Data Recovery System

DS
Data Set; Data Structure; Datagram Service; Development System (IBM)

DS-SSS
Direct-Sequence Spread-Spectrum System

DS-0
Digital Signal Level 0 (AT&T)

DS-1C
Digital Signal Level 1C (AT&T)

DSA
Digital Storage Architecture (DEC); Digitizing Signal Analyzer; Directory Service Agent

DSAB
Data Set Access Block

DSAF
Destination Subarea Field (IBM)

DSB
Defense Science Board (DOD)

DSCB
Data Set Control Block (IBM)

DSD
Data Set Definition (IBM)

DSDD
Double-Sided Double-Density (Refers to floppy disks)

DSDF
DSA [Direct Storage Architecture] Standard Disk Format (DEC)

DSDT
Data Set Definition Table (IBM)

DSE
Data Set Extension (IBM); Data Switching Exchange (IBM)

DSF
Data Set Function(s) (IBM); Device Support Facility (IBM)

DSI
Data Stream Interface (IBM)

DSIN
Digital Software Information Network (DEC)

dsk
disc (disk)

DSL
Data Set Label (IBM); Digital Subscriber Line (AT&T)

DSLO
Distributed Systems License Option (IBM)

DSM
Data Services Manager (IBM); Distributed Systems Management; Digitizing Scope Module (Tektronix Inc); Digital Standard MUMPS [Massachusetts General Hospital Utility Multi-Programming System] (DEC)

DSMO
Data Site Management Officer (AT&T)
DSN
Data Set Name (IBM); Defense Switched Network (DOD); Digital Service Node
DSP
Digital Signal Processing; Directory Service Protocol; Distributed System Program; Domain Specific Part
DSPU
Downstream Physical Unit (IBM)
dspl
display
DSR
Data Set Ready; Digital Standard Runoff (DEC); Document Structure Recognition
DSRB
Data Services Request Block (IBM)
DSRI
Digital Standard Relational Interface (DEC)
DSS
Decision Support System; DECnet System Service (DEC); Dynamic Support System; Distribution Scheduling System; Digital Simulation System
DSSA
Distributed System Security Architecture (DEC)
DSSD
Double-Sided Single-Density (refers to floppy disks)
DSSI
Digital Storage System Interconnect (DEC)
DST
Data Services Task (IBM)
DSU
Data Service Unit; Digital Service Unit
DSX
Digital Signal Cross-Connect; Distributed Systems Executive (IBM)
DS0
Digital Signal 0 [Zero]
DT
Data Table; Data Terminal; Digital Terminal; Dial Tone
DTB
Dynamic Transaction Backout (IBM)
DTAS
Data Transmission And Switching (System)
DTC
Desk Top Computer

DTE
Data Terminal Equipment
DTF
Data Transfer Facility (DEC)
DTG
Date-Time Group
DTIF
Digital Tabular Interchange Format (DEC)
DTL
Diode-Transistor Logic (Early IC technology family)
DTMF
Dual Tone Multiple Frequency (AT&T)
DTP
Desk Top Publishing; Distributed Transaction Processing (IBM)
DTR
Data Terminal Ready; Data Transfer Rate
DTS
Dedicated Transmission Service (AT&T); Digital Termination Service (AT&T)
DUA
Directory User Agent
DUAL
Dispatchable Unit Access List (IBM)
DUAT
Dual User Access Terminal (FAA)
dup
duplicate
DUP
Disk Utility Program
DUT
Device Under Test
DUV
Data Under Voice
DV
Dependent Variable
dvc
device
DVHSP
Digital Video High-Speed Processor
DVI
Digital Video Interface
DVM
Data/Voice Module (AT&T); Data/Voice Multiplexer (AT&T); Digital Voice Multiplexer (AT&T); Digital Voltmeter
DVN
Digital Video Network (DEC)
DVST
Direct View Storage Tube
DVT
Device Vector Table (IBM); Digital Video

Teleconferencing (Intel Corp, US)

DVX

Digital Voice Exchange

DW

Daisy Wheel; Double-Word

DWB

Direct Wafer Bonding

DWSS

DPPX [Distributed Processing Program Executive] Word Station Support (IBM)

DX

Directory Exchange; Distance [Commonly used in radiotelegraph); Duplex (Telecom-

munications)

DXAM

Distributed Indexed Access Method (IBM)

DXC

Data Exchange Control; Digital Cross-Connect system

DXF

Data Exchange Format

DXI

Data Exchange Interface

DYSTAL

Dynamic Storage Allocation

E

e
empty; error; enable; execute; expression; exponent; voltage; execution

E
Exa (SI prefix denoting 10^{18}); Voltage

E/D
Encode/Decode

E/D
Enhancement/Depletion

E-E
End-to-End

E-Mail
Electronic Mail

e-mail
electronic mail

E/R
Entity/Relationship

E-R
Entity-Relationship

E-TIME
Execution Time

e (E)
voltage

E&OE
Errors and Omissions Excepted

EA
Effective Address; Element Activity; Energy Analysis; Extended Address

EAD
Estimated Availability Date

EADAS
Engineering and Administration Data Acquisition System

EADS
Engineering and Analysis Data System (NASA)

EAE
Extended Arithmetic Element

EAM
Electrical Accounting Machine

EAN
European Article Numbering

EAP
Extended Arithmetic Processor

EAPROM
Electrically Alterable Programmable

Read-Only Memory

EAR
Extended Address Register

EARL
Easy Access Report Language

EARN
European Academic Research Network

EAROM
Electrically Alterable Read-Only Memory

EASL
External Applications Software Library (DEC)

EAU
Extended Arithmetic Unit

EAX
Electronic Automatic Exchange

EBAM
Electron Beam Addressable Memory

EBCD
Extended Binary-Code Decimal

EBCDIC
Extended Binary-Coded Decimal Interchange Code

E BEAM
Electronic Beam

EBES
Electron Beam Exposure System

EBIC
Electron Beam Induced Current

EBM
Extended Branch Mode

EBR
Electron Beam Recording; Employee Badge Reader (AT&T)

EBRS
Electronic Batch Records System (DEC)

EBT
Equipment-Based Training

EBV
Extended Binary Vectors

EC
European Community; Electronic Computer; Engineering Change (IBM); Echo Cancel; Erase Character (DOD); Error Correcting; Extended Control

ECA
Extended Contingent Allegiance; Electronics Control Assembly

ECAD
Enhanced Computer-Aided Design

ECAM
Extended Content-Addressable Memory

ECAP
Electronic Circuit Analysis Program
ECB
Event Control Block (IBM)
ECC
Error Checking and Correcting [or Correction] (IBM); Error Check and Control; Error Correcting [or Correction] Code (DEC); Error Correction Circuit; Error Correction Control
ECCM
Electronic Counter-Countermeasures
ECCNP
European Conference on Computer Network Protocols
ECE
Executive Communications Exchange
ECF
Enhanced Connectivity Facilities (IBM)
ECI
European Cooperation in Informatics
ECIF
Electronic Components Industry Federation
ECL
Emitter-Coupled Logic; Executive Control Language
ECM
Electric Coding Machine; Electronic Counter Measure(s); Extended Core Memory; Electrochemical Machining
ECMA
European Computer Manufacturers Association
ECN
Engineering Change Notice; Executive Computer Network
ECO
Engineering Change Order; Electron-Coupled Oscillator
ECOMA
European Computer Measurement Association
ECOS
Extended Communications Operating System
ECP
Embedded Control Processor (Intel Corp, US)
ECPS
Extended Control Program Support (IBM)
ECR
Electronic Cash Register
ECREEA
European Conference of Radio and Electronic Equipment Association
ECS
Extended Channel Support; Extended Character Set; Extended Control Storage
ECSA
Extended Common Storage [or System] Area (IBM)
ECSA
European Computing System Simulator
ECT
Estimated Completion Time
ECTEL
European Telecommunications and Professional Electronics Industry
ECTL
Emitter Coupled Transistor Logic
ECU
Electronic Control Unit
ed
edition; editor
ED
Encryption Device; Extra Density (Refers to floppy disk capacity)
EDA
Electronic Design Automation; Enterprise Data Access (IBM)
EDAC
Error Detection and Correction
EDBMF
Extended Data Base Management Facility (IBM)
EDBMS
Engineering Data Base Management System
EDBS
Educational Data Base Management System
EDC
Electronic Digital Computer; Estimated Date or Completion; Extended Device Control; Error Detection Code; Error Detection and Correction
EDCS
Electronic Data Control System (DEC)
EDD
Expert Data base Designer
EDF
Execution Diagnostic Facility (IBM)
EDFM
Extended Disk File Management System
EDGAR
Electronic Data Gathering, Analysis and Retrieval system

edi
editor
EDI
Electronic Data Interchange (CCITT); Electronic Document Interchange
EDIF
Electronic Design Interchange Format
EDINET
Educational Instruction Network
EDIS
Engineering Data Information System
edit
editor
EDL
Engineering Data Library; Emulation Design Language
EDM
Electrical Discharge Machining; Environment Description Manager (IBM); External Data Manager
EDMA
Extended Direct Memory Access
EDMICS
Engineering Data Management Information and Control System (DOD)
EDN
Enhanced Digital Networking
EDOS
Extended Disk Operating System
EDP
Electronic Data Processing; Extended Density Platform (NEC)
EDPE
Electronic Data Processing Equipment
EDPEP
Electronic Data Processing Education Program
EDPM
Electronic Data-Processing Machine
EDPS
Electronic Data Processing System
EDRAM
Enhanced Dynamic Random Access Memory
EDS
Electronic Data Systems Corp (US); Electronic Data System; Electronic Data Switching; Engineering Data System
EDSAC
Electronic Delay Storage Automatic Computer
EDSL
Enhanced Digital Subscriber Line (AT&T)

EDSX
Electronic Digital Signal Cross-Connect (CCITT)
edt
editor
EDT
Engineering Design Text
EDTV
Extended Definition Television
EDVAC
Electronic Discrete Variable Automatic Computer; Electronic Discrete Variable Calculator
EDX
Energy Dispersive X-Ray; Event-Driven Executive (IBM)
EDX/CF
Event-Driven Executive/Communications Facility (IBM)
EE
Electrical Engineer; Errors Excepted; Extended Edition (Refers to IBM's OS/2)
EE-PROMs
Electrically Erasable, Programmable Read-Only Memories
EEA
Electronic Engineering Association
EECL
Enhanced Emitter Coupled Logic; Emitter-to-Emitter Coupled Logic
EECMA
European Electronic Component Manufacturers Association
EEI
Essential Elements of Information
EEL
Edge-Emitting Laser
EEMC
Electronics Equipment Manufacturers Committee
EEMS
Enhanced Expanded Memory Specification
EEP
Electronic Evaluation and Procurement
EEPLD
Electronically Erasable Programmable Logic Device (Advanced Micro Devices, US)
EET
Edge Enhancement Technique (Dot matrix printer quality improvement technique)

EF
Execution Function; Extended Facility; External Flag

EFA
Extended Finite Automation

EFF
Expandable File Family

effect
effective

EFL
Effective [or Equivalent] Focal Length; Error Frequency Limit

EFOP
Expanded Function Operator Panel

EFS
Error-Free Seconds; End-of-Frame Sequence; External Function Store; Extended Frame Superformat (AT&T)

EFT
Electrical Fast Transient; Electronic Funds Transfer; Electronic Financial Transaction

EFTPOS
Electronic Funds Transfer at Point Of Sale

EFTS
Electronic Funds Transfer System

EGA
Enhanced Graphics Adapter

EGM
Enhanced Graphics Module

EGP
Exterior Gateway Protocol (DOD)

EHCN
Experimental Hybrid Computer Network

EHF
Extra [or Extremely] High Frequency (30 to 300 GHz band)

EHLLAPI
Emulator High-Level Language Application Program Interface (IBM)

EHP
Effective HorsePower

EHV
Extra [or Extremely] High Voltage

EI
Enable Interrupt; Error Indicator

EIA
Electronic Industries Association

EIA-J
Electronic Industries Association of Japan

EIAJ
Electronic Industries Association of Japan

EIB
Execute Interface Block (IBM)

EIC
Ethernet Interface Coupler; Equipment Identification Code

EIEMA
Electrical Installation Equipment Manufacturers Association

EIES
Electronic Information Exchange System (EPA, US)

EIN
European Informatics Network; Equivalent Input Noise

EIOS
Extended Input/Output System

EIRENE
European Information Researchers Network (EC)

EIS
Engineering Information System (USAF); Enterprise Integration Services (DEC); Executive Information System; Extended Instruction Set

EISA
Extended Industry Standard Architecture

EIT
Engineer In Training

EITS
Express International Telex Service

EL
Electroluminescent(ence); End of the Line; Erase Line (DOD); External Link

ELA
Equipment Leasing Association; Extended Line Adapter

ELAN
Enhanced Local Area Network; Error Logging and Analysis

ELD
Electroluminescent Display

ELED
Edge-Emitting Light-Emitting Diode

elem
element

ELF
Extra [or Extremely] Low Frequency (30 to 300 Hz band); Extensible Language Facility

Elint
Electronic Intelligence

ELINT
Electronic Intelligence

ELL
Excimer Laser Lithography

ELP
Electronic Line Printer
ELR
Error Logging Register
ELS
Entry Level System
ELSI
Extremely Large Scale Integration (IC)
elt
element
ELT
Emergency Locator Transmitter (FCC)
EM
Electronic Mail; End-of-Medium (Character, CCITT); Electromagnetic; Expandable(ed) [or Extended] Memory
EM&S
Equipment Maintenance and Support
EMA
Enterprise Management Architecture (DEC); Expanded [or Extended] Memory Area
EMB
Emulator Board
EMC
Electromagnetic Compatability; Electromagnetic Coupling; Emitter Coupled Logic; External Multiplexer Channel
EMD
Equilibrium Mode [or Modal] Distribution (Refers to fiber optic communications)
emf (EMF)
electromotive force
EMI
Electromagnetic Interference
EMIND
European Modular Interactive Network Designer
EML
Emulator Machine Language; Established Measured Loss
EMM
Ethernet Management Module
EMMS
Electronic Mail and Message System
EMOD
Erasable Memory Octal Dump
EMP
Electromagnetic Pulse
EMPL
Extensible Microprogramming Language
EMR
Electromagnetic Radiation

EMS
Electromagnetic Susceptibility; Electronic Mail Service (DEC); Electronic Mail System; Electronic Message Service; Electronic Messaging System; Element Management Service; Energy Management System; Enterprise Management Station (DEC); Extended Main Store; Expanded Memory Specification (Lotus-Intel-Microsoft. Also known as *LIM EMS*); Extended Memory Specification (AST Research Inc, US)
EMSS
Electronic Message Service System
EMU
Electromagnetic Unit; Extended Memory Unit
EMUG
European Manufacturing Automation Protocol Users' Group (EC)
enbl
enable
end
endorsement
endec
encoder/decoder
ENDS
Euratom Nuclear Documentation System (EC)
ENET
Enhanced Network
ENFIA
Exchange Network Facilities for Interstate Access
ENIAC
Electronic Numerical Integrater And Calculator (Early 1940's digital computer)
ENLG
Enable Level Group
ENN
Expand Nonstop Network
ENOB
Effective Number of Bits (A measure)
enq
enquiry
ENS
Enterprise Network Switch; Equivalent Noise Temperature
ENTELEC
Energy Telecommunications and Electrical Association
EO
Electro Optic(al, s); Enable Output; En-

gineering Order

EOA
End-Of-Address

EOB
End-Of-Block

EOC
End-Of-Chain (IBM); End-Of-Character; End-Of-Conversion

EOD
End-Of-Data; Entry-On-Duty

EOE
End-Of-Extent (IBM)

EOF
End-Of-File (IBM)

EOI
End Or Identify (IEEE); End-Of-Inquiry

EOJ
End-Of-Job

EOL
End-Of-Line; End-Of-List

EOLM
End-Of-Line Marker

EOM
End-Of-Medium; End-Of-Message [code]; Erasable Optical Memory

EON
End-Of-Number (Control character, CCITT)

EOP
End-Of-Page

EOPM
Electro Optic Phase Modulation

EOQ
End-Of-Query

EOR
End-Of-Record; Exclusive OR

EOS
Electrical Overstress; Electronic Office System; End-Of-String; End-Of-Screen; End-Of-Segment; End-Of-Sequence; End-Of-Step

EOT
End-Of-Tape; End-Of-Test; End-Of-Text; End-Of-Transmission (Character, CCITT)

EOV
End-Of-Volume (IBM)

EOW
End-Of-Word

EP
Environmentally Protected; Emulation(or) Program (IBM); Extended Platform

EPA
Environmental Protection Agency (US); Event Processor Array; Estimated Profile

Analysis; Extended Performance Analysis

EPBX
Electronic Private Branch Exchange

EPC
Editorial Processing Center

EPCAD
Electronics Packaging Computer-Aided Design

EPL
Encoder Programming Language

EPLANS
Engineering, Planning and Analysis Systems

EPLD
Erasable Programmable Logic Device (IC)

EPN
Expansion Port Network (AT&T)

EPO
Emergency Power Off

EPOS
Electronic Point-of-Sale

EPR
Error Pattern Register

EPRA
Electronic Representatives Association

EPRI
Electric Power Research Institute

EPROM
Electrically Programmable Read-Only Memory

EPS
Electronic Payments System; Encapsulated PostScript [file] (Page description language); Extended Protocol Specification; Even Parity Select

EPSCS
Enhanced Private Switched Communications Service [or System]

EPSF
Encapsulated PostScript File (Page description language)

EPT
Executive Process Table

eq
equal

eql
equal

EQL
English Query Language

eqpt
equipment

equ
equal

EQUATE
Electronic Quality Assurance Test Equipment

equip
equipment

equiv
equivalent

er
error

ER
Established Reliability; Exponent Register; Explicit Route (IBM)

ERA
Electrically Reconfigurable Array

ERATO
Exploratory Research in Advanced Technologies (Japan)

ERC
Engineering Research Center (NSF); Engineering Rule Check

ERCC
Error Checking and Correction

EREP
Environmental Recording, Editing, and Printing (IBM)

ERJE
Extended Remote Job Entry

ERMA
Electronic Recording Machine Accounting

EROM
Erasable Read-Only Memory

ERP
Error Recovery Procedures; Error Recovery Program (IBM); Extended Research Program (DEC)

err
error

ERRC
Expandability, Recoverability, Repairability Cost

ERS
Emergency Reporting System

ERT
Expected Run-Time

ES
End System; Expert System; External Store

ESA
European Space Agency; Enterprise Systems Architecture (IBM); Externally Specified Address

ESB
Electrical Standards Board

ESC
Enhanced Services Complex (AT&T)

esc (ESC)
escape (Keyboard key, CCITT)

ESCON
Enterprise Systems Connection architecture (IBM)

ESCS
Emergency Satellite Communications System

ESD
Electronic Software Distribution; Electrostatic Discharge; External Symbol Dictionary (IBM)

ESDI
Enhanced Small Device [or Disk] Interface

ESDS
Electrostatic Discharge Sensitivity; Entry Sequenced Data Set

ESE
Electronic Storage Element; Expert System Environment (IBM)

ESF
Extended Superframe Format; External Source Format (IBM); Extended Spooling Facility

ESFMU
Extended Superframe Monitoring Unit

ESI
Enhanced Serial Interface (Hayes Microcomputer Products, US); Externally Specified Index

ESL
European Systems Language

ESN
Emergency Service Network; External Segment Name

ESO
European Southern Observatory

ESP
Electrosensitive Paper; Engineering Support Processor (IBM); Enhanced Serial Port (Hayes Microcomputer Products, US); Enhanced Service Package (MCI); Enhanced Service Provider

ESPL
Electronic Switching Programming Language

ESPRIT
European Strategic Program for Research and Development in Information Technol-

ogy (EC)

ESR
Equivalent Series Resistance

ESS
Electronic Switching System (AT&T); Executive Support System; Event Scheduling System

est
estimated

EST
Earliest Start Time; Eastern Standard Time

ESTSC
Energy Science and Technology Software Center (DOE)

ESU
Electrostatic Unit

ET
Eastern Time; Electronic Typewriter; Emerging Technology; End of Text; Exchange Termination

ETB
End-of-Transmission-Block (CCITT)

ETC
Estimated Time of Completion

ETCOM
European Testing for Certification of Office and Manufacture

ETD
Estimated Time of Departure

ETDEF
Entry Table Descriptor Definition (IBM)

ETDL
Electronics Technology and Device Laboratory (US Army)

EtherNIM
Ethernet Network Integrity Monitor

ETLT
Equal To or Less Than

ETM
Element Test and Maintenance

ETN
Electronic Tandem Networks (AT&T)

ETR
Early Token Release; External Throughput Rate (IBM); Expected Time of Response

ETRR
External Throughput Rate Ratio (IBM)

ETS
Electronic Tandem Switching; Electronic Translator System; Electronic Typing Sys-

tem; Experimental Technologies Satellite; Engine Test Stand

ETSI
European Telecommunications Standards Institute (EC)

ETSPL
Extended Telephone Systems Programming Language

ETSS
Entry Time-Sharing System (IBM)

ETV
Educational Television

ETX
End-of-Text (CCITT); End-of-Transmission

EU
End-User; Execution Unit

EUCLID
Easily Used Computer Language for Illustration and Drawing (EC)

EUDG
European Datamanager User Group

EUF
End User Facility

EUIT
Educational Uses of Information Technology

EUROCOMP
European Computing Congress

EUROCON
European Conference on Electronics

EUROMICRO
European Association for Microprocessing and Microprogramming (EC)

EURONET
European Information Network (EC)

EUV
Extreme Ultraviolet

eV
electron Volt

EVA
Extensible VAX Editor (DEC)

EVFU
Electronic Vertical Format Unit

evid
evidence

EVIL
Extensible Video Interactive Language

EVM
Extended Virtual Machine

EVR
Electronic Video Recording

EW
Electronic Warfare

EWAN
Enterprise Wide Area Network
EWOS
European Workshop for Open Systems (EC)
ex
execute; executor
Ex
Exciter (Electronics)
EXCP
Execute Channel Program (IBM)
exctr
executor
EXD
External Device
EXDAMS
Extendable Debugging and Monitoring System
exec
execute; executive
EXEC
Execute
EXF
External Function

EXIP
Execute In Place (Memory card specification)
EXLST
Exit List
EXOR
Exclusive OR
exp
exponent; express; expression
expo
exposition
expr
expression
ext
external
EXTM
Extended Telecommunications Module
EXTRAN
Expression Translator
EXTRN
External Reference

F

f
false; farad; femto (SI prefix denoting 10^{-15}); fetch; file; fixed; flag; fraction; fractional; frequency; full; function; functional

F
Fahrenheit; Farad (The basic unit of capacitance); Faraday (Also called Faraday constant); Fast; Final (As subscript); Fermi (A small unit of length and wavelength); Fixed head; Flag (Refers to Synchronous Data Link Control [SDLC], IBM); Force; Focal length; Fluorine (Symbol); Filament; Fuse

F/B
Foreground/Background

F&E
Facilities and Equipment

F/L
Fetch/Load

F/R
Failure and Recovery

F-V
Frequency to Voltage

Fa
femtoampere (10^{-15} Ampere)

FA
Factory Automation; Field Address; Full Adder; Failure Analysis; Fatty Acid

FAA
Federal Aviation Administration (US)

FAAR
Forward Area Alerting Radar

FAB
File Access Block (DEC)

fac
facsimile; factual

FAC
File Access Channel; Floating Accumulator; Functional Authority Credential (IBM)

FACE
Field Alterable Control Element

FACETS
Factory Automation Control Environment Tool Set (CTS Corp)

FACS
Financial Accounting and Control System

FACT
Fast-Action Computer Terminal; Facility for Automation, Control and Test; Fully Automatic Compiling Technique

FADP
Federal Automatic Data Processing

FADS
FORTRAN Automatic Debugging System

FADUG
Federation Automatic Data Processing Users Group

FAM
File Access Manager

FAMHEM
Federation of Associations of Materials Handling Equipment Manufacturers

FAMOS
Floating-gate Avalanche-injection Metal-Oxide Semiconductor (MOS) (A type of erasable PROM)

FAP
Failure Analysis Program

FAPL
Formats and Protocols Language (IBM)

FAR
File Address Register

FARNET
Federation of American Research Networks

FAS
Flexible Access System

FASB
Financial Accounting Standards Board

FASR
Fast Acting Shift Register

FASS
Frequency Agile Signal Simulator (H-P)

FAST
Fairchild Advanced Schottky TTL (Fairchild Electronics, US); Fast Access Storage Technology; File Analysis and Selection Technique; Failure Analysis and Support Technology (IBM); First Application System Testing (Northern Telecom Inc, US); Flow Analysis Software Toolkit (NASA)

FAT
File Allocation Table

FATAR
Fast Analysis of Tape and Recovery

FATS
Fast Analysis of Tape Surface(s)

fax (FAX)
facsimile
FB
File Block; Fixed Block
FBA
Fixed-Block Architecture (IBM)
FBM
Foreground and Background Monitor
FC
Flow Controller; Flux Change; Font Change; Frame Control (IEEE); Function Code
FCB
File Control Block (DEC); Forms Control Buffer
FCBA
Fair Credit Billing Act
FCC
Federal Communications Commission (US); Flight Control Computer (NASA)
FCFS
First Come, First Serve(d)
fci (FCI)
flux changes per inch
FCIM
Farm, Construction and Industrial Machinery
FCL
Format Control Language
FCLA
Florida Center for Library Automation (US)
FCM
Firmware Control Memory; Field Coupling Mode
FCMS
Factory Control and Management System
FCP
File Control Processor; File Control Program
fcpi (FCPI)
flux changes per inch
FCPSI
Flux Changes Per Square Inch
FCPU
Flexible Central Processing Unit
FCS
File Control System (DEC); Frame Check Sequence (IEEE); Fixed Control Storage; Financial Control System; Finance Communication System
fct
function

FCU
File Control Unit
FD
File Definition; File Description; Flexible Disk; Floppy Disk; Full Duplex
FDAS
Flight Dynamics Analysis System
FDB
File Data Block
FDC
Floppy Disk Controller
FDCT
Factory Data Collection Terminal
FDD
Flexible Disk Drive; Floppy Disk Drive
FDDI
Fiber-Distributed Data Interface (IBM)
FDDL
File Data Description Language
FDL
Facility(ies) Data Link; Forms Description Language; File Definition Language (DEC)
FDM
Frequency Division Multiplex(ing)
FDMA
Frequency Division Multiple Access
FDOS
Floppy Disk Operating System
FDR
Fast Dump Restore; File Data Register
FDS
Flexible Disk System; Floppy Disk System
FDT
Formal Description Technique (CCITT); Functional Description Table
FDX
Full Duplex
FE
Field Editor; Field Engineer; Front End
FEA
Finite Element Analysis (Refers to a mathematical procedure)
FEBE
Far End Block Error
FEC
Forward Error Correction; Front-End Computer
FECN
Forward Explicit Congestion Notification (ANSI)

FECP
Front End Communications Processor
FED-STD
Federal Standard
FEDNET
Federal Information Network
FEDSIM
Federal Computer Performance Evaluation and Simulation Center
FEFO
First-Ended, First-Out [or First Ended/First Out]
FEI
Front End Interface
FELT
Full Etchstop Layer Transfer (TI)
FEM
Finite Element Modeling
FEP
Front End Processor
FERS
Facility Error Recognition System (IBM)
FET
Field-Effect Transistor (Electronics)
FETE
FORTRAN Execution Time Estimator
FF
Fast Forward; Flip-Flop; Form Feed
FFMS
Factory Floor Management Software
FFN
Full Function Node
FFS
Flash File System (Microsoft Corp, US); Formatted File System
FFT
Fast Fourier Transform
fg
foreground
FGA
Font Graphics Accelerator (Toshiba Electronics)
FH
File Handler; Fixed Head; Frequency-Hopped
FHP
Fractional Horsepower
FHSF
Fixed-Head Storage Facility
FI
Format Identifier
FIA
Field Image Alignment

FIB
File Information Block; Focused Ion Beam
FIC
First-In-Chain
FICON
File Conversion
FICS
Financial Control System [or Financial Information and Control System]; Factory Information Control System
FID
File Identifier (DEC); Format Identification (IBM)
FIDAC
Film Input to Digital Automatic Computer
FIE
File Interface Extension
FIF
Family Information Facility
FIFO
First In, First Out [or First In/First Out]
fig (FIG)
figure
FIGS
Figures Shift
FILEX
File Exchange
FILO
First In, Last Out [or First In/Last Out]
FILSYS
File System
FIMS
Forms Interface Management System; Financial Information Management System
FINAC
Fast Interline Non-active Automatic Control (AT&T)
FINAR
Financial Analysis and Reporting
FINMAN
Financial Management
FIO
For Information Only
FIPS
Federal(tion) Information Processing Standard (FCC)
FIR
Finite Impulse Response; File Indirect Register
FIRM
Financial Information for Resource Man-

agement

FIRMR
Federal Information Resources Management Regulations

FISO
Fast In/Slow Out (VLSIC)

FIT
File Inquiry Technique; Frame-Interline-Transfer

FIU
Federation of Information Users

FJA
Functional Job Analysis

fL
foot-Lambert (Unit of luminance)

fld
field

flg
flag

FLL
Frequency-Locked Loop

FLOPS
Floating Point Operations Per Second

FLP
Floating Point

FLPAU
Floating Point Arithmetic Unit

FLR
Flag Register

FLSF
Font Library Service Facility (IBM)

FM
Facilities Management; File Manager; File Management; Frequency Modulation; Function Management (IBM); Format Manager

FMD
Function Management Data

FMID
Function Modification Identification (IBM)

FML
File Manipulation Language

FMS
Flexible Manufacturing System; Forms Management System (DEC); File Management System

FN
Feature Node (CCITT); Functional Network

FNB
File Name Block

FNT
File Name Table

FO
Fiber Optic(s)

FOA
First Office Application (AT&T)

FOB
Friends Of Bill (Coined right after Bill Clinton's U.S. Presidential Election victory)

FOC
Fiber Optics Communications

FOCAL
Formula Calculator (DEC)

FOCIS
Fiber Optic Communication and Information Society

FOGM
Fiber-Optic Guided Missile (DOD)

fol
folio

FOM
Fiber-Optic Modem

FORTRAN
Formula Translator (IBM)

FOTS
Fiber-Optic Transmission System

FOV
Field Of View

FP
File Processor; Floating Point; Frame Pointer (DEC); Function Processor

FPA
Floating Point Arithmetic; Floating Point Accelerator (DEC)

FPC
Floating-Point Coprocessor; Functional Processor Cluster

FPD
First Part Done (DEC)

FPE
Floating Point Engine

FPGA
Field-Programmable Gate Array (IC)

FPLA
Field-Programmable Logic Array (IC)

FPM
File Protect Memory

FPP
Floating-Point Processor

FPPU
Floating Point Processor Unit

FPR
Floating Point Register (IBM)

FPROM
Field Programmable Read-Only Memory

fps
feet per second; frames per second

FPS
Fast Packet Switching; Frames Per Second

fps (FPS)
frames per second

FPU
File Processing Unit; Floating Point Unit (IBM)

FQL
Formal Query Language

FR
File Register; Final Report; Frame Relay (Telecommunications)

fract
fraction

FRAM
Ferroelectric Random Access Memory

FRL
Financial Reporting Language

FROM
Fusible Read-Only Memory

FRS
Financial Reporting System

FRU
Field Replaceable Unit (IBM)

fs
femtosecond (Denoted as 10^{-15} second)

FS
Field Separator; Field Service; File Separator (CCITT); Finite State; Full Scale; Frame Status (IEEE); Frame Sync; Function Select

FSA
Finite State Automation; Flexible System Architecture; Future Systems Architecture (IBM)

FSC
Federal Supply Code

FSCM
Federal Supply Code for Manufacturers

FSD
Functional Sequence Diagram; Fixed Shroud Duplex

fsec
femtosecond (Denoted as 10^{-15} second)

FSEC
Federal Software Exchange Center

FSK
Frequency-Shift Keying

FSM
Finite State Machine (IBM); Frequency-Shift Modulation

FSP
Full-Screen Processing; Full Screen Product

FSR
Feedback Shift Register; Full Scale Range

FSS
Flight Service Station (FAA)

FSU
Facsimile Server Unit; Facsimile Switching Unit; Field Select Unit; File Support Utility

ft
feet

FT
Format Type; Fault Tolerant; Fourier Transform

FTA
Fault Tree Analysis

FTAM
File Transfer Access and Management

ftc
footcandle

FTP
File Transfer Protocol

FTPI
Flux Transitions Per Inch

FTS
Federal Telecommunications System

FTSC
Federal Telecommunications Standards Committee

FU
Field Unit

func
function

FVC
Frequency to Voltage Converter

fw
firmware

FW
First Word

fwd
forward

fwdg
forwarding

FXM
Fiber Expansion Module (AT&T)

FXU
Fixed Point Unit (IBM)

FYI
For Your Information

G

g
gram; gain; conductance; group; graph; gravity; subscript for gate; subscript for generator

G
Gauss; Giga; Conductance; Gate; Generator; Deflection Factor (Symbol); Perveance (Symbol); Gravitational Constant (Symbol)

g (G)
conductance

g-byte
gigabytes

G/T
Gain/Temperature

Ga
Gallium (Element symbol)

GA
Go Ahead; General Average; Graphic Adapter; General Automation (Computer manufacturer); Global Address

GaAs
Gallium Arsenide chip (Semiconductor material)

GAB
Graphic Adapter Board

GADC
General Audio and Communications Ltd (UK)

GAELIC
Grumman Aerospace Engineering Language for Instructional Checkout

GAIC
Gallium Arsenide Integrated Circuit (IC)

GAIL
Gate Array Interface Language (High-level language, used in CAD applications)

GAL
Generic Array Logic

GALA
Gallium Aluminum Arsenide

GAM
Graphic(al) Access Method (IBM)

GAMA
Graphics Assisted Management Application

GAN
Global Area Network; Generating and Assembly Networks

GAO
General Accounting Office (US)

GAP
General Assembly Program; Graphics Application Program

GAPP
Geometric Arithmetic Parallel Processor (NCR)

GASP
General Activity Simulation Program; Graphic Applications Subroutine Package

GASS
Generalized Assembly System

GAT
Generalized Algebraic Translator; Graphic Arts Terminal

GATD
Graphic Analysis of Three-dimensional Data

GATE
Generalized Algebraic Translator Extended

Gb
Gigabit

GB
Giga Byte; General Business

GBF
Geographic Base file

GBIT
GigaBIT

GBT
Generalized Burst Trapping

GBTS
General Banking Terminal System

GBVS
Global Business Videoconferencing Service (AT&T)

GBW
Gain Bandwidth

gc
gigacycle

GC
Gas Chromatography; Garbage Collection; Generic Controller; Group Code (Searchable field)

GCAP
Generalized Circuit Analysis Program

GCC
Graphics Control Center

GCCA
Graphic Communications Computer Association (US)
GCD
Greatest Common Divisor
GCE
General Consumers Electronics (US)
gch
gigacharacters
GCI
General Component Interface; Graphics Command Interpreter; Generalized Communication Interface
GCOS
General Comprehensive Operating Supervisor (Honeywell, US)
GCP
Graphics Control Program
gcps
gigacycles per second
GCR
Group Code(d) Recording
GCS
Graphics Compatibility System; Global Communications Subsystem (IBM); General Communications System (Sperry Univac, US); General Computer Systems (US)
GCT
Graphics Communications Terminal
GD
Graphic(s) Display
GDB
Global DataBase
GDBMS
Generalized DataBase Management System
GDC
General Data Comm (US)
GDD
General Design Document
GDDL
Graphical Data Definition Language
GDDM
Graphical Data Display Manager (IBM)
GDE
Generalized Data Entry; Ground Data Equipment
GDF
Group Distribution Frame
GDG
Generation Data Group

GDI
Graphic Display Interface
GDL
Graphic Display Library
GDM
Global Data Manager
GDMS
Generalized Data Management System
GDS
Generic Digital Services; Graphic Data System; Graphic Design System; General Drafting System
GDT
Gas Discharge Tube; Generator Development Tools; Graphic Display Terminal
GDU
Graphic Display Unit
GE
General Electric Co (US); Gateway Exchange (Telecommunications)
GEC
General Electric Co (UK)
GECCS
General Electric Co Computer Services (UK)
GECOM
General Compiler
GEEP
General Electric Electronic Processor
GEESE
General Electric Electronic System Evaluator
GEFRC
General File/Record Control (Honeywell, US)
GEISCO
General Electric Information Services Company (US)
GEL
General Emulation Language
GELOAD
General Loader (Honeywell, US)
GEM
Graphics Environment Manager (Digital Research Inc, US); Generic Emulation Module
GEMCOS
Generalized Message Control System (IBM)
gen
general; generate; generation
GENESYS
Generalized System (Computer program)

GEPAC
General Electric Process Automation
Computer

GERT
Graphical Evaluation and Review Technique

GENIE
General Information Extractor

GENIO
General Input/Output

GERTS
General Remote Terminal System

GESC
Government Electronic Data Processing
Standards Committee (Canada)

GETEL
General Electric Test Engineering Language

GeV
Giga electron Volts (Denoting 10^9 volts)

GEVIC
General Electric Variable Increment Computer

GFA
Gas Fusion Analysis

GFCI
Ground Fault Circuit Interrupter (Electrical)

GFI
Ground Fault Interrupter (Electrical);
Guided Fault Isolation

GFLOPS
Giga Floating Point Operations Per Second

GFM
Graphics Function Monitor (Tektronix Inc,
US)

GFP
Generalized File Processor

ghz
gigahertz

GHz
Giga Hertz

GI
General Instrument Corp (US); Graded
Index (Optical fibre transmission)

GIC
General Input Channel; General Input/output Channel

GIDAP
Government Industry Data Exchange Program

GIDEP
Government-Industry Data Exchange Program (US)

GIF
Graphic Interchange Format

GIFS
Generalized Interrelated Flow Simulation

GIFT
General Internal FORTRAN Translator

GIGO
Garbage In, Garbage Out (Computing)

GIM
Generalized Information Management

GIMIC
Guard-ring Isolated Monolithic Integrated
Circuit

GIOP
General-purpose Input/Output Processor

GIPS
Ground Information Processing System

GIPSY
General(ized) Information Processing
System

GIRL
Generalized Information Retrieval Language; Graphic Information Retrieval
Language

GIRLS
Generalized Information Retrieval and
Listing System

GIS
General(ized) Information System (IBM);
Guidance Information System (IBM);
Geographic Information System

GJP
Graphic Job Processor

GKS
Graphical Kernal System (ANSI)

GL
Geographic Location

GLC
Gas-Liquid Chromatography

GLIPS
Giga Logical Inferences Per Second

GMAP
General Macro Assembly Program
(Honeywell, US); Generalized Macroprocessor

GM
General Manager; Graphic Machine;
Group Mark

GMF
Graphic Monitor Facility (IBM)
GMIS
Generalized Management Information System; Government Management Information Sciences
GML
Generalized Mark-up Language; Generic Mark-up Language; Graphic Machine Language
GMR
General Modular Redundancy; Graphics Metafile Resource
GMS
General Maintenance System; Geometric Modeling Software
GMSS
Graphical Modeling and Simulation System
GMT
Greenwich Mean Time; Generalized Multi-Tasking; Graphics Mouse Technology
GN
Grant Number; Group Number
GNC
Graphic Numerical Control
gnd
ground (Electrical, earth connection)
GNS
Global Network Services
GO
General Operations; General Order; Generated Output
GOC
Graphic Option Controller
GOCI
General Operator Computer Interaction
GOE
Ground Operation Equipment
GOL
General Operating Language; Goal Oriented Language
GOPS
Giga Operations Per Second
GOS
Grade of Service; Graphics Operating System (Tektronix Inc, US)
GOSIP
Government Open Systems Interconnect Protocol [or processor]
GP
General Purpose; Graphic Package;

Graphics Protocol [or Processor]; Gang Punch; General Processor; Generalized Programming
GPa
Giga Pascals
GPA
General Purpose Analysis; General Purpose Array
GPAX
General Purpose Automation Executive (IBM)
GPB
General Purpose Basic (Programming language)
GPC
Gas Phase Chromatography; General-Purpose Computer; General Peripheral Controller; General Precision Connector; Graphics Performance Characterization
GPCA
General Purpose Communications Adapter
GPD
General Protocol Driver
GPDA
General Purpose Data Acquisition
GPDC
General-Purpose Digital Computer
GPDS
General-Purpose Display System
GPGL
General Purpose Graphic Language
GPH
Gallons Per Hour
GPI
Graphical Programming Interface (Microsoft Corp, US)
GPIA
General Purpose Interface Adapter
GPIB
General Purpose Interface Bus
GPL
General Purpose Language; General Purpose Loader
GPM
Gallons Per Minute; General Purpose Macro-generator; General Purpose Module
GPO
Government Printing Office (US); General Post Office (UK)
GPOS
General Purpose Operating System

GPP
General Purpose Processor; General Print and Punch

GPR
General Purpose Register (IBM)

GPS
General Problem Solver

GPSS
General Purpose Simulation System; General Problem Statement Simulator; General Purpose System Simulator

GPSDW
General Purpose Scientific Document Writer

GPT
General Purpose Terminal

GPU
General Processing Unit

GQE
Generalized Queue Entry

GQL
Graphical Query Language; Guided Query Language

GR
General Records; General (purpose) Register (IBM); Growth Rate

gr
grade

GRAFTEK
Graphics Technology Corp (US)

GRASP
Generalized Read And Simulate Program; Generalized Remote Acquisition and Sensor Processing; Graphic Service Program

GRED
Generalized Random Extract Device

GRG
Graphical Rewriting Grammar

GRID
Graphical Interactive Display

GRIN
Graphical Input

GRINDER
Graphical Interactive Network Designer

GRIP
General Retrieval of Information Program (Personal indexing system)

grnd
ground

grp
group

GRP
Group Reference Pilot

GRO
Graphics Reporting Option

GRS
General Register Stack; General Reporting System; Generalized Retrieval System

GRTS
General Remote Terminal Supervisor

GS
Group Switch; Group Separator (CCITT); Graphics System

GSA
General Services Administration; General Syntax Analyzer

GSAM
Generalized Sequential Access Method (IBM)

GSC
Group Switching Center

GSD
General Services [or Systems] Division (IBM)

GSDN
Global Software-Defined Network (AT&T)

GSE
Graphics Screen Editor

GSI
Grand Scale Integration (IC); Graphic Structure Input

GSL
Generalized Simulation Language; Generation Strategy Language

GSM
Graphics System Module

GSP
Graphics Shading Processor (Toshiba Electronics); Graphics Subroutine Package; Graphics System Processor; General Syntactic Processor

GSPC
Graphics Standards Planning Committee (ACM)

GSS
Graphic Support Software

GST
Global Symbol Table (DEC)

GSTN
General Switched Telephone Network

GSVC
Generalized Supervisor Call

GT
Graphics Terminal; Greater Than; Ger-

man Title (Searchable field)

GTD
Graphic Tablet Display

GTF
Generalized Trace Facility (IBM); Greater
Than Flag

GTO
Gate Turn-Off; Graphics Text Organizer

GTOT
Gate Turn-Off Thyristor

GTP
Graphics Transform Package

GUI
Graphical User Interface

GULP
General Utility Library Program

GW
Giga Watt

H

h

hardware; head; hecto (SI prefix meaning hundred(s), i.e., denoting 10^2); hierarchy; home; horizontal; host; hour; Planck constant (Symbol, denoting 6.6256 x 10^{-27} erg sec)

H

Magnetic Field Strength (Symbol); Magnetic Force (Symbol); Hydrogen (Symbol); Half-Adder; Horizontal; Henry (The unit of inductance); Home Address; Harmonic (Symbol); Hexadecimal (Suffix); Unit Function (Symbol)

h (H)

horizontal

H-Band

H-Band

H/H

Host to Host

H/T

Head per Track

HA

Hazard Analysis; Half Adder

HAB

Home Address Block

HADA

High Availability Disk Array (Data General Corp, US)

HAIT

Hash Algorithm Information Table

HAL

Highly Automated Logic

HALSIM

Hardware Logic Simulator

HAM

Hierarchical Access Method

HAMT

Human-Aided Machine Translation

hand

handling

HANDS

Healthcare Application Network Delivery System (US Sprint)

HAP

Host Access Protocol

HAPUB

High-speed Arithmetic Processing Unit Board

HAR

Home Address Register

hardwr

hardware

HARM

High-Speed Anti-Radiation Missile (DOD)

HASQ

Hardware-Assisted Software Queue

HAU

Horizontal Arithmetic Unit; Hybrid Arithmetic Unit

hb

handbook; hybrid

HB

Hexadecimal to Binary

HBA

Host Bus Adapter

HBEN

High Byte Enable

HBO

Home Box Office (Cable TV)

HBW

Half Bandwidth

HC

Host Command; Host Computer; High-speed Complementary (IC); Hard Copy; Hardware Capability; Hybrid Computer

HCC

Hardware Capability Code

HCF

Host Command Facility (IBM)

HCG

Hardware Character Generator

HCI

Hybrid Computer Interface; Host Computer Interface

HCMOS

High-speed Complementary [logic] Metal-Oxide Semiconductor

HCP

Hard Copy Printer; High Speed Channel Processor; Host Communications Processor

HCR

Hardware Check Routine

HCS

Hard Copy System; Hazard Communications Standard; Health Care System; Hundred Call Seconds

HCT

High-power CMOS Transistor

HCTL
High-power CMOS TTL Logic (H-P)

HD
Half-Duplex (Telecommunications); Hierarchical Direct; High-Density (Refers to floppy [5.25"] or microfloppy [3.5"] disks)

HDA
Head/Disk Assembly

HDAM
Hierarchical Direct Access Method (IBM)

HDAS
High-Speed Data Acquisition System; Hybrid Data Acquisition System

HDB
High Density Bipolar

HDB$_3$
High-Density Binary 3

HDBV
Host Data Base View (IBM)

HDC
High-Speed Data Channel

HDD
High-Density Disk (Refers to floppy [5.25"] or microfloppy [3.5"] disks); Head Down Display

HDDR
High-Density Digital Recording

HDDS
High-Density Data System

HDF
High-Density Flexible

HDI
High-Density Interconnect; Head-Disc Interference (Head crash, or failure)

HDL
Hardware Description Language

HDLA
High-Level Data Link Control Adapter

HDLC
High-Level Data Link Control (IBM, protocol); Hierarchical Data Link Control

HDM
Hierarchical Development Methodology

HDMR
High-Density Multitrack Recording

HDMS
High-Density Modem System; Honeywell Distributed Manufacturing System

HDOS
Hard Disk Operating System

hdr
header

HDR
High Density Recording

HDS
Hybrid Development System

HDSC
High-Density Signal Carrier (DEC)

HDT
High Density Tape

HDTV
High-Definition Television

hdw
hardware

HDX
Half-Duplex (Telecommunications)

He
Helium (Symbol)

HEALS
Honeywell Error Analysis and Logging System

HECS
Higher Education Calling Service (AT&T)

HELP
Highly Extendable Language Processor

HEMT
High Electron Mobility Transistor

HERO
Health Educational Robot (Heath Co, US)

HERS
Hardware Error Recovery System (Sperry Univac, US)

Hex
Hexadecimal

hex (HEX)
hexadecimal

HEXFET
Hexagonal Field-Effect Transistor

Hf
Hafnium (Symbol)

HF
High Frequency (3 to 30 MHz band)

HFAS
Honeywell File Access System

HFDF
High-Frequency Distribution Frame

HFDL
Host Forms Description Language

HFFS
High Frequency Phase Shifter

HFE
Human Factors Engineering

HFET
Heterostructure Field-Effect Transistor

HFS
Hierarchical File Structure

Hg
Mercury (Symbol)

HHLS
Hand-Held Laser Scanner

HHS
Hand-Held Scanner

HHT
Hand-Held Terminal

hi
high

HI-RES
High-Resolution

HI-TECH
High Technology

Hi-Z
High Impedance

HiBiCMOS
Hitachi Bipolar CMOS

HIC
Hybrid Integrated Circuit; Highest Incoming Channel (CCITT)

HICAP
High Capacity

HICS
Hierarchical Information Control System

HIDAM
Hierarchical Indexed Direct Access Method (IBM)

HI FI
High Fidelity (Audio reproduction)

HiFI
High-Performance Fiber-Optic Interface

HIFT
Hardware Implemented Fault Tolerance

HIMOS
High-Injection Metal-Oxide Semiconductor

HIP
Host Interface Processor

HIPIC
High-Performance Integrated Circuit [IC]

HIPO
Hierarchy Input, Process, Output [or Hierarchical Input Process Output] (IBM)

hir
hierarchy

HISAM
Hierarchical Indexed Sequential Access Method (IBM)

HISDAM
Hierarchical Indexed Sequential Direct

Access Method

HIT
High-Isolation Transformer

HITAC
Hitachi Computer Services

HI/TC
Half Inch Tape Cartridge

HL
High Level; Host Language

HLAF
High(er) Level Arithmetic Function

HLAIS
High-Level Analog Input System

HLC
Host Language Call

HLDTL
High-Level Data Transistor Logic

HLI
Host Language Interface

HLL
High-Level Language

HLLAPI
High-Level Application Program Interface (IBM)

HLML
High-Level Microprogramming Language

HLPI
High Level Programming Interface

HLR
High-Level Representation

HLS
High-Level Scheduler

HLSE
High-Level Single Ended

HLQL
High Level Query Language

hlt
halt

HLU
House Logic Unit

HMAC
High-Performance Memory Array Controller (NCR)

HMI
Hub Management Interface; Hardware Monitor Interface

HMM
Hardware Multiply Module

HMO
Hardware Microcode Optimizer; Health Maintenance Organization

HMOS
High-performance [or High-speed] Metal-Oxide Semiconductor (Intel Corp, US)
HMR
Hybrid Modular Redundancy
HMW
High Molecular Weight
HN
Host to Network
HNA
Hierarchical Network Architecture; Hitachi Network Architecture
HNDT
Holographic Non-Destructive Testing
HNIL
High Noise Immunity Logic
HNPL
High Level Network Processing Language
Ho
Holmium (Symbol)
HO
High Order
HOC
Highest Outgoing Channel (CCITT)
HOF
Head of Form
HOL
High-Order Language
HOLWG
Higher Order Language Working Group
HOP
Hybrid Operating Program
HOQ
Home Office Quote
hor
horizontal
horitz
horizontal
HOS
Higher Order Software
HP
High Power; HorsePower; Host Processor; Hewlett Packard (Preferred form is H-P [Hewlett-Packard])
H-P
Hewlett-Packard
hp (HP)
horsepower
HP-UX
Hewlett-Packard UNIX
HPA
High Power Amplifier; Heuristic Path Al-

gorithm
HPCA
High Performance Communications Adapter
HPCC
High-Performance Computing and Communications
HPEGS
Hewlett-Packard Engineering Graphics System
HPF
High Pass Filter; Host Preparation Facility
HPFS
High-Performance File System
HPGL
Hewlett Packard Graphics Language (H-P)
HPGS
High Performance Graphics System
HPIB
Hewlett-Packard Interface Bus
HPIL
Hewlett-Packard Interface Loop
HPLC
High-Performance (or Pressure) Liquid Chromatography
HPO
High-Performance Option (IBM); Host Processing Option (IBM)
HPPCIB
Hewlett-Packard Personal Computer Instruments Bus
HPPI
High-Performance Parallel Interface (ANSI)
HPT
Head Per Track
hr
hour
HR
Holding Register; Hour; High Reduction of microforms; Hit Ratio
HRAM
Hierarchical Random-Access Memory
HRC
Horizontal Redundancy Check; Hypothetical Reference Circuit
HRDP
Hypothetical Reference Digital Path
HRIN
Human Resources Information Network

HRIS
House [U.S.] of Representatives Information System

HRM
Hardware Read-in Mode

HRMS
Human Resource Management System

HRNES
Host Remote Node Entry System

HRPM
High-Resolution Permanent Magnet

HRS
High-Resolution System (Refers to HDTV and similar video systems); Human Resources [management] System; Host Resident Software

HRSS
Host Resident Software System

HRV
High-Resolution Video

HRX
Hypothetical Reference Connection

HS
Hierarchical Sequential

HSAM
Hierarchical Sequential Access Method (IBM)

HSB
High Speed Buffer

HSBA
High Speed Bus Adapter

HSC
Hierarchical Storage Controller (DEC); High-Speed Channel; High-Speed Concentrator; High-Speed Controller (DEC)

HSD
High-Speed Data; Hard/Soft Display

HSDB
High-Speed Data Buffer

HSDA
High-Speed Data Acquisition

HSDMS
Highly Secure Database Management System

HSEL
High-Speed Selector Channel

HSLA
High-Speed Line Adapter

HSM
Hierarchical Storage Manager; High-Speed Memory

HSP
High-Speed Printer; High-Speed Shading

Processor

HSR
High-Speed Reader

HSRO
High-Speed Repetitive Operation

HSS
Hierarchy Service System (Toshiba Electronics); High-Speed Storage; High-Speed Steel

HSSI
High-Speed Serial Interface

HSSP
High-Speed Serial Processor

HT
Hand-held Terminal; Horizontal Tabulation (CCITT); Half Tone printing; High Tension; Head per Track

HTB
Hexadecimal To Binary

HTC
Hybrid Technology Computer

HTE
Hypergroup Translating Equipment

HTL
High Threshold Logic

HTS
Head, Track, and Sector; Host To Satellite

HTSC
High-Temperature Superconductor

HUD
Head Up Display

HUG
Honeywell Users Group

Humint
Human Intelligence

HV
High Voltage; Horizontal-Vertical; Hardware Virtualizer

HVG
High-Voltage Generator

HVIC
High-Voltage Integrated Circuit

HVR
Hardware Vector to Raster; Home Video Recorder

HVTS
High Volume Time-Sharing

hw
hardware

HW
Hard Wired

HWI
  Hardware Interpreter
HWM
  High Water Mark
hyb
  hybrid

hz
  hertz
Hz
  Hertz

I

i
current (Symbol); immediate; indirect; information; input; instruction; interrupt

I
Current (Symbol); Information (Refers to Synchronous Data Link Control [SDLC], IBM); Iodine (Symbol); Intrinsic Semiconductor (Symbol); Luminous Intensity (Symbol)

I-4
International Information Integrity Institute

I&A
Indexing and Abstracting

I-AMAP
Integrated Adaptive Multiple-Access Protocol

I&C
Installation and Checkout

I/C
Instrumentation/Control

I/D
Instruction/Data

I/O
Input/Output

I-TIME
Instruction Time

IA
Immediately Available; Incoming Access (CCITT); Instruction Address; Integrated Adapter

IAB
Internet Activities Board; Internet Advisory Board; Interrupt Address to Bus

IAC
Inter-Application Communication; Interactive Array Computer; International Association for Cybernetics

IACP
International Association of Computer Programmers

IACS
Integrated Access and Cross-Connect System (AT&T)

IAD
Interactive Debugging; Initial Address

Designator; Integrated Automatic Documentation

IAF
Interactive Facility

IALE
Instrumented Architectural Level Emulation

IAM
Indexed Access Method (IBM); Innovation Access Method

IAMACS
International Association for Mathematics and Computers in Simulation

IANET
Integrated Access Network

IAP
Image Array Processor

IAPS
International ASCII Publication Standard; International Accunet Packet Service (AT&T)

IAR
Instruction Address Register; Interrupt Address Register

IARN
International Amateur Radio Network

IAS
Institute of Advanced Study; Interactive Application System (DEC); ISDN Applications and Services; Immediate Access Storage

IASC
International Association for Statistical Computing

IATA
International Airline Telecommunications Association; International Air Transport Association

IAU
Interface Adaptor Unit

IAW
In Accordance With

IB
Identifier Block; Input Bus; Instruction Bus; Interface Bus; Integrated Broadband; Internal Bus; Internetwork Bridge

IBC
Integrated Block Channel; Integrated Broadband Communications

IBF
Input Buffer Full

IBFI
International Business Forms Industry
IBG
Inter-Block Gap
IBN
Interim Broadband Network
IBOL
Interactive Business Oriented Language
IBT
Integrated Broadband Termination; Integrated Business Terminal
IBX
Integrated Business Exchange
IC
Identification Code; Image Capture; Integrated Circuit; Interlook Code (CCITT); Instruction Counter; Instrumentation Control
IC/P
Intelligent Copier/Printer
ICA
Integrated Communications Adapter; Intercomputer Adapter; International Communication Association; Interapplication Communication Architecture (Apple Computer Inc, US)
ICAD
Integrated Control and Display
ICAE
Integrated Communications Adapter Extension
ICAM
Integrated Computer-Aided Manufacturing
ICAT
Intelligent Computer-Aided Training
ICB
Internal Common Bus; Incoming Calls Barred (CCITT)
ICC
Image Computer Controller; Intelligent Communications Controller; International Conference on Communications; Intermediate Cross-Connect
ICCAD
International Center for Computer Aided Design
ICCCM
International Conference on Computer Capacity Management
ICCDP
Integrated Circuit Communications Data Processor
ICCF
Interactive Computing and Control Facility (IBM)
ICCP
Institute for the Certification of Computer Professionals
ICCS
Integrated Communications Cabling System; Intercomputer Communications System
ICCU
Intercomputer Communications Unit
ICD
Interface Control Document; Interactive Cartridge Debugger; International Congress for Data Processing; Interactive Call Distribution
ICDDB
Internal Control Description Data Base
ICDL
Internal Control Description Language
ICDLA
Internal Control Description Language Analyzer
ICDS
Integrated Circuit Design System
ICE
In-Circuit Emulator; International Electro-Technical Commission
ICEA
International Consumer Electronics Association
ICES
Integrated Civil Engineering Software System
ICF
Intercommunication Flip-Flop; Integrated Catalog Facility (IBM)
ICI
Intelligent Communications Interface
ICLID
Incoming Call Line Identifier (AT&T)
ICM
Instruction Control Memory
ICMS
Integrated Circuit and Message Switch; Instrument Calibration and Maintenance Schedule; Intelligent Chassis Management System
ICN
Integrated Computer Network

117

ICOBOL
Interactive Common Business Oriented Language (Data General Corp, US)

ICP
In-Circuit Programming; Initial Connection Protocol; Intelligent Communications Processor; Integrated Channel Processor; Inventory Control Point

ICR
Input Control Register; Interrupt Control Register

ICS
Image Control System; Industrial Control System; Inbound Communications Server; Interactive Computer Systems (DEC); Information Collection System; Institute of Computer Science; Interactive Communications Software; International Computer Symposium

ICST
Institute for Computer Sciences and Technology

ICSTI
International Centre for Scientific and Technical Information

ICSU
Intelligent Channel Service Unit

ICT
In-Coming Trunk; In-Circuit Test(er)

ICU
Instruction Cache Unit (IBM); Industrial Control Unit; Interrupt Control Unit; Instruction Control Unit; Interface Control Unit

ICW
Interface Control Word

id
identification; identifier

ID
Intelligent Digitizer; Intelligent Device; Item Descriptor

id (ID)
identification

IDA
Interactive Debugging Aid; Institute for Defense Analysis; Interactive Data Analysis; Integrated Digital Access; Integrated Data Analysis; Intelligent Data Access

IDAM
Indexed Direct Access Method

IDAS
Industrial Data Acquisition System

IDB
Input Data Buffer; Instruction Decode Buffer (IBM); Integrated Data Base; Interrupt Dispatch Block (DEC)

IDBMS
Integrated Data Base Management System

IDC
Internal Data Channel

IDCC
Integrated Data Communications Controller

IDCMA
Independent Data Communications Manufacturers Association

IDD
Integrated Data Dictionary; International Direct Dial(ing)

IDDD
International Direct Distance Dialing

IDDS
International Digital Data Service

IDE
Independent Drive Electronics; Interactive Data Entry; Integrated Device Electronics

IDEA
Interactive Data Entry/Access; Interactive Design and Engineering Automation

IDEAS
Integrated Design and Engineering Automated System; Integrated Design and Analysis System

ident
identification

IDEPT
Image Document Entry Processing Terminal

IDES
Interactive Data Entry System

IDF
Image Description File; Intermediate Distribution Frame; Instrument Data Frame (NASA)

IDI
Improved Data Interchange

idl
idle

IDL
Information Description Language; Instruction Definition Language

IDMS
Interactive Database Management System; Integrated Database Management System
IDN
Intelligent Data Network
IDNX
Integrated Digital Network Exchange
IDP
Integrated Data Processing; Internet Datagram Protocol; International Data Processing
IDPS
Interactive Direct Processing System
IDRC
Improved Data Recording Capability (IBM)
IDRS
Integrated Data Retrieval System
IDS
Information Display System; Intelligent Disk Server; Integrated Data Store; Intelligent Display System; Interactive Display System
IDT
Intelligent Data Terminal; Integrated Device Technology; Interactive Data Terminal; Interface Development Tool (DEC); Interrupt Descriptor Table (Intel Corp, US)
IDU
Industrial Development Unit; Interface Data Unit
IE
Information Engineering; Interrupt Enable
IEC
International Electrotechnical Commission
IECI
Industrial Electronics and Control Instrumentation
IEEE
Institute of Electrical and Electronics Engineers
IEF
Information Engineering Facility
IERE
Institution of Electronic and Radio Engineers
IES
Illuminating Engineering Society
IETF
Internet Engineering Task Force
if
interface

IF
Instruction Field; Intermediate Frequency
IFA
Information Flow Analysis
IFAC
International Federation of Automatic Control
IFAM
Inverted File Access Method
IFC
Interface Clear (IEEE)
IFI
Instrumentation Facility Interface
IFIP
International Federation for Information Processing
IFIPS
International Federation of Information Processing Societies
IFM
Interactive File Manager; Instantaneous Frequency Measurement
IFORS
International Federation of Operations Research Societies
IFP
Integrated File Processor
IFR
Interface Register
IFRB
International Frequency Registration Board
IFS
Interactive File Sharing
IG
Interactive Graphics
IGA
Integrated Graphics Array
IGAS
Interactive Generalized Accounting System (NCR)
IGBT
Insulated Gate Bipolar Transistor
IGES
Initial Graphics Exchange Standard (ANSI)
IGFET
Insulated Gate Field Effect Transistor
IGL
Interactive Graphics Language
IGOSS
Industry Government Open Systems Speci-

fication (NIST)

IGRP
Internet Gateway Resolution Protocol (Internet)

IGS
Information Group Separator; Interactive Graphics System

IGT
Interactive Graphics Terminal

IH
Interrupt Handler

II
Integrated Circuit Interconnect (DEC); Interrupt Inhibit; Inventory and Inspection

IIA
Information Industries Association

IICIT
International Institute of Connector and Interconnection Technology

IIE
Institute of Industrial Engineers

IIL
Integrated Injection Logic

IIOP
Intelligent Input/Output Processor; Integrated Input/Output Processor

IIPACS
Integrated Information Presentation And Control System

IIS
Interactive Instructional System (IBM)

IITI
International Information Technology Institute

IJCAI
International Joint Conference on Artifical Intelligence

IKB
Intelligent Keyboard

IL
Instruction List; Intermediate Language

ILA
Integrated Laboratory Automation; Intelligent Line Adapter; Intermediate Level Amplifier

ILAN
Integrated Local Area Network

ILB
Initial Load Block

ILD
Injection Laser Diode; Intersection Loop Detection

ILF
Infra Low Frequency (300 to 3000 Hz band)

ILM
Intelligent Library Manager; Intermediate Language Machine

ILO
Individual Load Operation; Injection-Locked Oscillator

ILP
Intermediate Language Program

ILU
Initiate Logical Unit (IBM)

IM
Information Management; Index Marker; Interconnection Medium; Integrated Modem; Instruction Memory; Interrupt Mask; Intensity Modulation; Instrumentation and Measurement

IMA
Institute for Manufacturing Automation; Invalid Memory Address

IMACS
International Association for Mathematics and Computers in Simulation

IMARS
Information Management and Retrieval System

IMC
International Micrographics Congress; Information Management Center; Information Management Concepts; Interactive Module Controller; Integrated Multiplexer Channel

IMD
Intermodulation Distortion

IMDR
Intelligent Mark Document Reader

IME
International Microcomputer Exposition

IMG
International Mailgram

IMIS
Integrated Management Information System

IML
Interactive Matrix Language; Information Manipulation Language; Intermediate Machine Language

imm
immediate

IMM
Intelligent Memory Manager

IMOS
Interactive Multiprogramming Operating System

IMP
Image Management Processor; Information Management Package; Inventory Management Package; Interface Message Processor; Integrated Manufacturing Planning

IMPAC
Information for Management Planning Analysis and Coordination

IMPACT
Ion-Implanted Advanced Composed Logic (TI); Integrated Management Planning and Control Techniques

IMPROVE
Inventory Management, Product Replenishment and Order Validity Evaluation

IMR
Interrupt Mask Register; Integrated Multiport Repeater

IMRADS
Information Management, Retrieval and Dissemination System

IMS
Information Management System (IBM); Integrated Measurement System; Integrated Manufacturing System; Inventory Management System

IMS/VS
Information Management System/Virtual System (IBM)

IMSI
Information Management System Interface

IMSL
International Mathematics and Statistical Library

IMSLIDF
International Mathematics and Statistical Library Interactive Documentation Facility

IMTEC
Information Management and Technology

IMTS
Improved Mobile Telephone Service

IMU
Instruction Memory Unit

IMX
Inquiry Message Exchange

in
inch; increase; input

In
indium (Symbol)

IN
Information Network (IBM); Intelligent Network; Internal Node; Index Number; Interconnecting Network

INA
Integrated Network Architecture

inc
increment

Inc
Incorporated

INC
Incorporated; Intelligent Network Controller

INCA
Interactive Controls Analysis (NASA); Inventory Control and Analysis

incl
include; including; inclusive

incr
increment

incre
increment

INDAC
Industrial Data Acquisition and Control

info
inform; information; informational

info (INFO)
information

INFOBANK
Information Bank

INFOL
Information Oriented Language

INFONET
Information Network

INFOR
Information Network and File Organization

init
initialize

INMACS
Integrated Network Management Administration and Control System

inp
input

INP
Independent Network Processor; Integrated Network Processor; Intelligent Network Processor; Internet Nodal Processor

ins
  insert
Ins
  Insert
INS
  Instruction Set Simulator
inst
  instant; instruction; instrument
instr
  instruction
int
  integer; internal; interrupt
int (INT)
  interrupt; interpreter
INTA
  Interrupt Acknowledge
INTACK
  Interrupt-Acknowledge(ment) (Intel Corp, US)
INTE
  Interrupt Enable
INTELCOM
  International Telecommunications Exposition
INTELEC
  International Telecommunications Energy Conference
INTELSAT
  International Telecommunications Satellite
inten
  intensity
intermed
  intermediate
interp
  interpreter
INTFU
  Interface Unit
INTGEN
  Interpreter-Generator
INTIP
  Integrated Information Processing
intl
  international
Intl
  International
intr
  interrupt
INTR
  Interrupt Register; Interrupt Request
intro
  introduction

INTUG
  International Telecommunications Users Group
inv
  invalid
INV
  Invalid
inv (INV)
  invalid
INWATS
  Inward Wide Area Telecommunications Service
IO
  Immediate Order; Input/Output
IOA
  Input/Output Adapter
IOAU
  Input/Output Access Unit
IOB
  Input/Output Block; Input/Output Buffer
IOC
  Inter-Office Channel; Input/Output Channel; Input/Output Controller
IOCP
  Input/Output Control Program (IBM)
IOCS
  Input/Output Control System (IBM)
IOCTL
  Input/Output Control
IOCU
  Input/Output Control Unit
IOD
  Input/Output Device
IOGEN
  Input/Output Generation
IOIH
  Input/Output Interrupt Handler
IOLA
  Input/Output Link Adapter
IOLC
  Input/Output Link Control
IOM
  Information Output Management; Input/Output Microprocessor; Input/Output Module
IOMS
  Input/Output Management System
IOP
  Input/Output Processor
IOQ
  Input/Output Queue

IOR
Input-Output Read; Input-Output Register
IORC
Input-Output Read Control
IORT
Input-Output Remote Terminal
IOS
Input-Output Supervisor; Input-Output System; Interactive Operating System; Input/Output Subsystem
IOSB
Input/Output Status Block (DEC)
IOSYS
Input/Output System
IOT
Input/Output Transfer; Input/Output Trap; Interoffice Trunk
IOU
Input/Output Unit
IOW
Input/Output Write
IOWIT
International Organization of Women in Telecommunications
IOX
Input/Output Executive
ip
input
IP
Instrument Panel; Impact Printer; Information Processor; Information Processing; Initialize Program; Initial Permutation; Initial Phase; Interface Processor; Intelligent Peripheral; Interactive Processor; Input/Output Processor; Internet Protocol; Instruction Pointer; Interrupt Process; Interchangeable Parts
IPA
Integrated Peripheral Adapter; Integrated Printer Adapter
IPAC
Interface Protocol Asynchronous Cell
IPARS
International Passenger Airline Reservation System (IBM)
IPB
Integrated Processor Board; Instruction Prefetch Buffer (IBM); Interprocessor Buffer
IPC
Industrial Process Control; Information Processing Center; Integrated Peripheral

Channel; Integrated Peripheral Controller; Instructions Per Clock; Interprocess Controller
IPD
Information Processing Department; Intelligent Power Device
IPDS
Intelligent Printer Data Stream (IBM)
IPF
Information Processing Facility; Information Productivity Facility; Interactive Productivity Facility (IBM)
IPI
Intelligent Printer Interface; Intelligent Peripheral Interface
IPIC
Initial Production and Inventory Control; Intelligent Power Integrated Circuit
IPICS
Initial Production and Inventory Control System (IBM)
IPL
Information Processing Language; Initial Program Load (IBM); Initial Program Loader; Interrupt Priority Level (DEC)
IPM
Inventory Policy Model; Intelligent Power Module; Incremental Phase Modulation
IPN
Integrated Packet Network
IPO
Input, Process, and Output
IPP
Internetwork Packet Protocol (Xerox Corp, US)
IPPF
Instruction Preprocessing Function
IPS
Index Participation; Information Protection System (IBM); Information Processing System; Intelligent Power Supply; Intelligent Power System; Installation Performance Specifications; Item Processing System (Burroughs Corp, US); Invoice Processing Service (US Sprint)
IPSE
Integrated Project Support Environment (IBM)
IPSJ
Information Processing Society of Japan
IPSS
Information Processing System Simulator

IPSY
Interactive Planning System
IPTC
International Press Telecommunications Council
IPU
Instruction Processing Unit; Integrated Processor Unit; Interprocessor Unit
IPV
Inverse Peak Voltage
IQ
Information Quick; Intelligent Query
IQA
Institute of Quality Assurance
IQEC
International Quantum Electronics Conference
IQF
Interactive Query Facility
IQL
Interactive Query Language
Ir
Iridium (Symbol); Infrared
IR
Infrared; Instruction Register; Insulation Resistance; Index Register; Interrupt Request; Independent Research; Informal Report; Internet Router; Interim Report; Information Retrieval
IR&D
Independent Research and Development
IRA
Information Resource Administration
IRAD
Industry Research and Development (DOD)
IRAM
Indexed Random Access Method
IRAR
Integrated Random Access Reservation
IRAS
Infrared Astronomical Satellite (NASA)
IRB
Interruption Request Block
IRC
International Record Carrier; Immediate Response Chain (IBM); Inductance-Resistance-Capacitance (Refers to electrical circuitry)
IRCCD
Infrared Charge-Coupled Device

IRDS
Information Resource Dictionary System
IRED
Infrared Emitting Diode
IRF
Input Register Full
IRG
Inter-Record Gap
IRI
Industrial Research Institute
IRIG
Inter-Range Instrumentation Group
IRJE
Internet Remote Job Entry; Interactive Remote Job Entry
IRL
Information Retrieval Language
IRLD
Infrared Laser Diode
IRM
Information Resources Management; Intelligent Remote Multiplexer
IRMS
Information Resources Management Service
IRN
Internal Routing Network
IRP
I/O Request Packet; Inventory Requirements Planning (IBM)
IRQ
Interrupt Request
IRR
Interrupt Return Register
irreg
irregular
IRS
Information Retrieval System
IRTU
Intelligent Remote Terminal Unit
IS
Information Science; Information Separator; Immediate System; Information System; International Standard; Interrupt Stack (DEC); Indexed Sequential
IS-to-IS
Intermediate System-to-Intermediate System (DEC)
IS&R
Information Storage and Retrieval
ISA
Industry Standard Architecture (IBM)

ISAAC
Information System for Advanced Academic Computing
ISAL
Information System Access Line
ISAM
Indexed Sequential Access Method (IBM)
ISAR
Information Storage And Retrieval
ISBN
International Standard Book Number
ISC
International Service Carrier (AT&T); Intersystem Communication (IBM)
ISD
Information Structure Design; International Subscriber Dialing; Intermediate Storage Device
ISDN
Integrated Services Digital Network
ISDS
Integrated Software Development System
ISE
Integrated Storage Element (DEC); Interrupt System Enable; Institute for Software Engineering
ISEP
International Standard Equipment Practice
ISFM
Indexed Sequential File Manager
ISFMS
Indexed Sequential File Management System
ISHM
International Society for Hybrid Microelectronics
ISI
Institute for Scientific Information; Instrument Systems Installation; Intelligent Standard Interface; Information Structure Implementation
ISIC
International Standard Industrial Classification
ISK
Instruction Space Key
ISL
Interactive Simulation Language
ISMEC
Information Service in Mechanical Engineering

ISMM
International Society for Mini and Microcomputers
ISN
Information System Network (AT&T); Initial Sequence Number; Internal Sequence Number
ISO
International Standards Organization (International Organization for Standardization); Information Systems Office
ISODE
International Standards Organization Development Environment
ISP
Instruction Set Processor; In-Store Processor; Interrupt Stack Pointer (DEC)
ISPF
Interactive System Productivity Facility (IBM)
ISR
Information Storage and Retrieval; Interrupt Service Routine (DEC)
ISRM
Information Systems Resource Manager
ISS
Integrated Support System; Information System Services (IBM); Intelligent Support System; Integrated Switching System
ISSCC
International Solid-State Circuits Conference
ISSMB
Information Systems Standards Management Board
ISSN
International Standard Serial Number
ISSR
Information Storage, Selection, and Retrieval; Independent Secondary Surveillance Radar
ISSS
Initial Sector Suite System (FAA); Integrated Support System Sort
IST
Internal Standard
ISTA
International Society for Technology Assessment
ISTAB
Information Systems Technical Advisory

Board
ISTE
International Society of Technology in Education
ISU
Instruction Storage Unit; Integrated Service Unit; Interface Sharing Unit
ISV
Independent Software Vendor
IT
Information Technology; Indent Tab (Character); Incomplete Transmission; Intelligent Terminal; Inventory Turnover; Input Terminal; Inventory Transfer
ITAC
Information Technology Acquisition Center (US Navy)
ITB
Intermediate Text Block
ITC
Intelligent Traffic Controller; Integrated Transaction Controller; Intelligent Transaction Controller
ITDM
Intelligent Time Division Multiplexer
ITDS
Integrated Technical Data Systems
ITF
Integrated Test Facility
ITG
Interactive Test Generator (H-P)
itin
itinerary
ITL
Independent Testing Laboratory; Intermediate Transfer Language
ITN
Image Transmission Network; Integrated Teleprocessing Network; Integrated Telecommunications Network
ITP
Integrated Transaction Processor
ITPS
Interactive Text Preparation System; International Practical Temperature Scale
ITR
Internal Throughput Rate (IBM)
ITRC
Information Technology Requirements Council
ITS
International Temperature Scale (NIST);

Interactive Terminal Support; Institute for Telecommunication Science
ITU
International Telecommunications Union
ITV
Instructional Television
IU
Information Unit; Instruction Unit; Interface Unit
IUPAC
International Union of Pure and Applied Chemistry
IUPAP
International Union of Pure and Applied Physics
IUS
Information Unit Separator
IV
Interface Vector
IVAN
International Value-Added Network
IVD
Integrated Voice and Data
IVDT
Integrated Voice/Data Terminal
IVHS
Intelligent Vehicle Highway System
IVI
Interactive Video Instruction
IVM
Interface Virtual Machine
IVP
Installation Verification Procedure
IVR
Interactive [or Integrated] Voice Response
IVT
Integrated Video Terminal
IWDS
Interactive Wholesale Distribution System
IWPA
International Word Processing Association
IWS
Interactive Work Station; Instruction Work Stack
IX
Index Register
IXC
Interexchange Carrier (AT&T); Interexchange Channel

IXM
  Index Manager
IXR
  Intelligent Transparent Restore
IXU
  Index Translation Unit

J

j
job

J
Joule (Symbol, the SI unit of work, $= 10^7$ erg); Jack [or Connector]; Emissive Power (Symbol)

JA
Job Analysis; Jump Address; Journal Announcement (Searchable field)

JACC
Joint Automatic Control Conference

JACM
Journal of the Association for Computing Machinery (ACM)

JAD
Joint Application Development

JAERI
Japan Atomic Energy Research Institute

JAF
Job Accounting Facility

JAI
Job Accounting Interface

jam
jammed

JAN
Joint Army Navy (DOD)

JANET
Joint Academic Network

JAR
Jump Address Register

JARS
Job Accounting Report System

JAS
Job Analysis System

JASIS
Journal of the American Society for Information Science

JAT
Job Accounting Table

JAWS
Just Another Work Station (Computer jar-

gon)

JC
Journal Citation; Journal Coden; Journal Title Code (Searchable fields)

jc
junction

JCALS
Joint Computer-Aided Acquisition and Logistics Support (DOD)

JCB
Job Control Block

JCC
Job Control Card; Joint Computer Conference (US)

JCL
Job Command Language; Job Control Language (IBM)

JCLGEN
Job Control Language Generation

JCMST
Journal of Computers in Math-and Science Teaching (US)

jcn
junction

JCN
Jump on Condition

JCP
Job Control Processor; Job Control Program

JCS
Job Control Statement

jct
junction

JCT
Job Control Table

jctn
junction

JD
Job Description

JDL
Job Description Library; Job Descriptor Language

JDS
Job Data Sheet

JE
Job Entry

JECC
Japan Electric Computer Corp (Japanese computer manufacturer)

JECL
Job Entry Control Language

JECS
Job Entry Control Services (IBM)

JEDEC
Joint Electronic Device Engineering Council (US)

JEDI
Joint Education Initiative

JEIDA
Japan Electronic Industry Development Association

JEPS
Job Entry Peripheral Services (IBM)

JES
Job Entry Subsystem (IBM); Job Entry System

JET
Journal Entries Transfer

JETS
Job Executive and Transport Satellite (NCR)

JFCB
Job File Control Block

JFET
Junction Field-Effect Transistor

JFN
Job File Number (DEC)

JG
Junction Grammar (Machine translation term)

JI
Junction Isolation

JIB
Job Information Block (DEC)

JIC
Joint Information Center

JICST
Japan Information Center of Science and Technology

JIP
Joint Input Processing

JIPDEC
Japan Information Processing Development Center

JIRA
Japanese Industrial Robot Association

JIS
Japanese Industrial Standard; Job Information System; Job Input System

JIT
Just-In-Time

JL
Job Library; Job Lot

JM
Job Memory

jmp
jump

jmpr
jumper

JMSX
Job Memory Switch Matrix

JN
Journal Name (Searchable field)

jn
junction

jnc
junction

JND
Just Noticeably Difference (Unit of change in a displayed image)

jnl
journal

jnt
joint

JNT
Joint Network Team

JO
Job Order

JOC
Job Order Costing

JOL
Job Organization Language

jour
journal

journ
journal

JOVIAL
Jule's Own Version of International Algorithmic Language

JP
Job Processor

JPA
Job Pack Area

JPL
Jet Propulsion Laboratory

JPRA
Japanese Phonograph Record Association

JPU
Job Processing Unit

JPW
Job Processing Word

JR
Job Rotation; Joint Return

jrnl
journal

JRP
Joint Requirements Planning

JRS
Junction Relay Set (Telecommunications)

JSA
Japanese Standards Association

JSAT
Japan Communications Satellite Co

JSCLC
Joint Standing Committee on Library Co-operation (UK)

JSF
Job Services File

JSIA
Japan Software Industry Association

JSL
Job Specification Language

JSLS
Japan Society of Library Science

JSME
Japan Society of Mechanical Engineers

jt
joint

JT
Job Table

JTAG
Joint Test Action Group

K

k
Boltzmann('s) constant (Symbol, equals 1.380 x 10^{-16} erg per degree Celsius); keyboard; kilohm; constant (General symbol); dielectric constant (Symbol); key; kilo (SIO prefix denoting 10^3); kilobyte; kiloBIT

K
Cathode (Symbol); Deflection Parameter (Symbol); Potassium (Symbol); Kelvin (Symbol, SI unit of thermodynamic temperature); Stiffness Coefficient (Symbol); Go Ahead (Radiotelegraph symbol for, "over"); Symbol for measured, computer memory storage capacity of 1024 bits

k (K)
general symbol for constant

ka
kiloampere

KAPSE
Kernel Ada Programming Support Environment

KAR
Kodak Automated Registration System (Eastman Kodak Co, US)

kb
kilobyte; keyboard; kiloBIT

Kb
kiloByte

kbd
keyboard

KBDSC
Keyboard and/or Display Controller (Computing)

KBE
Keyboard Entry

KBENC
Keyboard Encoder (Computing)

KBPRC
Keyboard and Printer Controller (Computing)

kbit
kiloBIT

KBMS
Knowledge Base Management System

kbps
kilobits per second (Data rate, thousands of bits per second); kilobytes per second

KBPS
KiloBITs Per Second (Data rate, thousands of BITs per second); KiloBytes Per Second

kbs
kilobits per second

KBS
Knowledge Based System

kc
kilocycle

KCC
Keyboard Common Contact

kch
kilocharacter

kchr
kilocharacter

KCL
Keystation Control Language

KCP
Keyboard-Controlled Phototypesetter

KCS
Kilocharacters Per Second

KCU
Keyboard Control Unit

KD
Key Definition; Keyboard and Display

KDE
Keyboard Data Entry

KDOS
Key Display Operating System; Key to Disc Operating System

KDP
Keyboard Display and Printer

KDR
Keyboard Data Recorder

KDS
Key Data Station; Key Display System; Key to Disk(ette) System

KDT
Key Data Terminal

KEE
Knowledge Engineering Environment

KEEPS
Kodak Ektaprint Electronic Publishing System (Eastman Kodak, US)

KEK
Key-Encrypting Key

KEP
Key Entry Processing

KES
Knowledge Engineering System
keV
kiloelectron Volt(s) (Denoting 10^3 electron volts)
KEYTECT
Keyword Detection
keybd
keyboard
KF
Key Field
KFAS
Keyed File Access System
KFLOPS
Kilo Floating Point Operations Per Second
kg
kilogram
KGM
Key Generator Module
kh
kilohour
khz
kilohertz
kHz
kilohertz
KIC
Kernal Input Controller
KICU
Keyboard Interface Control Unit
KIL
Keyed Input Language
kilopac
kilopackets
KIMS
Kodak Image Management System (Eastman Kodak, US)
KIP
Kinetics Internet Protocol
KIPO
Keyboard Input PrintOut
KIPS
Knowledge Information Processing Systems; Kilo (or, Thousands of) Instructions Per Second (Denoting 10^3 instructions per second)
KIS
Keep It Simple; Keyboard Input Simulation
KISS
Keep It Simple, Sir; Keyed Indexed Sequential Search

KIST
Korea Institute of Science and Technology
KL
Key Length
KLIC
Key Letter In Context (Indexing method)
KLIPS
Kilo (or, Thousands of) Logical Inferences Per Second (Denoting 10^3 logical inferences per second)
KLU
Key and Lamp Unit (Telecommunications)
km
kilometer
KMC
Key Management Center
KMON
Keyboard Monitor (DEC)
KOPS
Kilo (or, Thousands of) Operations Per Second (Denoting 10^3 operations per second)
KORSTIC
Korea Science and Technological Information Center
kp
keypunch
KP
Key Pulsing; Key Punch
KPC
Keyboard/Printer Control
KPH
Keystrokes Per Hour
KPIC
Key Phrase In Context (Indexing method)
KPO
Key Punch Operator
KPR
Keypunch Replacement
KPS
Knowledge Processing System (Factory automation, expert system shell)
Kr
Krypton (Symbol)
KR
Key Register
KRL
Knowledge Representation Language
KSAM
Keyed Sequential Access Method; Keyfield Sequential Access Method (H-P)

KSDS
Key Sequenced Data Set
KSH
Key Strokes Per Hour
KSP
Kernel Stack Pointer (DEC)
KSPS
Kilo (or, Thousands of) Samples Per Second
KSR
Keyboard Send/Receive
KSR/T
Keyboard Send/Receive Terminal
KST
Known Segment Table
KT
Key Tape
KTDS
Key To Disc Software
KTM
Key Transport Module
KTP
Keyboard Typing Perforator
KTS
Key Telephone System
kv
kilovolt
kV
kilovolt (Denoting 10^3 Volts)
kVA
kilovolt-Amperes
KVA
Kilovolt-Amperes (Denoting 10^3 Volt-Amperes [VA])
kw
kilowatt; kiloword
kW
kilowatt (Denoting 10^3 Watts); Kilo Word
kWh
kilowatt-hour (Denoting 10^3 Watt-hours)
KWH
Kilowatt-Hour
KWAC
Key Word And Context (Indexing method)
KWADE
Key Word as a Dictionary Entry (IBM, indexing system)
KWIC
Keyword In Context (IBM, indexing method)
KWIP
Key Word In Permutation (Indexing method)
KWIT
Key Word In Title (Indexing method)
KWOC
Keyword Out of Context (IBM, indexing method)
KWOT
Key Word Out of Title (Indexing method)
KXU
Keyword Transformation Unit
kybd
keyboard

L

l
length (Symbol); language; liter (Metric unit of capacity); local; low (In the subscript); link; left; inductance; lumen

L
Inductance (Symbol); Length (Symbol); Mean Life (Symbol); Low; Laplace Transform (Symbol); Resembling the capital letter 'L' in physical shape; Lambert (Symbol, cgs unit of luminance); Liter

l (L)
length; liter; low; inductance

L-Air
Liquid Air

L/C
Line Control

L-He
Liquid Helium

L-R
Left to Right

L&T
Language and Terminal

L/V
Loader/Verifier

La
Lanthanum (Symbol)

LA
Local Address; Logical Address; Line Adapter

LAA
Locally Administered Address (IBM)

LAB
Logic Array Block

LAB-C
Line Attachment Base-C (IBM)

LAD
Listen Address Device (IEEE); Local Area Disk

LADD
Lens Antenna Deployment Demonstration (DOD); Local Area Data Distribution

LADDER
Language Access to Distributed Data with Error Recovery

LADS
Local Area Data Set

LADT
Local Area Data Transport (IBM)

LAG
Listen Address Group (IEEE)

LAM
LAN Access Module (AT&T); Lobe Access [or Attachment] Module

LAMA
Local Automatic Message Accounting

LAMN
Local Area Multiplexer Node

LAMP
Logic Analysis for Maintenance Planning

LAMPF
Los Alamos Meson Physics Facility (Los Alamos National Laboratory [LANL], US)

LAN
Local Area Network

LANA
Local Area Network Accelerator

LANL
Los Alamos National Laboratory (US)

LANRES
Local Area Network Resource Extension (IBM)

LANSP
Local Area Network Support Program (IBM)

LAP
Link Access Protocol; Link Access Procedure; Local Area Power

LAP-B
Link Access Protocol, Balanced

LAP-D
Link Access Protocol, D-channel

LAP-M
Link Access Procedure for Modems

LAPB
Link Access Protocol, Balanced

LAPD
Link Access Protocol, D-channel

LAPM
Link Access Procedure for Modems

LAR
Limit Address Register

LARPS
Local and Remote Printing Station

LARS
Laser Ranging System

LAS
Local Address Space; Land Analysis System (NASA)

Laser
Light Amplification by Stimulation of Emitted Radiation

LASER
Light Amplification by Stimulation of Emitted Radiation

LASL
Los Alamos Scientific Laboratory (DOD)

LASP
Local Attached Support Processor

LASS
Logistics Analysis Simulation System

LAST
Local Area System Transport

LAT
Local Access Terminal; Local Area Transport (DEC)

LATA
Local Access and Transport Area(s) (AT&T)

LATCP
Local Area Transport Control Protocol (DEC)

LATS
Low Altitude Target Satellite

LAU
Line Adapter Unit

LAVC
Local Area VAX Cluster (DEC)

LAVCS
Local Area VAX Cluster System (DEC)

LAWN
Local Area Wireless Network

lb
pound

LB
Line Buffer; Logical Block

LBA
Local Bus Adapter; Linear Bounded Automation

LBC
Local Bus Controller

LBEN
Low Byte Enable

lbl
label

LBL
Lawrence Berkeley Laboratory; Line by Line

LBMI
Lease Base Machine Inventory

LBN
Logical Block Number (DEC)

LBO
Line Build-Out

lbr
librarian

LBR
LASER Beam Recorder; Large Business Remote

LBRV
Low Bit Rate Voice

LBS
Line Buffer System

LC
Library of Congress (US); Liquid Crystal; Lower Case; Inductance-Capacitance (Refers to an electrical circuit); Location Counter; Line Concentrator; Line Control

LC/TC
Line Control/Task Control

LCA
Logic Cell Array; Line Control Adapter; Low Cost Automation

LCB
Line Control Block; Link Control Block; Logic Control Block

LCC
Life Cycle Costs; Leadless Chip Carrier; Ledger Card Computer; Local Communications Controller (IBM)

LCCC
Leadless Ceramic Chip Carrier

LCCPMP
Life Cycle Computer Program Management Plan

LCD
Liquid Crystal Display; Least Common Denominator

LCDS
Low Cost Development System

LCF
Least Common Factor

LCH
Logical Channel

LCHILD
Logical Child

LCL
Limited Channel Logout; Lower Control Limit

LCM
Least Common Multiple; Large Core Memory; Line Concentrator Module; Line

Control Module

LCN
Logical Channel Number (CCITT)

LCNTR
Location Counter

LCP
Language Conversion Program; Link Control Protocol; Link Control Procedure; Local Control Point

LCR
Least Cost Routing; Inductance-Capacitance-Resistance (Refers to an electrical circuit); Lead Calcium Rechargeable battery

LCS
Large Core Storage; Liquid Crystal Shutter

LCSP
Logical Channels Switching Program

LCT
Latest Completing Time; Line Control Table; Low Cost Technology; Logical Channel Termination

LCTV
Liquid Crystal Television

LCU
Lightweight Computer Unit (US Army); Local Control Unit; Line Control Unit; Level Converter Unit

LCW
Line Control Word

LD
Logical Design; Long Distance; Low Dispersion; Laser Diode; Laser Disk

LDA
Linear Discriminant Analysis; Local Data Administrator; Local Display Adapter; Live Data Analysis; Logical Device Address; Long Distance Adapter

LDB
Large Data Base; Logical Data Base

LDBS
Local Data Base System

LDC
Low Density Center; Local Display Controller

LDCS
Long Distance Control System

LDD
Lightly Doped Drain; Local Data Distribution

LDDC
Long Distance Direct Current dialing system

LDF
Local Distribution Frame

LDI
Local Data Interchange

LDL
Logical Data Base Level

LDLA
Limited Distance Line Adapter

LDM
Limited Distance Modem; Linear Delta Modulation; Local Data Manager; Logical Data Modeling

LDMX
Local Digital Message Exchange

LDO
Logical Device Order; Low Drop-Out

LDR
Local Distribution Radio

LDT
Language Dependent Translator; Local Descriptor Table (Intel Corp, US)

LDU
Line Drive Unit

LE
Leading Edge

LEADS
Law Enforcement Automated Data System

LEC
Local Exchange Carrier

LED
Light-Emitting Diode

LEF
Line Expansion Function

LEIS
Law Enforcement Information System (US Coast Guard)

LEM
Lobe Expansion Module; Logic Enhanced Memory; Logical End of Media

len
length

LEN
Low-Entry Networking (IBM)

LEO
Low Earth Orbit

LEOS
Low Earth-Orbiting Satellite

let
letter
LET
Linear Energy Transfer
lev
level
LEX
Line Exchanger; Leading Edge Extension
LF
Line Feed (CCITT); Low Frequency (30 to 300 kHz band)
LFC
Local Form Control
LFD
Local Frequency Distribution
LFM
Local File Manager
LFN
Logical File Name
LFS
Local Format Storage
LFSR
Linear Feedback Shift Register
lft
left
LG
Line Generator
LGA
Land Grid Array
LGI
Linear Gate and Integrator
LGN
Logical Group Number
LH
Light Helicopter (DOD)
LHC
Left-Hand Chain; Left-Hand Circular
LHF
List Handling Facility
LHS
Left-Hand Side
Li
Lithium (Symbol)
LIA
Laser Industry Association; Laser Institute of America; Laser Interferometric Alignment; Low Speed Input Adapter; Loop Interface Address
lib
librarian
LIB
Line Interface Bus (IBM); Line-Item Budget

LIBE
Library Editor
LIBMAN
Library Management
libr
librarian
LIBRIS
Library Information System
LIC
Linear Interface Circuit (TI); Line Interface Coupler (IBM); Lowest Incoming Channel (CCITT)
LIDAR
Laser Intensity Detection and Ranging
LIDO
Logic In, Documents Out
LIF
Line Interface Feature
LIFE
Long Instruction Format Engine
LIFO
Last In, First Out
LIH
Line Interface Handler
LILO
Last In, Last Out
LIM
Language Interpretation Module; Line Interface Module
LIMA
Logic-In-Memory Array
LIMS
Laboratory Information Management System
LINED
Line Editor
LINX
Logistics Information Exchange
LIOCS
Logical Input/Output Control System
LIOM
LAN I/O Module
LIOP
Local Input/Output Processor
LIPID
Logical Page Identifier
LIPS
Logical Inferences Per Second; Laboratory Interconnecting Programming System
lips (LIPS)
logical inferences per second

liquid
liquidation
LIRS
Library Information Retrieval System
LIS
Library Information System
LISA
Linked Index Sequential Access
LISP
List Processor(ing)
lit
literal
LIU
Line Interface Unit
LJE
Local Job Entry
LKED
Linkage Editor (IBM)
LKM
Low Key Maintenance
LL
Leased Line; Local Line; Local Loopback
LLA
Leased Line Adapter; Long Line Adapter
LLA
Library Look Aside (IBM)
LLB
Local Loop Back
LLC
Logical Link Control protocol (IEEE)
LLD
Local Longitude Difference
LLG
Logical Line Group
LLI
Low Level Interface
LLL
Lawrence Livermore Laboratory
LLM
Low Level Multiplexer
LLNL
Lawrence Livermore National Laboratory
LLO
Local Lock Out (IEEE)
LLP
Lowest Level Processor
LM
LAN Manager (IBM); Link Manager; Linear Module (National Semiconductor Inc, US); Logic Module; Local Memory; Loop Multiplexer
LM/X
LAN Manager X (H-P)

LMB
Left Most BIT; Logical Memory Block (DEC)
LMBI
Local Memory Bus Interface
LMCC
Land Mobil Communications Council
LMCSS
Letter Mail Code Sort System
LMF
License Management Facility (DEC)
LMI
Local Memory Image; Layer Management Interface; Local Management Interface; Link Management Interface
LML
Logical Memory Level
LMOS
Line Management Operating System; Loop Maintenance Operations System
LMRS
Land Mobile Radio Service (FCC)
LMS
List Management System; Laser Magnetic Storage; Learning Management System (DEC); Library Management Software
LMT
Local Mean Time; Logical Mapping Table
LMU
Line Monitor(ing) Unit
LMX
Local Multiplexer
ln
line; logarithm, natural [or Naperian]
LN
Link Number
LNA
Low-Noise Amplifier
LNB
Low-Noise Block; Local Name Base
LNE
Local Network Emulator
LNG
Liquefied Natural Gas
LNI
Line Network Interface
LNM
Logical Network Machine
LNR
Low-Noise Receiver

lo
low
LO
Local Oscillator
LOA
Low Speed Output Adapter
loc
local; location
LOC
Loss Of Carrier; Location Counter; Lowest Outgoing Channel (CCITT)
LOFAR
Low Frequency Analysis Recording
log
logarithm
LOGFED
Log File Editor
LONS
Local On-Line Network System (USAF)
LOP
Line Oriented Protocol; Loss of Power
LOR
Level Of Repair
LOS
Line Of Sight; Loss Of Signal
LOSR
Limit Of Stack Register
LOTS
Low Overhead Time-Sharing System
LOX
Liquid Oxygen
LP
Lead Programmer; Logic Probe; Light Pen; Line Printer; Line Protocol; Linear Programming; Liquid [or Liquified] Petroleum; Long-Play(ing) (Refers to audio or video recordings); Linear Polarization [or Linearly Polarized]
LPA
Line Powered Amplifier; Link Pack Area (IBM)
LPAR
Logical Partition (IBM)
LPCM
Linear Phase Code Modulation
LPF
Low Pass Filter
LPG
Liquid [or Liquified] Petroleum Gas
LPI
Lines Per Inch

LPL
List Processing Language; Local Processor Link
LPM
Lines Per Minute; Laser Processing Machinery; Linear Power Module
lpm (LPM)
lines per minute (Refers to speed rating of printers)
LPN
Logical Page Number
LPS
Linear Programming System; Lines Per Second
LPSA
Licensed Program Support Agreement (IBM)
LPT
Line Printer
LPU
Language Processor Unit; Line Printer Unit
LQ
Letter Quality (Refers to printers with printed copy of the highest quality)
Lr
Lawrencium (Symbol)
LR
Left to Right; Logical Record; Link Register (IBM); Limit Register; Inductance-Resistance (Symbol, refers to electrical circuitry); Longitudinal Recording; Limited Response
LRA
Logical Record Access
LRC
Inductance-Resistance-Capacitance (Symbol, refers to electrical circuitry); Local Register Cache; Longitudinal Redundancy Check
LRCC
Longitudinal Redundancy Check Character
LRECL
Logical Record Length (IBM)
LRIP
Low Rate Initial Production
LRL
Logical Record Length; Logical Record Location
LRP
Logical Request Package

LRSP
Long Range Strategic Planning
LRU
Least Recently Used
LRV
Lunar Roving Vehicle (NASA)
LS
Least Significant; Low Speed; Local Store; Linkage Stack (IBM); Low-Power Schottky (IC)
LS/TTL
Low-Power Schottky Transistor-Transistor Logic (IC)
LSA
Line-Sharing Adapter
LSAR
Local Storage Address Register
LSB
Least Significant Bit; Large-Scale Bypass (AT&T); Low Surface Brightness; Lower Sideband
LSD
Least Significant Difference; Least Significant Digit; Line Signal Detector
LSDR
Local Store Data Register
LSE
Language-Sensitive Editor (DEC); Linkage Stack Entry (IBM)
LSFR
Local Store Function Register
LSI
Large-Scale Integration (IC)
LSL
Ladder Static Logic
LSM
Line Switch Module; Letter Sorting Machine; Line Select Module
LSP
Local Store Pointer
LSR
Local Shared Resources (IBM); Local Storage Register; Low Speed Reader
LSS
Language for Symbolic Simulation
LSSD
Level-Sensitive Scan Detector (IBM)
LST
Latest Starting Time; Local Standard Time
LSTTL
Low-Power Schottky Transistor-Transistor Logic (IC)

LSU
Least Significant Unit; Laser Scanning Unit; Local Storage Unit; Library Storage Unit; Line-Sharing Unit
LT
Less Than; Line Terminator(ion); Large Lunar Telescope (NASA)
LTB
Local Token-Ring Bridge
LTC
Lowest Two-Way Channel (CCITT); Line Time Clock; Local Terminal Controller
Ltd
Limited
LTD
Line Transfer Device; Limited
LTH
Logical Track Header; Leaded Through Holes (Refers to IC boards)
LTM
Long Term Memory; LAN Traffic Manager
ltr
letter
LTRS
Letters Shift
LTS
Line Transient Suppression
LTSS
Lawrence Timesharing System (LLNL)
LTU
Line Termination Unit
Lu
Lutetium (Symbol)
LU
Logical Unit (IBM)
LU-LU
Logical Unit to Logical Unit
LUB
Logical Unit Block
LUF
Lowest Usable Frequency
LUI
Logical Unit Interface (IBM)
LUN
Logical Unit Number
LUT
Look-Up Table
LUW
Logical Unit of Work (IBM)
LV
Linear Video

LVA
Local Virtual Address
LVDT
Linear Variable Differential Transformer
[or Transducer]; Linear Velocity/Displace-
ment Transducer [or Transmitter]
LW
Last Word
LWA
Last Word Address

LWR
Laser Write Read
lx
lux (Unit of illumination)
LXMAR
Load External Memory Address Register
ly
light-year
LZA
Leading Zero/One Anticipator (IBM)

M

m

mass (Symbol); machine; mantissa; magnetization; master; mega; milli (SI prefix denoting 10^{-3}); memory; monitor; multiplier; modem; mode; meter (Metric unit of linear measure and of electrical wavelength); minute; mile; modulation coefficient (Symbol)

M

Mega (SI prefix denoting 10^6); Molar; Mutual inductance (Symbol); Modified index of refraction (Symbol); Roman numeral designation for 10^3 (1000)

M&A

Maintenance and Administration

M/O

Magneto-Optic

mA

milliampere(s) (Symbol, 10^{-3} Ampere[s])

MA

Materials Analysis; Manufacturing Assembly; Memory Address

mac

macro

MAC

Media Access Control; Maintenance Allocation Chart; Memory Access Controller; Message Authentication(or) Code; Multiplier Accumulator; Multiple Access Control; Multiplexed Analog Component

MACC

Micro Asynchronous Communications Controller

mach

machine; machinery

Mach

Mach number

macrol

macrolanguage

MACS

Multiline Automatic Calling System

MACSAT

Multiple Access Communications Satellite (NASA)

MAE

Memory Address Extension

MAF

Multiply-Add-Fused (IBM)

mag

magnetic

maint

maintenance

MAL

Memory Access Logic

MAM

Memory Allocation Manager

MAMS

Manufacturing Applications Management System

man

manual; manufacture

MAN

Metropolitan Area Network

MANDATE

Multiline Automatic Network Diagnostic and Transmission Equipment

manf

manufacture; manufacturer; manufacturing

MANIAC

Mechanical And Numerical Integrator And Computer

MAOS

Metal Alumina Dielectric Oxide Semiconductor

MAP

Manufacturing Automation Protocol; Maintenance Analysis Procedures; Management Analysis and Projection; Memory Allocation and Protection; Measurement Assurance Program (NIST)

MAPGEN

Map Generator

MAPI

Mail Applications Interface (Microsoft Corp, US); Messaging Application Programming Interface (Microsoft Corp, US); Machinery and Allied Products Institute

MAPS

Management Analysis and Planning System; Manufacturing and Production System

MAR

Memory Address Register

MARC

Machine-Readable Catalog(ing)

marg
margin; marginal
MART
Mean Active Repair Time
MASER
Microwave Amplification by Stimulated Emission of Radiation
MASIS
Management and Scientific Information System
MASK
Multiple Amplitude Shift Keying
MASM
Macro Assembler
MASS
Multiple Access Switching System
MASTER
Multiple Access Shared-Time Executive Routines
MAT
Memory Address Time
MATE
Modular Automated Test Equipment (IEEE)
MATS
Multiple-Access Time Sharing
MATV
Master Antenna Television
MAU
Memory Access Unit; Media Access Unit; Multistation Access Unit (IBM); Multiple Access Unit
max
maximum
MAXI
Modular Architecture for the Exchange of Information (DOD)
mb
megabit [or megaBIT]
Mb
Megabit
MB
Megabyte [or MegaByte]; Memory Buffer; Memory Bus
MBC
Memory Bus Controller; Message Broadcast Controller; Multiple Basic Channel
MBCD
Modified Binary Coded Decimal
MBE
Molecular Beam Epitaxy (AT&T)

MBI
Memory Bank Interface
MBM
Magnetic Bubble Memory
mbr
member
MBR
Master Boot Record; Memory Base Register; Memory Buffer Register
MBU
Memory Buffer Unit
m-byte
megabyte
mc
megacycle
MC
Magnetic Card; Master Control; Memory Control
MCA
Micro Channel Architecture (IBM); Multiprocessor Communications Adapter
MCAE
Mechanical Computer-Aided Engineering
MCBF
Mean Cycles Between Failure
MCC
Management Control Center (DEC); Multichip Carrier; Multiple Chip Carrier; Multichannel Communications Controller
MCD
Multichannel Communications Device
MCDBSU
Master Control and Data Buffer Storage Unit
MCDN
Marine Corps Data Network (US Marine Corps)
MCDS
Management Control Data System
MCGA
Multi-Color Graphics Adapter (IBM)
MCF
Magnetic Card File
mchr
megacharacter
MCI
Machine Check Interruption
MCIC
Machine Check Interruption Code
MCIS
Maintenance Control Information System; Materials Control Information System

MCL
Monitor Control Language
MCLK
Master Clock
MCM
Memory Control Module; Multichip Module
MCMS
Multichannel Memory System
MCOS
Microprogrammable Computer Operating System
MCP
Master Control Program (Burroughs Corp, US); Master Catalog Program (Burroughs Corp, US); Message Control Program; Modular Communications Processor; Macintosh Co-processor Platform (Apple Computer Inc, US)
MCPU
Multiple Central Processing Unit
MCR
Magnetic Card Reader; Magnetic Character Reader; Magnetic Character Recognition; Monitor Console Routine (DEC); Master Control Routine; Memory Control Register
MCRR
Machine Check Recording and Recovery (IBM)
MCS
Maintenance Control System; Master Control System; Management Control System; Multichannel Communications Support; Multichip System (Intel Corp, US); Message Control System; Multifunction Communication Service (AT&T)
MCT
Metal-oxide-Controlled Thyristor
MCU
Maintenance Control Unit; Management Control Unit; Memory Control Unit (TI); Master Control Unit; Multichip Unit (DEC); Micro-Controller Unit; Microprocessor Communications Unit
Md
Mendelevium (Symbol)
MDA
Multidimensional Access; Modulation-Domain Analysis (H-P); Monochrome Display Adapter (IBM)

MDAC
Multiplying Digital-to-Analog Converter
MDB
Master Data Bank
MDC
Memory Disk Controller; Multiple Device Controller
MDCU
Magnetic Disk Control Unit
MDD
Magnetic Disk Drive
MDE
Modular Design Environment
MDF
Main Distributing(on) Frame
MDLC
Multiple Data Link Controller
MDOS
Multi-User Disk Operating System
MDP
Main Data Path
MDPSK
Multilevel Differential Phase Shift Keying
MDR
Memory Data Register
MDS
Maintenance Data System; Management Display System; Multiple Data Set; Modular Data System
MDT
Mean Down Time; Mobile Data Terminal
MDX
Multi-Indexing
ME
Mechanical Engineering (Official monthly publication of the ASME); Memory Element
meg
megabyte
MEGAFLOP
One Million Floating-Point Operations Per Second
mem
memory; memorandum
MESFET
Metal Enhancement Semiconductor Field Effect Transistor
mesg
message
MET
Management Engineering Team

MeV
Million Electron Volts

mf
microfarad

MF
Master File; Medium Frequency (300 to 3000 kHz band)

MFCA
Multifunction Communications Adapter

MFCM
Multifunction Card Machine

MFCU
Multifunction Card Unit

mfd
manufactured

MFD
Master File Directory (DEC)

MFDC
Main Facility Device Controller (AT&T)

MFDSUL
Multifunction Data Set Utility Language

MFE
Multifunction Equipment

MFF
Match Flip Flop

mfg
manufacturing

MFLOPS
Million [or Millions of] Floating Point Operations Per Second

MFM
Modified Frequency Modulation

MFP
Multifunction Printer

mfr
manufacture; manufactured; manufacturer

MFR
Multifrequency Receiver

MFS
Macintosh File Structure (Apple Computer Inc, US); Message Format Services (IBM)

MFSK
Multiple Frequency Shift Keying

MFT
Metallic Facility Terminal (AT&T); Multiprogramming with a Fixed Number of Tasks (IBM)

Mg
Magnesium (Symbol)

mg
milligram

MG
Motor Generator

MGA
Monochrome Graphics Adapter

mgr
manager

mgt
management

MH
Materials Handling; Message Handler

MHD
Moving Head Disk

MHE
Materials Handling Equipment

MHI
Materials Handling Institute

MHS
Message Handling Service; Message Handling System; Multiple Host Support

mHz
millihertz (Denoting 10^{-3} Hertz)

mhz
megahertz

MHz
Megahertz (Denoting 10^6 Hertz, preferred form)

MI
Machine-Independent; Maskable Interrupt; Memory Interface; Memory Interconnect (DEC); Maintenance Interface

MIAS
Management Information and Accounting System

MICR
Magnetic Ink Character Recognition

micro
micro; microcomputer; microprocessor

MICS
Management Information and Control System; Marketing Information and Communication System

MIDAS
Management Interactive Data Accounting System; Microprogrammable Integrated Data Acquisition System

MIDS
Management Information Decision Support; Management Information Decision System

MIF
Master Index File

MIG
Metal-In-Gap; Metal Inert Gas welding

mil
one thousandth of an inch (In the United States, a small unit of thickness measurement [chiefly used in wire diameter and tape thickness]; 1 mil= 10^{-3})

MIL
Military; Module Interconnection Language

MIL-HDBK
Military Standardization Handbooks (Prefix letters are followed by an assigned serial number)

milli
SI prefix denoting 10^{-3} (Letter symbol m, meaning thousandth[s])

MIL-STD
Military Standard(s)

MILNET
Military Network

MIM
Metal-Insulator-Metal; Modem Interface Module

MIMD
Multiple Instruction, Multiple Data processor

min
minium; minute

MIND
Modular Interactive Network Designer

mini
mini; minicomputer

MINI
Minicomputer Industry National Interchange

MIO
Multiple Input/Output

MIOP
Master Input/Output Processor; Multiplexer Input/Output Processor

MIOS
Metal Insulator Oxide Silicon; Modular Input/Output System

MIP
Material In Process; Mixed-Integer Programming (IBM)

MIPS
Million [or Millions of] Instructions Per Second

MIR
Management Information Repository

(DEC); Memory Input Register

MIS
Management Information Service(s); Management Information System; Metal-Insulator-Semiconductor; Modular Interconnect System

misc
miscellaneous

MISC
Minimum Instruction Set Computer

MISAM
Multiple Index Sequential Access Method

MISD
Multiple Instruction, Single Data processor

MISP
Microelectronics Industry Support Program (UK)

MISR
Multiple-Input Signature Register (IBM)

MISSION
Manufacturing Information System Support Integrated Online

MIT
Massachusetts Institute of Technology (US); Master Instruction Tape

MITA
Microcomputer Industry Trade Association

MITI
Ministry of International Trade and Industry (Japan)

MIU
Modem Interface Unit

MIW
Microinstruction Word

MIX
Microprogram Index Register; Modular Interface Extension (Intel Corp, US)

MJD
Management Job Description

mk
mask

mks (MKS)
meter-kilogram-second (Metric system of units in which the meter is the unit of length; the kilogram, mass; and the second, time)

mksa (MKSA)
meter-kilogram-second-ampere (Electromagnetic system of units, also called the Giorgi system)

mkt
market

ml
milliliter (A Metric unit of capacity, or volume, equal to 10^{-3} liter); multileaving

ML
Machine Language; Memory Location

MLA
Multiple Line Adapter

MLB
Multi-Layer [or Multilayer] Board

MLC
Magnetic Ledger Card; Multi-Layer [or Multilayer] Ceramic; Multi-Line [or Multiline] Controller; Multi-Link Control field (CCITT)

MLCP
Multi-Location Calling Plan (AT&T); Multi-Line [or Multiline] Communications Processor

MLCU
Magnetic Ledger Card Unit

MLD
Machine Language Debugger

MLFS
Master Library File System

MLG
Macro Layout Generator (IBM)

MLI
Machine Language Instruction

MLP
Machine Language Program; Multi Link Procedure (CCITT)

MLOCR
Multi-Line Optical Character Reader

MLPA
Modified Link Pack Area

MLS
Multi-LAN Switch; Maximum Length Sequence (NIST); Machine Literature Searching

mlt
mass, length, time

MLTA
Multiple Line Terminal Adapter

mm
millimeter (Metric unit of linear measure denoting 10^{-3} meter)

MM
Main Memory; Machine Model; Mass Memory; Memory Module

MMA
Multiple Module Access; Microcomputers Managers Association

MMAS
Manufacturing Management Accounting Systems; Material Management and Accounting System (DOD)

MMC
Main Memory Controller

MMF
Magnetomotive Force

MMFS
Manufacturing Message Format Standard

MMI
Main Memory Interface

MMIC
Monolithic Microwave Integrated Circuit

MMIS
Maintenance Management Information System

MMM
Main Memory Module; Monolithic Main Memory

MMP
Main Microprocessor

MMPS
Manufacturing Material Planning System

MMPU
Memory Management and Protection Unit

MMR
Main Memory Register; Memory Management Register

MMS
Man-Machine System; Memory Management System; Module Management System (DEC); Message Management System

MMSE
Minimum Mean Square(d) Error

MMU
Main Memory Unit; Memory Management Unit; Memory Mapping Unit

MN
Message Number

Mn
Manganese (Symbol)

MNN
Main Network Node

MNOS
Metal-Nitride Oxide Semiconductor

Mo
Molybdenum (Symbol)
mo
month
MO
Manually Operated; Magneto-Optic; Memory Output
MOCA
Mixed Object Document Content Architecture (IBM)
MOI
Moment of Inertia
mod
model; modification; modulate
MOD
Magneto-Optic Disk; Message Output Descriptor (IBM)
MODEM
Modulator-Demodulator
Modem
Modulator-Demodulator
MODI
Modular Optical Digital Interface
mol
mole (Symbol)
MOL
Machine-Oriented Language
mol wt
molecular weight
mon
monitor
MOP
Maintenance Operation Protocol (DEC)
MOPS
Million [or Millions of] Operations Per Second
MOR
Memory Output Register
MOS
Management Operating System; Macintosh Operating System (Apple Computer Inc, US); Margin Of Safety; Metal-Oxide Semiconductor; Metal-Oxide Silicon; Memory Oriented System
MOSFET
Metal-Oxide Semiconductor Field-Effect Transistor
MOSROM
Metal-Oxide Semiconductor Read-Only Memory
MOV
Metal-Oxide Varistor

mp
microprocessor; multiprocessing [or multiprocessing]; multiprocessor [or multi-processor]; microprogram; melting point
MP
Mathematical Programming; Metal Particle; Multi-Processing(or)
MP/OS
Microprocessor Operating System (Data General Corp, US)
MPa
Megapascals
MPB
Memory Processor Bus
MPC
Microprogram Control; Multi-Personal Computer
MPCM
Microprogram Control Memory
MPD
Missing Pulse Detector
MPF
Manufacturing Progress Function
MPG
Microwave Pulse Generator
mpg
miles per gallon
MPGS
Microprogram Generating System
mph
miles per hour
MPI
Multibus Peripheral Interface (Intel Corp, US); Microprocessor Interface
MPL
Message Processing Language; Microprogramming Language
mplxr
multiplexer
MPM
Microprogram Memory
MPMCU
Microprogram Memory Control Unit
MPN
Manufacturer's Productivity Network (H-P); Most Probable Number
MPP
Message Processing Program
MPR
Microprogram Register; Multi-Port Repeater; Multi-Protocol Router

MPROM
Mask Programmed Read-Only Memory
MPS
Mathematical Programming System;
Microprocessing System
MP/SCM
Multiport Semiconductor Memory
MPSK
Multiple Phase Shift Keying
MPSX
Mathematical Programming System Extended
mpt
multipoint
MPT
Ministry of Posts and Telecommunications
(Japan); Memory Processing Time
MPU
Memory Protection Unit; Microprocessing
Unit
mpx
multiplexer
MPX
Multiprogramming Executive
MQ
Multiplier-Quotient
M&R
Maintainability and Reliability; Maintenance and Repair
MR
Magnetic Resonance; Maintenance Report; Master Reset; Modem Ready; Multiple Register
MRA
Materials Requirement Analysis
MRAM
Mapping Random Access Memory
MRC
Machine Readable Code
MRD
Memory Read
MRDF
Machine Readable Data File
MRDY
Message Ready
MRI
Magnetic Resonance Imaging; Memory
Reference Instruction
MRO
Maintenance, Repair and Operating [or
Operational]; Multiple Region Operation
(IBM)

MROM
Macro Read-Only Memory
MRP
Manufacturing Resource(s) Planning;
Material(s) Requirements Planning
MRS
Management Reporting System; Magnetic Resonance Spectrometry
MRT
Mean-Repair-Time
M&S
Materials and Services
ms
manuscript; millisecond (Denoting 10^{-3}
second)
MS
Main Storage; Message Store; Margin of
Safety; Management Science; Mass Storage; Multi-Spectral; Metric System; Material Specification; Manufacturing System
MS-DOS
MicroSoft Disk Operating System
(Microsoft Corp, US)
MSA
Mass Storage Adapter
MSB
Most Significant Bit
MSBY
Most Significant Byte
MSC
Mass Storage Control; Multisystem Coupling; Multiple System Coupling (IBM)
MSCP
Mass Storage Control Protocol (DEC)
MSCU
Modular Store Control Unit
MSD
Mass Storage Device; Most Significant
Digit; Modem Sharing Device
MSDS
Material Safety Data Sheet; Message
Switching Data Service
MSE
Mean Square Error
msec
millisecond (Denoting 10^{-3} second)
MSF
Mass Storage Facility
msg
message

MSI
Medium Scale Integration

MSIO
Mass Storage Input-Output

MSITTL
Medium Scale Integration Transistor-Transistor Logic

MSK
Minimal Shift Keying; Multi-Shift Keying

MSM
Memory Storage Module

MSNF
Multiple Systems Networking Facility (IBM); Multisystem Networking Facility

MSO
Multistage Operations; Main Storage Occupancy (IBM); Multivendor Support Operation (H-P)

MSOS
Mass Storage Operating System

MSPS
Megasamples per Second

MSS
Mass Storage System (IBM); Multispectral [or Multi-Spectral] Scanner

mssg
message

MST
Mean Service Time; Mountain Standard Time

mstr
master

MSU
Mass Storage Unit; Memory Storage Unit

MT
Machine Translation; Message Transfer (CCITT); Mountain Time; Magnetic Tape

mt
multitasking

MTACP
Magnetic Tape Ancillary Control Process (DEC)

MTBCF
Mean-Time-Between-Component-Failure; Mean-Time-Between-Critical-Failures

MTBD
Mean-Time-Between-Defects

MTBE
Mean-Time-Between-Errors

MTBF
Mean-Time-Between-Failures

MTBI
Mean-Time-Between-Interrupts

MTBM
Mean-Time-Between-Maintenance

MTBO
Mean-Time-Between-Overhauls

MTBR
Mean-Time-Between-Repairs

MTBSE
Mean-Time-Between-Software Errors

MTBSF
Mean-Time-Between-Significant-Failures; Mean-Time-Between-System-Failure

MTBUM
Mean-Time-Between Unscheduled-Maintenance

MTBUR
Mean-Time-Between Unscheduled-Removal

MTC
Magnetic Tape Controller; Manufacturing Technology Center (NIST)

MTCU
Magnetic Tape Control Unit

MTDA
Mean Time for Data Availability

MTF
Mean-Time-to-Failure; Modulation Transfer Function; Multitasking Facility (IBM)

MTH
Magnetic Tape Handler

MTIRA
Machine Tool Industry Research Association

MTO
Made-To-Order; Master Terminal Operator

MTOS
Magnetic Tape Operating System

mtr
monitor

MTR
Magnetic Tape Reader

MTS
Message Telephone Service; Message Transfer System; Message Telecommunication Service; Multiple Terminal System

MTSF
Mean-Time-to-System-Failure

MTT
Magnetic Tape Transport; Magnetic Tape

Terminal; Message Transfer Time

MTTF
Mean-Time-To-Failure

MTTR
Mean-Time-To-Repair; Mean-Time-To-Restore

MTTSF
Mean-Time-To-System-Failure

MTU
Magnetic Tape Unit; Memory Transfer Unit

MTX
Multitasking Executive

MU
Machine Unit; Memory Unit

MUD
Master User Directory

MUF
Maximum Usable Frequency

mul
multiplexer

mult
multiple; multiplier

MUMPS
Massachusetts General Hospital Utility Multi-Programming System (Programming language)

mux (MUX)
multiplexer

MUST
Multipurpose User-Oriented Software Technology

mV
millivolt (A unit of low voltage denoting

10^{-3} Volt[s])

MV
Mean Variation

MVM
Manager Virtual Machine; Multiple Virtual Modem

MVL
Metal Vapor Laser

MVS
Multiple Virtual Storage (IBM); Multiple Virtual Systems (IBM)

MVS/SP
Multiple Virtual Storage/System Product (IBM)

MVS/XA
Multiple Virtual Systems/Extended Architecture (IBM)

MVT
Multiprogramming with Variable Number of Tasks (IBM)

mW
milliwatt (A small unit of electric power denoting 10^{-3} Watt[s])

MW
Megawatt (A unit of high power denoting 10^6 Watt[s]); Microwave; Molecular Weight

MXA
Main Exchange Area

MX
Mail Exchange

MZR
Multi-Zone Recording

N

n
nano (SI prefix denoting 10^{-9}); number (Symbol); node; negative; numeric; numerical; symbol for a term (e.g., a multiplier) having an assigned value; symbol for part of an expression or operator (as in $2n$, $n-1$, n, n^2, etc.); index of refraction (Symbol)

N
Newton (Symbol, SI unit of force); Nitrogen (Symbol); Symbol for Number; Abbreviation of Number (Also, No)

N/A
Name and Address

n-p-n
negative-positive-negative

N(R)
Number [Receive] (CCITT)

N(S)
Number [Send] (CCITT)

Na
Sodium (Symbol)

NA
Not Accessible (CCITT); No Action; Not Accurate; Not Available; Not Applicable; Not Authorized; Numerical Aperture

NAA
Noise Analysis Approach

NAB
National Association of Broadcasters (US)

NAC
Network Access Controller

NACK
Negative Acknowledgment

NAE
National Academy of Engineering

NAED
National Association of Electrical Distributors (US)

NAF
Network Access Facility

NAG
Numerical Algorithms Group programs

NAI
No Action Indicated

NAICC
National Association of Independent Computer Companies

NAIS
National Association for Information Systems

NAK
Negative Acknowledge (CCITT)

NAL
National Agricultural Library (US); New Assembly Language

NAM
Network Access Method

NAMPS
Narrowband Advanced Mobile Phone Service (Motorola Inc, US)

NAN
Network Application Node

NAND
NOT-AND (Circuitry)

NANP
North American Numbering Plan (AT&T)

NANPA
North America Numbering Plan Administration

NAP
Network Access Program (IBM); Network Access Protocol; Noise Analysis Program; Network Applications Platform

NAR
No Action Required

NARA
National Archives and Records Administration (US)

NARTE
National Association of Radio and Telecommunications Engineers

NAS
Network Application Support (DEC)

NASA
National Aeronautics and Space Administration (US)

NASTRAN
NASA Structural Analysis System (NASA, US)

NAT
No Action Taken

NATA
North American Telecommunications Association

NAU
Network Addressable Unit (IBM)

Nb
Niobium (Symbol)
NB
Narrow Band; Noise Block
NBFM
Narrow Band Frequency Modulation
NBPM
Narrow Band Phase Modulation
nbr
number
NBS
National Bureau of Standards (Obsolete, now referred to as National Institute of Standards and Technology [NIST]); Numeric Backspace character
NBVC
Narrow Band Video Conferencing
NC
Network Congestion (CCITT); Network Control; Noise Cancelling; No Connection; Normally Closed; Numerical Control; Numerically Controlled
NCAM
Network Communication Access Method
NCB
Network Connect Block; Network Control Block
NCC
National Computer Conference; National Computer Center; Network Communications Controller; National Control Center; Network Control Center; Network Control Console
NCCF
Network Communications Control Facility (IBM)
NCCCD
National Center for Computer Crime Data (NIST)
NCDS
Numerical Control Distribution System
NCF
Network Configuration Facility (IBM); National Communications Forum; Neutral Code Format
NCGA
National Computer Graphics Association
NCL
Network Control Language
NCM
Network Configuration Management (DEC); Network Control Module

NCMS
Network Control and Management System (NEC)
NCN
Network Control Node
NCO
Numerically Controlled Oscillator
NCP
Network Control Point (AT&T); Network Control Program (IBM); Network Control Processor
NCPAS
National Computer Program Abstract Service
NCS
National Communications System; Network Control System; Network Communication [or Control] Server; Network Computing Services; Network Computing System
NCSA
National Center for Supercomputing Applications; National Computer Security Association
NCSC
National Computer Security Center (DOD)
NCSL
National Council of Standards Laboratories
NCTE
Network Channel Terminating Equipment (AT&T)
NCU
Network Control Unit; Number Crunching Unit; Node Coupling Unit
NCUG
National Centrex Users Group
Nd
Neodymium (Symbol)
ND
No Date; No Defects; Not Dated
NDAC
No Data Accepted (IEEE)
NDBMS
Network Data Base Management System
NDC
Network Diagnostic Control
NDE
Non-Destructive Evaluation
NDF
NCP/EP [Network Control Program/Emu-

lation Program] Definition Facility (IBM)

NDIS
Network Device Interface Specification (IBM); Network Driver Interface Standard (Microsoft Corporation, US)

NDLC
Network Data Link Control

NDR
Non-Destructive Read

NDRO
Non-Destructive Read-Out

NDT
Network Description Table; Non-Destructive Test(ing)

Ne
Neon (Symbol)

NE
Not Equal [to]; Network Equipment (CCITT)

NEA
National Electronics Association

NEARnet
New England Academic and Research Network

NEAT
National Electronic Autocoding Technique; New Enhanced Advanced Technology

NEC
National Electrical Code (Register trade mark of the National Fire Protection Association [NFPA])

NECA
National Exchange Carriers Association (FCC)

NEF
Noise Equivalent Flux

neg
negative

NEI
Noise Equivalent Irradiance; Not Elsewhere Indicated

NELC
Naval Electronics Laboratory Center

NELINET
New England Library Information Network

NEMA
National Electrical Manufacturers Association (US)

NEMOS
Network Management Operational Sup-

port system (AT&T)

NERSC
National Energy Research Supercomputer Center

net
network

NETA
New England Telecommunications Association

NETBIOS
Network Basic Input/Output System (IBM)

NETCON
Network Control

NETGEN
Network Generation

NETID
Network Identification

NETOP
Network Operator Process

NETS
Nationwide Emergency Telecommunications System

NETT
Network for Environmental Technology Transfer (EC)

NEU
Network Extension Unit

NEXT
Near-End Cross-Talk

NF
Normal Form

NFAIS
National Federation of Abstracting and Indexing Services

NFAM
Network File Access Method

NFAP
Network File Access Protocol

NFB
Negative Feedback

NFEA
National Federated Electrical Association

NFS
Network File System [or Server]

NFT
Network File Transfer

NGMF
NetView Graphic Monitor Facility (IBM)

NGP
Network Graphics Protocol

nHz
nanohertz
Ni
Nickel (Symbol)
NIA
No Input Acknowledge
NIBL
National Industrial Basic Language
NIC
Network Information Center; Network Interface Control; Network Interface Card; Numerically Intensive Computing
NICE
National Information Conference and Exposition; Network Information and Control Exchange (DEC)
NIF
Network Information File; Network Interface
NIFO
Next-In, First-Out
NIM
Network Interface Monitor
NIOSH
National Institute of Occupational Safety and Health (Centers for Disease Control [CDC], US)
NIP
Negative Intrinsic Positive diode; Non-Impact Printer; Nucleus Initialization Program (IBM)
NIS
Network Information Service; Network Interface System
NIST
National Institute of Standards and Technology (US Dept of Commerce, formerly, National Bureau of Standards [NBS])
NIU
Network Interface Unit
NIT
Network Interface Task
NJCL
Network Job Control Language
NJE
Network Job Entry (IBM)
NJEF
Network Job Entry Facility
NJI
Network Job Interface
NJOBS
Number of Jobs

NLA
Normalized Local Address
NLDM
Network Logical Data Manager (IBM)
NLM
National Library of Medicine (US)
NLOS
Natural Language Operating System
NLQ
Near-Letter Quality (Refers to typeface output produced by some dot-matrix printers [9-pin] that does not look as readable [low resolution] as that produced by letter-quality printers [24-pin], daisy wheel, or laser)
NLS
National Language Support (IBM); Network License System (DEC)
nm
nanometer (Metric unit of linear measure denoting 10^{-9} meter)
NM
Network Manager; Network Management
NMA
National Micrographics Association
NMC
Network Monitoring (or Management) Center
NMCC
Network Management Control Center; Non-digital Management Control Center (DEC)
NMF
New Master File
NMO
Number of critical Microoperations
NMOS
N-Channel [or Negative] Metal Oxide Semiconductor
NMS
Network Management Server (H-P); Network Management Services; Network Management System (Northern Telecom Inc, US); Network Management Software (DEC)
NMSE
Normalized Mean Square Error
NMVT
Network Management Vector Transport (IBM)
NNA
New Network Architecture

NNI
Next Node Index; Network Node Interface
No
Nobelium (Symbol); Number
no
number
NO
Normally Open; Not Obtainable (CCITT)
NOAA
National Oceanic and Atmospheric Administration (US)
NOCP
Network Operator Control Program
NOMA
National Office Management Association
NOMDA
National Office Machine Dealers Association
noncoll
noncollinear
NONSTD
Nonstandard
no-op
no-operation instruction (Pass instruction; do-nothing instruction)
NO OP
No-Operation instruction (Pass instruction; do-nothing instruction)
NOP
No-Operation instruction (Pass instruction; do-nothing instruction); Not Otherwise Provided for
NOPA
National Office Products Association
NOR
NOT-[or Negative-] OR [circuit or logic gate] (Contraction, the logical negation [inverse] of the OR function); Nucleolar-Organizing Region (Biology)
NORRD
No Reply Received
nos
numbers
NOS
Network Operating System (Control Data Corp, US); Not Otherwise Specified
NOS/BE
Network Operating System/Basic Environment (Control Data Corp, US); Network Operating System/Batch Environment
NOS/VE
Network Operating System/Virtual (Con-

trol Data Corp, US)
NOSC
Naval Ocean Systems Center
NOSP
Network Operating Support Program
NOT
NOT circuit or logic gate (In digital systems, a logic operation that effectively means "not 1 but zero" or "not zero but 1")
N-P
Negative-Positive
Np
Neptunium (Symbol)
NP
New Page; No Parity; Number Plan (CCITT)
NPA
Numbering Plan Area
NPD
Network Protective Device
NPDA
Network Problem Determination Application (IBM)
NPIU
Numerical Processing and Interface Unit
NPL
National Physical Laboratory (UK); New Programming Language
NPM
Network Performance Monitor (IBM)
n-p-n (N-P-N)
negative-positive-negative
npn
negative-positive-negative
NPR
National Public Radio; Noise Power Ratio; Nonprocessor Request
NPS
Numerical Plotting System
NPSI
NCP [Network Control Program] Packet Switching Interface (IBM)
NPSTN
National Public Switched Telecommunications Network
NPT
Network Planning Tool
NPU
Network Processing Unit
NQS
Network Queueing System

NRC
Nuclear Regulatory Commission (Washington, DC, US); National Replacement Character (ASCII); Network Routing Center; Noise Reduction Coefficient

nretn
nonreturn

NRFD
Not Ready For Data (IEEE)

NRI
National Research Institute

NRL
Normal Rated Load; Naval Research Laboratory (US Navy)

NRM
Normal Response Mode

NRP
Network Resource Planning

NRTZ
Non-Return to Zero (Preferred form is NRZ)

NRU
Network Resource Unit

NRZ
Non-Return to Zero (In transmission and recording of data, a method of encoding such data on magnetic tape)

NRZI
Non-Return to Zero Inverted (Method of encoding on magnetic tape)

ns
nanosecond(s) (Denoting 10^{-9} second[s]); nonsequenced

NS
New Signal; Network Support (IBM); Not Specified; Not Sufficient; Nonstandard

NSA
National Security Agency (DARPA)

NSAP
Network Service Access Point

NSC
National Supercomputer Center; Network Switching Center; Nodal Switching Center

NSD
National Service Division (IBM)

nsec
nanosecond(s) (Denoting 10^{-9} second[s])

NSF
National Science Foundation (US)

NSFNET
National Science Foundation Network

(NSF, US)

NSI
NASA Science Internet (NASA, US); Next Sequential Instruction; Nonstandard Item

NSL
Nonstandard Label

NSM
Network Security Module; Network Security Monitor; Network Services Manager

NSMB
National Standards Management Board (US)

NSN
NASA Science Network (NASA); National Stock Number

NSOS
N- [or Negative-] Channel Sapphire on Silicon

NSP
Network Services Protocol; Numeric Subroutine Package

NSR
Normal Service Request

NSTL
National Software Testing Laboratories

NSW
National Software Works

NT
Not True; Network Termination; Number of Tracks

NT-1
Network Terminator type One

NTA
National Telecommunications Agency

NTC
National Telecommunications Conference; Negative Temperature Coefficient

NTCA
National Telephone Cooperative Association

NTIA
National Telecommunications and Information Administration

NTIS
National Technical Information Service

NTN
National Telecommunications Network

NTO
Network Terminal Option (IBM)

NTP
  Network Terminal Protocol; Network Termination Processor
NTSC
  National Television Standards Committee
NTT
  Nippon Telegraph and Telephone
NTU
  Network Terminating Unit
NUA
  Network User Address; Network Users Association
NUI
  Network User Identification [or Identity] (CCITT)
NUL
  Null character (CCITT)

num
  number; numeric
nv
  nanovolt(s) (Denoting 10^{-9} volt[s])
NVRAM
  Non-Volatile Random Access Memory
NVT
  Network Validation Testing (AT&T); Network Virtual Terminal
NWD
  Network Wide Directory
NWS
  National Weather Service
NZT
  Non-Zero Transfer

O

o
open; operand; operation; operator; output (Symbol, used in the subscript); origin (Symbol)

O
Oxygen (Symbol); Output

o (O)
output

O&E
Operations and Engineering

O&M
Operations and Maintenance; Operation and Maintenance (DARPA)

O&R
Overhaul and Repair

OA
Office Automation; Operational Amplifier; Operational Analysis

OA&M
Operations, Administration and Maintenance

OABETA
Office Appliance and Business Equipment Trades Association

OAC
Office Automation Conference

OACS
Open Architecture CAD System (Motorola Inc, US)

OAF
Origin Address Field

OAM
Operations, Administration and Maintenance

OAP
Orthogonal Array Processor

OAR
Operand Address Register; Operations Analysis Report

OASYS
Office Automation System

OATS
Office Automation Technology Services (AT&T)

OB
Official Business; On Board; Output

Buffer; Output Bus

OBB
On-Board Buffer

OBD
On-Board Diagnostics

OBC
On-Board Computer

obj
object

OBO
Official Business Only

OBP
On-Board Processor

OBS
Optical Beam Scanner; Object-Based Systems

OC
Office Copy; Open Circuit; Open Connect; Optical Carrier; Open Collector; Output Computer

OCA
Open Communication Architecture

occ
occupation

OCC
Operator Control Command; Other Common Carrier

OCCA
Open Cooperative Computing Architecture (NCR)

OCCF
Operator Communications Control Facility (IBM)

OCDD
On-line Call Detail Delivery (AT&T)

OCE
Open Collaborative Environment (Apple Computer Inc, US)

OCF
Operator Console Facility

OCL
Operation Control Language

OCO
Operations Control Operator

OCP
Operational Control Panel; Over-Current Protection; Output Control Program; Optical Character Printing

OCR
Optical Character Reader; Optical Character Recognition; Output Control Register

OCR-A
Optical Character Recognition - ANSI Standard [Font A]

OCR-B
Optical Character Recognition - ANSI Standard [Font B]

OCRA
Optical Character Recognition - ANSI Standard [Font A]

OCRB
Optical Character Recognition - ANSI Standard [Font B]

OCRE
Optical Character Recognition Equipment

OCRUA
Optical Character Recognition Users Association

OCS
Office Computing System; On-Card Sequencer; Optical Character Scanner; Operator Control Station (Burroughs Corp, US); Open Connect Server

oct
octal

OCTS
Open Cooperative Test System (NCR)

OCU
Operational Control Unit; Office Channel Unit

OD
Outside Diameter; Optical Density; Original Design; Output Disable

ODA
Operational Data Analysis; Office Document Architecture

ODB
Output Data Buffer

ODBC
Open Database Connectivity (Microsoft Corp, US)

ODBMS
Object-Oriented Database Management System

ODBR
Output Data Buffer Register

ODC
Operational Document Control; Output Data Control

ODD
Optical Data Digitizer

ODESY
On-Line Data Entry System

ODI
Open Driver Interface

ODP
Optical Data Processing; Open Distributed Processing; Original Document Processing

ODR
Optical Data Recognition; Output Definition Register

ODT
Open Desktop; Octal Debugging Technique

OE
Office Equipment; Output Enable; Opto-Electronic

OEF
Original Element Field (IBM)

OEM
Original Equipment Manufacturer

OEP
Original Element Processor

OER
Original Equipment Replacement

OF
On File

OFA
Optical Fiber Amplifier

OFC
Optical Fiber Communication; Oscillation Frequency Control (H-P)

ofl
overflow

OFN
Open File Number

OFR
Open File Report; Over Frequency Relay

OFU
Object File Utility

OG
OR Gate

OGL
Overlay Generation Language (IBM)

oh
overhaul; overhead

OH
Off Hook

OI
Operating Instructions

OIE
Optical Incremental Encoder

OIF
Office Interconnect Facility (IBM)

OIP
Optical Image Processor
OIPS
Optical Image Processing System
OIS
Operating Information System; Optical Image Sensor
OIT
Operations Integration Testing (AT&T)
OL
On Line; Open Loop; Operations/Logistics
OLC
On-Line Computer; Open-Loop Control
OLDB
On-Line Data Base
OLDC
On-Line Data Collection
OLO
On-Line Operation
OLP
On-Line Programming
OLPS
On-Line Programming System
OLQ
On-Line Query; Outstanding Load Queue (IBM)
OLR
Open Loop Receiver; Open Loop Response
OLT
On-Line Test
OLTS
On-Line Test System
OM
Office Master; Operating Memory; Operation Manual; Operations Manager
OMA
Open Management Architecture
OMAR
Optical Mark Reader
OMC
Operations Monitoring Computer; Optical Memory Card
OMEF
Office Machines and Equipment Federation
OMI
Open Messaging Interface; Operations Maintenance Instructions; Open MUMPS Interconnect (Massachusetts General Hospital, US)

OMPR
Optical Mark Printer
OMR
Optical Mark Reader; Optical Mark Recognition
OMRC
Optical Mark Reader Card
OMS
Operating Management System; Optical Modulation System
ONA
Open Network Architecture
ONI
Operator Number Identification; Optical Network Interface
ONS
Off-Normal Switch; Open Networking System (NCR)
ONX
Open Network Exchange
OOA
Object-Oriented Analysis
OOD
Object-Oriented Design
OOL
Object-Oriented Language; Operator-Oriented Language
OOP
Object-Oriented Programming
OOPS
Off-Line Operating Simulator; Object-Oriented Programming Style (IBM); Object-Oriented Programming System (DEC)
op
open; operand; operation; operator; output
OP
Open Position; Operation Procedure
Op Amp
Operational Amplifier
OPAL
Operational Performance Analysis Language
OPC
Operations Planning and Control
OPCOM
Operator Communications
opd
operand
oper
operational

OPEX
Operational Executive
opl
operational
OPM
Operations Per Minute; Optical Power Meter; Operator Programming Method
opnl
operational
opns
operations
opr
operand; operator
OPR
Optical Page Reader; Optical Pattern Recognition
OPREQ
Operation Request
oprnl
operational
OPSCON
Operations Control
OPSER
Operator Service
OPSREP
Operations Report
OPSYS
Operating System
opt
optimization; optimizer; optional
OPU
Operations Priority Unit
OQPSK
Offset Quaternary Phase Shift Keying
OQL
On-Line Query Language
OR
OR circuit or logic gate; On Return; Operations Research
ORA
Output Register Address
ORB
Object Request Broker
ORC
Operations Research Center
ord
order; ordinary
ordd
ordered
ORE
Output Register Empty

org
organization; origin
orgl
organizational
orgn
organization
ORNL
Oak Ridge National Laboratory (US)
OROM
Optical Read-Only Memory
OROS
Optical Read-Only Storage
ORSA
Operations Research Society of America
ORT
Operational Readiness Testing (AT&T); Ongoing Reliability Test (DEC)
os
overstocked
Os
Osmium (Symbol)
OS
Office System; Operating System (IBM); Optical Scanning; Order Sheet
OS/2
Operating System/2 (IBM, a multitasking operating system for IBM PC-compatible computers)
OS/VS
Operating System/Virtual Storage
OSA
Open Systems Architecture; Optical Spectrum Analyzer
OSAM
Overflow Sequential Access Method
osc
oscillator
OSC
Ohio Supercomputer Center (US)
OSCAR
Optically Scanned Character Automatic Reader; On-Line Supreme Court Automated Resource
OSD
Optical Scanning Device
OSDP
On-Site Data Processing; Operational System Development Program
OSE
Open Systems Environment; Operational Support Equipment

OSF
Open Software Foundation
OSHA
Occupational Safety and Health Administration (US)
OSI
Open Systems Interconnection; Office of Scientific Information (NSF); On-Screen Instrument(ation); Operating System Interface
OSI/CS
OSI [Open Systems Interconnection] Communications Subsystem (IBM)
OSINet
OSI [Open Systems Interconnection] Network
OSL
Open System Language
OSM
Operating System Monitor
OSME
Open Systems Message Exchange
OSN
Output Sequence Number
OSR
Operand Storage Register; Optical Scanning Recognition
OSS
Operational Support System; Operations Support System; Operating System Supervisor
OSSF
Operating System Support Facility
OST
Office of Science and Technology (Terminated 1973, functions transferred to National Science Foundation [NSF])
OSTD
Off-Site Technical Director
OSTP
Office of Science and Technology Policy (The White House, Executive Office of the President, Washington, DC, US)
OT
Over Time; On Time; On Track; Operating Time; Output Terminal
OT&E
Operational Test and Evaluation
OTA
Office of Technology Assessment (US)
OTCC
Operator Test Control Console

OTF
Optical Transfer Function
OTHR
Over-The-Horizon Radar
OTL
On-Line Task Loader; OSI [Open Systems Interconnection] Testing Liaison
OTM
Office of Telecommunications Management
OTP
Office of Telecommunications Policy (US); One-Time Programmable (TI)
OTPROM
One-Time Programmable Read-Only Memory
OTS
On-Line Terminal System
OTU
Operational Test Unit
OU
Operation Unit; Operational Unit
oupt
output
out
outgoing; output
OUTRAN
Output Translator
outstg
outstanding
ov
overflow
OV
Overvoltage
OVD
Optical Video Disk; Optically Variable Device; Over-Voltage Detector
ovf
overflow
ovfl
overflow
ovld
overload
OVLO
Over-Voltage Lock-Out
OVP
Over-Voltage Protection
ovr
overflow
OWM
Office Work Measurement
oz
ounce

163

P

p

pico (SI prefix denoting 10^{-12}); positive; pair; parallel; parity; page; program; primary (In the subscript); fluid density (Symbol); parallel; process; punch; peak (In the subscript); pound; point (often capitalized, however); plate [of an electron tube] (In the subscript); pitch; per

P

Peta (SI prefix denoting 10^{15}); Power (Symbol); Phosphorus (Symbol); Plate [of an electron tube] (Symbol); Pressure; Permeance (Symbol); Primary (Symbol); Point

P/A

Pilotless Aircraft; Programmer/Analyst

P/AR

Peak to Average Ratio

P&C

Purchasing and Contracting

P/F

Poll/Final (CCITT)

P&FA

Program and File Analysis

P/FM

PBX [Private Branch Exchange] Facilities Management (DEC)

p-MOS

p-channel [or positive] Metal-Oxide Semiconductor

p-n-p (P-N-P)

positive-negative-positive

P&O

Planning and Operations

P&R

Planning and Review

P/ROM

Programmable Read-Only Memory

P/S

Parallel to Serial

P&S

Planning and Scheduling

Pa

Pascal (Symbol, the SI unit of pressure or stress); Protactinium (Symbol)

pA

picoampere (A small unit of current denoting 10^{-12} ampere[s])

PA

Performance Analysis; Program Analysis; Program Access key (IBM); Program Address; Project Analysis; Public Address system; Preamble

PAAC

Program Analysis Adaptable Control

PABX

Private Automatic Branch Exchange

PAC

Performance Analysis and Control; Planned Availability Concept; Pneumatic Analog Computer; Polled Access Circuit; Primary Address Code; Project Analysis and Control; Programmable Array Controller; Public Access Computer

PACE

Performance And Cost Evaluation; Programmed Automatic Communications Equipment

PACM

Pulse Amplitude Code Modulation

PACS

Program Authorization Control System; Picture Archiving and Communication System

PaCT

PBX [Private Branch Exchange] and Computer Teaming

PACT

Pay Actual Computer Time; Private Access Communication Terminal; Programmed Analysis Computer Transfer; Programmed Automatic Circuit Tester

PACX

Private Automatic Computer Exchange

PAD

Packet Assembler/Disassembler; Packet Assembly/Disassembly; Positioning Arm Disk

PADLA

Programmable Asynchronous Dual Line Adapter

PADS

Personnel Automated Data System

PAF

Page Address Field; Production Assembly Facility

PAI
Parts Application Information; Precise Angle Indicator

PAL
Paradox Applications Language (Borland International, US); Precision Artwork Language; Process Assembler Language; Phase Alteration by Line; Programmable Array Logic; Postal Answer Line (USPS); Privileged Architecture Library (DEC); Public Access Line (FCC); Programmed Application Library

PAM
Panel Monitor; Patent Application Management; Pulse Amplitude Modulation; Primary Access Method; Pulse Address Modem

PAM/D
Process Automation Monitor/Disk

PAN
Personal Account Number

PAP
Phase Advance Pulse

par
parameter

PAR
Page Address Register; Parameter Request (CCITT); Program Address Register

param
parameter

PARASYN
Parametric Synthesis

parm
parameter

part
participating; participation

PARS
Passenger Airline Reservation System (IBM)

PAS
Phase Address System; Processed Array Signal

PASLA
Programmable Asynchronous Line Adapter

PASN-AL
Primary Address Space Name Access List (IBM)

PASS
Planning And Scheduling System; Private Automatic Switching System; Personal Access Satellite System (NASA)

pat
patent

PAT
Performance Analysis Tool (Intel Corp, US); Prediction Analysis Technique; Production Acceptance Testing; Programmer Aptitude Test

patd
patented

PATE
Programmed Automatic Test Equipment

PATPEND
Patent Pending

patt
patent; pattern

PAX
Parallel Architecture Extended (Intel Corp, US); Physical Address Extension; Private Automatic Exchange

PATX
Private Automatic Telegraph Exchange

PAU
Pattern Articulation Unit

Pb
Plumbum (Symbol, Latin name for lead)

PB
Page Buffer; Peripheral Buffer; Push Button

PBC
Parallel Board Connector; Peripheral Bus Computer; Personal Business Computer

PBE
Prompt By Example

PBIC
Programmable Buffer Interface Card

PBN
Physical Block Number

PBO
Push-Button Operation

PBP
Push Button Panel

PBS
Public Broadcasting System; Push Button Switch

PBW
Parts By Weight; Proportional Bandwidth

PBX
Private Branch Exchange

pc
percent; percentage; photoconductor

PC
Personal Computer; Printed Circuit; Profes-

sional Corporation; Path Control; Path Controller; Per Cent; Perspective Control; Phase Contrast; Photoconductive(tion); Plug Compatible; Program Call (IBM); Program Counter; Protocol Controller; Portable Computer; Printed Copy; Production Control; Production Cost; Pulse Counter; Project Control; Punched Card

PC²
Personal Computer Connection

PC-DOS
Personal Computer Disk Operating System (IBM)

PCA
Performance Coverage Analyzer (DEC); Personal Computer Architecture; Printed Circuit Assembly; Process Control Analyzer; Pulse Counter Adapter

PCAM
Punched Card Accounting Machine

PCAS
Punch Card Accounting System

PCB
Printed Circuit Board; Polychlorinated Biphenyl; Page Control Block; Process Control Block; Program Communication Block (IBM); Program Control Block

PCBA
Printed Circuit Board Assembly

PCBS
Printed Circuit Board Socket

PCC
Personal Computer Connection; Program Control Counter; Program Controlled Computer

PCCU
Punched Card Control Unit

PCD
Program Control Document

PCDP
Punched Card Data Processing

PCE
Process Control Equipment; Program Cost Estimate; Punched Card Equipment

PCEO
Personal Computer Enhancement Operation (Intel Corp, US)

PCET
Personal Computer Extended Technology

PCF
Packet Control Facility; Program Complex

File; Program Control Facility

pch
punch

PCI
Peripheral Controller Interface; Process Control Interface; Pulsed Current Injection; Protocol Control Information; Program Check Interruption; Programmable Communications Interface; Personal Computer Instrumentation; Personal Computer Interface

PCIOS
Processor Common Input-Output System

PCK
Phase Control Keyboard; Printed Control Keyboard

PCKB
Phase Control Keyboard; Printed Control Keyboard

PCKT
Printed Circuit

PCL
Portable Common Loops (DEC); Printer Command Language (H-P); Print Control Language; Process Control Language

PCLK
Program Clock

PCM
Photo Chemical Machining; Physical Connection Management; Protocol Converting Multiplexer; Punch(ed) Card Machine; Primary Control Program; Pulse Code Modulation; Plug-Compatible Mainframe; Plug-Compatible Manufacturer; Plug-Compatible Memory

PCMD
Pulse Code Modulation Digital

PCMM
Plug-Compatible Mainframe Manufacturer

PCMS
Punched Card Machine System

PCN
Personal Communications Network; Personal Computer Network

PCO
Program Controlled Output

PCOS
Process Control Operating System

PCP
Peripheral Control Pulse; Plug-Compat-

ible Peripheral; Primary Control Program (IBM); Primary Communications Processor; Program Change Proposal; Programmable Communications Processor

PCR

Page Control Register; Print Command Register; Program Change Request; Punched Card Requisition

PCS

Password Connection Security; Patient Care System (IBM); Print Contrast Signal; Personal Computing System; Personal Communications Services (FCC)

Personal Communications System; Personal Computer Support (IBM); Production Control System; Punched Card System; Programmable Communications Subsystem

PCSA

Personal Computing Systems Architecture (DEC)

pct

percent; percentage

PCT

Personal Communications Terminal; Peripheral Control Terminal; Personal Computer Terminal; Process Control Table (DEC); Program Control Table (IBM)

PCTR

Program Counter

PCU

Peripheral Control Unit (NCR); Power Control Unit; Peripheral Control Unit; Processor Control Unit; Program Control Unit; Programmable Control Unit; Punch Card Unit; Punched Card Utility

PCW

Program Control Word

PCX

Process Control Executive

Pd

Palladium (Symbol)

PD

Panel Display; Physical Distribution; Proportional/Derivative; Plasma Display; Product Design; Potential Difference; Pulse Dialing

PD&P

Project Definition and Planning

PDA

Parallel Data Adapter; Parallel Drive Array; Product Departure Authorization

PDAS

Process Design Analysis System

PDB

Physical Data Base

PDC

Parallel Data Communicator; Parallel Data Controller; Program Designator Code (DARPA); Photo-Data Card; Programmable Data Controller; Programmable Desk Calculator

PDCS

Parallel Digital Computer System; Processing Distribution and Control System

PDD

Past Due Date; Priority Delivery Date; Performance Design and Debug; Program Description Document

PDDS

Program Definition Data Sheet

PDES

Product Data Exchange Specification [or Standard] (IEEE)

PDF

Packet-Data FIFO [First In/First Out] buffer; Power Division Factor; Program Development Facility (IBM); Program Data File

PDGS

Product Design Graphics System (ITT)

PDI

Picture Description Instruction

PDL

Page Description Language; Program Design Language; Picture Description Language; Process Design Language; Programmable Data Logger

PDM

Physical Distribution Management; Physical Data Modeling; Practical Data Manager; Print Down Module; Program Design Manual; Push Down Memory; Pulse-Duration Modulation

PDMA

Pipelined Direct Memory Access

PDMM

Push Down Memory Modem

pdn

production

PDN

Public Data Network

PDP

Plasma Display Panel; Program Development Plan; Programmed Data Processor (DEC); Programmed Digital Processor

PDR

Physicians' Desk Reference (A publication); Page Data Register; Preliminary Data Report; Processing Data Rate

PDS

Partitioned Data Set (IBM); Personal Data System; Premises Distribution System (AT&T); Photo-Digital Store; Power Distribution System; Problem Definition/Solution; Product Development System; Professional Development Series; Program Data Set; Programmable Data Station

PDT

Peripheral Device Type; Parallel Data Transmission; Pushdown Transducer; Programmable Data Terminal

PDU

Protocol Data Unit; Plasma Display Unit; Power Distribution Unit

PDX

Program Development Executive

PE

Professional Engineer; Performance Enhancement (IBM); Parity Error; Page-End character; Phase Encoded(ing); Processing Element; Pulse Encoding; Plasma Enhanced(ment); Protocol Emulator (DEC)

PEBS

Pulsed Electron Beam Source

PEC

Program Element Code; Photoelectrochemical cell

PECL

Pseudo Emitter-Coupled Logic (Motorola Inc, US)

PEDS

Packaging Engineering Data System

PEE

Photoferroelectric Effect

pel (PEL)

picture element (Diminutive and variant of *pixel*, lower-case spelling most common, an older acronym)

PEL

Picture Element (Diminutive and variant of PIXEL, lower-case spelling most common, an older acronym); Permissible Exposure Level

PELTS

Personal Emergency Locator Transmitter

Service (FCC)

PEM

Performance Enhancement Module; Privacy Enhanced Mail; Program Element Monitor; Processing Element Memory

PEO

Program Executive Officer

PEP

Partitioned Emulation Program(ming) (IBM); Peripheral Event Processor; Peak Envelope Power; Paperless Electronic Payment

pF

picofarad (A small unit of capacitance denoting 10^{-12} farad[s])

pf

preferred

PER

Program Error Report; Program Event Recording; Program Execution Request

PERCOM

Peripheral Communications

perf

performance

perif

peripheral

PERM

Programmed Evaluation for Repetitive Manufacture

PERS

Performance Evaluation Reporting System

PERT

Program Evaluation Review Technique

PES

Program Execution System; Positional Error Signal

PESY

Peripheral Exchange Synchronization

PET

Process Evaluation Tester; Program Evaluator and Tester

PF

Page Format; Permanent File; Program Function key; Programmable Function key; Programmable Format

PFAM

Programmed Frequency Amplitude Modulation

PFB

Parallel Filter Bank; Prefetch Buffer

PFC

Power Factor Correction

PFDA
Pulse Frequency Distortion Analyzer
PFK
Program Function Key; Programmable Function Key; Programmed Function Keyboard
PFN
Permanent File Name
PFP
Prefetch Processor; Program File Processor
PFS
Programmable Frequency Standard
PFT
Page Frame Table
pg
page
PG
Power Gain; Program Generator
PGA
Pin Grid Array; Programmable Gate Array; Programmable Gain Amplifier
PGC
Programmed Gain Control
PGIA
Programmable Gain Instrumentation Amplifier
pgm
program
PGN
Performance Group Number
PGS
Program Generation System
PGT
Program Global Table
ph
phase
PH
Packet Handler (CCITT)
PHA
Pulse Height Analyzer
PHD
Parallel Head Disk
phse
phase
pi
pi [π] (The 16th letter of the Greek alphabet, the mathematical constant [3.14159...] that appears in a multitude of engineering formulas)
PI
Power Input; Processor Interface; Program

Interrupter(ion); Programmed Information; Programmed Instruction; Polarization Intensity; Proportional Integral
PIA
Peripheral Interface Adapter; Programmable Interconnect Array
PIC
Portable Industrial Computer; Power Integrated Circuit; Program Interrupt Control; Programmable Integrated Circuit; Program Interrupt Controller; Production Inventory Control
PICS
Personnel Information Communication System
PICU
Parallel Instruction Control Unit
PID
Process Identification number (DEC); Personal Identification Device; Personal Identification number; Pictorial Information Digitizer; Proportional/Integral/Derivative
PIE
Parallel Interface Element
PIK
Programmer's Imaging Kernel (ANSI)
PIL
Processing Information List
PIM
Processor Interface Module; Personal Information Manager; Process Inactivity Monitor (DEC)
PIN
Personal [or Personnel] Identification Number
PIO
Parallel Input-Output; Peripheral Input-Output controller; Process Input-Output; Processor Input-Output; Programmed Input-Output
PIOU
Parallel Input-Output Unit
PIP
Path Independent Protocol; Parallel Image Processor; Peripheral Interchange Program (DEC); Personal Identification Project
PIQ
Parallel Instruction Queue
PIT
Peripheral Input Tape; Programmable In-

terval Timer

PIU
Path Information Unit (IBM); Process Interface Unit

PIV
Peak Inverse Voltage

pix
picture

pixel (PIXEL)
picture element (Lower-case spelling most common, diminutive spelling is *pel*)

pk
peak

PK
Public Key

PK/PK
Peak to Peak

PKA
Public Key Algorithm

PKC
Position Keeping Computer; Public Key Cryptographic system

pkg
package

pl
plus

PL
Private Line; Production Language; Program Library; Programming Language

PL/360
Programming Language 360 (IBM)

PL c /1 (or PL/I)
Programming Language 1 [One] (IBM)

PL/E
Programming Language/Edit

PLA
Print Load Analyzer; Programmable Line Adapter; Programmed Logic Array (H-P)

PLANIT
Programming Language for Interaction and Teaching

PLANS
Programming Language for Allocation and Network Scheduling

PLAR
Private Line Automatic Ringdown

PLAS
Program Logical Address Space

PLATO
Programmed Logic for Automatic Teaching Operations

PLC
Programmable Logic Controller; Program Level Change; Power Line Conditioner (AT&T); Programmed Logic Controller

PLCP
Physical Layer Convergence Procedure (IEEE)

plcy
policy

PLD
Physical Logical Description; Programmable Logic Device

PLEX
Programming Language Extension

PLF
Page Length Field

PLI
Paper-Like Interface (IBM); Private Line Interface (DARPA)

PLIMS
Programming Language for Information Management System

PLL
Phase-Locked Loop

PLM
Passive Line Monitor; Programming Logic Manual; Pulse-Length Modulation

PLO
Phase-Locked Oscillator

PLP
Procedural Language Processor; Presentation Level Protocol (AT&T)

PLS
Private-Line Service; Programmable Logic Sequencer (TI)

PLU
Primary Logical Unit (IBM)

Pm
Promethium (Symbol)

PM
Preventive Maintenance; Performance Management; Performance Monitor; Presentation Manager (IBM); Permanent Magnet; Phase Modulation; Process Manual; Process Module; Program Memory

PMA
Performance Measurement and Accounting system; Physical Memory Address; Priority Memory Access; Protected Memory Address

PMACS
Project Management and Control System
PMAP
Procedure Map
PMAR
Page Map Address Register
PMC
Performance Management Computer;
Plug-In Memory Card
PMDF
Pascal Memo Distribution Facility (DEC)
PME
Processor Memory Enhancement
PMEM
Processor Memory
PMF
Performance Monitor Function; Parameter
Management Frame; Panel Modification
Facility (IBM)
PML
Physical Memory Loss; Programmable
Macro Logic
PMM
Pulse Mode Multiplex
PMMI
Packaging Machinery Manufacturers In-
stitute
PMMU
Paged Memory Management Unit
PMN
Program Management Network
PMOS
P-channel [or Positive] Metal Oxide Semi-
conductor
PMP
Performance Management Package; Pro-
gram Management Plan
PMRS
Performance Management and Recogni-
tion System
PMS
Project Management System (IBM); Per-
formance Management System; Process
Management System; Processor Memory
Switch; Program Management System;
Public Message Service
PMSS
Preventive Maintenance Scheduling Sys-
tem
PMT
Process Maturity Test (DEC); Prepare
Master Tape; Program Master Tape; Photo

Multiplier [or Photomultiplier] Tube
PMU
Portable Memory Unit; Power Manage-
ment Unit
PMX
Protected Message Exchange
pn (PN)
pseudonoise
PN
Packet Number; Peripheral Node;
Pseudonoise; Page Number; Processor
Number; Programmable Network; Posi-
tive-Negative; Performance Number; Pol-
ish Notation
PNCC
Partial Network Control Center
pnch
punch
pnd
pending
pnp
positive-negative-positive
PNX
Private Network Exchange
Po
Polonium (Symbol)
PO
Parity Odd; Planning Objectives; Power
On; Post Office; Pulse Output; Purchase
Order
POC
Power On Clear
PODAPS
Portable Data Processing System
PODAS
Portable Data Acquisition System
POE
Point Of Entry
POF
Point Of Failure; Plastic Optical Fiber;
Programmed Operator Facility
POGO
Program Oriented Graphics Operation
POI
Probability of Intercept; Plan Of Instruc-
tion; Program Of Instruction
pol
policy
POL
Problem Oriented Language; Procedure
Oriented Language

POM
Program Operation Mode
POMS
Process Operations Management System
(IBM); Professional Office Management
System; Plain Old Mail Service
PON
Power On; Passive Optical Network
POP
Picture-Outside-Picture; Point Of Pres-
ence; Point-Of-Purchase; Power On/Off
Protection
pos
position; positive
POS
Point Of Sale; Program Option Select
(IBM); Primary Operating System; Pro-
gram Order Sequence
POSE
Picture-Oriented Software Engineering
POSIX
Portable Operating System Interface stan-
dard (IEEE)
poss
possible
POST
Production Oriented Scheduling Tech-
niques; Point-Of-Sale Terminal
postp
postprocessor
postpro
postprocessor
POT
Picture Object Table
POTS
Plain Old Telephone Service (AT&T)
POWER
Performance Optimization with Enhanced
RISC [Reduced Instruction Set Computer]
(IBM); Priority Output Writers, Execution
Processors, and Input Readers
pp
pages; preprinted; preprocessor
PP
Parallel Processing; Push-Pull; Partial Pro-
gram; Peripheral Processor; Print Position
PP/E
Parallel Print/Extract
PPA
Parallel Port Adapter; Physical Page Address
PPB
PROM [Programmable Read-Only

Memory] Programmer Board
PPC
Parallel Poll Configure (IEEE); Platform
Position Computer; Personal Program-
mable Calculator; Print Position Counter;
Parallel Protocol Controller (TI); Produc-
tion Planning and Control; Program Plan-
ning and Control
PPBM
Pulse Polarization Binary Modulation
PPDL
Postscript Page Description Language
(Adobe Systems Inc, US)
PPDS
Personal Printer Data Stream (IBM)
PPE
Premodulation Processing Equipment
PPEP
Pen Plotter Emulation Program
PPF
Plain Paper FAX [Facsimile]
PPFA
Page Printer Formatting Aid (IBM)
PPI
Program Position Indicator; Programmable
Peripheral Interface; Plan Position Indi-
cator
PPIU
Programmable Peripheral Interface Unit
PPL
Polymorphic Programming Language; Pro-
cess-to-Process Link; Print Positions Per
Line; Program Production Library
ppm (PPM)
parts per million
PPM
Parts Per Million; Pulse Position Modu-
lation; Pit Position Modulation; Pulses Per
Minute; Planned Preventive Maintenance
PPN
Processor Port Network (AT&T)
PPOLL
Parallel Poll (IEEE)
PPP
Point-to-Point Protocol; Parallel Pattern
Processor
pps (PPS)
packets per second; pulses per second
PPS
Packets Per Second; Parallel Processing
System; Programmable Power Supply;
Programmed Processor System; Project

Planning and Control System

PPSFP
Parallel-Pattern Single-Fault Propagation (IBM)

PPT
Processing Program Table (IBM); Punched Paper Tape; Programmer Productivity Techniques

PPTR
Punched Paper Tape Reader

PPU
Parallel Poll Unconfigure (IEEE)
Peripheral Processing Unit; Primary Physical Unit (IBM)

PPX
Packet Protocol Extension; Private Packet Exchange

pr
print; printer; program

Pr
Praseodymium (Symbol)

PR
Pattern Recognition; Performance Report; Physical Record; Print Restore; Program Register; Progress Report

PR/SM
Processor Resource/Systems Manager (IBM)

PRA
Page Replacement Algorithm; Primary Rate Access; Program Reader Assembly

PRAM
Programmable Random Access Memory; Program Requirements Analysis Method

PRBS
Pseudo-Random Bit Sequence; Pseudorandom Binary Sequence

PRC
Printer Control; Programmed Route Control

prcessn
processing

pre
prefix

prec
precedent; preceding

prepak
prepackaging; prepacked

PRF
Pulse Repetition Frequency; Permanent Requirements File; Potential Risk Factor

prfm
performance

prgm
program

prgmr
programmer

pri
primary; priority

PRI
Primary Rate Interface (AT&T); Printer Interface; Processing Research Institute; Pulse Repetition Interval

PRIDE
Programmed Reliability in Design Engineering

PRIME
Prescribed Right to Income and Maximum Equity

PRINCE
Programmed International Computer Environment

prio
priority

PRISM
Personnel Record Information System for Management; Program Integrated System Maintenance

prl
parallel

PRM
Performance Report Message

prn
printer

PRN
Pseudorandom Number

PRNET
Packet Radio Network

prntg
printing

prntr
printer

pro
procedure; processor; procurement

proc
procedure; processing; processor

procd
procedure

PROCLIB
Procedure Library (IBM)

PROCOMP
Process Compiler

procsd
processed

PROCSEQ
Processing Sequence

PRODOC
Procedure Documentation
PROFS
Professional Office System (IBM)
prog
program; programmer; programming
PROGDEV
Program Device
progr
programmer; programming
proj
project
PROLOG
Programming in Logic (IBM)
PROM
Programmable Read-Only Memory
PROMICE
Programmable Read-Only Memory In-Circuit Emulator
PROMIS
Project Management Information System; Problem-Oriented Medical Information System
PROMISE
Programming Managers Information System
PROMPT
Project Management and Production Team Technique
PROP
Programmable Operator (IBM)
PRONTO
Programmable Network Telecommunications Operating System
prot
protect
PRR
Pulse Repetition Rate
PRS
Program Requirements Summary; Pseudo-random Sequence
prt
printer
PRT
Program Reference Table
prtr
printer
prty
priority
PRU
Packet Radio Unit; Printer Unit

ps
picosecond (Denoting 10^{-12} second[s])
PS
Packet Switch; Packet switching; Physical Sequential; Picture System; Power Supply; Program Start; Programming System
PS/1
Personal System/1 (IBM)
PS/2
Personal System/2 (IBM)
PS&DS
Program Statistics and Data Systems
PSAF
Print Services Access Facility (IBM)
PSAM
Partitioned Sequential Access Method
PSB
Parallel System Bus (Intel Corp, US); Program Specification Block
PSC
Pittsburgh Supercomputer Center; Production Scheduling and Control; Program Schedule Chart; Program Status Chart
PSCL
Programmed Sequential Control Logic
PSCS
Program Support Control System; Packet-Switched Communication System
PSD
Position Sensing Detector; Packed Switched Data
PSDS
Postal Source Data System (US Postal Service)
PSE
Packet-Switching Exchange; Project Support Environment (IBM)
psec
picosecond (Denoting 10^{-12} second[s])
PSF
Point Spread Function; Print Services Facility (IBM)
PSG
Programmable Sequence Generator (TI); Planning Systems Generator
psi (PSI)
pounds per square inch
PSI
Packetnet System Interface (DEC); Pounds per Square Inch; Personal Security Identifier; Program Status Information

psia
pounds per square inch, absolute
psig
pounds per square inch, gauge
PSK
Phase-Shift Keying
PSKM
Phase-Shift Keying Modem
PSL
Program Support Library
PSLI
Packet Switch Level Interface
PSM
Packet Switched Signaling Message; Power Supply Module; Program Support Monitor
psn
position
PSN
Packet Switched Network; Packet Switched Node
PSO
Programmable Storage Oscilloscope
PSP
Packet Switching Processor
PSPDN
Packet-Switched Public Data Network
PSR
Page Send-Receive; Program Status Register; Program Status Report
PSS
Packet-Switched Service (AT&T); Printer Storage System
PST
Pacific Standard Time; Partition Specification Table
PSTN
Public Switched Telephone Network (CCITT)
PSU
Packet Switching Unit; Peripheral Switching Unit; Power Supply Unit; Processor Storage Unit; Program Storage Unit
PSW
Program Status Word (IBM)
pt
point
Pt
Platinum (Symbol)
PT
Paper Tape; Performance Test; Printer Terminal; Processor Terminal; Programmable

Terminal; Processing Time
PTA
Paper Tape Accessory; Programmable Translation Array
PTBR
Punched Tape Block Reader
PTBX
Private Telegraph Branch Exchange
PTC
Positive Temperature Coefficient
ptd
printed
PTD
Parallel Transfer Disk [or Drive]
PTDA
Per Task Data Area (Intel Corp, US)
PTDOS
Processor Technology Disk Operating System
PTE
Page Table Entry
PTF
Phase Transfer Function; Program Temporary Fix (IBM)
PTH
Plated Through Hole (IBM); Project Team Head
PTI
Program Transfer Interface
PTIOS
Paper Tape Input/Output System
PTIP
Pluribus Terminal Interface Processor (DARPA)
PTL
Parameter Table Load
PTM
Phase Time Modulation; Pulse Time Modulation; Programmable Terminal Multiplexer; Pulse Transmission Mode
PTO
Public Telecommunications Operator
PTOS
Paper Tape-Oriented Operating System
ptout
printout
PTP
Paper Thin Package; Paper Tape Perforator; Paper Tape Punch; Processor To Processor
ptr
pointer; printer

PTR
Pulse Time Reference; Paper Tape Reader; Punched Tape Reader

PTS
Processor Transaction Server; Paper Tape System; Public Telephone Service

PTT
Post, Telephone and Telegraph

PTTC
Paper Tape and Transmission Code

PTU
Package Transfer Unit

PTV
Punched Tape Verifier

Pu
Plutonium (Symbol)

PU
Peripheral Unit; Physical Unit (IBM); Processing Unit

PUB
Physical Unit Block

PUC
Processing Unit Cabinet; Peripheral Unit Controller; Public Utility Commission (US)

PUCP
Physical Unit Control Point (IBM)

PUD
Physical Unit Directory

PUL
Program Update Library

PUMS
Physical Unit Management Services (IBM)

pun
punch; punctuation

PUP
Peripheral Unit Processor; Peripheral Universal Processor; Principal User Processing [or Processor]

PUT
Program Update Tape

PV
Path Verification; Programmable Via (IBM); Process Variable; Photovoltaic

PV-WAVE
Precision Visuals Workstation Analysis and Visualization Environment (Software from Precision Visuals Inc, US)

PVAX
Personal Virtual Address Extension (DEC)

PVC
Permanent Virtual Circuit; Polyvinyl Chloride; Program and Velocity Computer

PVD
Plan View Display; Physical Vapor Deposition

PVI
Programmable Video Interface

PVR
Process Variable Record; Photovoltaic Relay

PVT
Parameter Variable Table; Performance Validation Test

pw
password

PW
Printed Wiring; Private Wire; Processor Write; Pulse Width

PWA
Posted Write Array; Printed Wire Assembly

PWB
Printed Wiring Board

PWBA
Printed Wiring Board Assembly

PWM
Pulse Width Modulation

pwr
power

PWS
Programmer Work Station

Q

q

quarterly; query; queue; quotient; electrical quantity (Symbol, expressed in units of coulombs [C]); charge carried by an electron (Symbol); value of a quantum (Symbol); quart (Occasional abbreviation of)

Q

Figure of merit [or Quality factor] (i.e., of a capacitor, inductor, or LC circuit. Hence, refers to an electronic circuit efficiency figure); Electrical charge (Symbol); Selectivity (Occasional symbol for); Q Band (36 to 46 GHz band); Q Output (The reference output of a flip-flop); Quality (General)

Q&A

Questions and Answers (General); Questions and Answers (Software developed by Symantec Corp, US, for IBM PC-compatible computers, an integrated word processing program and flat-file database manager which is designed for novice users)

Q&D

Quick and Dirty

Q&RA

Quality and Reliability Assurance

QA

Quality Assessment; Quality Assurance

QADS

Quality Assurance Data System

QAM

Quadrature Amplified Modulation (Data transmission); Queued Access Method (Data Processing)

QAS

Question Answering System

QASK

Quadrature Amplitude Shift-Keying

QASP

Quality Assurance Surveillance Plan

QBD

Quasi-Bidirectional

QBE

Query By Example (Search technique)

QBT

Quad Bus Transceiver

QC

Quality Control; Queue Control; Quick Code; (Searchable field); Quantum Counter

QCB

Queue Control Block

QCC

Quality Control Center

QCD

Query Complexity Degree; Quantum Chromodynamics

QCIF

Quarter Common Intermediate Format (CCITT)

QCM

Quantitative Computer Management (IEEE)

QCPE

Quantum Chemistry Program Exchange

QCR

Queue Control Record

QCS

Quality Control Specification

QDPSK

Quaternary Differential Phase Keying (Telecommunications)

QE

Queue Empty; Quantum Efficiency; Qualifier Entry version (Searchable field)

QED

Quick Editor (Text editing software); Quantec Executive Package; Quantum Electrodynamics

QEL

Quality Element; Queue Element

QF

Quality Factor; Queue Full

QFA

Quick File Access

QFET

Quantum Field-Effect Transistor

QFM

Quantized Frequency Modulation

QFP

Quad Flat Pack

QIC

Quarter Inch Cartridge

QIL

Quad-In-Line

QIO
Query Input/Output; Queue(d) Input/Output

QISAM
Queued Indexed Sequential Access Method (IBM)

QL
Query Language; Quantum Leap

QL/1
Query Language/One

QLLC
Qualified Logical Link Control (IBM)

QLP
Query Language Processor

QLSA
Queue Line Sharing Adapter

QLV
Quantized Linear Velocity

QMF
Query Management Facility (IBM)

QMR
Qualitative Material Requirement

QN
Query Normalization

QNDE
Quantitative Non-Destructive Evaluation

QOS
Quality of Service

QPAM
Quadrature Phase and Amplitude Modulation

QPL
Qualified Parts [or Products] List

QPR
Quadrature Partial Response

QPRS
Quadrature channel modulation using PRS [Partial Response Signalling]

QPSK
Quadrature Phase-Shift Keying; Quaternary Phase-Shift Keying

QR
Quadratic Residues; Quality and Reliability

QRC
Quick Response Controller

QRL
Quick Relocate and Link

QRP
Query and Reporting Processor

QRSS
Quasi-Random Signal Sequence; Quasi-

Random Signal Source

QRT
Queue Run-Time; Quick Response Team

QS
Query Similarity; Query System; Queue Select; Quiet Series

QSA
Quad Synchronous Adapter

QSAM
Quadrature Sideband Amplitude Modulation; Queued Sequential Access Method (IBM)

QSL
Queue Search Limit

qt
quart; quotient

QT
Qualifier Type (Searchable field)

QTAM
Queued Telecommunications Access Method (IBM); Queued Terminal Access Method

QTAT
Quick Turn Around Time (IBM)

Qtest
Quantitative Test of performance

QTH
Queued Transaction Handling

QTP
Quality Test Plan

QTR
Quality Technical Requirement

QTS
Quantizer Threshold Spacing

qu
quality

QUAD
Quadrophonic sound recording; Quadruplex (Video recording technique)

qual
quality

QUALTIS
Quality Technical Information Service

QUALTA
Quad Asynchronous Local Terminal Adapter

QUAM
Quantized Amplitude Modulation

QUEL
Query Language

QUEST
Query Evaluation and Search Technique;

Quality Electrical System Test

QUICKTRAN

Quick FORTRAN (Computer programming language)

QUICO

Quality Improvement through Cost Optimization

QUIP

Quick-Inline Package (Intel Corp, US)
Quad In-Line Package; Query Interactive Processor; Quota Input Processor

QVT

Qume Video Terminal

QW

Quantum Well

QWERTY

QWERTY (Pronounced "kwertee", or "kwerty". A keyboard layout named for the 'six leftmost characters' in the top row of alphabetic characters on most keyboards. The standard typewriter keyboard layout, also used for computer keyboards.)

QWIP

Quantum Well Infrared Photodetector

R

r

radius; range; ratio; read; reader; receive; receiver; record; register; relation; reliability; report; request; research; reset; resistance; correlation coefficient (Symbol for); reverse; revolution; roentgen (Symbol); right; ring; routine

r (R)

radius; roentgen (Symbol); resistance (Symbol)

R

Radical (Symbol, chemistry); Reluctance (Symbol); Resistor (Symbol); Resistance (Symbol); Roentgen (Symbol); Solidly received message [or Message received] ["Roger"] (Radio-telegraph abbreviation for); Rise time factor in transistors

R&A

Reports and Analysis; Research and Analysis

R&D

Research and Development

R/D

Resolver to Digital converter

R&E

Research and Engineering

R-L

Right to Left

R&M

Reports and Memoranda

R/M

Reliability/Maintainability

R/M/W

Read/Modify/Write

R/MOS

Refractory Metal-Oxide Semiconductor

R&QA

Reliability and Quality Assurance

R&QC

Reliability and Quality Control

R&R

Reliability and Response

R&S

Reliability and Serviceability

R-S

Reset-Set; Run-Stop

R&T

Research and Technology

R/V

Recreational Vehicle; Research Vessel

R/W

Read/Write

R/WM

Read/Write Memory

R&X

Register and Indexed

Ra

Radium (Symbol)

RA

Random Access; Right Ascension (Astronomy); Ratio Actuator; Read Amplifier; Receiver Attenuation; Record Address; Reimbursement Authorization; Relative Address; Rotary Assembly; Return Address; Reliability Analysis

RAC

Radio Adaptive Communications; Reflective Array Compressor; Rapid Action Change; Reliability Analysis Center; Read Address Counter; Remote Asynchronous Concentrator; Resolved Acceleration Control

RACE

Random Access Computer Equipment; Research and Development for Advanced Communications in Europe (EC); Research and Development in Advanced Communications for Europe (EC); Results Analysis, Computation and Evaluation; Random Access Control Equipment (IEEE)

RACF

Resource Access Control Facility (IBM)

racon (RACON)

radar beacon

RACS

Random Access Communications System; Remote Access Computing System; Remote Automatic Calibration System (NASA); Remote Automatic Control System

rad

rad [radiation absorbed dose] (The amount of radiation that delivers 100 ergs of energy to 1 gram of a substance); radian (diminutive of); radio (diminutive of); radical (diminutive of); radix (diminutive of); radiac [radioactive detection, identification, and computation] (Diminutive of)

RAD
Random Access Device; Random Access Data; Random Access Disk; Rapid Access Device; Rapid Access Disk; Rapid Application Development; Repository and Application Development (IBM)

RADA
Random Access Discrete Address

RADACS
Random Access Discrete Address Communications System

radar (RADAR)
radio detection and ranging

RADAR
Radio Detection and Ranging; Receivable Accounts Data-entry And Retrieval

RADAS
Random Access Discrete Address System

RADEM
Random Access Delta Modulation

radiac
radioactive detection, identification, and computation (Diminutive is **rad**)

RADIC
Research and Development Information Center

RADIR
Random Access Document Indexing and Retrieval

RADIUS
Research and Development for Image Understanding Systems (DARPA)

RADL
Robotic Applications Development Laboratory (NASA)

RAF
Remote Access Facility; Requirements Analysis Form

RAG
ROM [Read-Only Memory] Address Gate

RAI
Random Access and Inquiry

RAID
Redundant Array of Inexpensive Disks

RAIR
Remote Access Immediate Response

RAIS
Range Automated Information System

RAL
Rapid Access Loop

RALA
Registered Automatic Line Adapter

RALU
Register and Arithmetic Logic Unit

RAM
Random Access Memory; Relative Access Method (IBM); Remote Access Monitor; Remote Area Monitoring; Reliability, Availability and Maintainability

RAMAC
Random Access Method of Accounting and Control

RAMB
Random Access Memory Buffer

RAMD
Random Access Memory Device

RAMDAC
Random Access Memory Digital-to-Analog Converter

RAMIS
Rapid Access Management Information System

RAMM
Random Access Memory Module

RAMS
Random Access Measurement System

RANCOM
Random Communication Satellite

RAND
Research and Development

RANDAM
Random Access Non-destructive Advanced Memory

RAP
Random Access Program; Relational Associative Processor; Remote-Access Point; Resident Assembler Program

RAPID
Relative Address Programming Implementation Device; Reusable ADA Products for Information Systems Development (DOD); Remote Access Planning for Institutional Development; Retrieval And Processing Information for Display; Retrieval And Production for Integrated Data; Retrieval through Automated Publication and Information Digest

RAPIDS
Rapid Automated Problem Identification System

RAPPI
Random Access Plan Position Indicator

RAPS
Retrieval Analysis and Presentation System

RAPTAP
Random Access Parallel Tape

RAR
Return Address Register

RARP
Reverse Address Resolution Protocol

RAS
Reliability, Availability, Serviceability (IBM); Requirements Audit System; Row Address Select [or Strobe]

RASI
Reliability, Availability, Serviceability and Improvability

RASIS
Reliability, Availability, Serviceability, Integrity and Security

RASP
Remote Access Switching and Patching; Retrieval And Sort Processor

RASSR
Reliable Advanced Solid-State Radar (TI)

RASTAC
Random Access Storage and Control

RASTAD
Random Access Storage and Display

RAT
Remote Area Terminal

RATC
Rate-Aided Tracking Computer

RATFOR
Rational FORTRAN

RATO
Rocket-Assisted Take-Off (USAF)

RAVE
Random Access Video Editing; Random Access Viewing Equipment; Real-time Audio/Video Environment

RAW
Read After Write

RAX
Random Access; Remote Access; Rural Automatic Exchange

Rb
Rubidium (Symbol)

RB
Relay Block; Request Block; Return to Bias

RBA
Relative Byte Address

RBBS
Remote Bulletin Board Service

RBE
Remote Batch Entry

RBF
Remote Batch Facility

RBHC
Regional Bell Holding Company(ies)

RBHCs
Regional Bell Holding Companies

RBI
Remote Bus Isolator

RBM
Real-time Batch Monitor; Relative Batch Monitor; Remote Batch Module; Repository-Based Methodology

RBOC
Regional Bell Operating Company(ies)

RBOCs
Regional Bell Operating Companies

RBS
Remote Batch System; Rules-Based System

RBT
Remote Batch Terminal

RBW
Resolution Bandwidth

RC
Reader Code; Receive Card; Remote Computer; Remote Control; Return Code; Resistance-Coupled; Resistance-Capacitance circuit; Resistor-Capacitor

RCA
Remote Control Adapter

RCAC
Remote Computer Access Communications Service

RCC
Remote Center Compliance; Remote Communications Complex; Reset Control Center

RCCAM
Remote Computer Communications Access Method

RCCB
Remote Controlled Circuit Breaker

rcd
record

RCE
Reliability Control Engineering; Remote Control Equipment

RCF
Remote Call Forwarding; Remote Console Facility (IBM)

RCI
Remote Control Interface

RCIU
Remote Computer Interface Unit

rcl
recall

RCL
Resistance-Capacitance-Inductance circuit; Reliability Control Level

RCM
Remote Control Module

RCN
Record Control Number; Report Control Number

RCP
Receive Clock Pulse; Remote Control Panel; Recognition and Control Processor; Remote Communications Processor

RCS
Radar Cross-Section; Radio Command System; Reaction Control System [or Subsystem] (IEEE); Reloadable Control Storage; Remote Computing Service; Remote Control Switch; Remote Control System; Reentry Control System

RCSDF
Reconfigurable Computer System Design Facility

RCT
Regional Control Task

RCTL
Resistor-Capacitor-Transistor Logic; Resistance-Coupled Transistor Logic

RCU
Remote Control Unit

rcv
receive

RCV
Remote Controlled Vehicle

rcvd
received

RCW
Return Control Word

rd
read; road

RD
Read Data; Receive Data; Request Disconnect (IBM); Reference Document; Register Drive; Required Data; Research and

Development

RD&D
Research, Development, and Demonstration

RD&E
Research, Development, and Engineering

RD/I
Research, Development, and Innovation

rda (RDA)
recommended daily allowances

RDA
Radar Data Acquisition; Remote Database Access (ANSI); Register Display Assembly

RDAU
Remote Data Acquisition Unit

Rdb
Relational database (DEC)

RDB
Relational Data Base [or Database]

RDBA
Remote Data Base Access

RDBMS
Relational Data Base Management System

RDC
Remote Data Collection; Remote Data Concentrator

RDE
Receive Data Enable

RDF
Record Definition Field; Recirculating Document Feeder

RDI
Remote Data Input

RDIU
Remote Device Interface Unit

rdj
readjustment

RDL
Report Definition Language; Resistor Diode Logic

RDM
Remote Digital Multiplexer; Remote Device Module

RDMS
Relational Data Management System

RDOS
Real-time Disk Operating System (Data General Corp, US)

RDP
Remote Data Processor

rdr
  reader
RDR
  Receive Data Register; Remote Digital Readout
RDS
  Raster Display System; Remote Data Services (IBM)
RDT
  Remote Date Transmitter; Resource Definition Table
RDTL
  Resistor Diode Transistor Logic
RDVM
  Remote Digital [or Data] Voice Multiplexer (AT&T)
rdy
  ready
Re
  Rhenium (Symbol)
RE
  Request Element
REAC
  Reeves Electronic Analog Computer
REACT
  Register Enforced Automated Control Technique
READ
  Real-time Electronic Access and Display
REAL
  Relocatable Assembler Language
REB
  Remote Ethernet Bridge
rec
  receipt; receive; record; recover
RECAP
  Reformatter Electronic Circuit Analysis Program
RECAPS
  Read Encode/Capture/Proof/Sort
recd
  received
RECMF
  Radio and Electronic Component Manufacturers Federation
recov
  recovery
red
  reduction
REDAC
  Real-Time Data Acquisition

ref
  reference
REFS
  Remote Entry Flexible Security
reg
  register; regular
REG
  Range Extender with Gain
regis
  register
ReGIS
  Remote Graphics Instruction Set (DEC)
REGIS
  Relational General Information System
regs
  regulations
rej
  reject
REJ
  Reject (CCITT)
REJEN
  Remote Job Entry
rel
  relative; release; relocatable
RELP
  Residual-Excited Linear Predictive coding
rem
  remark
REM
  Ring Error Monitor (IBM); Recognition Memory; Remark [or Remark statement] (MS-DOS)
REM statement
  Remark statement (In the BASIC programming language and the MS-DOS and OS/2 batch file languages, explanatory text [statement] that is ignored when the computer executes the commands. Also useful in a macro or source code.)
REMICS
  Real-Time Manufacturing Information Control System
REMS
  Rohm Electronic Message System
rep
  reply; representative
REP
  Re-Entrant Processor
REP-OP
  Repetitive Operation
repr
  representation

184

REPROM
Reprogrammable Read-Only Memory
REN
Remote Enable (IEEE)
REPO
Remote Emergency Power Off
req
request
reqd
required
reqs
requires
reqt
requirement
RER
Residual Error Rate; Reverse Explicit Route (IBM)
res
reserve; reset; restore
RES
Remote Entry Service
RESLOAD
Resident Loader
RESQ
Research Queuing [or Queueing]
resrt
restart
ret
return
RET
Resolution Enhancement Technique (H-P); Return (Alternate form for Carriage Return [CR])
retd
returned
RETMA
Radio Electronics Television Manufacturers Association
REU
Ready Extension Unit
rev
reverse; revolution
REVS
Requirements Engineering and Validation System
REX
Real-Time Executive Routine; Regression Expert
REXX
Restructured Extended Executor (IBM)
RF
Radio Frequency; Rating Factor; Read

Forward; Register File; Reporting File; Remote File; Reliability Factor
RFA
Remote File Access; Record File Address (DEC)
RFAM
Remote File Access Monitor
RFB
Reliability Functional Block; Recording For the Blind
RFC
Radio Frequency Choke; Request for Comment
RFD
Ready For Data
RFI
Radio Frequency Interference; Request for Information
RFID
Radio Frequency Identification
RFIU
Radio Frequency Interface Unit
RFMS
Remote File Management System
RFNM
Ready For Next Message
RFOT
Remote Fiber-Optic Terminal
RFP
Request for Proposal
RFQ
Request for Quotation
rfrsh
refresh
RFS
Ready for Sending; Random Filing System; Remote File Sharing; Remote File System (AT&T); Report Forwarding System
rfsh
refresh
RFT
Radio Frequency Terminal; Report Format Table (IBM); Request for Test
RGA
Regenerative Amplifier
RGB
Red-Green-Blue [or Red/Green/Blue; Red, Green and Blue] (A mixing model, or method of describing colors [the three primary color signals], used with many color monitors)

RGB display
Same as RGB monitor

RGB monitor
A color monitor that uses color "guns" for Red, Green, and Blue [RGB] to produce a high-quality picture.

RGIS
Remote Graphics Instruction Set

RGP
Raster Graphics Processor; Remote Graphics Processor

Rh
Rhodium (Symbol)

RH
Relative Humidity; Request/Response Header (IBM)

RHA
Records Holding Area

RHC
Radio High-density Circuit; Regional Holding Company (AT&T)

RHEED
Reflectance High Energy Electron Diffraction

RHS
Right Hand Side

RI
Radio Interference; Radio Inspector; Radio Influence; Radio Inertial; Radio Interface; Register Immediate; Reliability Index; Ring Indicator

RIC
Radar Interface Control; Read-In Counter; Remote Interactive Communications (Xerox Corp, US); Repeater Interface Controller (National Semiconductor Inc, US)

RIF
Reliability Improvement Factor; Routing Information Field

RIFF
Resource Interchange File Format

RIG
Raster Image Generator

RII
Routing Information Indicator (IEEE)

RIM
Request Initialization Mode (IBM); Radio Imaging Method; Ring Interface Module; Read-In Mode; Read Interrupt Mask

RIMS
Remote Information Management System; Resource Information Management System; Requestor-Oriented Information Management System

RIN
Relative Intensity Noise

RIOC
Remote Input/Output Controller

RIOS
Rotating Image Optical Scanner

RIOT
RAM Input/Output Timer; Real-Time Input-Output Transducer [or Translator]; Remote Input/Output Terminal

RIP
Random Input Sampling; Raster Image Processor; Routing Information Protocol

RIPE
Robot-Independent Programming Environment

RIQS
Remote Information Query System

RIR
Request Immediate Reply; ROM Instruction Register

RIS
Radiological Information System; Record Input Subroutine; Remote Information System; Rotating Image Scanner

RISC
Reduced Instruction Set Computer(ing); Remote Information Systems Center

RISLU
Reduced Instruction Set Logical Unit

RJE
Remote Job Entry (IBM)

RJET
Remote Job Entry Terminal

RJETS
Remote Job Entry Terminal System

RJEX
Remote Job Entry Executive

RJO
Remote Job Output

RJP
Remote Job Processing

RJS
Remote Job System

RL
Record Length

RLC
ROM Location Counter; Run Length Coding

RLE
Request Loading Entry

RLG
Research Libraries Group
RLIN
Research Libraries Information Network
RLL
Relocating Linking Loader; Run Length Limited
RM
Register Memory; Resource Manager; Routine Maintenance
RMA
Random Multiple Access; Reliability, Maintainability, Availability
RMATS
Remote Maintenance and Testing Service (AT&T)
RMAX
Range Maximum
RMC
Rack-Mounted Computer; Read Modify Cache signal
rmdr
remainder
RME
Request Monitor Entry
RMF
Reduced Magnetic Field; Resource Management Facility; Resource Measurement Facility (IBM)
RML
Radar Microwave Link; Relational Machine Language
RMM
Read-Mostly Memory; Read-Mostly Mode; Remote Maintenance Monitor
RMMU
Removable Media Memory Unit
RMON
Remote Monitor(ing); Resident Monitor
RMOS
Refractory Metal-Oxide Semiconductor
RMPI
Remote Memory Port Interface
rms (RMS)
root mean square
RMS
Random Mass Storage; Record Management Services (DEC); Record Management System; Resource Management System; Recovery Management Support; Root Mean Square

RMSD
Root Mean Square Deviation
RMSE
Root Mean Square Error
RMSR
Recovery Management Support Recorder
rmt
remote
RMTS
Remote Mode Transfer Switch
RMU
Remote Multiplexer Unit; Resource Management Unit
RMW
Read-Modify-Write
RMX
Remote Multiplexer
Rn
Radon (Symbol)
RN
Reception Node; Record Number (IBM); Requisition Number
RNAC
Remote Network Access Controller
RNC
Reflective Null Corrector; Request Next Character
RNET
Remote Network; Republic Network
rngt
renegotiate
RNID
Record Number Identifier (IBM)
RNMC
Regional Network Measurement Center
RNP
Remote Network Processor
RNR
Receive Not Ready (CCITT)
RNS
Residue Number System
RNSC
Reference Number Status Code
RO
Read Only; Receive Only; Regional Office; Register Output
ROBAR
Read-Only Back-up Address Register
ROC
Recovery Operations Center; Remote Operator's Console; Reliability Operating Characteristic

ROCR
Remote Optical Character Recognition

ROCS
Resource-Oriented Computer System

ROF
Remote Operator Facility

ROI
Region of Interest

ROLS
Remote On-Line Subsystem

ROM
Read-Only Memory

ROMM
Read-Only Memory Module

ROP
Receive-Only Printer

ROPP
Receive-Only Page Printer

ROS
Read-Only Storage; Real-time Operating System; Resident Operating System; Remote Operation Service

ROSAR
Read-Only Storage Address Register

ROSDR
Read-Only Storage Data Register

ROSE
Remote Operation Service Element; Retrieval by On-Line Search

rot
rotate

ROT
Remaining Operating Time

ROTH
Read-Only Tape Handler

ROTHR
Relocatable Over-the-Horizon Radar

ROTL
Remote Office Test Line (IBM)

RP
Reader-Printer; Reader/Punch; Receive Processor

RPC
Regional Processing Center; Remote Position Control; Remote Power Controller; Remote Procedure Call; Registered Protective Circuit; Rotary Power Conditioner

RPE
Remote PABX [Private Automatic Branch Exchange] Exchange; Remote Procedure Error (CCITT); Required Page-End character

RPG
Report Program Generator; Radar Product Generation

RPI
Rows Per Inch

RPL
Remote Program Loader; Robot Programming Language

rpm (RPM)
revolutions per minute

RPM
Remote Processing Module; Repeater Performance Monitor; Read Program Memory; Repeats Per Minute; Revolutions Per Minute

RPMC
Remote Performance Monitoring and Control

RPN
Real Page Number; Regular Processor Network; Reverse Polish Notation

RPOA
Recognized Private Operating Agency

RPQ
Request Price Quotation

RPROM
Reprogrammable Read-Only Memory

RPS
Ring Parameter Server (IBM); Real-time Programming System; Records Per Sector; Remote Printing System; Rotational Position Sensing

RPS/CMI
Real-time Programming System/Communications Monitor (IBM)

rpt
repeat

RPT
Records Per Track; Request Programs Termination

RPU
Regional Processing Unit; Remote Processing Unit

RQ
Repeat Request

RQBE
Relational Query By Example

RQL
Rejectable Quality Level

RQM
Real-time Quality Measurement

RR
Receive Ready [or Ready to Receive];
Register to Register; Research Report;
Return Register
RRA
Remote Record Access
RRAR
ROM Return Address Register
RRDS
Relative Record Data Set
RRN
Relative Record Number; Remote Request
Number
RRT
Relative Retention Time
RRTS
Remote Radar Tracking System
RS
Reader Stop; Real Storage; Record Sepa-
rator (CCITT); Register Select; Remote
Site; Request to Send; Recommended
Standard (EIA)
RS&I
Rules, Standards and Instructions
RS-*nnn*
Recommended Standard *nnn* (EIA, e.g.,
RS-422/423/449, which are standards for
serial communications with transmission
distances over 50 feet)
RSA
Remote Storage Activities; Requirements
Statement Analyzer; Rural Service Area
(FCC)
RSC
Remote Store Controller
RSCS
Remote Spooling Communication Sub-
system (IBM)
RSDP
Remote Site Data Processor
RSE
Record Selection Expression; Request
Select Entry; Removable Storage Element
RSET
Register Set
RSEXEC
Resource Sharing Executive system
RSM
Real Storage Management; Remote
Switch Module (AT&T); Remote System
Manager (DEC)

RSP
Reader/Sorter Processor; Record Select
Program
RSS
Real-time Switching System; Relational
Storage System
rst
reset
RST
Readability, Strength, Tone; Read Sym-
bol Table
RSTS
Resource Sharing Timesharing System
(DEC)
RSTS/E
Resource Sharing Timesharing System/
Extended (DEC)
RSX
Realtime resource Sharing Executive
(DEC)
rt
right
RT
Real-Time; Register Transfer; Remote
Terminal; Run-Time (IBM)
RTA
Real-Time Accumulator; Real-Time Ana-
lyzer; Resident Transient Area
RTAC
Real-Time Advisory Control; Real-Time
Adaptive Control
RTAM
Remote Telecommunications Access
Method
RTAP
Real-Time Applications Platform (H-P)
RTB
Real Time BASIC; Remote Token Bridge
RTC
Real-Time Clock; Real-Time Computer;
Remote Terminal Controller
RTCF
Real-Time Computer Facility
RTD
Resistance Temperature Detector
RTE
Real-Time Executive; Remote Terminal
Emulator; Run-Time Evaluator
RTEID
Real-Time Executive Interface Definition
(Motorola Inc, US)

RTES
Real-Time Executive System
RTF
Real-Time FORTRAN; Remote Tape Facility (DEC)
RTI
Real-Time Interface; Remote Terminal Interface
RTIC
Real-Time Interface Coprocessor (IBM)
RTIP
Remote Terminal Interface Package
RTJ
Return Jump
RTL
Real-Time Language; Run-Time Library (DEC); Register Transfer Level; Resistor-Transistor Logic
RTM
Real-Time Management; Real-Time Monitor; Register Transfer Module; Response Time Monitor
RTMS
Real-Time Memory System
RTMP
Routing Table Maintenance [or Management] Protocol
rtn
return; routine
RTN
Remote Terminal Network
RTO
Real-Time Operation
RTOS
Real-Time Operating System
RTP
Real-Time Processor; Remote Terminal Processor; Remote Test Processor; Rapid Thermal Processing; Run Time Package
RTPS
Real-Time Programming System
RTR
Real-Time Reliable; Response Time Reporting
RTS
Real-Time System; Remote Terminal System; Register Transfer Scan; Remote Terminal Stores; Request To Send
RTSI
Real-Time System Integration
RTT
Request To Talk

RTU
Real-Time UNIX; Remote Terminal Unit; Remote Transmission Unit
RTV
Real-Time Video
RTVS
Run Time Variable Stack
RTX
Real-Time Executive
RTZ
Return To Zero
Ru
Ruthenium (Symbol)
RU
Are You...?; Remote Unit; Request Unit (IBM); Response Unit (IBM); Request/Response Unit
RUF
Resource Utililazation Factor
RUG
Resource Utilization Graph
RUM
Resource Utilization Monitor
RUN
Running (DEC)
RUP
Remote Unit Processor
RUT
Resource Utilization Time
RVA
Relative Virtual Address
RVDT
Rotational Velocity/Displacement Transducer [or Transmitter]
RVI
Remote Visual Inspection; Reverse Interrupt
RVN
Requirements Verification Network
RVT
Resource Vector Table
RW
Read-Write
RWM
Read/Write Memory
rwnd
rewind
RWR
Read Writer Register; Radar Warning Receiver
RWX
Read Write Execute

Rx
  Receive [or Receiver]
rx
  receive [or receiver]
RXM
  Read/write Expandable Memory
RZ
  Return to Zero (IBM); Reset to Zero

RZM
  Return to Zero Mark
RZ(NP)
  Return to Zero [Non-Polarized] recording
RZ(P)
  Return to Zero [Polarized] recording

S

s
scalar; second; distance [or displacement] (Symbol); standard deviation (Symbol); screen [of an electron tube] (Symbol); sender; server; set; sign; single; slave; software; source; stack; state; storage; switch; switching; synchronous; system

S
Screen [of an electron tube] (Symbol); Sulfur (Symbol); Switch (Symbol); Shell [of a tube or semiconductor device] (Symbol); Sync; Elastance (Symbol); Secondary (Symbol); Siemens (Symbol); Entropy (Symbol); Sine; Schottky (Symbol); Supervisory (CCITT)

S-D
Synchro to Digital

S/D
Synchro-to-Digital converter

S&DP
Systems and Data Processing

S&F
Store and Forward

S/H
Sample and Hold

S&H
Sample and Hold

S&M
Service and Maintenance; Supply and Maintenance

S/M
Sort-Merge

S/N
Signal-to-Noise ratio; Serial Number

S-P
Serial to Parallel

S&P
Systems and Procedures

S-P/ROM
Slave Programmable Read-Only Memory

S/R
Send/Receive; Set/Reset; Storage/Retrieval

S&R
Storage and Retrieval

S-S
Satellite-Switched; Storage to Storage

S/S
Source/Sink; Start/Stop

S-SEED
Symmetric Self Electro-optic Effect Device (AT&T)

S&T
Scientific and Technical

S/TS
Simulator/Test Set

sa
semiannual(ly)

SA
Sample Array; Scaling Amplifier; Security Assistance; Servo Amplifier; Shift Advance; Signal Analyzer; Signal Attenuation; Source Address (IEEE); Stack Access; Store Address; Structured Analysis; Swing Arm; Synchro Amplifier; System Administrator; Systems Address; Systems Analysis; Systems Analyst

SA&D
Structured Analysis and Design

SA/MS
Special Access/Management System

SA-RT
Structured Architect-Real Time

SAA
Systems Application Architecture (IBM); Slot Array Antenna; Servo-Actuated Assembly; Satellite Attitude Acquisition

SAAM
Simulation, Analysis, And Modeling

SAB
Stack Access Block; System Advisory Board

SABE
Society for Automation in Business Education

SABM
Set Asynchronous Balanced Mode (CCITT)

SABME
Set Asynchronous Balanced Mode Extended

SABRE
Semiautomated Business Research Environment; Semi-Automatic Business-Related Environment (IBM)

SAC
Set Address [space] Control (IBM); Serv-

ing Area Concept; Servo Adapter Coupler; Slanted Array Compressor; Single Address Code; Special Area Code; Strategic Air Command; Storage Access Channel; Storage Access Control; Store And Clear

SACE
Semiautomatic Checkout Equipment

SACK
Selection Acknowledge

SACS
Secure Access Control System (AT&T); Simulation for the Analysis of Computer Systems

SAD
Silicon Avalanche Diode; Store Address Director; System Analysis Drawing

SADC
Sampling Analog-to-Digital Converter; Sequential Analog-Digital Computer

SADD
Semiautomatic Detection Device

SADF
Semi-Automatic Document Feeder

SADP
System Architecture Design Package

SADT
Structured Analysis and Design Technique

SAE
Society of Automotive Engineers; Self-Addressed Envelope; Stand Alone Executive

SAF
Segment Address Field; System Administration Facility

SAFER
Split Access Flexible Egress Routing (AT&T); Structural Analysis, Frailty Evaluation and Redesign

SAFRAS
Self-Adaptive Flexible Format Retrieval and Storage System

SAG
Systems Analysis Group

SAGE
Semi-Automatic Ground Environment

SAIM
Systems Analysis and Integration Model

SAL
Structured Assembly Language; Symbolic Assembly Language; Systems Assembly Language

SALINET
Satellite Library Information Network

SALT
Symbolic Algebraic Language Translator

SAM
Sequential Access Method (IBM); Service Attitude Measurement; Selective Automatic Monitoring; Sample and Analysis Management; Sequential Access Memory; Scanning Acoustic Microscope; Security Access Monitor (DEC); Semi-Autonomous Mobility; System Activity Monitor; System Analysis Machine; Stratospheric Aerosol Measurement; Serial [or Sequential] Access Memory ("Sequential" more common); Systems Adapter Module; Sort and Merge

SAMA
Scientific Apparatus Makers Association

SAMIS
Structural Analysis and Matrix Interpretation System

SAMMS
Standard Automated Material Management System (DOD)

SAMON
SNA [Systems Network Architecture] Applications Monitor (IBM)

SAMOS
Silicon-Aluminum Metal Oxide Semiconductor (IBM)

samp
sample

SAMS
Sampling Analog Memory System; Satellite Automatic Monitoring System; Storage Automation Management System; Student Aid Management System

SAMSON
Strategic Automatic Message-Switching Operational Network

SAN
Small Area Network

SANDS
Structural Analysis Numerical Design System

SAO
Select Address and Operate; Systems Analysis Office; Smithsonian Astrophysical Observatory

SAP
Share Assembly Program; Soon As Possible; Structural Analysis Program; Service Access Point; Service Advertising

Protocol; Symbolic Assembly Program

SAPI
Service Access Point Identifier

SAR
Stand Alone Restore; Segment Address Register; Source Address Register; Storage Address Register; Synthetic Aperture [or Array] Radar; Semiannual Report; Successive Approximation Register; Search and Rescue (US Coast Guard)

SARA
Systems Analysis and Resource Accounting

SARLANT
Search and Rescue, Atlantic (US Coast Guard)

SARM
Set Asynchronous Response Mode (CCITT)

SARME
Set Asynchronous Response Mode Extended

SARMIS
Search and Rescue Management Information System (US Coast Guard)

SARP
Standards And Recommended Practices

SARSIM
Search and Rescue Simulation (US Coast Guard)

SARTEL
Search and Rescue, Telephone (US Coast Guard)

SARTS
Switched Access Remote Test System

SAS
Statistical Analysis System; Switched Access System; Single Attachment Station; Service Activation System

SASE
Special Application Service Elements

SAT
Scholastic Aptitude Test; System Access Technique

SATF
Shortest Access Time First

SatLAN
Satellite Local Area Network

SATNET
Satellite Network

SATO
Self-Aligned Thick Oxide (TI)

SAU
Smallest Addressable Unit

SAW
Software Analysis Workstation; Surface Acoustic Wave

sb
sideband; standby

Sb
Stibium (Symbol)

SB
Stack Base; Straight Binary; Synchronous Bit

SBA
Shared Batch Area; Shipping and Billing Authorization

SBB
Store Back Buffer (IBM)

SBC
Single-Board Computer; Small Business Computer; Sub-Band Coding

SBCU
Sensor Based Control Unit

SBD
Structured Block Diagram; Schottky Barrier Diode

SBI
Synchronous Backplane Interconnect (DEC); Single Byte Interleaved

SBIR
Storage Bus In Register; Small-Business Innovative Research

SBM
Space Block Map

sbmdl
submodel

SBNR
Signed Binary Number Representation

SBR
Storage Buffer Register

SBS
Satellite Business Systems; Subscript Character; Silicon Bilateral Switch

SBU
System Bus Unit (NCR); Station Buffer Unit

sc
semiconductor

Sc
Scandium (Symbol)

SC
Satellite Communication; Satellite Computer; Selector Channel; Secondary Chan-

nel; Self Contained; Send Common; Set Clear; Short Circuit; Sequence Controller; Suppressed Carrier; Single Column; Signal Comparator; Source Code; Start Computer; Statistical Control; Storage Capacity; Symbolic Code; System Control; System Controller; Switched Capacitor

SCA
Source Code Analyzer (DEC); Security, Control, and Auditing system; Synchronous Communications Adapter; System Control Area

SCAD
Schedule, Capability, Availability, Dependability

SCADA
Supervisory Control And Data Acquisition

SCAM
Scheduling Content-Addressable Memory; Synchronous Communications Access Method

SCAN
Switched Circuit Automatic Network (AT&T); Schedule Analysis

SCANNET
Scandinavian Network

SCARS
Status, Control Alerting and Reporting System

SCAT
Symbolic Code Assembly Translator (IBM); Schottky Cell Array Technology

SCATRAN
Symbolic Code Assembly Translator

SCB
Stack Control Block; Station Control Block; Stream Control Block

SCBA
Self-Contained Breathing Apparatus

SCC
Separation Control Character (CCITT); Satellite Communications Concentrator; Satellite Communications Controller; Sequential Control Counter; Specialized Common Carrier; Serial Communications Controller [or Channel] (Motorola Inc, US); Security Commodity Code; Standards Council of Canada; System Control Center; Synchronous Communications Controller

SCCB
Software Configuration Control Board

SCCS
Source Code Control System

SCCU
Single Channel Control Unit

SCD
Serial Cryptographic Device

SCDC
System Control Distribution Computer

SCDP
Society of Certified Data Processors

SCDT
Special Committee on Data Transmission

SCEU
Selector Channel Emulation Unit

SCF
Satellite Control Facility; Switched Capacitor Filter

SCG
Secondary Command Group (IEEE)

sch
schedule; scheduler

SCI
Serial Communications Interface; Source Code Input; Stacker Control Instruction; System Control Interface

SCILIB
Science Library

SCIP
System Control Interface Package

SCL
Screen Control Language (DEC); Sequential Control Logic; System Control Language; Supervisory Control Language

SCM
Single Channel Monitoring; Software-Configuration Management; Small Core Memory; Station Configuration Management

scn
scanner

SCOM
System Communication

SCOPE
Scientific Committee on Problems of the Environment; Supervisory Control of Program Execution

SCORE
System Cost and Operational Resource Evaluation

SCP
Supervisory Control Program; Secondary Communications Processor; Service Con-

trol Point; System Control Program (IBM)

SCPC
Single-Channel-Per-Carrier

SCPI
Standard Commands for Programmable Instrumentation (IEEE)

SCR
Silicon-Controlled Rectifier; Scan Control Register; Single Character Recognition; Software Change Report; System Change Request

SCS
Secondary Clear to Send; Shared Communications Service; Small Computer System; Silicon-Controlled Switch; Society for Computer Simulation; SNA [Systems Network Architecture] Character String (IBM); System Communications Services

SCSI
Small Computer System Interface

SCSR
Single-Channel Signalling Rate

SCT
Suppressed Carrier Transmission; Service Counter Terminal; Step Control Table

SCU
Storage Control Unit (IBM); System Control Unit (DEC); Station Control Unit; Sequence Control Unit

SCUG
Smart Card Users Group

SCX
Selector Channel Executive

SD
Sample Data; Send Data; Start Delimiter; Single Density; Switch Driver; Standard Deviation; Systems Design

SDA
Signal Design and Analysis; Software Disk Array; Source Data Acquisition; Source Data Automation

SDAL
Switched Data Access Line

SDB
Segment Descriptor Block; Software Development Board; Storage Data Bus

SDBD
Software Data Base Document

SDBN
Software-Defined Broadband Network (AT&T)

SDC
Selected Device Clear (IEEE); Signal Data

Converter; Software Distribution Center; Synchro-to-Digital Converter

SDD
Stored Data Description; System for Distributed Databases

SDDL
Stored Data Definition Language

SDDN
Software-Defined Data Network (AT&T)

SDDS
Structured Description Data Set (IBM)

SDE
Source Data Entry

SDF
Screen Definition Facility (IBM); Software Distribution Facility (IBM); Software Development Facility

SDFS
Standard Disk Filing System

SDH
Synchronous Digital Hierarchy

SDI
Standard Disk Interconnect (DEC); Selective Dissemination of Information; Switched Digital service International (AT&T)

SDIF
SGML [Standard Generalized Markup Language] Document Interchange Format

SDILINE
Selective Dissemination of Information On-Line

SDIP
Shrink Dual In-Line Package

SDIS
Switched Digital Integrated Service (AT&T); Structured Description Index Set (IBM)

SDK
Software Development Kit (Microsoft Corp, US); System Design Kit

SDL
Specification and Description Language (CCITT); Software Design Language; System Design Language; System Directory List

SDLC
Synchronous Data Link Control (IBM)

SDLDS
Structured Description Log Data Set (IBM)

SDM
Selective Dissemination on Microfiche; Semiconductor Disk Memory; Sub-rate Data Multiplexing; Synchronous Digital Machine

SDMAC
Shared Direct Memory Access Controller

SDMSS
Software Development and Maintenance Support System

SDN
Software-Defined Network (AT&T); Synchronous Digital Transmission Network

SDNI
Software-Defined Network International (AT&T)

SDNS
Software-Defined Network Services (AT&T)

SDP
Source Data Processing; Service Delivery Point

SDR
Statistical Data Recorder; Storage Data Register; System Design Review

SDS
Software Development System; Switched Data Service (AT&T); Software Distribution Services

SDSF
System Display and Search Facility (IBM)

SDSI
Shared Data Set Integrity

SDSU
Switched Data Service Unit

SDU
Service Data Unit (AT&T); Synchronous Data Unit (AT&T); Signal Distribution Unit; Source Data Utility; Station Display Unit

SDX
Satellite Data Exchange

Se
Selenium (Symbol)

SE
Service Element; South-East (As in direction or location); Shield Effectiveness; Single End; Single Entry; Special Equipment; Software Engineering; Stack Empty; Standard Error; System Element; System Engineer; Systems Engineering; System Extension

SE/ME
Single Entry/Multiple Exit

SE/SE
Single Entry/Single Exit

SEA
System Extension Assist; Static Error Analysis

SEAM
Software Enhancement and Maintenance; Software Engineering and Management

sec
second; secondary; secant; section

SEC
Secondary Electron Conduction; Single Error Correcting

sech
hyperbolic secant

sech^{-1}
inverse hyperbolic secant

SECS
Severe Environment Controller System

SEE
Standard Error of Estimate; Systems Effectiveness Engineering; Simultaneous Engineering Environment; Software Engineering Environment

SEEA
Software Error Effects Analysis

SEED
Self-Excited Electro-Optic Device (AT&T); Self-Explaining Extended DBMS [Data Base Management System]; Software Engineering Environment Development

SEER
Systems Engineering, Evaluation, and Research

SEF
Software Engineering Facility

seg
segment

SEI
Software Engineering Institute

sel
select; selector

SEL
Surface-Emitting Laser

SELDAM
Selective Data Management system

SEM
Scanning Electron Microscope; Standard Electronics Module; Systems Engineering

Management
SEMI
Semiconductor Equipment and Materials
Institute
SEMICON
Semiconductor Conference
SEN
Software Error Notification
seq
sequence; sequential
SEQUEL
Structured English Query Language
ser
serial
SER
Sequential Events Recorder
SERLINE
Serials On-Line
SES
Severely Errored Seconds; Ship Earth Station; System External Storage; Strategic Engineering Support; Systems Engineering Services
SET
Set parameters (CCITT); Stepped Electrode Transistor
SETA
South Eastern Telecommunications Association (US)
SEU
Single-Event Upset; Source Entry Utility
sev
several
SF
Safety Factor; Select Frequency; Shift Forward; Stack Full; Signal Frequency; Superframe Format; Short Format
SFA
Segment Frequency Algorithm
SFB
Silicon Fusion Bonding
SFC
Sectored File Controller; Selector File Channel; Supercritical Fluid Chromatography
SFD
Start Frame Delimiter (IEEE); Software Functional Description
SFH
Simple Forwarding Header
SFIS
Small Firms Information Service

SFM
Sum Frequency Mixer(ing)
SFMS
Supercomputer Facilities Management Services
SFP
Security Filter Processor
SFS
Start of Frame Sequence; Symbolic File Support
sft
shift
SFU
Special Function Unit
SFUN
Special Functions library
SG
Scanning Gate; Signal Ground; Single Ground; Signal Generator; Specific Gravity; System Gain
SGD
Self-Generating Dictionary
SGEN
System Generator
SGML
Standard Generalized Markup Language
SGT
Segment Table
SGVS
Self-Guided Vehicle System
SH
Session Handler; Source Handshake
SHA
Sample and Hold Amplifier
SHF
Super High Frequency (3 to 30 GHz band)
shf
shift
shipmt
shipment
SHOP
Sequential Heuristic Optimization Programming
SHP
Standard Hardware Program
SHPi
Super High Pi
shr
share
si
superimpose

Si
Silicon (Symbol)

SI
Système International (International System of units); Scientific Instrument; Serial Input; Shift-In character (CCITT); Signal Interface; Single Instruction; System(s) Integration

SIA
Semiconductor Industry Association; Software Industry Association; Standard Interface Adapter

SIAM
Society of Industrial and Applied Mathematics

SIB
Screen Image Buffer; Serial Interface Board; System Interface Bus

SIC
Semiconductor Integrated Circuit; Special Interest Committee; Standard Industrial Classification system; Switchgear Interface Controller

SiCB
Silicon Circuit Board

SIDF
Standard Interchange Data Form

SIF
Storage Interface Facility

sig
signal

SIG
Special Interest Group

SIG/AH
Special Interest Group/Arts and Humanities (American Society for Information Science)

SIG/ALP
Special Interest Group/Automated Language Processing (American Society for Information Science)

SIG/BSS
Special Interest Group/Behavioral and Social Sciences (American Society for-Information Science)

SIG/CBE
Special Interest Group/Costs, Budgeting, and Economics

SIG/CR
Special Interest Group/Classification Research (American Society for Information Science)

SIG/DAT
Signal/Data

SIG/ES
Special Interest Group/Education for Information Science (American Society for Information Science)

SIG/FIS
Special Interest Group/Foundations of Information Science (American Society for Information Science)

SIG/IAC
Special Interest Group/Information Analysis Centers (American Society for Information Science)

SIG/ISE
Special Interest Group/Information Services to Education (American Society for Information Science)

SIG/LA
Special Interest Group/Library Automation and Networks (American Society for Information Science)

SIG/RT
Special Interest Group/Reprographic Technology (American Society for Information Science)

SIG/SDI
Special Interest Group/Selective Dissemination of Information (American Society for Information Science)

SIGACT
Special Interest Group on Automata and Computability Theory

SIGADA
Special Interest Group on Ada

SIGAPL
Special Interest Group on APL Programming Language

SIGBIO
Special Interest Group on Biomedical Computing
(American Society for Information Science)

SIGCOMM
Special Interest Group on Data Communication

SIGCOSIM
Special Interest Group on Computer Systems, Installation Management (ACM)

SIGCPR
Special Interest Group on Computer Personnel Research

SIGCS
Special Interest Group for Computers and Society (ACM)

SIGDOC
Special Interest Group for Systems Documentation

SIGFIDET
Special Interest Group on File Description and Translation (ACM)

SIGGRAPH
Special Interest Group on Computer Graphics

SIGI
System of Interactive Guidance and Information

SIGIR
Special Interest Group on Information Retrieval

SIGLASH
Special Interest Group on Language Analysis and Studies in the Humanities (ACM)

SIGMAP
Special Interest Group for Mathematical Programming

SIGMINI
Special Interest Group on Minicomputers (ACM)

SIGMOD
Special Interest Group on Management of Data

SIGOA
Special Interest Group on Office Automation

SIGOUT
Signal Output

SIGPC
Special Interest Group on Personal Computing (ACM)

SIGPLAN
Special Interest Group on Programming Languages

SIGREAL
Special Interest Group on Real Time Processing (ACM)

SIGSIM
Special Interest Group on Simulation

SIGSMALL
Special Interest Group on Small Computing Systems and Applications

SIGSOC
Special Interest Group on Social and Behavioral Science Computing (ACM)

SIGSOFT
Special Interest Group on Software Engineering

SIGSPAC
Special Interest Group on Urban Data Systems, Planning, Architecture, and Civil Engineering (ACM) Applications (ACM)

SIGTRAN
Special Interest Group on Translation

SIGUCCS
Special Interest Group for University and College Computing Services

SIL
Scanner Input Language; System Information Library

sim
simulator; simulation

SIM
Set Initialization Mode (IBM); Set Interrupt Mask; Synchronous Interface Module; System Information Management; Strategic Information Management

SIMCON
Simulation Control

SIMD
Single Instruction/Multiple Data processor

SIML
Simulation Language

SIMM
Single In-Line Memory Module

SIMOS
Stacked-gate Injection Metal Oxide Semiconductor

SIMOX
Silicon-Implanted Oxide

SIMP
Satellite Information Message Protocol

SIMPAC
Simulation Package

SIMSYS
Simulation System

simul
simultaneous

sin
sine

SIN
Symbolic Integrator

sin⁻¹
arc sine

SINAD
Signal-to-Noise-And-Distortion
sinh
hyperbolic sine
sinh^{-1}
inverse hyperbolic sine
SIO
Serial Input/Output; Start Input/Output
(IBM); Systems Interconnect Operation
(Intel Corp, US)
SIOC
Serial Input/Output Channel
SIOP
Selector Input/Output Processor
SIP
SMDS [Switched Multi-Megabit Data
Service] Interface Protocol; SMDS
[Switched Multi-Megabit Data Service]
Internet Protocol; Simulated Input Proces-
sor; Single In-line Package
SIPMOS
Single In-line Package Metal-Oxide Semi-
conductor
SIPS
Statistical Interactive Programming Sys-
tem
SIR
Segment Identification Register; Selective
Information Retrieval; Surface Insulation
Resistance
SIS
Scientific Information System; Strategic
Information System; Student Information
System; Software Integrated Schedule;
Standard Instruction Set; Superconductor/
Insulator/Superconductor (NASA); System
Interrupt Supervisor
SISD
Single Instruction, Single Data processor
SIT
Stand-alone Intelligent Terminal; Static In-
duction Transistor; System Initialization
Table (IBM)
SITC
Standard International Trade Classifica-
tion
SIU
System Interface Unit
SJ
Single Job
sk
skip

SKIL
Scanner Keyed Input Language
Skynet
Sky Network (AT&T)
SL
Section List; Signal Level; Simulation Lan-
guage; Standard Label; Systems Language
SLA
Serial Link Adapter (IBM); Shared-Line
Adapter; Stored Logic Array; Synchronous
Line Adapter
SLAM
Scanning Laser Acoustic Microscope;
Simulation Language for Alternative Mod-
eling; Symbolic Language Adapted for Mi-
crocomputers
SLB
Single-Layer Board
SLC
Selector Channel; Surface Laminar Circuit
(IBM); Systems Life Cycle; Subscriber
Line Charge
SLCU
Synchronous Line Control Unit
SLD
Super-Luminescent Diode; Synchronous
Line Driver
SLDM
Synchronous Long-Distance Modem
SLED
Surface Light-Emitting Diode
SLI
Synchronous Line Interface
SLIB
Source Library; Subsystem Library
SLIC
Subscriber Line Interface Circuit; Silent
Liquid Integral Cooler
SLIH
Second Level Interrupt Handler
SLIMS
Supply Line Inventory Management Sys-
tem
SLIP
Serial Line Internet Protocol; Symbolic
List Processor; Symmetric List Processor
SLM
Synchronous Line Module
SLP
Single-Link Procedure (CCITT)
SLR
Single-Lens Reflex; Storage Limits Reg-

201

ister
sls
sales
SLS
Source Library System; Station Logic Switch
SLSI
Super Large-Scale Integration
SLT
Solid-Logic Technology
SLU
Secondary Logic Unit; Serial Line Unit
Sm
Samarium (Symbol)
SM
Session Manager (IBM); Semiconductor Memory; Sequence Monitor; Service Manual; Set Mode; Surface Mount; Sort Merge; Structure Memory; Synchronous Modem
SMAC
Store Multiple Access Control
SMAE
System Management Application Entity
SMAP
System Management Application Process
SMART
Scheduling Management and Allocating Resources Technique; Systems Management Analysis, Research and Test
SMB
Sever Message Block (IBM); System Monitor Board; Systems Message Block; Structured Message Block
SMC
Storage Module Controller; System Monitor Controller
SMD
Single instruction/Multiple Data; Surface Mount Device; Storage Module Drive [or Device]
SMDI
Simplified Message Desk Interface
SMDR
Station Message Detail Recorder [or Recording] (AT&T)
SMDS
Switched Multi-megabit Data Service
SME
Society of Manufacturing Engineers
SMF
Single-Mode Fiber; Systems Management

Facility (IBM); Systems Measurement Facility
SMG
Screen Management Guidelines (DEC); System Management Group
SMI
Static Memory Interface; System Memory Interface; System Management Interrupt; Structure of Management Information
SMIP
Structure Memory Information Processor
SMIS
Society for Management Information Systems; Symbolic Matrix Interpretation System; Specific Management Information-passing Service
sml
small
SML
Symbolic Machine Language
SMM
Semiconductor Memory Module; System Management Mode (Intel Corp, US)
SMP
Shared Memory Processor; Symmetrical Multi-Processing (H-P); System Modification Program (IBM)
SMP/E
System Modification Program/Extended (IBM)
smpl
sample
SMS
Service Management System; Shared Mass Storage; Standard Modular System; Site Management Station (DEC); Storage Management Services; Systems Managed Storage (IBM)
SMT
Standard Mean Time; Systems Management Team; Surface Mount Technology; Storage Management Task
SMTP
Simple Mail Transfer Protocol
Sn
Stannum (Symbol)
SN
Sector Number; Sequence Number; Serial Number; Signal Node; Systems Network
SNA
Systems Network Architecture (IBM)

SNAC
SNA [Systems Network Architecture] Network Access Controller; Single Number Account Control

SNADS
Systems Network Architecture Distributed Services (IBM)

SNAFS
Systems Network Architecture File Services

sngl
single

SNI
Selective Notification of Information; Subscriber Network Interface; Systems Network Interconnection; SNA [Systems Network Architecture] Network Interconnection (IBM)

SNMP
Simple Network Management Protocol

SNOBOL
String-Oriented Symbolic Language

SNP
Statistical Network Processor

SNR
Signal-to-Noise Ratio

SNRM
Set Normal Response Mode

SNRME
Set Normal Response Mode/Extended

SO
Shift-Out character (CCITT); Send Only; Serial Output; Stop Order; System Operation; Systems Orientation

SOA
Start Of Address; Semiconductor Optical Amplifier; State Of the Art

SOAP
Symbolic Optimum Assembly Program (IBM)

SOB
Start Of Block

SOD
Serial Output Data

SODA
System Optimization and Design Algorithm

SOEMI
Serial Original Equipment Manufacturer Interface (IBM)

SOF
Start-Of-Format control; Start Of Frame

soft
software

Soft World
Software World (A publication)

SOG
Sapphire on Garnet

SOH
Start Of Header(ing) character (CCITT)

SOI
Silicon-On-Insulator

SOICS
Special Operations Improved Cryptographic System (ITT)

SOM
Start of Message; Satellite Office Microfilm

sonar (SONAR)
sound navigation and ranging

Sonet
Synchronous Optical Network

SONET
Synchronous Optical Network

SOP
Standard Operating Procedure

SOR
Specific Operational(ing) Requirement

SORM
Set Oriented Retrieval Module

SOS
Silicon On Sapphire (H-P); Station Operator Support

SOS CMOS
Silicon-On-Sapphire Complementary Metal-Oxide Semiconductor; Special Ordered Sets (IBM)

SOT
Start Of Text

SOUP
Software Updating Package

sp
special; single-pole; space

sp (SP)
single-pole; space

SP
Space (CCITT); Satellite Processor; Send Processor; Sequence Processor; Sequential Phase; Sequential Processing; Set Point; Signal Processor; Single-Phase; Special Purpose; Stack Pointer; Start Permission; Structured Programming; Switch Panel; System Parameter; Systems Procedures; System Product (IBM); Scratch Pad

SP3T
Single-Pole, Triple-Throw
SPA
Shared Peripheral Area; Single Parameter Analysis
SPAD
Scratch Pad Memory
SPAN
System Performance Analyzer
SPARC
Scalable Processor Architecture; Standards Planning and Requirements Committee (ANSI)
SPAU
Signal Processing Arithmetic Unit
SPB
Stored Program Buffer
SPC
Small Peripheral Controller; Stored Program Control; Switching and Processing Center; Statistical Process Control
SPCS
Service Point Command Service (IBM); Storage and Processing Control System
SPD
Serial Poll Disable (IEEE); Software Product Description; System Program Director
spdt (SPDT)
single-pole, double-throw
SPDU
Session Protocol Data Unit
SPE
Serial Poll Enable (IEEE); Single Processing Element; Special Purpose Equipment; System Performance Effectiveness
spec
specification
SPEC
Systems Performance Evaluation Cooperative (H-P)
SPECOL
Special Customer Oriented Language
SPEED
Systematic Plotting and Evaluation of Enumerated Data
SPF
Shortest Path First; Structured Programming Facility
SPI
Single Program Initiator (IBM); Shared Peripheral Interface; Single Processor Interface; Specific Productivity Index
SPIC
Spare Parts Inventory Control
SPICE
Simulation Program with Integrated Circuit Emphasis
SPID
Service Profile Identifier (AT&T)
SPIE
Society of Photo-Optical Instrumentation Engineers
SPIKE
Science Planning Interactive Knowledge Environment system (NASA)
SPL
Signal Processing Language; Sound Pressure Level; Simulation Programming Language; Structured Programming Language; System Program Loader; System Programming Language
SPM
Scratch Pad Memory; Scanning Probe Microscope(scopy); Source Program Maintenance; System Planning Manual; Self-Phase Modulation; Statistical Packet Multiplexing
SPMAR
Scratch Pad Memory Address Register
SPNS
Switched Private Network Service
SPOOL
Simultaneous Peripheral Operation(s) On-Line
SPP
Signal Processing Peripheral; Simultaneous Print/Plot; Special Purpose Processor; Sequenced Packet Protocol; Serial Pattern Processor
SPR
Statistical Pattern Recognition; Storage Protection Register; System Parameter Record
SPRINT
Strategic Program for Innovation and Technology Transfer
SPREAD
Supercomputer Project Research Experiment for Access and Development (Stanford University, US)
SPROM
Switched Programmable Read-Only Memory

SPS
Symbolic Program(ing) System; String Process System; Samples Per Second; Serial-Parallel-Serial; Standard Positioning Service; Standby Power Supply [or System]

SPSS
Statistical Package for the Social Sciences

spst (SPST)
single-pole, single-throw

SPT
Sectors Per Track; Symbolic Programming Tape; Structured Programming Techniques

SPU
Slave Processing Unit; System Processing Unit

SPX
Sequenced Packet Exchange

spx
simplex (Circuit)

sq
square

SQA
Software Quality Assurance

SQAP
Software Quality Assurance Procedure

SQD
Signal Quality Detector

SQE
Signal Quality Error

SQPSK
Staggered Quadriphase Shift Keying

SQR
Square Root

sr
senior; steradian; subroutine

Sr
Strontium (Symbol)

SR
Sample Rate; Slew Rate; Scientific Report; Service Record; Shift Register; Special Report; Speech Recognition; Status Register; Standard Requirement; Storage Register; Switch Register

SR-TB
Source-Routing Transparent Bridge

SRA
Systems Requirements Analysis; Source Routing Accelerator; Selective Routing Arrangement (AT&T)

SRAM
Static Random Access Memory; Sort Re-

entrant Access Method

SRB
Service Request Block; Scheduler Request Block (IBM); Single Route Broadcast

src
source

SRC
Stored Response Chain (IBM); Synchronous Remote Control; Supercomputer Research Center

SRCR
System Run Control Record

SRD
Software Requirements Document; Step Recovery Diode

SRDM
Sub-Rate Data Multiplexer (AT&T)

SRE
Society of Reliable Engineers

SREJ
Selective Reject

SREM
Software Requirements Engineering Methodology

SREP
Software Requirements Engineering Program; Source Representation

SRF
Self-Resonance Frequency; Software Recording Facility; Software Recovery Facility

SRIC
Switching-Regulator Integrated Circuit

SRL
Shift Register Latch

SRM
Short-Range Modem; Shared Resource Manager (H-P); Standard Reference Material; Storage and Resource Management system; System Reference Manual (DEC); Systems Resources Manager (IBM)

SRN
Software Release Notice (DARPA); System Reference Number

SRP
Shared Resources Processing

SRPI
Server-Requester Programming Interface (IBM)

SRQ
Service Request (IEEE)

SRR
System Requirements Review
SRS
Software Requirements Specification (NASA); Slave Register Set
SRT
Source Routing-Transparent (IBM); System Recovery Table (IBM)
SRTB
Source Routing-Transparent Bridge (IBM)
SRTM
Simplified Real-Time Monitor
ss
substructure
SS
Sampled Servo; Satellite Switched(ing); Signal-Signal; Solid State; Samples per Second; Satellite System; Signal Selector; Single Sideband; Start-Stop; Support System; System Specifications; System Supervisor
SSB
Single Sideband modulation; Social Security Bulletin
SSB AM
Single-Sideband Amplitude Modulation
SSBLT
Source Synchronous Block Transfer
SSC
Superconductor Super Collider (DOE); Station Selection Code
SSCP
System Services Control Point (IBM)
SSD
Solid-State DASD [Direct Access Storage Device]; Solid-State Disk; Solid-state Storage Device
SSDA
Synchronous Serial Data Adapter
SSDD
Single-Sided Double-Density (Refers to data storage on a floppy disk)
SSE
Special Support Equipment
SSEC
Selective Sequence Electronic Calculator (IBM)
SSES
Software Specification and Evaluation System
SSG
Symbolic Stream Generator

SSI
Small-Scale Integration; Synchronous Serial Interface; Synchronous Systems Interface
SSL
Software Specification Language; Storage Structure Language; System Specification Language
SSLC
Synchronous Single Line Controller
SSM
Small Semiconductor Memory
SSMA
Spread Spectrum Multiple Access
SSMP
Shared Symmetric Multiprocessor
SSN
Segment Stack Number; Social Security Number
SSOP
Shrink Small Outline Package (TI)
SSP
Scientific Subroutine Package (IBM); System Support Program (IBM); Service Switching Point (CCITT); System Status Panel
SSPA
Solid-State Phased Array (TI)
SSPLIB
Scientific Subroutine Package Library
SSR
Software Specification Review; Solid-State Relay; System Status Report
SSRS
Source Storage and Retrieval System
SSS
Solid-State Storage
SSSD
Single-Sided Single-Density (Refers to data storage on a floppy disk)
SST
Spread Spectrum Technology [or Transmission]; Super Sonic Transport; System Segment Table
SSTV
Slow Scan Tele-Video [or Television]
SSU
System Services Unit
SSW
Satellite-Switched
st
status

ST
Stream Protocol; Self-Test; Sequence Timer; Storage Tube; Straight Time; System Test

ST-LCD
Super Twist Liquid Crystal Display

sta
station; status

STA
Spanning Tree Algorithm

STACK
Start Acknowledge

STAIRS
Storage And Information Retrieval System (IBM)

STAM
Shared Tape Allocation Manager

STAMIS
Standard Army Management Information System (US Army)

stan
standard; standardization

STAR
Self-Testing And Repairing

STARS
Surveillance Target Attack System (USAF); Standard Time And Rate Setting; Status And Revision System

stat
status

STAT
Status request (CCITT)

STAT-PACK
Statistical Package

STATDSB
Status Disable

STATMON
Status Monitor (IBM)

STATPAC
Statistical Package

STATPAK
Statistical Package

STB
Strobe

STC
Serving Test Center; Start Conversion; Science and Technology Center (NSF); Society for Technical Communications (US); Society of Telecommunications Consultants (US)

STCK
Store Clock

std
standard

STD
Science and Technology for Development (EC); Subscriber Trunk Dialing

STDM
Statistical Time-Division Multiplexer; Synchronous Time-Division Multiplexer

STDMA
Slotted Time-Division Multiple Access

STE
Segment Table Entry; Signalling Terminal (CCITT); Special Test Equipment; Standard Test Equipment; Subscriber Terminal Equipment

STEP
Specification Technology Evaluation Program; Systematic Test and Evaluation Process

STESD
Software Tool for Evaluating System Designs

STF
Supervisory Time Frame

STFF
Schmitt Trigger Flip-Flop

STH
Satellite To Host

STI
Standard Tape Interconnect (DEC); Scientific and Technical Information

STIDC
Scientific and Technical Information and Documentation Committee (EC)

STIS
Science and Technology Information System (NSF)

STL
Schottky Transistor Logic

STM
Short Term Memory; Self-Test Module; Scanning Tunneling Microscope; Synchronous Transfer Mode

stmt
statement

STN
Switched Telecommunication Network; Scientific and Technical Network; Super-Twisted Nematic display

stnd
standard

STO
Segment Table Origin; Standing Order
STOKEN
Space Token (IBM)
STOL
Short Takeoff and Landing; Systems Test and Operation Language
STOQ
Storage Queue
stor
storage; store
STORET
Storage and Retrieval
STP
Shielded Twisted Pair; Standard Temperature and Pressure; Stop character; Signal [or Service] Transfer Point (AT&T)
stp
stop
STR
Segment Table Register; Synchronous Transmit(ter) Receive; Status Register
STRAIN
Structural Analytical Interpreter
STRAM
Self-Timed Random Access Memory
strd
stored
STRESS
Structural Engineering System Solver
STRIDE
Strategically Tiered Regionally Integrated Data Environment
strt
start
STRUBAL
Structured Basic Language
struc
structure
STRUDL
Structural Design Language
sts
status
STS
Synchronous Transport Signal
STSCI
Space Telescope Science Institute (Research Center, Johns Hopkins University, US)
STSI
Space Telescope Science Institute (NASA)

STSN
Set and Test Sequence Number
STSTB
Status Strobe
STSX
Synchronous Transport Signal Cross-Connect (CCITT)
STTL
Schottky Transistor-Transistor Logic
STU
Segment Time Unit; Secure Telephone Unit
STV
Subscription Television
STX
Start of Text (CCITT)
su
supply
SU
Selectable Unit; Signaling Unit; Storage Unit; Switching Unit
sub
subroutine; subscriber; substitute; subtraction; subtractor
SUB
Substitute Character (CCITT)
SUBS
Single-User Benchmark Set (DEC)
substn
substitution
SUI
Standard Universal Identifying Number
SUM
System Utilization Monitor
sup
supervisory
Super VGA
Super Video Graphics Array (Alternate form = SVGA)
supvr
supervisor
sur
surplus
SURANet
Southeastern Universities Research Association Network
SURP
Service and Unit Record Processor
SUS
Silicon Unilateral Switch
SUT
System Under Test

SV
Status Valid
SVA
Shared Virtual Area
svc
service
SVC
Supervisor Call (IBM); Switched Virtual Circuit
SVD
Simultaneous Voice/Data
SVDF
Segmented Virtual Display File
SVGA
Super Video Graphics Array
SVID
System "V" Interface Definition (AT&T)
SVP
Service Processor; Surge Voltage Protector
SVR
Super Video Recorder
SVS
Single Virtual Storage (IBM); Single Virtual System; Switched Voice Service (AT&T)
SVSPT
Single Virtual Storage Performance Tool
SVT
System Validation Testing
sw
software; switch
SW
South-West (As in direction or location); Specific Weight; Short Wave; Status Word
SWA
System Work Area
SWAMI
Software-Aided Multifont Input
SWAP
Standard Wafer Array Programming
swch
switch
SWE
Status Word Enable
SWI
Software Interrupt
SWIFT
Society for Worldwide Interbank Financial Telecommunication
SWIR
Short-Wave Infrared

SWL
Software Writer's Language; Short-Wave Listener
swp
swapper
SWP
Software Write/Protect
SWU
Switching Unit
sy
system
SYLCU
Synchronous Line Control Unit
sym
symbol; system
SYMGUG
Symbolic Debugger
symp
symposium
syn
synchronous
SYN
Synchronous Idle (CCITT)
sync
synchronization; synchronous
synch
synchronous
sys
system
SYSADMIN
System Administrator
SYSCOM
System Communication
SYSEX
System Executive
SYSGEN
System Generation (IBM)
SYSIN
System Input (IBM)
SYSLOG
System Log
SYSMON
System Monitor
SYSOUT
System Output
SYSRDR
System Reader
SYSRES
System Residence
syst
system; systematic

T

t

time (Symbol); ton; celsius temperature (Symbol for); terminal; troy system [or weight]; transformation; target; technical; tree; tension; period (Symbol for, i.e., unit, second); transaction

T

Temperature [or Celsius Temperature] (Symbol for); Transformer (Symbol); Tritium (Symbol); Tesla (Symbol); Tera (SI prefix denoting 10^{12}); Ton; True

t (T)

ton; temperature [or celsius temperature]

T0

Telecommunications Level 0 (AT&T)

T&A

Taken and Accepted

T-D

Transmitter-Distributor

T&E

Test and Evaluation

T/H

Track and Hold

T&H

Track and Hold

T&I

Test and Integration

T&M

Time and Materials

T&R

Transmit and Receive

T-R

Transmit-Receive

T/S

Terminal Server

T/T

Telegraphic Transfer

T&UG

Telephone and Utilities Group

Ta

Tantalum (Symbol)

TA

Tape Adapter; Technical Analysis; Technology Assessment; Terminal Access; Terminal Adapter (CCITT); Transfer Address

TAB

Tape-Automated Bonding; TAB Books (Publisher, a division of McGraw-Hill Inc, US)

TABS

Telemetry Asynchronous Block Serial protocol

TAC

Terminal Access Controller; Transistorized Automatic Computer; Tactical Advanced Computer; Telecommunications Associations Council

TACADS

Tactical Automated Data Processing System

TACOS

Tool for Automatic Conversion of Operational Software

TAD

Talk Address Device (IEEE); Terminal Address Designator; Time Available for Delivery; Transaction Applications Driver

TAF

Terminal Access Facility (IBM); Time And Frequency; Transaction Facility

TAG

Talk Address Group (IEEE); Transfer Agent; Technical Advisory Group; Time Automated Grid

TAGS

Time-Automated Grid System

TAL

Terminal Application Language; Transaction Application Language

TAM

Task Analysis Method; Terminal Activity Monitor (DEC); Telecommunications Access Method; Telephone Answering Machine; Terminal Access Method

TAMOS

Terminal Automatic Monitoring System

tan

tangent

tan⁻¹ tan^{-1}

inverse tangent (arctangent)

tanh

hyperbolic tangent

tanh⁻¹ $tanh^{-1}$

inverse hyperbolic tangent

TAP

Test Access Port; Terminal Access Processor; Time-sharing Assembly Program

TAPS
Terminal Application Processing System
TAR
Terminal Address Register; Test Accuracy Ratio; Track Address Register; Transfer Address Register; Turnaround Ratio
TARAN
Test And Repair [or Replace] As Necessary
TARP
Test And Repair Processor
TAS
Terminal Automation System; Test And Set
TASI
Time Assignment Speech Interpolation
TAT
Time and Attendance Terminal; Trans-Atlantic Telecommunications
TAT-X
Trans-Atlantic Telecommunications Cable
TAU
Trunk Access Unit
TAZ
Transient Absorption Zener diode
Tb
Terbium (Symbol)
TB
Terabyte (Denoting 10^{12} bytes); Transmitter-Blocker; Terminal Block; Time Base; Tone Burst
TBAM
Tone Burst Amplitude Modulation
TBE
Time Base Error
TBEM
Terminal Based Electronic Mail
TBI
Time Between Inspections
TBM
Tone Burst Modulation
TBR
Table Base Register
tc
telecommunications
Tc
Technetium (Symbol)
TC
Tabulating Card; Technical Committee; Terminal Computer; Terminal Concentrator; Terminal Control; Terminal Controller; Temperature Compensated(tion);

Transmission Control (CCITT); Test Conductor; Test Coordinator; Time Clock; Transfer Count; Trunk Control
TCA
Task Control Architecture; Task Control Area (IBM); Terminal Communication Adapter; Tele-Communications [or Telecommunications] Association
TCAM
Telecommunications Access Method (IBM)
TCAP
Transaction Capabilities Application (AT&T)
TCB
Thread Control Block (IBM); Trusted Computing Base (AT&T); Task Control Block; Transaction Control Block; Transfer Control Block
TCC
Technical Control Center; Technology Coordination Center
TCCC
Technical Committee for Computer Communications (IEEE)
TCE
Top Computer Executive; Thermal Coefficient of Expansion
TCIS
TELEX Computer Inquiry Service
TCK
Test Clock
TCL
Terminal Command Language; Terminal Control Language
TCM
Telecommunications Manager; Telecommunications Monitor; Thermal Conduction Module; Time Compression Multiplexing; Terminal, Computer and Multiplexer
TCMS
Telecommunications Management System
TCO/IP
Transmission Control Protocol/Internet Protocol
TCP
Tape Conversion Program; Task Control Program; Terminal Control Program; Transmission Control Program; Transmission Control Protocol; Transmitter Clock Pulse

TCPC
Telephone Cable Process Controller

TCS
Telecommunications Control System; Terminal Control System; Transaction Control System

TCT
Take Control--Transfer (IEEE); Task Control Table (IBM); Terminal Control Table; Transaction Control Table

TCU
Tape Control Unit; Telecommunications Control Unit; Terminal Control Unit; Timing Control Unit; Transmission Control Unit

TCXO
Temperature-Compensated Crystal Oscillator

TD
Tape Drive; Technical Data; Test Data; Time Delay; Track Data; Time Division; Transmit Data; Tunnel Diode

TDA
Tunnel Diode Amplifier

TDBI
Test During Burn-In

TDC
Tape Data Controller; Total Distributed Control

TDCAM
Table-Driven Computer Access Method (IBM)

TDCC
Transportation Data Coordinating Committee

TDCS
Time-Division Circuit Switching

TDD
Telecommunications Device for the Deaf (AT&T)

TDDL
Time-Division Data Link (Radio)

TDDM
Time-Division Digital Multiplexer

TDE
Time Displacement Error; Total Data Entry; Total Dynamic Error

TDG
Test Data Generator

TDHS
Time-Domain Harmonic Scaling

TDI
Test Data In; Time Delay and Integration; Telecommunications Data Interface

TDL
Test and Diagnostic Language; Transaction Definition Language

TDM
Time-Division Multiplexing; Template Descriptor Memory

TDM-VDMA
Time-Division Multiplex--Variable Destination Multiple Access

TDMA
Time-Division [or Time-Domain] Multiple Access; Tape Direct Memory Access

TDMD
Time-Division Multiplex Device (Radio)

TDMS
Time-shared Data Management System

TDO
Test Data Out

TDOS
Tape and Disk Operating System (IBM)

TDP
Test Data Package

TDPL
Top-Down Parsing Language

TDR
Tape Data Register; Time Delay Relay; Thermal Delay Relay; Time-Domain Reflectometry; Tone Dial Receiver; Transmit Data Register

TDRS
Tracking and Data Relay Satellite (NASA)

TDRSS
Tracking and Data Relay Satellite System (NASA)

TDS
Test Development Software; Transaction Distribution System

TDSP
Top-Down Structured Programming

TDWR
Terminal Doppler Weather Radar

TDX
Time-Division Exchange

Te
Tellurium (Symbol)

TE
Task Element; Terminal Equipment (CCITT); Technical Engineer; Text Edi-

tor; Trailing Edge; Thermoelectric; Tracking Error; Transverse Electric mode

TE1
Terminal Endpoint Type 1 (AT&T)

TE2
Terminal Endpoint Type 2 (AT&T); Terminal Equipment 2 (CCITT)

TEAM
Terminology, Evaluation and Acquisition Method

TEBOL
Terminal Business-Oriented Language

TEC
Transparent Electrical Conductor; Triple Erasure Correction

tech
technical

TECO
Text Editor and Corrector (DEC)

TED
Text Editor

TEI
Terminal Endpoint Identifier

tel
telegraph; telephone

TEL
Task Execution Language; Telephone; Terminal Emulation Language

telco (TELCO)
telephone company (Generic term)

tele
telegraph; telephone

telec
telecommunication

telecc
telecommunication

telecom
telecommunication

Telecom
Telecom (French satellite communications system)

telecomm
telecommunication

teleg
telegram

TELEMUX
Telegraph Multiplexer

Telex
Teleprinter [or Teletype] Exchange

TELEX
Teleprinter [or Teletype] Exchange (The international network of teleprinter sub-

scribers)

TELNET
Telecommunications Network

TELOPS
Telemetry On-Line Processing System (IBM)

TEM
Test Equipment Manufacturing; Transmission Electron Microscope; Transverse Electromagnetic Mode; Tunneling Electron Microscope

TEMA
Telecommunication Engineering and Manufacturing Association

temp
temporary

TEO
Technical Electronic Office (Data General Corp, US)

TEP
Twisted Wire Pair; Terminal Error Program

TEPE
Time-sharing Event Performance Evaluator

TEPOS
Test Program Operating System

teraops
tera operations per second (Denoting 10^{12} operations per second[s])

term
terminal; termination

TES
Terminal Emulation Server; Text Editing System

TeV
Tera electron-Volts (Denoting 10^{12} electron volt[s])

tex
telex; text

TF
Tape Feed; Terminal Frame; Time Frame; Transfer Function; Transmitter Frequency

TFA
Test Form Analyzer

TFE
Tetrafluoroethylene (Teflon)

TFM
Tape File Management

TFMS
Text and File Management System

TFS
Tape File Supervisor
TFT
Thin-Film Transistor
TFTP
Trivial File Transfer Protocol
tg
telegraph
TG
Task Group; Terminator Group; Test Group
TGA
Thermogravimetric Analysis
TGC
Terminator Group Controller
Th
Thorium (Symbol)
TH
Temporary Hold; Transmission Header
THD
Total Harmonic Distortion
THP
Terminal Handling Processor
THF
Tremendously High Frequency (300 to 3000 GHz band)
THG
Third Harmonic Generation
THT
Token Holding Timer
THz
Tera Hertz (Denoting 10^{12} Hertz)
Ti
Titanium (Symbol)
TI
Texas Instruments Inc (US); Test Instrumentation; Transmission Identification; Test Indicator; Terminal Instruction; Terminal Interface; Temporary Instructions; Tape Inverter; Technical Integration; Technical Information;
TIA
Task Item Authorization; Telecommunications Information Administration (US); Telecommunications Industry Association (US)
TIAC
Texas Instruments Automatic Computer (TI)
TIBTPG
Texas Instruments Bourdon Tube Pressure Gauge (TI)

TIC
Token-Ring Interface Coupler (IBM); Terminal's Identification Code; Time Interval Counter
TICCIT
Time-shared Interactive Computer-Controlled Information Television
TICR
Transmit Interrupt Control Register
TICS
Telecommunication Information Control System
TIDAR
Texas Instruments Digital Analog Readout (TI)
TIDMA
Tape Interface Direct Memory Access
TIF
Tape Inventory File; The Information Facility (IBM); Terminal Independent Format
TIGA
Texas Instruments Graphics Architecture (TI)
TII
Texas Instruments Incorporated (US)
TINDX
Texas Instruments, Inc Index Access Method (TI)
TIOLR
Texas Instruments Online Reporting System (TI)
TIPACS
Texas Instruments Planning and Control System (TI)
TIPC
Texas Instruments Pressure Controller (TI)
TIG
Tungsten-Inert Gas welding
TIGS
Terminal Independent Graphics System
TIH
Trunk Input Handler
TIM
TCP/IP [Transmission Control Protocol/Internet Protocol] Integration Module; Terminal Inactivity Monitor (DEC); Table Input to Memory
TIMS
The Institute of Management Science; Text Information Management System;

Thermal Infrared Multispectral Scanner; Transmission Impairment Measuring Set

TIO
Test Input/Output

TIOT
Task Input/Output Table

TIP
Terminal Interface Processor; Transaction Interface Processor

TIPS
Text Information Processing System

TIQ
Task Input Queue

TIR
Target Instruction Register

TIRS
The Integrated Reasoning Shell (IBM)

TIU
Terminal Interface Unit

TJID
Terminal Job Identification

tk
track

Tl
Thallium (Symbol)

TL
Target Language; Technical Library; Transaction Language; Transmission Level; Transmission Line

TLA
Transmission Line Adapter; Transmission Line Assembly

TLB
Table Look-aside Buffer; Translation Look-aside Buffer

TLC
Task Level Controller; Thin-Layer Chromatography

TLI
Transport Layer Interface

TLM
Transmission Line Matrix

TLMS
Tape Library Management System

TLN
Trunk Line Network

TLP
Telephone Line Patch; Transmission Level Point

TLU
Table Look-Up

TM
Tabulating Machine; Tape Mark; Termi-

nal Monitor; Test Mode; Test Model; Time Monitor; Transaction Manager; Transverse Magnetic mode

TMC
Tape Management Catalog (IBM)

TMF
Transaction Monitoring Facility

TMG
Test Message Generator

TMIS
Telecommunications Management Information System (US Gov); Technician Maintenance Information System

tml
terminal

TMOS
Telecommunications Management and Operations Support

TMP
Terminal Monitor Program (IBM)

TMS
Table Management System; Text Management System; Test Mode Select; Tape Management System; Tape Monitoring System; Transport Management System

TMSCP
Tape Mass Storage Control Protocol (DEC)

TMSL
Test and Measurement System Language (H-P)

TMU
Test Maintenance Unit; Transmission Message Unit

TMX
Transaction Management Executive

tn
ton

TN
Terminal Node; Test Number; Twisted Nematic (LCD); Transport Network

TNC
Transport Network Controller

TNM
Transmission Network Manager (IBM)

TNS
Transaction Network Service

to
turnover

TO
Technical Order; Test Operation; Time Out; Transfer Order

TOADS
Terminal-Oriented Administrative Data System

TOC
Table Of Contents

TOCS
Terminal-Oriented Computer System

TODS
Test-Oriented Disk System

TOF
Top Of File; Top Of Form

TOL
Test-Oriented Language

TOLTEP
Teleprocessing On-Line Test Executive Program

TOOL
Test-Oriented Operator Language

TOP
Technical and Office Protocol

TOPS
Time-sharing Operating System

TOS
Tape Operating System; Top Of Stack

TOSL
Terminal-Oriented Service Language

TOSS
Terminal-Oriented Support System

tot
total

tp
teleprinter; teleprocessing

TP
Teleprocessing; Teleprinter; Teletype Printer; Terminal Point; Terminal Packet (CCITT); Thermopile; Terminal Printer; Terminal Processor; Terminal Protocol; Test Procedure; Transaction Period; Transaction Processor; Transaction Processing; Transmission Priority (IBM)

TPA
Telephone Pioneers of America (Organization); Transient Program Area

TPAD
Terminal Packet Assembler/Disassembler

TPAM
Teleprocessing Access Method

TPAP
Transaction Processing Applications Program

TPD
Transaction Processing Description

TPDDI
Twisted Pair Distributed Data Interface

TPE
Twisted Pair Ethernet (Intel Corp, US); Transaction Processing Executive

TPG
Telecommunication Program Generator

tph
telephone

tpi (TPI)
track per inch

TPI
Twisted Pair Interface

TPL
Terminal Processing Language; Terminal Programming Language; Test Procedure Language; Transaction Processing Language

TPM
Teleprocessing Monitor; Total Passivation Module

TPNS
Teleprocessing Network Simulator

TPS
Thermal Protection System; Terminal Programming System; Transactions Per Second; Transaction Processing System

TPU
Telecommunications Processing Unit; Terminal Processing Unit; Text Processing Utility (DEC)

TQC
Total Quality Control

TQM
Total Quality Management

tr
track

TR
Tape Reader; Tape Resident; Test Request; Test Run; Terminal Ready; Technical Requirement; Technical Report; Technical Reference; Token Ring; Transfer Reset; Translation Register

tra
transfer

TRACE
Total Remote Access Center

TRAM
Test Reliability And Maintainability

tran
transaction; transmit

TRAN-PRO
Transaction Processing
trans
translator
TRANSET
Transportation Network Set
TransLAN
Transparent Local Area Network
TRC
Transmit/Receive Control Unit
TRC-AS
Transmit/Receive Control Unit-Asynchronous Start/Stop
TRC-SC
Transmit/Receive Control Unit-Synchronous Character
TRC-SF
Transmit/Receive Control Unit-Synchronous Framing
trf
transfer
TRF
Tuned Radio Frequency
Triac
Triode AC switch
TRIB
Transfer Rate of Information BITs
TRIM
Tailored Retrieval and Information Management
trk
track
TRL
Transistor-Resistor Logic
TRM
Terminal Response Monitor; Transmission Resource Manager
TRN
Token Ring Network
TROS
Transformer Read-Only Storage
trp
trap
TRQ
Task Ready Queue
TRR
Tape Read Register
TRS
Terminal Receive Side; Turbo Reflow Solder system
TRT
Token Rotation Timer

TRU
Tape Restore Unit
trx
transaction
ts
teletypesetting
TS
Technical Specification; Telecommunication System; Time Sharing; Time Switch; Transit Storage; Transport Station
TS/DMS
Time-Shared/Data Management System
TSA
Technical Support Alliance; Time Slot Access
TSAP
Transport Service Access Point
TSAU
Time Slot Access Unit
TSB
Terminal Status Block
TSC
Time Share Control; Transmitter Start Code
TSCA
Terminal Simulator Communications Area (IBM)
TSD
Transmission System Dependent (IEEE)
TSE
Time-Sharing Executive
TSF
Time to System Failure
TSI
Test Structure Input; Test System Interface; Time Slot Interchange
TSID
Track Sector Identification
TSIU
Telephone System Interface Unit
tsk
task
TSL
Time Series Language; Time Sharing Library; Tri-State Logic
TSM
Terminal Server Manager (DEC); Terminal Support Module; Time-Sharing Monitor (IBM); Time-Sharing Modulation
TSMS
Time Series Modeling System

TSNS
Telecommunications Services, Network Support (IBM)
TSO
Time-Sharing Option (IBM); Technical Standards Orders
TSODB
Time Series Oriented Database
TSOP
Thin Small-Outline Package
TSP
Time Series Processor; Terminal Simulator Panel (IBM); Technical Support Package
TSPL
Telephone Systems Programming Language
TSR
Translation State Register; Terminal Surveillance Radar; Temporary Storage Register; Telecommunications Service Request (DARPA); Terminate-and-Stay-Resident [program]
TSS
Task State Segment (Intel Corp, US); Time-Sharing Service; Time-Share System (IBM); Time-Sharing System; Time-Sharing Subsystem; Terminal Send Side; Transparent Semiconductor Shutter
TSSOP
Thin-Scaled Small-Outline Package (TI)
tst
test
TST
Transaction Step Task; Temporary Storage Table (IBM); Transparent Spanning Tree
TSX
Time-Sharing Executive
tt
teletype
TT
Teller Terminal; Touch Tone (AT&T); Transaction Telephone; Transaction Terminal; Tracking Telescope
TT&C
Tracking, Telemetry, and Command; Tracking, Telemetry, and Control
TTC
Tracking, Telemetry, and Command; Tracking, Telemetry, and Control (NASA)
TTC&M
Telemetry, Tracking, Command, and Monitoring; Tracking, Telemetry, Control and Monitoring
TTD
Temporary Text Delay
TTDR
Tracking Telemetry Data Receiver
TTF
Time to Time Failure
TTI
Transmitter Terminal Identification
TTL
Transistor-Transistor Logic; Through The Lens (Image Technology)
TTL/LS
Transistor-Transistor Logic/Low-power Schottky
TTLS
Transistor-Transistor Logic Schottky
TTP
Telephone Twisted Pair
TTR
Timed Token Rotation
TTRT
Target Token Rotation Time
TTS
Transmission Test Set
tty
teletype; teletypewriter
TTY
Telephone-Teletypewriter; Teletypewriter
TU
Tape Unit; Technology Utilization; Time Unit; Timing Unit; Transfer Unit; Transmission Unit; Transport Unit
TUC
Technology Utilization Center
TUD
Technology Utilization Division (NASA)
TUO
Technology Utilization Office (NASA)
TUP
Technology Utilization Program (NASA); Telephone User Part
TUT
Transistor Under Test
tv
television
TV
Transfer Vector
TVC
Television Camera; Thermal Voltage Conversion(ter)

TVI
Transient Voltage Indicator; Television Interference

TVM
Transistor Voltmeter

TVRO
Television Receive Only (A "receive only" satellite earth station)

TVS
Transient Voltage Suppressor

TVSS
Transient Voltage Surge Suppressor

tw
typewriter

TW
Terawatt (Denoting 10^{12} watts); Time Word

TWA
Transaction Work Area (IBM); Typewriter Adapter

TWR
Tape Writer Register

TWT
Traveling Wave Tube

TWX
Teletypewriter Exchange

tx
telex; transmit; transmitter

TX
Terminal Executive

Tx
Transmit; Transmitter

TXA
Terminal Exchange Area

txt
text

typ
type; typewriter; typical(ly)

typwrtr
typewriter

U

u
unified atomic mass unit (Symbol for);
micro (Typewritten or print substitute for
Greek letter μ [mu], denoting 10⁻⁶); unified; unit; universal; update; user

U
Uranium (Symbol); Unit; Universal set
(Symbol for); Union of sets (Symbol for);
Unnumbered (CCITT)

U/L
Upper/Lower

uA
microampere (Denoting 10⁻⁶ Ampere[s])

UA
Unnumbered Acknowledgement (CCITT);
User Area; User Agent

UAA
User Action Analyzer

UAC
Uninterrupted Automatic Control

UACTE
Universal Automatic Control and Test
Equipment

UADP
Uniform Automated [or Automatic] Data
Processing

UADPS
Uniform Automated [or Automatic] Data
Processing System

UADS
User Attribute Data Set

UAF
Unit Authorization File

UAI
User Application Interface

UAL
Unit Authorization List; User Adaptive
Language

UALI
Unit Authorization List Item

UAP
User Area Profile

UAR
Unit Address Register

UART
Universal Asynchronous Receiver/Trans-
mitter

UAT
User Accounting Table; Unaligned Address Transfer

UATE
Universal Automatic Test Equipment

UB
User Board

UBC
Universal Block Channel; Universal
Buffer Controller

UBHR
User Block Handling Routine

uc
unichannel

UC
Upper Case; Usable Control; Utilization
Control

UCA
Utility Communications Architecture;
Upper Control Area

UCB
Unit Control Block; Universal Character
Buffer

UCBT
Universal Circuit Board Tester

UCC
Uniform Commercial Code; Utility Control Console

UCD
Uniform Call Distribution

UCF
Utility Control Facility

UCG
Universal Command Group (IEEE)

UCI
Utility Card Input

UCIC
Universal Counter Integrated Circuit (H-
P)

UCM
Universal Communications Monitor

UCN
Uniform Control Number

UCP
Uninterruptable Computer Power

UCS
Universal Call Sequence; Universal Character Set; User Control Store

UCSB
Universal Character Set Buffer

UCSTR
Universal Code Synchronous Transmitter

Receiver
UCW
Unit Control Word
UD
Ultra-low Dispersion; Usage Data
UDAC
User Digital Analog Controller
UDAS
Unified Direct Access Standards
UDC
Universal Decimal Classification; Universal Digital Control
UDE
Universal Data Entry
UDF
User Danger Factor (DEC); User-Defined Function; Unit Development Folder; Utility and Data Flow
UDI
Universal Development Interface
UDL
Uniform Data Language; Universal Data Link
UDP
Uniform Delivered Price; UNIX Datagram Protocol; Universal Data Protocol; User Datagram Protocol
UDR
Utility Data Reduction
UDRC
Utility Data Retrieval Control
UDRO
Utility Data Retrieval Output
UDS
User-Defined Sequence
UDTS
Universal Data Transfer Service
UE
Unit Equipment; User Equipment
UET
Universal Emulating Terminal
UF
Utility File
UFAM
Universal File Access Method
UFC
Universal Frequency Counter
UFD
User File Directory
UFF
Universal Flip-Flop

UFI
User-Friendly Interface
UFM
User-to-File Manager
UFO
Unidentified Flying Object; User Files On-line
UFP
Utility Facilities Program
UG
User Group
UGT
User Group Table
UH
Unit Head
UHD
Ultra-High Density
UHECL
Ultra-High-Speed Emitter Coupled Logic
UHF
Ultra-High Frequency (300 to 3000 MHz band)
UHM
Universal Host Machine
UHV
Ultra-High Vacuum
uHz
microhertz (Denoting 10^{-6} Hertz)
UI
User Interface
UIC
Unreferenced Internal Count (IBM); User Identification Code (DEC)
UICP
Uniform Inventory Control Program
UIG
User Instruction Group
UIL
UNIVAC Interactive Language; User Interface Language
UIO
Universal Input/Output
UIOD
User Input/Output Devices
UIR
User Instruction Register
UIS
Universal Information Service (AT&T); Unit Identification System
UJCL
Universal Job Control Language

UJT
Unijunction Transistor
UK
United Kingdom
UKB
Universal Keyboard
UKITO
United Kingdom Information Technology
Organization
UL
Underwriters Laboratories (US); Upper
Limit; User Language
ULANA
Unified Local Area Network Architecture
ULC
Underwriters' Laboratories of Canada;
Uniform Loop Clock; Universal Logic Circuit
ULE
Unit Location Equipment; Ultra-Low Expansion
ULM
Universal Line Multiplexer; Universal
Logic Module
ULS
Unit Level Switchboard
ULSI
Ultra Large-Scale Integration
UM
User Module; Universal Monitor; Unscheduled Maintenance
UMASS
Unlimited Machine Access from Scattered
Sites
UMB
Upper Memory Block
UMF
Ultra Microfiche
UMLC
Universal Multiline Controller
UMOD
User Module
UMS
Universal Multiprogramming System
UNADS
UNIVAC Automated Documentation System
UNALC
User Network Access Link Control
UNAMACE
Universal Automatic Map Compilation
Equipment

UNCM
User Network Control Machine
uni
universal; university
UNI
User Network Interface
UNIBUS
Universal Bus
UNIDATS
Unified Data Transmission Service
UNIMOD
Universal Module
UNIPOL
Universal Procedure Oriented Language
UNIPRO
Universal Processor
UNISAP
UNIVAC Share Assembly Program
(Sperry Univac)
UNISTAR
UNIVAC Storage and Retrieval System;
User Network for Information Storage,
Transfer Acquisition, and Retrieval
Univac
Universal automatic computer
UNIX
UNIX operating system (AT&T)
UNL
Unlisten (IEEE)
UNMA
Unified Network Management Architecture (AT&T)
unprot
unprotect(ed)
UNT
Untalk (IEEE)
UOA
Used On Assembly
UOC
Universal Output Computer
UODDL
User-Oriented Data Display Language
UOS
Universal Operations Systems
up
uniprocessing; uniprocessor
UPA
Units Per Assembly
UPC
Universal Peripheral Control; Universal
Product [or Price] Code (Inventory control)

UPDATE
Unlimited Potential Data through Automation Technology in Education
UPI
Universal Peripheral Interface
UPIC
Universal Personal Identification Code
UPL
Universal Programming Language; User Programming Language
UPS
United Parcel Service Inc (US); Uninterruptible Power Supply [or System]; Universal Processing System
UPT
User Process Table
UPTP
Universal Package Test Panel
UPU
Universal Postal Union
UR
Unit Record; Unit Register; Utility Register
URC
Unit Record Control
URD
Unit Record Device (DEC)
UREP
UNIX RSCS [Remote Spooling Communications Subsystem] Emulation Program (DEC)
URL
User Requirements Language
URM
Unlimited Register Machine
URP
Unit Record Processor
us
underscore
US
United States [of America]; Underscore; Unit Separator (CCITT)
USA
United States of America
USACSC
United States Army Computer Systems Command
USAM
Unique Sequential Access Method
USAN
University Satellite Network

USART
Universal Synchronous/Asynchronous Receiver/Transmitter
USB
Upper Sideband
USC
User Service Center; Universal Serial Controller
USDA/CRIS
United States Department of Agriculture/Current Research Information System
USE
UNIVAC Scientific Exchange
usec
microsecond (Denoting 10^{-6} second[s])
USG
United States Government
USI
User/System Interface
USIA
United States Information Agency
USIC
United States Industrial Council; United States Information Center
USIO
Unlimited Sequential Input/Output
USIS
United States Information Service
USITA
United States Independent Telephone Association
USN
United States Navy; Universal Services Node
USNO
United States Naval Observatory (US Navy)
USOC
Universal Service Order Code
USOP
Ultra-Small-Outline Package
USPO
United States Post Office
USPS
United States Postal Service
USR
User Service Routine; Unsatisfactory Service Report (DARPA)
USRT
Universal Synchronous Receiver/Transmitter

UST
User Symbol Table
USVR
User Security Verification Routine (IBM)
UT
Universal Time; User's Terminal
UTA
User Transfer Address
UTC
Utilities Telecommunications Council (US)
util
utility; utilization
UTOL
Universal Translator Oriented Language
UTP
Unshielded Twisted Pair
UTR
Unprogrammed Transfer Register
UTS
Universal Time-sharing System
UUA
UNIVAC Users Association
UUT
Unit Under Test

uv
ultraviolet
UV
Ultraviolet; Undervoltage
UV-EPROM
Ultraviolet-Eraseable Programmable Read-Only Memory
UV-PROM
Ultraviolet Programmable Read-Only Memory
UVD
Undervoltage Detector
UVEPROM
Ultraviolet-Eraseable Programmable Read-Only Memory
UVL
Undervoltage Lockout; Ultraviolet Laser; Ultraviolet Light
UVPROM
Ultraviolet Programmable Read-Only Memory
UWA
User Working Area

V

v
variable; vector; velocity; verification; vertical; virtual;

V
Vanadium (Symbol); Volt; Voltage [or Potential] (Symbol); Volume (Symbol); Vertical; Reluctivity (Symbol for)

V/A
Video/Analog; Video/Audio

V&DA
Voice and Data Acquisition

V-F
Voltage-to-Frequency

V/F
Voltage to Frequency converter

V-H
Vertical-Horizontal

V/M
Volts per Mil

V/mil
Volts per Mil

V&R
Validation and Recovery

V/REG
Voltage Regulator

V+TU
Voice plus Teleprinter Unit

V/V
Volume/Volume

V&V
Verification and Validation

VA
Volt-Ampere; Value Analysis; Virtual Address

VAA
Voice Access Arrangement

VAB
Voice Answer-Back

VAC
Value-Added Carrier; Volts Alternating Current; Vector Analog Computer

VACC
Value-Added Common Carrier

VAD
Value-Added Dealer; Value-Added Distributor; Value-Added Driver; Voltmeter

Analog-to-Digital converter

VADAC
Voice Analyzer Data Converter

VADC
Video Analog to Digital Converter

VADE
Versatile Automatic Data Exchange

VADS
Value Added and Data Services

VAES
Voice-Activated [or Actuated] Encoding System

VAI
Value-Added Installer

val
valuation; value

VAN
Value-Added Network

VANA
Vector-Automated Network Analyzer

VANS
Value Added Network Service

VAP
Value-Added Process

VAPC
Vector-Adaptive Predictive Coding

var
variable; variation

VAR
Value-Added Remarketer [or Reseller, or Retailer]; Voice-Activated [or Actuated] Recorder

VAS
Value-Added Service; Value-Added Statement; Vector Addition System; Voice-Activated [or Actuated] System

VAST
Virtual Archival Storage Technology

VAT
Virtual Address Translator (IBM); Voice-Activated [or Actuated] Typewriter

VATE
Versatile Automatic Test Equipment

VAU
Vertical Arithmetic Unit

VAWS
Vector Arbitrary Waveform Synthesizer (H-P)

VAX
Virtual Address Extension (DEC)

VAXBI
Virtual Address Extension Backplane In-

terconnect (DEC)

VAXft
Virtual Address Extension, fault tolerant (DEC)

VAXSIM
Virtual Address Extension System Integrity Monitor (DEC)

VB
Voice Band

VBD
Voice Band Data

VBI
VAX Bus Interface (DEC

VBL
Vertical Block Line

VBN
Virtual Block Number (DEC)

VBOMP
Virtual Base Organization and Maintenance Processor

VBP
Virtual Block Processor

VC
Voltage Comparator [or Compensator]; Vector Control; Verification Condition; Virtual Call; Virtual Circuit; Virtual Computer; Volume Control

VCA
Voltage Control of Amplification [or Voltage-Controlled Amplifier]; Voice Connecting Arrangement

VCBA
Variable Control Block Area

VCC
Voltage-Controlled Capacitor; Video Compact Cassette

VCCS
Voltage-Controlled Current Source

VCD
Voltage Crossing Detector; Variable Capacitance Diode

VCDRO
Voltage-Controlled Dielectric Resonator Oscillator

VCF
Voltage-Controlled Filter; Voltage-Controlled Frequency; Verified Circulation Figure

VCG
Voltage-Controlled Generator; Verification Condition Generator

VCLO
Voltage-Controlled Local Oscillator

VCM
Voice Coil Motor; Voltage-Controlled Multivibrator

VCO
Variable-Coupled Oscillator; Voltage-Controlled Oscillator

VCP
Voltage-Controlled Potentiometer

VCPI
Virtual Control Program Interface (Intel Corp, US)

VCR
Video Cassette Recorder

VCS
VAXcluster Console System (DEC); Virtual Circuit Switch (AT&T); VMS [Virtual Memory System] Command Substitution; Validation Control System; Video Communications System; Voltage-Current-Sequence

VCSR
Voltage-Controlled Shift Register

VCT
Voltage Curve Tracer

VCTCA
Virtual Channel to Channel Adapter

VCTCXO
Voltage-Controlled Temperature-Compensated Crystal Oscillator

VCTV
Viewer-controlled Cable Television (AT&T)

VCU
VAX Calendar Utility (DEC)

VCV
Variable Compression Vector

VCVS
Voltage-Controlled Voltage Source

VCXO
Voltage-Controlled Crystal Oscillator

VD
Virtual Data; Vacuum Deposition; Voltage Detector

VDA
Visual Data Analysis; Vendor Data Article

VDAM
Virtual Data Access Method

VDB
Vector Data Buffer; Video Display Board

VDC
Volts Direct Current; Vendor Data Control; Video Display Controller; Voltage Doubler Circuit

VDD
Visual Display Data

VDDL
Virtual Data Description Language

VDDP
Video Digital Data Processing

VDE
Variable Display Equipment

VDETS
Voice Data Entry Terminal System

VDFM
Virtual Disk File Manager

VDG
Video Display Generator

VDI
Video Display Input; Video Display Interface; Visual Display Input; Virtual Device Interface

VDL
Virtual Database Level; Visible Diode Laser

VDM
Video Display Module; Voice-Data Manager (NCR); Voice-Data Multiplexer

VDP
Vertical Data Processing; Video Data Processor; Video Display Processor

VDPS
Voice Data Processing System

VDR
Vendor Data Request

VDRG
Vendor Data Release Group

VDS
Vendor Direct Shipment; Voice/Data Switch; Variable Depth Sonar

VDT
Video [or Visual] Display Terminal; Video Data Terminal

VDU
Video [or Visual] Display Unit

VE
Value Engineering; Virtual Environment

VEA
Value Engineering Audit

VEC
Vector Analog Computer

VEDR
Value Engineering Design Review

VEFCA
Value Engineering Functional Cost Analysis

VEM
Value Engineering Model; Vendor Engineering Memorandum

VENDAC
Vendor Data Control

VEP
Value Engineering Program

VEPC
Voice-Excited Predictive Coding

VEPR
Value Engineering Program Requirements

ver
verify

vert
vertical

VET
Value Engineering Training

VEX
Video Extension to X-Windows

VF
Variable Factor; Variable Frequency; Video Frequency; Visual Field; Voice Frequency; Vertical Form; Vector Facility (IBM); Vertical File; Vertical Flight (NASA); Visual Flight

VFB
Vertical Format Buffer

VFC
Voltage-to-Frequency Converter; Variable File Channel; Vertical Format Control; Voltage Frequency Channel

VFD
Vacuum Fluorescent Display

VFEA
VME [Virtual Memory Extended] Futurebus Extended Architecture

VFFT
Voice-Frequency Facility Terminal

VFL
Variable Field Length

VFMED
Variable Format Message Entry Device

VFO
Variable Frequency Oscillator

VFU
Vertical Forms Unit; Vertical Format Unit; Vocabulary File Utility

VG
Vector Generator; Voice Grade
VGA
Video Graphics Array
VGAM
Vector Graphics Access Method
VGCA
Voice Gate Circuit Adapters
VGPL
Voice Grade Private Line (AT&T)
VH
Vertical-Horizontal
VHD
Video High Density; Very High Density
VHDF
Very High Density Floppy diskette
VHDL
VHSIC [Very-High-Speed Integrated Circuit] Hardware Description Language
VHE
Very-High Energy
VHF
Very-High-Frequency (30 to 300 MHz band)
VHF/AM
Very-High-Frequency, Amplitude Modulated
VHF/DF
Very-High-Frequency Direction-Finding
VHF/FM
Very-High-Frequency, Frequency Modulated
VHFJ
Very-High-Frequency Jammer
VHFO
Very-High-Frequency Oscillator
VHFR
Very-High-Frequency Receiver
VHFT
Very-High-Frequency Termination
VHLL
Very-High-Level Language
VHM
Virtual Hardware Monitor
VHO
Very High Output
VHOL
Very-High-Order Language
VHS
Video Home System; Video Helical Scan format
VHSI
Very-High-Speed Integrated(tion)

VHSIC
Very-High-Speed Integrated Circuit
VHSOC
Very-High-Speed Optic Cable
VI
Variable Interval; Volume Indicator
VIA
Videotex Industries Association (US); VAX Information Architecture (DEC)
VIC
VME [Virtual Memory Extended]-Bus Interface Controller; Variable Instruction Computer; Virtual Interaction Controller
VICAM
Virtual Integrated Communications Access Method
VICAR
Video Image Communication And Retrieval
VICC
Visual Information Control Console
vid
video
VIDA
VAX IBM Data Access (DEC)
VIDAT
Visual Data Acquisition
VIDEO
Visual Data Entry On-Line
VIDPI
Visually Impaired Data Processors International (Organization)
VIEW
Virtual Interface Environment Workstation (NASA)
VIFF
Visualization and Image File Format
VIL
Vendor Item List; Vertical In-Line
VIM
Vendor Independent Messaging; Vendor Initial Measurement
VIMTPG
Virtual Interactive Machine Test Program Generator
VIN
Vehicle Identification Number; Vendor Identification
VINES
Virtual Network System
VIO
Video Input/Output; Virtual Input/Output

VIP
Value in Performance; Variable Information Processing; Variable Interest Plus; Vector Instruction Processor; Versatile Information Processor

VIPS
Variable Item Processing System

VIR
Vendor Information Request; Vendor Item Release

VIS
Vector Instruction Set; Verification Information System; Visible Infrared Spectrum; Voice Information Services

VISAM
Variable-length Indexed Sequential Access Method

VISCA
Video Systems Control Architecture

VISDA
Visual Information System Development Association

VISPA
Virtual Storage Productivity Aid

VITA
VME [Virtual Memory Extended] International Trade Association; Volunteers in Technical Assistance

VIURAM
Video Interface Unit Random Access Memory

VL
Vector Length

VLA
Very Large Area; Very Large Array

VLAM
Variable Level Access Method

VLAT
Very Large Array Telescope (NASA)

VLB
Very Long Baseline

VLBA
Very Long Baseline Array

VLCBX
Very Large Computer(ized) Branch Exchange

VLD
Visible Laser Diode

VLDB
Very-Large Data Base

VLDBS
Very-Large Data Base System

VLDS
Very Large Data Store

VLF
Variable Length Field; Very-Low-Frequency (3 to 30 kHz); Virtual Lookaside Facility (IBM)

VLFJ
Very-Low-Frequency Jammer

VLFR
Very-Low-Frequency Receiver

VLM
Virtual Library Manager

VLS
Virtual LAN Server; Virtual Linkage Subsystem

VLSI
Very-Large-Scale Integration

VLSIC
Very-Large-Scale Integrated Circuit

VLSW
Virtual Line Switch(ing)

VLT
Video Layout Terminal; Very Large Telescope

VLTP
Variable Length Text Processor

VM
Virtual Machine (IBM); Vertical Merger; Virtual Memory; Voice Mail

VM-Assist
Virtual Machine Assist (IBM)

VM/ESA
Virtual Machine/Enterprise Systems Architecture (IBM)

VM/IS
Virtual Machine/Integrated System (IBM)

VM/SP
Virtual Machine/System Product

VM/XA
Virtual Machine/Extended Architecture

VMA
Valid Memory Address; Virtual Machine Assist

VMAPS
Virtual Memory Array Processing System

VMB
Voice Mail Box

VMC
Virtual Memory Computer

VMCF
Virtual Machine Communication Facility

VME
Virtual Memory Extended; Virtual Memory Environment

VMEbus
Virtual Memory Extended bus (Motorola Inc, US)

VMF
Virtual Machine Facility

VML
Virtual Memory Level

VMM
Virtual Machine Monitor; Vector Matrix Multiplication

VMOS
Virtual Memory Operating System

VMR
Violation Monitor and Remover

VMS
Virtual Memory System (DEC); Voice Message System

VMT
Virtual Memory Technique

VMX
Voice Message Exchange

VNA
Vector Network Analyzer (H-P)

VNC
Voice Numerical Control

Vnet
Virtual network

VNET
Virtual Network

VOA
Voice Of America

VOB
Vacuum Optical Bench

voc
vocational

VOC
Variable Output Circuit; Volatile Organic Compound

vocab
vocabulary

VODACOM
Voice Data Communications

VODAT
Voice-Operated Device for Automatic Transmission

VOF
Variable Operating Frequency

VOGAD
Voice-Operated Gain-Adjusting Device

(NASA)

vol
volume

volt
voltage

VOM
Volt-Ohm-Milliammeter

VOS
Virtual Operating System; Voice-Operated Switch

VOTS
VAX OSI Transport Services (DEC)

vox
voice

VOX
Voice-Operated Keying; Voice-Operated Transmission

VP
Virtual Program (IBM); Vector Processor; Vertical Parity; Virtual Processor

VPA
VAX Performance Advisor (DEC)

VPDN
Virtual Private Data Network

VPDS
Virtual Private Data Services

VPE
Vector Processing Element

VPF
Vector Parameter File

VPI
Virtual Path Interconnect; Vendor Parts Index

VPK
Volts Peak

VPL
Virtual Private Line

VPM
Vendor Part Modification; Versatile Packaging Machine; Vibrations Per Minute; Virtual Processor Monitor; Virtual Protocol Machine; Volts per Meter [or Mil]

VPN
Virtual Private Network; Vendor Parts Number; Virtual Page Number

VPRF
Variable Pulse Repetition Frequency

VPS
VTAM [Virtual Telecommunications Access Method] Printer Support (IBM); Vacuum Plasma System; Vector Processing System; Vibrations Per Second; Va-

por Phase Soldering; Voice Processing Station; Virtual Print Spool

VPSS
Vector Processing Subsystem Support

VPT
Voice plus Telegraph

VPU
Virtual Processing Unit

VPWM
Variable Pulse-Width Modulation

VPZ
Virtual Processing Zero

VQA
Vendor Quality Assurance

VQD
Vendor Quality Defect

VQFP
Very Fine-Pitch Quad Flatpack

VR
Virtual Route (IBM); Visible Record; Virtual Reality; Vertical Recording; Voltage Regulator

VRA
Value Received Analysis; Virtual Route Analyzer (IBM)

VRAM
Variable Random Access Memory; Variable Rate Adaptive Multiplexing; Video Random Access Memory

VRC
Vertical Redundancy Check

VREF
Voltage Reference

VRM
Voice Recognition Module; Version Release Modification (IBM); Virtual Resource Manager

VRP
Visual Record Printer

VRS
Voice Recognition System; Voice Recording System

VRTX
Virtual Real-Time Executive

VRU
Voice Response Unit

VRX
Virtual Resource Executive

VS
Vendor Supplier; Virtual Storage (IBM); Virtual System; Vocal Synthesis

VS-1
Virtual Storage One (IBM)

VSA
Value Systems Analysis; Voltage Sensitive Amplifier

VSAM
Virtual Storage Access Method (IBM); Virtual Sequential Access Method; Virtual System Access Method

VSAT
Very Small Aperture Terminal

VSB
Vestigial Side-Band

VSBS
Very Small Business System

VSC
Virtual Subscriber Computer; Virtual Storage Constraint; Virtual System Control

VSCR
Virtual Storage Constraint Relief (IBM)

VSCS
Virtual SNA [Systems Network Architecture] Console Support (IBM); Virtual System Console Support (IBM)

VSD
Variable Slope Delta

VSDM
Variable Slope Delta Modulation

VSE
Virtual Storage Extended (IBM)

VSF
Voice Store and Forward system

VSI
Visual Simulator Interface

VSL
Variable Specification List

VSLAN
Very Secure Local Area Network

VSM
Video Switching Matrix; Virtual Storage Management; Virtual Storage Memory

VSMF
Visual Search Microfilm File

VSOP
Very-Small-Outline Package

VSP
Video Signal Processor

VSPC
Virtual Storage Personal Computing (IBM)

VSS
Video Storage System; Virtual Storage

System; Voice Signaling System

VSW
Voltage Standing Wave

VSWR
Voltage Standing-Wave Ratio

VSYNC
Vertical Synchronous

VT
Variable Time; Vertical Tabulation (CCITT); Video Terminal; Virtual Terminal; Virtual Tributary

VTA
Variable Transfer Address; Virtual Terminal Agent

VTAB
Vertical Tabulation

VTAC
Video Timing and Controller

VTAM
Virtual Telecommunications Access Method (IBM); Virtual Terminal Access Method; Vortex Telecommunications Access Method

VTAME
Virtual Telecommunications Access Method Entry (IBM)

VTB
Video Terminal Board

VTC
Video Tele-Conferencing; Virtual Terminal Control

VTCC
Video Terminal Cluster Controller (DEC)

VTD
Variable Time Delay; Vertical Tape Display

VTDI
Variable Threshold Digital Input

VTE
Visual Task Evaluation [or Evaluator]

VTFS
Visual Technology Flight Simulator

VTI
Video Terminal Interface

VTLC
Virtual Terminal Line Controller

VTNS
Virtual Telecommunications Network Service (AT&T)

VTO
Voltage-Tuned Oscillator

VTOC
Visual Table Of Contents; Volume Table

Of Contents (IBM)

VTP
Verification Test Plan; Virtual Terminal Protocol

VTR
Video Tape Recorder(ing)

VTRC
VME [Virtual Memory Extended] Token Ring Controller (Data General Corp, US)

VTRS
Video Tape Recording System; Video Tape Response System

VTRU
Variable Threshold Recently Used

VTS
Video Transmission Service (AT&T); Virtual Terminal System

VTVM
Vacuum Tube Voltmeter

vtx
videotex

VU
Voice Unit; Volume Unit

VUE
Visual User Environment

VUIT
Visual User Interface Tool (DEC)

VUP
VAX Units of Performance (DEC)

VUV
Visible Ultraviolet

VV
Vertical-Vertical; Volume in Volume

VV & C
Verification, Validation, and Certification

VVA
Voltage Variable Attenuator

VVCR
VSAM [Virtual Sequential Access Method] Volume Control Record (IBM)

VVDS
VSAM [Virtual Sequential Access Method] Volume Data Set (IBM)

VVR
VSAM [Virtual Sequential Access Method] Volume Record (IBM)

VWS
Variable Word Size

vx
videotex

VZ
Virtual Zero

w
wait; weight; week; wide; width; word; write

W
Watt; Work (Symbol); Energy (Symbol for); West; Width; Wolfram [or Tungsten] (Symbol for); Wait Time; Wait State

W&C
Write and Compute

W-DCS
Wideband Digital Cross-Connect Signal

W/E
Writer/Editor

W-ISDN
Wideband Integrated Services Digital Network

W/O
Write-Off

W/R
Write/Read

W/W
Wire Wrap

WA
Weighted Average; Will Advise; Word Added

WAAN
Wide Area AppleTalk Network (Apple Computer Inc, US)

WABCR
Wide Area Bar Code Reader

WAC
Wage Analysis and Control; Weapon Arming Computer; Working Address Counter

WACK
Wait Acknowledge

WACS
Wire Automated Check System; Weather Analysis Computer System

WAD
Work Authorization Document

WAD/SO
Work Authorization Document/Shop Order

WADS
Wide Area Data Service

WAF
Word Address Format

WAI
Wait for Interrupt

WAK
Wait Acknowledge; Write Access Key

WAM
Words A Minute; Work Analysis and Measurement

WAN
Wang Laboratories Inc (AMEX symbol); Wide Area Network; Work Authorization Number

WAP
Work Assignment Procedure; Wideband Acoustical Processor

WAPA
Western Area Power Administration (DOE)

WAR
With All Risks; Work Authorization Report [or Request, or Routine]

WARC
World Administrative Radio Conference

WARES
Workload And Resources Evaluation System

WARF
Weekly Audit Report File

WARP
Worldwide AUTODIN [Automatic Digital Information Network] Restoral Plan

WARS
Wide-Area Remote Sensors

WAS
Wideband Antenna System

WASAR
Wide Application System Adapter

WASP
Work Activity Sampling Plan; Workshop Analysis and Scheduling Programming

WATBOL
Waterloo Business-Oriented Language (University of Waterloo, Canada)

WATCIM
Waterloo Centre for Integrated Manufacturing (Research center, University of Waterloo, Canada)

WATFOR
Waterloo FORTRAN (University of Waterloo, Canada)

WATS
  Wide Area Telecommunications Service;
  Wide Area Telephone Service (AT&T)

Wb
  Weber (The SI unit of magnetic flux)

WB
  Wideband; Write Buffer

WBA
  Wire Bundle Assembly; Wideband Amplifier

WBAT
  Wideband Adapter Transformer

WBC
  Wideband Coupler

WBCT
  Wideband Current Transformer

WBD
  Wideband Data

WBDA
  Wideband Data Assembly

WBDI
  Wideband Data Interleaver

WBDL
  Wideband Data Line [or Link]

WBDR
  Wideband Data Recorder

WBDX
  Wideband Data Switch

WBS
  Work Breakdown Structure

WBTS
  Wideband Transmission System

WC
  Word Count; Work Card; Work Control;
  Write Control

WCB
  Will Call Back

WCC
  Work Center Code; Work Control Center

WCDB
  Work Control Data Base

WCF
  Workload Control File

WCGM
  Writable Character Generation Module

WCL
  Word Control Logic

WCM
  Wired-Core Matrix; Wired-Core Memory;
  Word Combine and Multiplexer; Writable
  Control Memory

WCP
  Work Control Plan

WCPD
  Waterloo Centre for Process Development
  (Research center, University of Waterloo,
  Canada)

WCR
  Word Control [or Count] Register

WCS
  Work Control System; Writeable Control
  Storage; Writeable Control Store; Wang
  Computer System (Wang Laboratories
  Inc, US)

wd
  width; word

WD
  Work Description; Work Directive; Write
  Data; Write Direct

WDB
  Word Driver BIT; Working Data Base

WDC
  Write Data Check; Wideband Directional Coupler; World Data Center (National Academy
  of Sciences)

WDCS
  Writable Diagnostic Control Store

WDF
  Weather Data Facility

WDIR
  Working Directory

WDL
  Wireless Data Link

WDM
  Wavelength Division Multiplexing

WDMA
  Wave Division Multiple Access

WDP
  Work Distribution Policy

wdt
  width

WDT
  Watch Dog Timer

WE
  Write Enable

WEFAX
  Weather Facsimile

WEP
  Weather Processor

WETARFAC
  Work Element Timer and Recorder for
  Automatic Coupling

WEX
Wavelength Extender
WF
Write Fault; Write Forward; Wrong Font
WFC
Wide Field [or Field-of-view] Camera
WFL
Work Flow Language
WFOV
Wide Field-Of-View (Image technology)
WG
Working Group; Write Gate
WGS
Working Group Standards
wgt
weight
WHIP
Wafer Hybrid Interconnection Packaging
WI
Word Intelligibility
wid
width
WIIS
Wang Integrated Image System (Wang Data Systems Inc, US)
WILCO
Will Comply (Radio term, used after "Roger")
WIN
Wireless In-building Network; Wireless Information Network; Worldwide Intelligent Network
WIND
Weather Information Network and Display
WINDS
Weather Information Network and Display System
WIP
Work In Place; Work In Process; Work In Progress
WIPS
Word Image Processing System
WIRDS
Weather Information Remoting and Display System
WISC
Writable Instruction Set Chip [or Computer]
WISE
Wang Intersystem Exchange (Wang Laboratories Inc, US)

WISS
Workstation-Independent Segment Storage
WIT
Women in Telecommunications (Defunct organization)
WITIS
Weather Integration with Tactical Intelligence System
wk
week; work
wkg
working
wl
workload
WL
Word Line; Work Level
WLCT
Washington Legislative Council on Telecommunications
WLR
Wrong Length Record
WNL
Within Normal Limits
WNP
Will Not Process; Wire Non-Payment
wo
without
WO
Wait Order; Wipe Out; Write-Off; Write Only; Write Out
WOA
Work Order Authorization
WOCS
Work Order Control System
WOLAP
Workplace Optimization and Layout Planning
WOM
Write-Only Memory; Write Optional Memory
WOPAST
Work Plan Analysis and Scheduling Technique
WOR
Work Order Release
WORAM
Word-Oriented Random Access Memory
WORM
Write-Once, Read-Many [or Mainly, or Mostly] ("Read-Many" is preferred)

WORN
Write-Once, Read-Never
WOROM
Write-Only, Read-Only Memory
WORP
Word Processing
WOSUS
Wang Office Systems User Society (Wang Laboratories Inc, US)
WOUDE
Wait-On-User-Defined Event
WP
WordPerfect (WordPerfect Corp, US); Word Processing; Word Processor; Workspace Pointer; Write Protect(ion)
WP/AS
Word Processing/Administrative Support
WPB
Write Printer Binary
WPC
Wired Program Computer; Word Processing Center
WPD
Write Printer Decimal
WPDA
Writing Pushdown Acceptor
WPI
World Patent Index
wpm (WPM)
words per minute
WPM
Words Per Minute; Work Package Management; Write Program Memory; Write-Protect Memory
WPN
Write Punch
WPOE
Word Processing and Office Equipment
WPR
Work Planning and Review
wps (WPS)
words per second
WPS
Word Processing System; Words Per Second; Wideband Packet Switch
WPU
Write Punch
WPWM
Wide Pulse Width Modulation
wr
write

WR
Wire Recorder; Word Request; Work Request; Working Register
WRAIS
Wide Range Analog Input Subsystem
WRAPS
World Bank Retrieval Array Processing System
WRE
Write Enable
WRIU
Write Interface Unit
WRO
Work Release Order
WRP
Weighted Random Pattern (IBM)
WRPT
Write Protect(ion)
WRS
Word Recognition System
wrt
write
WRTC
Write Control
ws
worksheet
WS
Waveguide Slab; Word Station; Word Sync; Work(ing) Space; Work Station; Working Storage
WSDCU
Wideband Satellite Delay Compensation Unit
WSF
Work Station Facility
WSI
Wafer Scale Integration; Weather Services International Corp
WSR
Weather Surveillance Radar
WST
Word Study; Word Synchronizing Track
WSTA
Wall Street Telecommunications Association
WSU
Work Station Utility
wt
weight
WT
Wait(ing) Time; Waveguide Transmis-

sion; Word Terminal

WTA
World Teleport Association

WTD
World Telecommunications Directory

WTO
Write-To-Operator

WTOR
Write-To-Operator with Reply (IBM)

WTR
Work Transfer Record; Work Transfer Request

WTS
Word Terminal, Synchronous

WTT
Working Timetable

WTTY
World Trade Teletypewriter

WU
Work Unit; Western Union Telegraph Company

WUDB
Work Unit Data Bank

WUEMI
Western Union Electronic Main, Inc.

WUI
Western Union International

WULDS
Western Union Long Distance Service

WUSCI
Western Union Space Communications, Inc

WUTC
Western Union Telegraph Company

WUTELCO
Western Union Telegraph Company

WUX
Western Union Exchange (Teleprinter)

WV
Weight in Volume; Working Voltage

WW
Wire Wrap

WXR
Weather Radar

X

x
abscissa (Symbol for); unknown quantity (Symbol for); number of carriers [drawn from collector to base of a transistor, for each carrier collected] (Symbol for); x-axis [or horizontal axis] (Symbol for, of a graph or screen in the Cartesian coordinate system); multiplication; experiment; express; transmission; index(ed)

X
Roman numeral designation for "10"; Reactance (Symbol for); No connection (Symbol for); Unknown quantity (Symbol for); X-Axis [or Horizontal axis] (Symbol for, of a graph or screen in the Cartesian coordinate system); X-Windows (A windowing environment software commonly used on UNIX-based workstations); Multiplication; Abscissa (Symbol for); Designation prefix of CCITT data communications recommendations (e.g., X.25 is a packet-switching network protocol)

x amplifier
horizontal amplifier [or x-axis amplifier] (Of an oscilloscope or recorder)

x (X)-axis
horizontal axis

X-bar
A crossbar [or rectangular bar] usually cut from a Z-section

X-balance
Reactance balance

X-band
A radio-frequency band extending from 5200 to 11000 MHz

X-bridge
An AC bridge for measuring reactance

X-channel
Horizontal channel (Of an oscilloscope or recorder)

X-component
Reactive component (In a complex impedance)

x-coordinate
An abscissa

X-deflection
Horizontal deflection

X-direction
Horizontal direction

X-factor
Unknown quantity

x-irradiate
To expose to X-rays

X-line
Horizontal line (In a computer memory matrix)

X-meter
An instrument for measuring reactance and phase angle

X.*nn*
Designation prefix of CCITT data communications recommendations

X-off (OFF)
transmitter off

X-on (ON)
transmitter on

X-POP
X-Body Axis Perpendicular to Orbit Plane (Aerospace)

X-radiation
Radiation composed of X-rays

X-section
Cross-section

X switch
Crossover switch (For reversing compatible devices)

X-wave
Extraordinary wave

X-Windows
A windowing environment software commonly used on UNIX-based workstations

X-Y
Cartesian Coordinate System

XA
Auxiliary Amplifier; Cross-Assembler; Transmission Adapter; Extended Architecture

XACT
X Automatic Code Translation

XALC
Extended Assembler Language Coding

XAM
External Address Modifier

XASM
Cross-Assembler

xb (XB)
crossbar

xbar
crossbar

XBC
External Bus Controller; External Block Controller

XBM
Extended Basic Mode

XBT
Crossbar Tandem (Telecommunications)

XC
Xerox Copy

XCL
Executive Command Language

XCONN
Cross-Connection

xcp
except

xcpt
except

XCS
Xerox Computer Services (Xerox Corp, US)

XCT
X-Band Communications Transponder

XCU
Crosspoint Control Unit (Telecommunications)

xcvr
transceiver

xd
crossed (Telecommunications)

XD
Ex-Directory (Telecommunications, unlisted subscriber); Examined; Crossed (Telecommunications)

XDFLD
Secondary Index Field

XDM
Xerox Dry Microfilm

XDMS
Experimental Data Management System

XDOS
UNIX Disk Operating System

XDP
X-Ray Density Probe

XDPS
X-Band Diode Phase Shifter

xdr
transducer

XDR
External Data Representation

XDS
Xerox Data Systems

xducer
transducer

XDUP
Extended Disk Utilities Program

Xe
Xenon (Symbol)

XE
Experimental Engine

xec
execute

XEC
Extended Emulator Control

xeq
execute

XER
Exception Register (IBM); Xerox Reproduction

XES
X-Ray Energy Spectrometry

XESS
X-Windows Engineering and Scientific Spreadsheet

XFC
Extended Function Code; Transferred Charge Call (Telecommunications)

xfer
transfer

Xfer
Transfer

XFES
Xerox Family Education Services

xfd
crossfeed (NASA)

XFM
X-Band Ferrite Modulator

xfmr
transformer

xformer
transformer

Xformer
Transformer

XFQH
Xenon-Filled Quartz Helix

xg
crossing

XGA
Extended Graphics Array (IBM)

xge
exchange

XGP
Xerox Graphic Printer (Xerox Corp, US)
XHAIR
Cross Hair (IEEE)
XHR
Extra-High Resolution
XHV
Extreme High Vacuum
XI
X.25 Interface (IBM)
XI/O
Execute Input/Output
XIC
Transmission Interface Converter
XICS
Xerox Integrated Composition System
(Computer typesetting system)
XID
Exchange Identification
XIM
Extended I/O Monitor
xing
crossing
XIO
Executive Input/Output (Computing)
XIP
Execute In Place
xistor
transistor
Xistor
Transistor
XIT
Extra Input Terminal
XL
Cross-Reference List; Execution Language
XLIST
Execution List
XLP
Extra Large-scale Packaging
XLPE
Cross-Linked Polyethylene (Cable insulation material)
XLPS
Xenon Lamp Power Supply
XLS
Xerox Learning Systems
XM
Expanded Memory
XMAS
Extended Mission Apollo Simulation
xmfr
Transformer

XMI
Extended Memory Interconnect (DEC)
xmission
transmission
xmit
transmit; transmitter
xmitter
transmitter
XMOS
Cross Metal-Oxide Semiconductor
XMP
Experimental Mathematical Programming System
XMS
Xerox Memory System
xmsn
transmission
xmt
transmit; transmitter
Xmt
Transmit
XMT
X-Band Microwave Transmitter
xmt-rec (XMT-REC)
transmit-receive
xmtr
transmitter
Xmtr
Transmitter
xmtr-rec (XMTR-REC)
transmitter-receiver
XN
Execution Node
XNOS
Experimental Network Operating System
XNREN
X-400 National Research and Education Network (NSF)
XNS
Xerox Network System [or Services] (Xerox Corp, US)
XO
Crystal Oscillator
XOFF
Transmitter Off
XON
Transmitter On; Cross-Office Highway (Telecommunications)
XOP
Extended Operation
XOR
Exclusive OR (Circuit or logic gate)

XOS
Xerox Operating System; Cross-Office Slot (Telecommunications)

XOT
Extra Output Terminal

xover
crossover

XP
Expandable [or Expansion] Processor (IBM)

XPA
X-Band Parametric Amplifier

xpd
expedite

XPD
Cross-Polarization Discrimination (Telecommunications, antenna characteristic)

xpdr
transponder

XPI
Cross-Polarization Interference (In radio transmission)

XPIC
Cross-Polarization Interference Canceller

xponder
transponder

Xponder
Transponder

XPPA
X-Band Pseudopassive Array

XPS
X-ray Photo-electron Spectrometry

XPSW
External Processor Status Word

xpt
cross-point (Switching element)

XQ
Cross-Question

XQP
Extended QIO [Queued Input/Output] Processing (DEC)

XR
External Reset; Index Register

Xray
Phonetic alphabet communications code word for the letter X

xrds
crossroads

XREF
Cross-Reference

XREP
Extended Reporting

XRF
Extended Recovery Facility (IBM)

XRM
Extended Relational Memory

XRS
X-Ray Spectrometry

xs
excess

XS3
Excess 3 code (Binary arithmetic transformation code)

XSA
Extended Storage Architecture

XSECT
Cross-Section

XSI
X/Open System Interface

xso
crystal-stabilized oscillator

XSP
Extended Set Processor

XSTDA
X-Band Stripline Tunnel Diode Amplifier

xstr
transistor

XSTT
Excess Transit Time

XT
Extended Technology (e.g., an IBM PC/XT computer based on the Intel 8088 microprocessor that was introduced in 1983); Extended Processor (Honeywell, business personal computer); Cross Talk (IEEE)

XTA
X-Band Tracking Antenna

xtal
crystal

Xtal
Crystal

xtalk
cross-talk

Xtalk
Cross-talk

XTC
External Transmit Clock

XTE
X-Ray Timing Explorer (NASA)

XTEL
Cross Tell (IEEE)

XTEN
Xerox Telecommunications Network
(Xerox Corp, US)
XTI
X/Open Transport Interface
XTLK
Cross Talk (Aviation)
XTPA
Extended Transaction Processing Archi-
tecture
xtr
transmitter
Xtr
Transmitter
xtrm
extreme
XTS
Cross-Tell Simulator (IEEE)
XU
X Unit; X-ray Unit
XUI
X-Windows User Interface (DEC)
XUV
Extreme Ultraviolet

XV
X-Ray Vision
xvers
transverse
xvtr
transverter
XWAVE
Extraordinary Wave
XXX
A signal indicating urgency (Used in ra-
diotelegraphy)
XY
Cartesian Coordinate System
XYA
X-Y Axis
XYAT
X-Y Axis Table
XYL
Ex-Young Lady (Amateur radio operator's
slang for "wife")
XYP
X-Y Plotter
XYR
X-Y Recorder

Y

y
yield; yaw; year; yard; y-axis [or vertical axis] (Symbol for, of a graph or screen in the Cartesian coordinate system); yellow; you

Y
Admittance (Symbol for); Yttrium (Symbol); Young's Modulus (Symbol)

Y-adapter or connector
So called from its resemblance to the letter "Y"

y-amplifier
vertical amplifier (Of an oscilloscope or recorder)

Y-antenna
Delta matched antenna

y-axis
vertical axis (Of a chart, graph, or screen in the Cartesian coordinate system)

y-axis amplifier
See y-amplifier

Y-capacitor
A radio interference suppression capacitor

y-coordinate
an ordinate

Y-connection
A Wye [or Star] connection

Y-current
Wye [or Star] current (Of a three-phase circuit)

y-deflection
vertical deflection

y-direction
the "vertical direction" in deflections and in graphical presentations of data

y-line
a "vertical line" of a computer memory matrix

Y-match
Delta match

Y/N
Yes/No (Response prompt)

Y-parameters
The "Admittance" parameters of a four-terminal network or device

Y-point
Wye [or Star] point (Of a three-phase circuit)

Y-POP
Y-Body Axis Perpendicular to Orbit Plane (Aerospace)

Y-position
"Vertical" position

Y-potential
Wye [or Star] potential (Of a three-phase circuit)

Y-rectifier
Wye [or Star] rectifier (Of a three-phase circuit)

Y-winding
A Wye [or Star] connection winding (Of a three-phase circuit)

Y-Y
Yaw Axis

Y-Y circuit
A Wye-Wye [or Star-Star] circuit (Of a three-phase circuit)

YA
Year Authorized (Searchable field); Yaw Axis

YAC
Young Astronaut Council (Organization); Yet Another Compiler

YACC
Yet Another Compiler-Compiler

YACTOFF
Yaw Actuator Offset

YAG
Yttrium-Aluminum-Garnet (Stimulated material in some lasers)

YAGL
Yttrium-Aluminum-Garnet Laser

YAL
Yttrium-Aluminum Laser

YAP
Yield Analysis Pattern

YAS
Yaw Attitude Sensor

YAWP
Yet Another Word Processor

Yb
Ytterbium (Symbol)

YBCO
Yttrium Barium Copper Oxygen

YBPC
Young Black Programmers Coalition (Organization)

YC
Yaw Channel; Yaw Coupling
YCP
Yaw Coupling Parameter
YDB
Yield Diffusion Bonding
YDC
Yaw Damper Computer
Yds
Yards
YDS
Yards
YEA
Yaw Error Amplifier
YEC
Youngest Empty Cell
Yel
Yellow
yel
Yellow
YES
Young Executive Society (Automotive Warehouse Distributors Association)
YGL
Yttrium-Garnet Laser
YIG
Yttrium-Iron-Garnet
YIL
Yellow Indicating Light
yl (YL)
yellow
Yl
Yellow
YLF
Yttrium Lithium Fluoride
YLR
YAG [Yttrium-Aluminum-Garnet] Laser Range-finder
YLRL
Young Ladies Radio League
ylw (YLW)
yellow
YM
Yield Map
YME
Young's Modulus of Elasticity

YMS
Yield Measurement System; Yaw Microwave Sensor
YOE
Year of Entry
YP
Year of Publication (Searchable field); Yellow Pages; Yield Point
YPA
Yaw Precession Amplifier
YPD
Yaw Phase Detector
YPS
Yellow Pages Service; Yards per Second
yr
year
YR
Year (Searchable field)
YRC
Yaw Ratio Controller
Yrly
Yearly
YRLY
Yearly
YS
Yard Stick; Yield Strength; Yield Stress
YS/E
Yield Strength to Elastic Modulus Ratio density
YSB
Yield Stress Bonding
YSDB
Yield Stress Diffusion Bonding
YSF
Yield Safety Factor
YSLF
Yield Strength Load Factor
Yt
Yttrium (Symbol)
YTC
Yield to Call
YTD
Year to Date
YTF
YIG [Yttrium-Iron-Garnet] Tuned Filter

Z

z
electrochemical equivalent (Symbol for); zero; zone

Z
Impedance (Symbol for); Atomic number (Symbol for); Zenith distance (Astronomy); Z-fold [or fan-fold] paper (Computer paper);

Z-amplifier
The "intensity-modulation" amplifier of an oscilloscope; zenith; zinc

Z-angle meter
An instrument for measuring impedance and phase angle in a electric circuit

Z-Axis:
Zilog microprocessor (As prefix)

z-axis
The "intensity-modulation" input of an oscilloscope; The third axis in a three-dimensional coordinate system that represents "depth"

z-axis modulation
intensity modulation

Z-bar
Z-cut crystal

Z of C
Zones of Communications (Military)

Z/CAL
Zero Calibration

Z-fold paper
Fan-fold paper (Computer paper)

Z-gain
The gain [or gain control] of the "intensity channel" of an oscilloscope

Z-LV
Z-Axis along Local Vertical

Z-marker
Zone-marker

Z-meter
An "impedance" meter

Z-parameters
Device or network parameters expressed as "impedances"

Z&S
Zero and Subtract

Z-signals
A collection of letter groups, each starting with the letter "Z" (Used for simplification in telegraphy and radiotelegraphy by the military services)

Z&Z
Zero and Add

ZA
Zero-Adjusted; Zone of Action; Zenith Angle; Zero and Add; Zero Adder; Zero Adjuster

ZAA
Zero Angle of Attack

ZAAP
Zero Antiaircraft Potential

ZAD
Zenith Angle Distribution

ZADCC
Zone Air Defense Control Center

ZAI
Zero Address Instruction

ZAM
Z-Axis Modulation

ZAP
Zero and Add Packed; Zero Antiaircraft Potential

ZAPP
Zero Assignment Parallel Processor

ZAS
Zero Access Storage

ZB
Zero Beat (Radio)

ZBID
Zero Bit Insertion/Deletion

ZBLAN
Zirconium, Barium, Lanthanum, Aluminum, Sodium Fluoride (Chemistry)

ZBR
Zero Beat Reception (Radio); Zone Bit Recording

ZBTSI
Zero Byte Time Slot Interchange (AT&T)

ZCR
Zero-temperature Coefficient Resistor

ZCR
Zero Crossing Rate

ZCD
Zero Crossing Detector

ZCR
Zero Crossing Rate

ZD
Zero Defect; Zenith Distance; Zener Di-

ode; Zero Defects

ZDP
Zero Defects Program; Zero Delivery Pressure

ZDPA
Zero Defects Program Audit

ZDR
Zoned Data Recording

ZDS
Zilog Development System (Zilog Inc, US)

ZDT
Zero-Ductility Transition

ZEC
Zero Energy Coefficient

ZED
Zero Express Dialing

ZEG
Zero Economic Growth; Zero Energy Growth

ZELMAL
Zero-Length Launch and Mat Landing (Missiles)

ZF
Zero Frequency

ZFC
Zero Failure Criteria

ZFW
Zero Fuel Weight (Aviation)

ZG
Zero Gravity

ZGF
Zero Gravity Facility (NASA)

ZGS
Zero Gradient Synchrotron (Nickname is Ziggy)

ZHF
Zone Heat Flux

ZI
Zinc Institute; Zero Input; Zoom In (Image technology)

ZICON
Zone of the Interior Consumers Network

ZIF
Zero Insertion Force [connector or socket]

Ziggy
Nickname for Zone Gradient Synchrotron

ZIP
Zip-Code; Zinc-Impurity Photodetector; Zone Improvement Plan

zkW
Zero Kilowatt

ZLL
Zero-Length Launch (Missiles)

ZLTO
Zero-Length Takeoff

ZM
Zero Marker

ZMKR
Zone Marker

ZMR
Zone-Melt Recrystallization

zn
zenith; zone

Zn
Zinc (Symbol)

ZNR
Zinc Resistor

ZO
Zero Output

ZOD
Zero Order Detector

ZODIAC
Zone Defense Integrated Active Capability

ZOE
Zero Energy

ZOH
Zero Order Hold

ZOR
Zinc Oxide Resistor

ZPB
Zinc Primary Battery

ZPG
Zero Population Growth

ZPI
Zone-Position Indicator; Zigzag In-line Package; Zone Information Protocol (USPS)

ZPR
Zero Power Reactor

ZPT
Zero Power Test

Zr
Zirconium (Symbol)

ZRC
Zenith Radio Corp (US)

ZRE
Zero Rate Error

ZRM
Zone Reserved for Memory

ZS
Zero Shift; Zero and Subtract

ZSA
Zero-Set Amplifier
ZSB
Zinc Storage Battery
ZSG
Zero-Speed Generator
ZSL
Zero-Slot LAN
ZSPG
Zero-Speed Pulse Generator
ZST
Zone Standard Time
ZT
Zone Time (Navigation)
ZTAT
Zero Turn-Around Time
ZTC
Zero-Temperature Coefficient
ZUM
Zoned Usage Messaging
ZVR
Zener Voltage Regulator

ZVRD
Zener Voltage Regulator Diode
ZVS
Zero Voltage Switch
ZW
Zero Wait
ZWC
Zero Word Count; Zone Wind Computer
ZWP
Zone Wind Plotter
ZWL
Zero Wavelength
ZXMP
Zero Transmission Power
zz
zigzag [or zig-zag]
ZZC
Zero-Zero Condition
ZZD
Zig-Zag Diagram
ZZR
Zig-Zag Rectifier

Appendix

Numbers & Symbols

* **asterisk** [wildcard symbol, or character] (A symbol used to represent a multiplication operator in many programming languages; in DOS, OS/2 and other operating systems, the wildcard symbol that can be used in place of "one or more" other characters. Cf. question mark [?])

@ **at sign** [suppress display, batch-file command] (In DOS batch file techniques, suppresses the display of the command line on-screen [DOS 3.3 and later]. For example, you may use the @ symbol to suppress the display of the REM [Remark] command itself. This is done by simply writing the command as "@REM")

\ **back slash** [pathname & root directory symbols] (Pathname: in DOS, a statement that indicates precisely where a file is located on a hard disk. Root directory: the top-level directory on a disk, the one DOS creates when you format the disk)

[**left bracket** [escape sequence character] (ASCII)

[] **pair of brackets** [may be found in DOS Shell window, directory tree area] (The directory tree area, in the upper left quadrant of the window, graphically depicts your directory structure. At the top of this area, the root directory of the logged disk is shown as a folder-shaped icon, or "as a pair of brackets []" if the DOS Shell is in text mode)

: **colon** [label symbol] (In DOS batch files, a string of characters [labels may be longer than eight characters, but DOS recognizes only the first eight] preceded by a colon [:] that marks the destination of a "GOTO" command)

$ **dollar sign** [metastring symbol] (Special characters that display specific types of information can be used after the DOS PROMPT command. All of these special characters [t, d, p, v, n, g, l, b, q, and e] are preceded by the $ character)

.$$$ **dot, triple-dollar signs** [temporary file extension] (In DOS, a temporary or incorrectly stored file. This might be the case if only a portion of a file were saved)

. **dot** [current directory symbol] (The directory that DOS or an application uses by default to store and retrieve files)

.@@@ **dot, triple at signs** [old DOS BACKUP file extension] (In DOS versions before 3.3 [6.0 currently], BACKUP created a heading file called "BACKUPID.@@@" on each floppy disk. That file held the date, time, and disk number of the backup)

.. **dot-dot** [parent directory symbol] (In DOS directories, the directory above the current subdirectory in the tree structure)

... **set of three dots** [ellipsis] (Usually used to indicate incompleteness. In printed text, indicates the omission of one or more words. In software with a graphical interface [as in many windowing programs], an ellipsis following a menu command indicates that choosing the command will produce a dialog box)

/ **forward slash** [switch symbol] (An addition to a DOS command that affects the way the command performs its function, the switch symbol is generally followed by a letter [such as /s, /m, or /a]; a parameter)

/? **forward slash-question mark** [DOS online help facility switch] (Every DOS command supports the /? switch, which provides a short description of the command and its syntax, e.g., type the DOS command that you want, followed by the switch /?)

> **greater-than character** [redirect command output, operator] (In DOS control device commands, the > symbol redirects a command's output)

>> **two greater-than characters** [redirect command output/append as target, operator] (In DOS control device commands, when using the >> symbols, redirects a command's output and appends the output [new information] to the target [a file], if one exists)

- **hyphen** [en dash] (A punctuation mark [half the width of an em] used to indicate a range of dates or numbers [e.g., 1980-90] or to separate the elements of a compound adjective, one part of which is hyphenated or consists of two words [e.g., pre-Civil War]

-- **two hyphens** [em dash] (A punctuation

mark, generally used to signify a change or an interruption in the train of thought expressed in a sentence or to set off an explanatory comment)

< **less-than character** [redirect command input, operator] (In DOS control device commands, redirects a command's input, i.e., keyboard input is redirected using the < symbol. Input that normally comes from the keyboard can be redirected so as to come from either a file or a device)

% **percent sign** [DOS batch file replaceable parameter] (All replaceable parameters begin with the percent sign [%], followed by a number from 0 to 9)

%% **two percent signs** [DOS batch file variable parameter] (The variable is a single upper or lowercase letter and it represents a "dummy filename")

+ **plus sign** [expands current branch of the directory tree by one level] (DOS keystroke command; DOS assigns special functions to some keys when you use them within the DOS Shell; the plus sign [+] is one of them)

? **question mark** [wildcard symbol, or character] (In some operating systems and applications, a wildcard character often used to represent any other "single" character. Cf. asterisk [*])

} **right brace** [used in DOS Shell configuring] (Useful when creating custom color schemes by editing the DOS Shell configuration file, "DOSSHELL.INI")

. **star-dot-star** [wildcard symbol, or character] (A file specification using the asterisk wildcard that means "any combination of filename and extension" in operating systems such as DOS)

~ **tilde** [used in DOS Shell configuring when adding custom help features] (Useful when building "links" to the built-in DOS Shell help messages from your custom help messages, i.e., type the help-message reference number, enclosed in tildes [~], just to the right of the link word[s])

| **vertical line** [pipe symbol] (In DOS, OS/2, and UNIX, the symbol that tells the operating system to send the output of one command to another command, rather than displaying this output on the screen)

|| **double vertical lines** [command separator symbol] (This symbol, which is generally used in the DOS Shell program start-up command, [generated by the <F4> key] separates certain commands in a series)

0-0 zero-zero. no ceiling, no visibility for an aircraft

0-g zero gravity

000 emergency services (Australia)

0 deg lat zero degrees latitude. The equator, encircling widest part of the earth

0TLP Zero Transmission Level Point

0° zero degrees (the Equator)

0°lat zero degrees latitude (the Equator)

1/2 t half title

1/2 gr half-gross

1/2 h half-hard

1/2 rd half-round

1/4" Generally refers to a 1/4" data cartridge tape

1/4 h quarter-hard

1/4 ly quarterly

1/4 ph quarter-phase

1/4 rd quarter-round

1/4s quarters

01/102-key the 101/102-key "enhanced" keyboard, introduced by IBM

1° solo

1/c single-conductor

1C member or former member of US armed forces with honorable discharge

1ce once

1D Refers to a single-density floppy disk

1DD Refers to a single-sided double-density floppy disk

1/e first edition

1NF First Normal Form (In a relational database, an approach to structuring information)

1/O First Officer

1-p single pole

1 ph single-phase

1Q first quarter

1S single-sided disk. Refers to a floppy disk on which data can be reliably stored on only one side

1st first

1st Asst Engr First Assistant Engineer

1st Asst Pur First Assistant Purser

1st cl hon first-class honors (in academic

degrees)

1st Lieut First Lieutenant

1st Off First Officer

1st Sgt First Sergeant

1-striper ensign (USN)

1 1/2 striper naval lieutenant, junior grade

1-wd one-wheel drive

1-y-o one-year-old (child, pet, racehorse, etc.)

1-yTs one-year Treasury securities

1-2-3 Lotus 1-2-3 (Spreadsheet program introduced in 1982 by Lotus Development Corp, US)

1.2M 1.2 Meg, or Megabyte (Generally refers to the 1.2M high-density 5.25" floppy disk used on PCs

1.2MB Refers to a 5 1/4" high-density floppy disk

1.44M 1.4 Meg, or Megabyte (Generally refers to the 1.4M high-density 3.5" microfloppy disk used on PCs)

1.44MB Refers to a 3 1/2" high-density floppy disk

10^2 hecto (symbol h)

10^6 mega (symbol M)

10^9 giga (symbol G)

10^{12} tera (symbol T)

10^{-1} deci (symbol d)

10^{-2} centi (symbol c)

10^{-3} milli (symbol m)

10^{-6} micro (symbol μ)

10^{-9} nano (symbol n)

10^{-12} pico (symbol p)

10^{-15} femto (symbol f)

10^{-18} atto (symbol a)

1Base5 Refers to wiring options for IEEE 802 Specifications. Referred to as the Starlan (AT&T) specification

10Base3 Refers to wiring options for IEEE 802 Specifications. 10 MHz, baseband, with 300-meter segments

10Base-F 10Base-Fiber

10Base-T 10Base-Twisted (pair)

10BT 10Base-Twisted (pair)

16-bit 16-bit computer, or machine

16-bit computer A computer that works with information in groups of 16 bits (binary digits) at a time

16-bit machine Same as 16-bit computer

110Base2 Refers to wiring options for IEEE 802 Specifications. Specification for thinwire coax Ethernet using RG-58-C/U

coaxial cable

111 emergency services (New Zealand)

170 Derived from standard RS-170. The standard for NTSC composite video signals

1001 Derived from FED-STD-1001. High-speed synchronous signaling rates between data terminal equipment and DCE

1003.1 Derived from IEEE standard 1003.1. POSIX systems calls, programmer's interface

1003.10 Derived from IEEE standard 1003.10. POSIX WG—Supercomputing Applications Profile

1003.15 Derived from IEEE standard 1003.15. POSIX WG—Batch Extensions to POSIX Group

1003.18 Derived from IEEE standard 1003.18. Standardized Profile for a POSIX Platform

1003.2 Derived from IEEE standard 1003.2. POSIX commands and command interpreter, limited to commands used in batched command shell scripts

1003.4 Derived from IEEE standard 1003.4. POSIX real-time extensions

1003 Derived from FED-STD-1003. Bit-oriented data link control procedures

1005 Derived from FED-STD-1005. 2400 bps modems

1010 Derived from FED-STD-1010. ASCII bit sequencing for serial transmission

1011 Derived from FED-STD-1011. Character structure for serial-by-bit ASCII transmission

1012 Derived from FED-STD-1012. Character structure for parallel-by-bit ASCII transmission

1013 Derived from FED-STD-1013. DTE to DCE synchronous signaling rates using 4kHz circuits

1020 Derived from FED-STD-1020. Electrical characteristics of unbalanced voltage digital interface circuits

1030 Derived from FED-STD-1030. Electrical characteristics of balanced voltage digital interface circuits

1401 A second-generation IBM computer system that was introduced in 1959 and used until the late 1960s

1408K Refers to 1408 kilobytes of extended memory. A memory upgrade so that 2M of **RAM** can be obtained on the mother board

1553 Derived from MIL-STD-1553. A data bus used in all major US military aircraft

2B1Q Two binary, one quaternary

2/c two-conductor

2ce twice

2-d two-dimensional

2-D Refers to a double-density floppy disk

2d second

2D Refers to a double-density (DD) floppy disk

2DD Refers to a double-sided double-density floppy disk

2/e second edition

2-F two-seater fighter aircraft (naval symbol)

2HD Refers to a double-sided high-density floppy disk

2-HD Refers to a double-sided high-density floppy disk

2/M Second Mate

2nd Asst Engr Second Assistant Engineer

2nd Asst Pur Second Assistant Purser

2nd Lieut Second Lieutenant

2nd Off Second Officer

2nd Stwd Second Steward

2NF Second Normal Form (In a relational database, an approach to structuring information)

2/O Second Officer

2-p double pole

2 ph two-phase

2Q second quarter

2S/2D Refers to a double-sided double-density floppy disk

2S/HD Refers to a double-sided high-density floppy disk

2S double-sided disk. Refers to a floppy disk that can hold data on both its top and bottom surfaces

2S 2D Refers to a double-sided double-density floppy disk

2-striper corporal (US Army); lieutenant (USN); second assistant engineer or second mate (merchant marine)

2T double throw

2-wd 2-wheel drive

2 1/2 striper naval lieutenant commander

24/7 24 hours a day, 7 days a week

24-bit video adapter A Macintosh color video adapter that can display more than

16 million colors simultaneously

24-pin Refers to dot-matrix printers that can produce dot patterns fine enough to approach the print quality of daisy wheel or laser printers, i.e., Letter Quality [LQ] output

232 Derived from EIA standard RS-232. A standard adopted by the *EIA* for connecting data terminal equipment (DTE) to data circuit-terminating equipment (DCE)

232-C Derived from EIA standard RS-232-C. An interface specification for connecting DTE and DCE used for the serial exchange of data

232-D Successor of EIA RS-232-C. A specification supposedly compatible with CCITT V.24

287 See 80287

2780, 3780 Standard communications protocols for transmitting batch data

3B2T Three Binary, Two Tertiary

3C Computer Control Company

3 C's, The Calculate, Compare and Copy (By calculating, comparing, and copying, the computer accomplishes all forms of data processing. The 3 C's is a registered service mark of The Computer Language Company Inc, US)

3/c three-conductor

3ce thrice

3Com3+ A network operating system from 3Com Corp that is based on MS/Net and supports PC and Macintosh workstations

3d third

3D Three-Dimensional

3-D Three-Dimensional

3de three-day event

3/e third edition

3GL Third Generation Language

3M Minnesota Mining and Manufacturing Company

3/M Third Mate

3-M Maintenance and Material Management (USN)

3NF Third Normal Form (In a relational database, an approach to structuring information)

3/O Third Officer

3-p triple pole

ph three-phase

3Q third quarter

3rd Asst Engr Third Assistant Engineer

3rd Off Third Officer

3rd Stwd Third Steward

3-striper commander (USN); first assistant engineer or first mate (merchant marine); sergeant (US Army)

33T triple throw

3 x 5 3-inch by 5-inch filing card

3 1/2" DS/DD Refers to a double-sided double-density (720KB capacity) floppy disk

3 1/2" DS/ED Refers to a double-sided "extra-density" (4 MB rather than 1.44 MB typically found on high-density [HD]) floppy disk

3 1/2-inch 3 1/2-inch microfloppy disk

3 1/2" DS/HD Refers to a double-sided high-density (1.44MB capacity) floppy disk

32-bit 32-bit computer, or machine

32-bit computer A computer that works with information in groups of 32 bits (binary digits) at a time

32-bit machine Same as 32-bit computer

35mm Generally refers to a 35 millimeter camera

37xx Refers to a series of communications controllers from IBM

303x A series of medium to large-scale IBM mainframes introduced in 1977

308x A series of large-scale IBM mainframes introduced in 1980

309x A series of large-scale IBM mainframes introduced in 1986

360, 370 series The System/360 series and System/370 series introduced by IBM in 1964 and 1970, respectively

360K 360 Kilobyte (Generally refers to the 360K low-density 5.25" floppy disk used on PCs)

366-A Derived from EIA standard RS-366-A. Specification for interface between DTE and automatic calling equipment for data communication

370 architecture Refers to a computer that will run programs written for the IBM System/370 mainframe series

384K Refers to 384 kilobytes of extended memory. A memory upgrade so that 1M of **RAM** can be obtained on the mother board

386 See 80386

386DX See 80386DX

386 Enhanced mode An operating mode of Microsoft Windows that takes full advantage of the technical capabilities of Intel 80386 and later microprocessors

386^{Max} A memory management program for 386-based PCs from Qualitas

386SX See 80386SX

387 See 80387

387SX See 80387SX

3270 The communications protocol for interactive terminals connected to IBM mainframes, which includes the 3278 monochrome and 3279 color terminals

34010, 34020 Graphics coprocessors from Texas Instruments

3456K Refers to 3456 kilobytes of extended memory. A memory upgrade so that 4M of **RAM** can be obtained on the mother board

3705 Derived from IBM 3705. The IBM communication's frontend processor that is used in an SNA network

3770 A standard communications protocol for batch transmission in an IBM SNA environment

3780 See 2780,3780

4-AS American Association for the Advancement of Science

4B3T Four Binary, Three Tertiary

4/c four-conductor

4-class fourth-class (mail)

4-col p four-color page

4/e fourth edition

4GL Fourth Generation Language

4mm Generally refers to a 4 millimeter data cartridge tape

4/O Fourth Officer

4-p's product, place, promotion, price

4-p quadruple pole

4Q fourth quarter

4R Ceylon aircraft

4th Asst Engr Fourth Assistant Engineer

4-striper captain (merchant marine or USN); chief engineer (merchant marine)

4-wd four-wheel drive

4X Israeli aircraft

43xx A series of medium-scale IBM mainframes initially introduced in 1979

422 Derived from EIA standard RS-422. An interface specification for connecting DTE to DCE using unbalanced-voltage digital interface circuits

423 Derived from EIA standard RS-423. An interface specification for connecting DTE to DCE using unbalanced-voltage digital interface circuits

442 Derived from EIA standard RS-442. Specification for serial communications interface featuring DB-15 connectors

449-1 Derived from EIA standard RS-449-1. Specification for data interchange protocol using RS-449 interface

449 Derived from EIA standard RS-449. A general purpose 37-pin and 9-pin interface specification for connecting DTE to DCE using a serial binary data interchange

45's 45 rpm phonograph records

453 Derived from EIA standard 453. Dimensional, Mechanical, and Electrical Characteristics Defining Phone Plugs and Jacks

458 Derived from EIA standard 458. Standard Optical Waveguide Material and Preferred Sizes

485 Derived from EIA standard RS-485. A specification for multidrop, or multipoint, communications lines

486 See 80486

486DX See 80486DX

486SX See 80486SX

488 Derived from IEEE standard 488. The electrical definition of the General-Purpose Interface Bus (GPIB)

4004 The first microprocessor designed by Marcian E. "Ted" Hoff at Intel

5A Libyan aircraft

5BX five basic exercises (Royal Canadian Air Force physical fitness program)

5 by 5 radio reception loud and clear (volume and clarity measured on a scale from 1 to 5)

5/e fifth edition

5ESS Five Electronic Signalling System

5 1/4" DS/HD Refers to a double-sided high-density (1.2MB capacity) floppy disk

5 1/4-inch 5 1/4-inch floppy disk

5 1/4" DS/DD Refers to a double-sided double-density (360KB capacity) floppy disk

5100 The first desktop computer from IBM, introduced in 1974

6/c six-conductor

6/e sixth edition

6-mcd six-month certificate of deposit

6-mTs six-month Treasury securities

64-bit computer A computer that works with information in groups of 64 bits (binary digits) at a time

64-bit machine Same as 64-bit computer

66 Phillips Petroleum Company

640K Refers to a computer's base, or conventional memory. In an IBM PC or compatible machine operating in real mode; the first 640K (kilobytes) of the computer's **RAM** memory that is accessible to programs running under *DOS*

650 IBM's first major computer success, introduced in 1954

680x0 Refers to the Motorola 68000 family of microprocessors

696/S-100 Derived from IEEE standard 696/S-100. The electrical definition of the S-100 bus used by early personal computer systems based on the Intel 8080, Zilog Z-80, and Motorola 6800 microprocessors

6502 An 8-bit microprocessor developed by Rockwell International

6800 An 8-bit microprocessor developed by Motorola Inc

6845 A programmable video controller from Motorola

65816 A 16-bit microprocessor from Western Digital Design used in the Apple IIGS

68000 0 A line of 32-bit microprocessors from Motorola Inc that are the CPUs in Macintoshes and a wide variety of workstations. The original microprocessor in the 680x0 family

68020 A 32-bit microprocessor in the 680x0 family from Motorola

68030 A 32-bit microprocessor in the 680x0 family from Motorola

68040 A 32-bit microprocessor in the 680x0 family from Motorola

68881 The math coprocessor used with the Motorola 68000 and 68020 microprocessors

7ber September

7/c seven-conductor

7/e seventh edition

7-track Refers to older magnetic tape formats that record 6-bit characters plus parity, or seven tracks

7/24 7 days a week, 24 hours a day

70mm Generally refers to a 70 millimeter camera

720K 720 Kilobyte (Generally refers to the 720K low-density 3.5" microfloppy disk used on PCs)

767-300 Boeing 767 300-passenger airliner

78's 78 rpm phonograph records

8-bit computer A computer that works with information in groups of 8 bits (binary digits) at a time

8-bit machine Same as 8-bit computer

8-bit video adapter A color video adapter that can display 256 colors simultaneously

8-DPSK Octal Differential Phase Shift Keying

8/e eighth edition

8mm Generally refers to an 8 millimeter data cartridge tape

8 1/2 x 11 paper size 8 1/2" by 11" (standard letter size)

84-key the 84-key keyboard introduced with the IBM PC/AT

802.1 Derived from IEEE standard 802.1. Specification for communications management in all OSI levels (LAN standard relating internetworking)

802.2 Derived from IEEE standard 802.2. Logical link control layer for LANs.

802.3 Derived from IEEE standard 802.3. CSMA/CD LAN standard

802.4 Derived from IEEE standard 802.4. Arcnet (token bus) LAN standard

802.5 Derived from IEEE standard 802.5. Token ring (IBM), twisted pair LAN standard

802.6 Derived from IEEE standard 802.6. Metropolitan area network (MAN) LAN specification

802.7 Derived from IEEE standard 802.7. Broadband

802.8 Derived from IEEE standard 802.8. Fiber optic

802.9 Derived from IEEE standard 802.9. Integrated Data and Voice Networks

802.10 Derived from IEEE standard 802.10. Standard for Interoperable LAN Security

802.11 Derived from IEEE standard 802.11. Wireless Local Area Networks

8100 A minicomputer from IBM that was introduced in 1978

8080 An 8-bit microprocessor from Intel Corp that was introduced in 1974

8086 A 16-bit microprocessor from Intel Corp that was introduced in 1978

8087 A math, floating-point (or numeric) coprocessor from Intel Corp designed to work with the Intel 8086/8088 and 80186/80188 microprocessors

8088 A 16-bit microprocessor from Intel Corp that was introduced in 1978

8514 A monitor from IBM that is used with its 8514/A display adapter

8514/A A high-resolution display adapter from IBM that provides an interlaced display of 1024x768 pixels with up to 256 colors or 64 shades of gray

80286 Also called the 286. A 16-bit microprocessor from Intel Corp, introduced in 1982

80287 Also called the 287. A math coprocessor from Intel Corp designed for use with the 80286 family of microprocessors

80386 See 80386DX

80386DX Also called the 386, and 386DX. A 32-bit microprocessor from Intel Corp, introduced in 1985

80386SX Also called the 386SX. A 16-bit microprocessor from Intel Corp, introduced in 1988

80387 Also called the 387. A math coprocessor from Intel Corp designed for use with the 80386 family of microprocessors

80387SX Also called the 387SX. A math coprocessor from Intel Corp designed for use with the 80386SX family of microprocessors

80486 See 80486DX

80486DX Also called the i486, and 486DX. A 32-bit microprocessor from Intel Corp, introduced in 1989

80486SX Also called the 486SX. A version of the 32-bit, 80486DX microprocessor from Intel Corp, introduced in 1990, that omits the math coprocessor circuitry

80860 Also called the i860 or 860. A 64-bit *RISC*-based microprocessor from Intel Corp

82385 A cache controller chip that governs

cache memory using the Intel 80386 and 80486 family of microprocessors

88000 A family of 32-bit *RISC* microprocessors from Motorola Inc, first introduced in 1988

9-pin Refers to dot-matrix printers which can only produce dot patterns of low resolution, i.e., Near-Letter Quality [NLQ] output

9-track Refers to magnetic tape that records 8-bit bytes plus parity, or nine parallel tracks

9 to 5 everyday 9 A.M. to 5 P.M. job

911 emergency telephone number (US)

914 9 inches by 14 inches

999 emergency services (UK)

9370 A series of entry-level mainframes from IBM, introduced in 1986, that uses the 370 architecture

I-A available for military service

I-D member of reserve component or student taking military training

---

Chronology of Computing & Information Technology

1642 French mathematician and philosopher, Blaise Pascal, develops a calculating machine, which in turn, is named after him (the Pascaline).

1815 World's first female computer scientist, and colleague of Charles Babbage, Augusta Ada Byron, Countess of Lovelace and daughter of poet Lord Byron is born. Ada, the Pascal-based, high-level programming language developed by the U.S. Department of Defense is named in honor of her. She died in 1852.

1828 Noah Webster published his *American Dictionary of the English Language.*

1837 Samuel F.B. Morse invents the telegraph.

1841 Dun & Bradstreet Corp founded.

1844 "First telegraph message" over 'first telegraph line' sent by inventor, Samuel F.B. Morse from Washington to Baltimore: "What hath God wrought!"

1858 First trans-Atlantic submarine cable completed by Cyrus W. Field Aug. 5th; cable failed Sept. 1st.

1865 International Telegraph Union formed.

1866 Post Roads Act--assigned regulatory responsibility for the telegraph industry to the U.S. Postmaster General.

1868 First appearance (edition) of *The World Almanac*, a publication of the New York World.

1874 French engineer and telegrapher, Jean-Maurice-Emile Baudot develops the 5-bit (uses 5 bits to make up a character) "Baudot code", which is a coding scheme used principally for telex transmissions.

1877 Bell Telephone Co formed.

1878 Edison Electric Light Co founded, by Mr. Edison.

1878 First commercial telephone exchange (switchboard, 21 subscribers) opened, New Haven, CT.

1883 Heinrich Hertz detects electromagnetic waves.

1884 John Henry Patterson purchases the National Manufacturing Company of Dayton, OH, and renames it National Cash Register (NCR). Today, NCR Corp is a major manufacturer of computers and financial terminals.

1885 AT&T formed from Bell Telephone and Western Electric.

1886 Well known maker of calculating machines and cash registers, Burroughs Corp founded.

1889 Thomas A. Edison invents the "kinetoscope" (motion pictures), given first public showing April 14, 1894.

1890 Developed by Herman Hollerith, a statistician who had worked for the Census Bureau, the first automatic data processing system (Hollerith tabulating machine) is used to count the 1890 U.S. census.

1895 Guglielmo Marconi invents the radio.

1901 First transatlantic radio transmission by Marconi.

1906 International Electrotechnical Commission (IEC) is founded as an organization that sets international electrical and electronics standards, and headquartered in Geneva.

1911 The Computing-Tabulating-Recording Co (CTR) is created by a merger of The Tabulating Machine Co, International Time Recording Co, Computing Scale Co, and Bundy Manufacturing. This company went on to be renamed IBM Corp.

1912 Radio Act—allocated frequencies, established licensing of radio stations, and provided rules for radio use.

1915 First "telephone talk" from New York to San Francisco by Alexander Graham Bell and Thomas A. Watson.

1916 Membership organization, Computer and Business Equipment Manufacturers Association (CBEMA) founded.

1918 Nonprofit, privately-funded membership organization, American National Standards Institute (ANSI) founded.

1921 Leading electronics manufacturer, Radio Shack founded. It was acquired in 1963 by Tandy Corp.

1924 Membership organization, Electronic Industries Association (EIA) founded.

1924 A successful international enterprise called CTR (Computing-Tabulating-Recording Co), which started out in 1911, is renamed and known as IBM (International Business Machines Corp).

1928 Leading manufacturer of semiconductor devices, Motorola Inc founded in Chicago by Paul V. Galvin.

1930 Geophysical Service Inc is founded, and goes on to be renamed as (TI) Texas Instruments Inc (1951).

1931 First commercial microwave across the English Channel.

1933 Involved in the navigational guidance and control equipment business, Sperry Corp founded.

1934 Communications Act—formed the Federal Communications Commission (FCC) as the regulatory body for interstate and international telecommunications.

1939 Major manufacturer of computers and electronics, Hewlett-Packard Co (H-P) is founded by William Hewlett and David Packard in a garage behind the Packard's California home.

1942 First digital calculating machine that used vacuum tubes was completed (started in 1939). Known as ABC (Atanasoff-Berry Computer). Named in honor of Iowa State Professor John Atanasoff and graduate student, Clifford Berry.

1946 International organization (that sets international standards), International Standards Organization (ISO) founded.

1946 Developed for the U.S. Army by John Eckert and John Mauchly at the Moore School of Electrical Engineering, University of Pennsylvania, ENIAC (Electronic Numerical Integrator And Calculator) was completed.

1947 International membership organization, Association for Systems Management (ASM) founded.

1947 Membership organization, Association for Computing Machinery (ACM) founded.

1949 The EDSAC (Electronic Delay Storage Automatic Calculator), developed by Maurice Wilkes at Cambridge University in England was completed. It was in use until 1958.

1951 Membership organization, Data Processing Management Association (DPMA) founded.

1951 Geophysical Service Inc is renamed and called Texas Instruments Inc (TI), a leading semiconductor manufacturer.

1951 Remington Rand introduces the UNIVAC I (Universal Automatic Computer), the first commercially successful, general-purpose computer.

1951 Major manufacturer of computers, Wang Laboratories Inc founded by Dr. An Wang, who started the company only six years after coming from China to study applied physics at Harvard.

1952 UNIVAC I (by Remington Rand) predicts Eisenhower's victory over Stevenson.

1955 Sperry Corp merges with Remington Rand to form Sperry Rand.

1956 First transatlantic telephone cable (TAT-1) went into operation.

1956 IBM introduces RAMAC (Random Access Method of Accounting and Control), the first computer with a disk drive.

1957 IBM develops (1954) and releases the first "well suited to scientific, mathematical, and engineering applications" high-level programming language and compiler called FORTRAN (Formula Translator).

1957 Major computer company, Control Data Corp is founded.

1957 Major computer manufacturer, Digital Equipment Corp (DEC) founded by Kenneth Olson.

1959 Texas Instruments (TI) develops integrated circuitry (IC).

1959 An organization devoted to the development of computer languages, Conference on Data Systems Languages (CODASYL) was founded.

1960 Membership organization, Association of Data Processing Service Organizations (ADAPSO) founded.

1960 LISP (List Processing), a list-oriented, high-level programming language, is developed (1959-60) by John McCarthy and his colleagues at the Massachusetts Institute of Technology (MIT). One of the oldest programming languages still in use.

1961 Membership organization, American Federation of Information Processing Societies Inc (AFIPS) founded.

1963 First transpacific submarine telephone cable went into operation.

1963 Professional membership organization, Institute of Electrical and Electronics Engineers (IEEE) founded.

1964 International organization (involved in launching and operating commercial satellites), International Telecommunications Satellite Corp (INTELSAT) formed, with only 11 countries participating (today, over 114 nations have ownership).

1964 Extended Binary Coded Decimal Interchange Code (EBCDIC), a binary code for representing data was developed by IBM Corp for its 360 series.

1964 IBM introduces RPG (Report Program Generator), one of the first program generators designed for business reports.

1964 IBM introduces a high-level programming language called Programming Language 1 (PL/I) with its System/360 family.

1968 Datapoint Corp introduces the first local area network technology called ARCNET, or ARCnet (Attached Resource Computer Network).

1968 Computer manufacturer, Data General Corp founded by Edson de Castro.

1968 Leading manufacturer of semiconductor devices, Intel Corp founded by Bob Noyce and Gorden Moore in Mountain View, CA.

1968 MCI Decision—FCC ruling that permitted MCI (Microwave Communications Inc) (and any other carrier) to construct long distance facilities in competition with AT&T.

1969 Leading independent software vendor, CompuServe Inc founded.

1970 Amdahl Corp, a computer manufacturer is founded by Gene Amdahl, chief architect of the IBM System/360.

1970 Edgar Codd coins the term "relational database", which became a popular buzzword in the mid 1980s.

1970 Centronics Corp (maker of the first commercially successful dot matrix printers) introduces the Centronics printer.

1971 "Open Skies Policy"—a policy established by the FCC that allowed free competition in satellite communication.

1971 Intel Corp develops first microprocessor.

1972 Supercomputer manufacturer, Cray Research Inc founded by Seymour Cray, a leading designer of large-scale computers at Control Data Corp.

1972 Computer manufacturer, Prime Computer Inc, founded by seven engineers from Honeywell.

1972(3) PROLOG (Programming in Logic), a high-level programming language used in the development of AI research and applications, expert systems, and abstract problem solving, was developed by French scientist Alain Colmerauer and logician Philippe Roussel, at the University of Marseilles.

1974 Manufacturer of fault tolerant computers, Tandem Computers Inc founded.

1975 IBM introduces the first laser printer, called the 3800.

1975 Leading microcomputer software company, Microsoft Corp founded by Paul Allen and Bill Gates.

1976 Leading independent software vendor, Digital Research Inc founded.

1976 Professional organization, Data Entry Management Association (DEMA) was organized.

1976 Leading independent software vendor, Computer Associates International Inc is founded by Charles Wang and three associates.

1976 Apple Computer Inc, a major manufacturer of personal computers is founded on April Fool's Day, in a garage by Steve Wozniak and Steve Jobs. The Apple I was introduced soon after.

1977 Digital Equipment Corp (DEC) introduces the VAX (Virtual Address eXtension) machine, a family of 32-bit computers.

1977 Personal computer industry begins when Apple, Radio Shack, and Commodore introduce the first off-the-shelf computers as consumer products.

1977 Nonprofit membership organization, The Boston Computer Society (BCS) founded by Jonathan Rotenberg.

1978 Leading independent software vendor, WordStar International Inc founded.

1979 Leading independent software vendor, WordPerfect Corp founded.

1980 Workstations manufacturer, Apollo Computer founded.

1981 Leading independent software vendor, Lotus Development Corp founded.

1981 IBM introduces a series of personal computers called IBM PC.

1981 Microsoft Corp introduces MS-DOS (Microsoft Disk Operating System), the standard, single-user operating system of IBM PCs and compatibles.

1981 Data General Corp introduces an integrated office software called Comprehensive Electronic Office (CEO).

1981 Digital Equipment Corp (DEC) introduces a family of computer systems called DECmate, that are specialized for word processing.

1982 Compaq Computer Corp (first maker of IBM PC clones), a Houston manufacturer of high-performance personal computers founded by Rod Canion, Bill Murto and Jim Harris.

1982 Commodore Business Machines Inc introduces a home computer called Commodore 64.

1982 Leading independent software vendor, Autodesk Inc founded.

1982 Lotus Development Corp introduces Lotus 1-2-3, a very popular spreadsheet program for IBM PCs and compatibles, VAXs, and IBM mainframes.

1982 MAP (Manufacturing Automation Protocol), a communications protocol is introduced by General Motors.

1983 Hewlett-Packard was first major vendor to make commitment to the OSI standard, AdvanceNet.

1983 Leading independent software vendor, Novell Inc founded.

1983 Iomega Corp introduces the Bernoulli Box, an innovative removable mass storage system. The name comes from the 18th century Swiss scientist, Daniel Bernoulli, whose principle of fluid dynamics (aerodynamic lift) is demonstrated in the disk mechanism.

1983 IBM introduces a series of personal computers called IBM PC/XT.

1983 Apple Computer introduces a corporate-aimed marketable computer called the Lisa. But, because the machine was far too expensive for its market and slow, it was soon dropped in favor of the Macintosh.

1983 Leading independent software vendor, Borland International Inc, is founded by Philippe Kahn.

1983 Compact discs (CDs) introduced in the United States.

1984 Divestiture--the 13-year-old lawsuit against AT&T by the U.S. Justice Dept was finally settled and gave way to the breakup of AT&T's 22 Bell System companies and reformation of AT&T into seven regional holding companies. In return, AT&T was allowed to expand into previously prohibited areas including data processing, telephone and computer equipment sales, long distance, research, and computer communications devices.

1984 Borland International introduces Sidekick, a desktop accessory program for

PCs.

1984 Jointly developed by Lotus Development Corp, Intel Corp, and Microsoft Corp, Expanded Memory Specification (EMS), a description of a technique for adding (expanding) memory beyond one megabyte to IBM PCs running under MS-DOS is introduced. Also called LIM EMS. LIM is for Lotus/Intel/Microsoft.

1984 Leading independent software vendor, Aldus Corp founded.

1984 Hewlett-Packard (H-P) introduces the first desktop laser printer, called the LaserJet.

1984 Apple Computer introduces a family of personal computers that features a graphical user interface, and calls it Macintosh.

1984 IBM introduces a series of personal computers called IBM PC/AT.

1984 Computer manufacturer, Dell Computer Corp founded by Michael Dell in Austin, TX.

1985 Apple Computer introduces AppleTalk, a local area networking environment.

1986 Nonprofit, international research and development consortium, Corporation for Open Systems (COS) founded.

1986 Computer company, Unisys Corp formed as a merger of the Burroughs and Sperry Corporations.

1987 Apple Computer introduces an open-bus, high-performance family of personal computers, and calls it Macintosh II.

1987 IBM introduces SAA (Systems Application Architecture), a set of standards for the appearance and operation of application software that will give programs written for all IBM computers--from micro to mainframe--a similar look and feel.

1987 IBM introduces a series of personal computers called IBM PS/2.

1988 Computer Security Act—a first step in improving the security and privacy of information contained in federal computer systems is signed January 8th by President Ronald Reagan.

1988 In August, Philips, Sony, and Microsoft announce a jointly developed compact disk data storage standard called Compact Disc Read-Only Memory extended Architecture (CD-ROM XA).

1988 As a counter to IBM's Micro Channel, EISA (Extended Industry Standard Architecture) is announced.

1988 Nonprofit, research and development organization, Open Software Foundation (OSF) formed.

1989 Corel Systems Corp introduces a Windows-based, sophisticated and elegantly designed illustration program for IBM PCs and compatibles called CorelDRAW!.

1989 Borland International introduces a speedsheet program which provides advanced graphics and presentation capabilities called Quattro Pro.

1989 Seymour Cray, founder of Cray Research Inc (1972), leaves and starts-up Cray Computer Corp.

1990 IBM introduces a series of home computers called PS/1.

1992 Intel Corp introduces the 'next generation' of microprocessors called Intel® Pentium™ (or 586) processor. The following lists the significant features of the Pentium. (1) Increased number of transistors: packing more than 3 million transistors on a single silicon chip—can integrate components such as math coprocessors and caches right onto the CPU—dramatically cutting access time; (2) Redesigned floating-point unit: offers five times the performance of the i486 CPU—excellent for math-intensive applications; (3) Cache memory (on-chip cache): separate 8K code and data write-back caches that reduce cache conflicts and increase system performance; (4) Bus size doubled (64 bit): this allows twice as much information to be fetched at once—a 64-lane freeway inside your CPU; (5) Branch prediction: an intelligence of its own—a small cache known as the Branch Target Buffer, which predicts which way an execution will branch; (6) Increased number of executions per clock cycle: using new superscalar technology (enables information to be processed simultaneously through dual pipelines), the processor has two side-by-side pipelines for integer instructions—the pipelines divide up an instruction, then send it through five stages—as it passes from one stage to the next, the pipeline is free to begin another instruction—enables the processor to execute two instructions per clock cycle (at once). Source: Intel Technology Briefing, Pentium™ processor. ©1993 Intel Corp.

Commonly Used Extensions [1]

An extension is a file category created under DOS and OS/2. All programs and most data files use extensions. However, many word processing files do not, and users can set up their own filing system by making up their own. File name and extension are separated with a dot, for example, ANSI.SYS, SALES.DBF, and GLOSS.EXE.

Commonly Used Extensions

Extension	Type of File Created by These Programs
.ARC /.PKARC	Compressed file
.ASM	Source program Intel Assembly language
.BAK	Backup version Common
.BAS	Source program BASIC
.BAT	Batch DOS and OS/2
.C	Source program C
.CAP	Captions Ventura Publisher
.CDR	Graphics file CorelDRAW!
.CFG	Configuration Common
.CGM	Graphics Common vector & raster format
.CHP	Chapter Ventura Publisher
.CIF	Chapter information Ventura Publisher
.COB	Source program COBOL
.COM	Executable program Compilers and assemblers
.DB	Database Paradox

Extension	Type of File Created by These Programs
.DBF	Database dBASE
.DBT	Text dBASE
.DCA	Text IBM
.DOC	Document MultiMate, Microsoft Word, WordPerfect
.DOX	Document MultiMate v4.0
.DRW	Graphics Micrografx products
.DXF	Graphics AutoCAD common
.DWG	Graphics AutoCAD proprietary
.EPS	Graphics/Text Encapsulated PostScript
.EXE	Executable program Compilers and assemblers
.FMT	Screen format dBASE
.FRM	Report layout dBASE
.GEM	Graphics GEM draw format (vector)
.GRF	Graphic file Micrografx products
.HP	Graphics Hewlett-Packard (vector)
.IMG	Graphics GEM paint format (raster)
.LBL	Label description dBASE
.NDX	Index dBASE
.OBJ	Object module Compilers and assemblers
.OVL	Executable program Compilers and assemblers
.PCT	Graphics Macintosh
.PCX	Graphics PC Paintbrush
.PDF	Printer file WordStar
.PDV	Printer file PC Paintbrush
.PIC	Graphics Lotus 1-2-3, Micrografx products
.PIF	Program information Microsoft Windows

Extension	Type of File Created by These Programs
.PM	Graphics/text PageMaker
.PM3	Graphics/text PageMaker v3.0
.PRD	Printer file Microsoft Word
.PRN	Printer file XyWrite, DisplayWrite
.PRS	Printer file WordPerfect
.PRG	Source program dBASE
.PS	Page description PostScript
.SC	Source program Paradox
.SCR	Screen layout dBASE
.SLD	Graphics AutoCAD slide format
.STY	Style sheet Ventura Publisher
.SYS	System DOS and OS/2
.TIF	Graphics Common vector format
.TMP	Temporary Common
.TXT	ASCII Text Common
.VGR	Chapter information Ventura Publisher
.VUE	Relational view dBASE
.WK1	Spreadsheet Lotus 1-2-3 v2
.WKS	Spreadsheet Lotus 1-2-3 v1a
.WMF	File transfer Microsoft Windows
.XLS	Spreadsheet Excel
.XLC	Chart Excel
.ZIP	Compressed file PKZIP
.$$$	Temporary Common

MS-DOS 6.0 COMMAND REFERENCE

Types of Commands (an overview defined)

Utilities:

Utilities commands are basic instructions provided with MS-DOS 6.0. Utilities are designed to perform a particular function, especially those related to computer system management. In general, these may be referred to as "command-line basics".

Batch:

Batch commands are *internal commands* that you can use to direct how a batch program runs. A batch file provides a shortcut for executing one or many MS-DOS commands. Batch files consist entirely of ASCII text characters. You can create batch files in the DOS Editor, in Edlin, and in nearly any other text-editing or word-processing program. Batch files can automate long or repetitive instructions.

CONFIG.SYS:

CONFIG.SYS commands are commands that you can use to customize your system. They provide a method to load device drivers (such as those for printers, keyboard, and memory), set the number of open files and buffers to use, install some memory-resident programs into HMA or upper memory blocks, for example, and carry out utilities (or MS-DOS) commands during Config.Sys processing. Here's how it works: after DOS starts but before it runs AUTO-EXEC.BAT, DOS looks in the root directory of the boot disk for a file called CONFIG.SYS. If DOS finds CON-FIG.SYS, DOS attempts to carry out the commands in the file. In short, CON-FIG.SYS commands define to the operating system how your system will be configured.

(Internal):

Internal commands are stored in the

COMMAND.COM file, which is loaded into memory when you start your system. They include the simpler, more commonly used commands you need on a regular basis. Because internal commands are part of COMMAND.COM, you never see their names in a directory listing. These commands remain resident in memory and are available to you at all times.

(External):

External commands exist as separate files on your disk. When you use the "Dir" command to view the files on your MS-DOS system disk, you see the external commands in the list of filenames and directory names. The filename of an external command has a .COM, .EXE, or .BAT extension. Additionally, it is a command that cannot be used unless the program file is present in the current drive, directory, or path.

NOTE: The *commands* in this Reference are divided into six (6) groups: DOS Utilities Commands, Batch Commands, Configuration Commands, Debug Commands, DOS Editor Commands, and Edlin Commands. The commands are listed alphabetically within each group.

MS-DOS Utilities Commands[1]

APPEND (Set directory search order): (External command) Instructs MS-DOS to search the specified directories on the specified disks for data (nonprogram/nonbatch) files. In recent versions of MS-DOS, you can also search for executable files.

ASSIGN (Assign disk drive): (External command) Instructs MS-DOS to use a drive other than the one specified by a program or command. ASSIGN is included on the MS-DOS Supplementary Program disk, not in the standard DOS 6.0 package.

ATTRIB (Change/show file attributes): (External command) Displays, sets, or clears a file's read-only, archive, system, or hidden attributes.

BACKUP (Back up floppy disks or hard disks): (External command) Backs up one or more files from a hard disk or a floppy disk onto a floppy disk or another hard disk. MS-DOS 6.0 provides backward compatibility with this command. (See MSBACKUP).

BREAK: (Internal command) Determines when MS-DOS looks for a Ctrl+Break sequence to stop a program.

CHCP (Change code page): (Internal command) Displays or sets code page (character set or font) used by MS-DOS for all devices that display fonts.

CHDIR or CD (Change directory): Changes the current directory or shows the path of the current directory.

CHKDSK (Check disk): (External command) Checks the directory and the file allocation table (FAT) of the disk and reports disk and memory status. CHKDSK also can repair errors in the directories or the FAT.

CLS (Clear screen): (Internal command) Erases or clears the display screen.

COMMAND (Invoke secondary command processor): (External command) Invokes another copy of COMMAND.COM, the command processor.

COMP (Compare files): (External command) Compares two sets of disk files of the same name and length. MS-DOS 6.0 provides backward compatibility with this command. (See FC).

COPY (Copy files): (Internal command) Copies files between disk drives or devices, either keeping the same file name or changing it. COPY can concatenate (join) two or more files into another file or append one or more files to another file. Options in this command support special handling of text files and verification of the copying process.

CTTY (Change console): (Internal command) Changes the standard input and output device to an auxiliary console, or changes the input and output device back from an auxiliary console to the keyboard and video display.

DATE (Set/show date): (Internal command) Displays and/or changes the system date.

DBLSPACE (DoubleSpace, disk compression utility): (External command) Starts the full-screen interface to the "DoubleSpace" disk Compression capability. DoubleSpace automatically compresses information on hard disks or floppy disks and configures many aspects of the compression. The general target is to "double" the amount of information. Note: You must compress a disk drive by running BDLSPACE.EXE before you can use the DBLSPACE.SYS device driver. After you compress the disk drive, MS-DOS updates your CONFIG.SYS file to include the driver. In conclusion, with switches and parameters, you can control each aspect of DoubleSpace from the DOS command line. The many possible combinations are covered in the forthcoming sections of this Command Reference that deal with specific DoubleSpace commands.

DBLSPACE/AUTOMOUNT: (External command) Automatically mounts a compressed drive.

DBLSPACE/CHKDSK: (External command) Checks the structure (i.e., directory and the file allocation table [FAT]) of a compressed drive. The command reports errors (such as lost clusters and cross-linked files) and can correct some errors.

DBLSPACE/COMPRESS: (External command) Compresses the files on an existing hard disk, floppy disk, or other removable disk, making more space available.

DBLSPACE/CREATE: (External command) Creates a new compressed drive by using free space on an uncompressed drive.

DBLSPACE/DEFRAGMENT or /DEF: (External command) Defragments a compressed drive by moving all the drive's free space to the end of the drive. This command enables you to get the maximum reduction in the size of the drive when you issue the DBLSPACE/SIZE command.

DBLSPACE/DELETE or /DEL: (External command) Deletes (removes) a compressed drive and its associated compressed volume file (CVF).

DBLSPACE/FORMAT or /F: (External

command) Formats a compressed drive.

DBLSPACE/INFO: (External command) Displays information about a compressed drive.

DBLSPACE/LIST or /L: (External command) Shows a listing of all compressed volumes and uncompressed drives currently installed, including RAM drives and floppy disk drives.

DBLSPACE/MOUNT or /MO: (External command) Associates a drive letter with a compressed volume file (CVF) so that you can access the files in the CVF as though they were on a disk. Normally, DoubleSpace mounts CVFs for you, so you need to mount a CVF only if you have explicitly "unmounted" it or if the CVF is on a floppy disk.

DBLSPACE/MOVE: (External command) Loads the DBLSPACE.SYS driver with Quarterdeck QEMM's LOADHI.SYS program.

DBLSPACE/RATIO or /RA: (External command) Changes the estimated compression ratio of a compressed drive.

DBLSPACE/SIZE or /SI: (External command) Changes or adjusts the size of a compressed drive. Examples: you may want to make a compressed drive "smaller" if you need more free space on its host drive. You may want to make a compressed drive "larger" if its host drive has a great deal of free space.

DBLSPACE/UNMOUNT or /U: (External command) Breaks the association between a drive letter and a compressed volume file (CVF), temporarily making a compressed drive unavailable. In short, "dismounts" a compressed volume.

DBLSPACE.SYS: (External command) Specifies whether the DoubleSpace driver, DBLSPACE.BIN, ends up in conventional or upper memory.

DEBUG (Run, Test, Edit Programs): (External command) A utility that tests and edits programs. DEBUG also assembles the machine code from assemble-language mnemonics, unassembles bytes into source statements, and allocates EMS (expanded memory). For more information on associated DEBUG commands, see "MS-DOS Debug Commands", which follows "MS-DOS Configuration Commands".

DECOMP (File decompression utility): (External command) Decompresses program files from the DOS distribution floppy disks. (See also EXPAND).

DEFRAG (Defragment files utility): (External command) Defragments (moves files and clusters within files) files on disks to "optimize" your disk's performance.

DEL or ERASE (Delete files): (Internal command) Deletes files from the disk. DEL is an alternative command for "ERASE" and performs the same function. (See also ERASE).

DELOLDOS (Delete Old DOS Files): (External command) Removes from the hard disk all files from a previous (older) version of MS-DOS after a MS-DOS 5.0 or 6.0 installation. MS-DOS 6.0 provides backward compatibility with this command.

DELTREE (Delete subdirectory and all files inside): (External command) Deletes a directory, and any and all files and subdirectories in the named directory.

DIR (Directory): (Internal command) Lists any or all files and subdirectories in a disk's directory. By default, the DIR command displays a list, which includes the following information: volume label and serial number; one directory or file name per line; file size (in bytes); date and time of the last modification; number of files listed; total bytes listed; number of available bytes remaining on the disk.

DISKCOMP (Compare floppy disks): (External command) Compares two floppy disks on a track-for-track, sector-for-sector basis to see whether their contents are identical. MS-DOS 6.0 provides backward compatibility with this command. (See FC).

DISKCOPY (Copy entire floppy disk): (External command) Copies the entire contents of one floppy disk to another floppy disk on a track-for-track basis. DISKCOPY works with floppy disks only.

DOSHELP (DOS On-line Help): (External command) Provides an on-line help summary for basic DOS commands and syntax. MS-DOS provides backward compatibility with this command. (See also HELP).

DOSKEY (Review command line/Create macros): (External command) Remembers a history of commands typed from the command line for reuse or editing. You also can use DOSKEY macros to create custom DOS commands.

DOSSHELL (Start the Shell program): (External command) Starts the Shell (a graphical user interface) that accompanies MS-DOS.

EDIT (Full-screen text editor): (External command) Activates the MS-DOS Editor, which enables you to create and edit ASCII text files (such as batch files) in a full-screen mode. This mode gives you much of the editing capability of a simple word processor. *Note*: EDIT is the text editor that QBASIC uses. This program is helpful for creating and editing batch files, as well as other text files. (See also EDLIN and QBASIC). For more information on associated EDIT commands, see "MS-DOS Editor Commands", which follows "MS-DOS Debug Commands".

EDLIN (ASCII text editor): (External command) Starts Edlin, which enables you to edit short batch, text, and data files. MS-DOS 6.0 provides backward compatibility with this limited, line-oriented ASCII text editor. (See also EDIT). For more information on EDLIN commands, See "Edlin Commands" which follows "MS-DOS Editor Commands".

EMM386 (EMS/UMB provider): (External command) Emulates expanded memory (EMS 4.0) on an 80386 or higher processor. This command also enables you to place device drivers and TSRs in reserved memory.

ERASE or DEL (Erase files): (Internal command) Removes (deletes) one or more files from a directory. ERASE is an alternative command for DEL and performs the same functions. (See also DEL).

EXE2BIN (Change EXE files into BIN or COM files): (External command)

Changes suitably formatted EXE files into BIN or COM files. MS-DOS 6.0 provides backward compatibility for this command.

EXIT (Leave secondary command processor): (Internal command) Quits COMMAND.COM and returns to the program that started COMMAND.COM. Stated in simpler terms, leaves a secondary command processor and returns to the primary command processor.

EXPAND (Expand compressed files): (External command) Copies a compressed, unusable file from the DOS distribution (installation or update) disks that accompanied MS-DOS 5.0 and 6.0 to uncompressed, "usable" form. (See also DECOMP).

FASTHELP (DOS On-line Help): (External command) Provides an on-line brief description or summary of help for basic DOS commands and syntax. (See also HELP).

FASTOPEN (Fast opening of files): (External command) Keeps directory information in memory so that DOS can find and use frequently needed files quickly.

FC (Compare files): (External command) Compares two disk files or two sets of disk files. Note: Although FC has a function similar to COMP's, FC is a more intelligent file compare utility because it makes determinations about the files that it compares and assumes that EXE, COM, SYS, OBJ, LIB, and BIN files are binary. It compares other files as ASCII files.

FDISK (Create a hard disk partition): (External command) Prepares or partitions a hard disk to accept an operating system such as MS-DOS.

FIND (Find string filter): (External command) Displays all the lines of the designated files that match (or do not match, depending on the switches used) the specified string. This command also can display the line numbers.

FORMAT (Format disk): (External command) Initializes a disk to accept MS-DOS information and files. FORMAT also checks the disk for defective tracks and (optionally) places MS-DOS on the floppy disk or hard disk.

GRAFTABL (Load graphics table): (External command) Loads into memory the additional character sets to be displayed on the IBM Color Graphics Adapter (CGA). MS-DOS 6.0 provides backward compatibility with this command.

GRAPHICS (Graphics screen print): (External command) Prints the contents of the graphics screen on a suitable printer.

HELP (On-line help system): (External command) Provides on-line, context-sensitive command help. Hence, displays syntax, notes, and examples for a DOS command. (See also FASTHELP).

INTERLNK (Link computers to share resources): (External command) Allows two computers connected by parallel or serial ports to share printers, disk drives, and files.

INTERSVR (Start INTERLNK Server): (External command) Starts the INTERLNK server that cooperates with an INTERLNK.EXE in a client system to enable the client to use the server's drives and printers. (See also INTERLNK).

JOIN (Join disk drives): (External command) Produces a single directory structure by connecting a disk drive to a subdirectory of a second disk drive. MS-DOS 6.0 provides backward compatibility with this command.

KEYB (Enable foreign language Keys): (External command) Changes (configures) the keyboard layout and characters to one of 18 languages.

LABEL (Volume Label): (External command) Creates, changes, or deletes a volume label for a disk.

LOADFIX (Fix program load): (External command) Loads and executes a program just above the first 64K of RAM (or conventional memory) for compatibility. (See also SETVER).

LOADHIGH or LH (Load program in reserved memory): (Internal command) Loads device drivers or memory-resident programs (TSRs) in reserved memory on an 80386 or greater processor. (See also DEVICEHIGH).

MEM (Display memory usage): (External

command) Displays the amount of used and unused memory, allocated and open memory areas, and all programs currently running in memory.

MEMMAKER (Optimize memory use): (External command) Attempts to optimize your computer's conventional memory by moving device drivers and memory-resident programs (TSRs) to upper memory. Note: You must have an 80686SX or greater processor and extended memory to use this command.

MIRROR (Protects against data loss): (External command) Records information about the file-allocation table (FAT) and the root directory to enable you to use the UNFORMAT and UNDELETE commands. In simpler terms, saves information about a disk drive so that you can recover accidentally lost data. MS-DOS 6.0 provides backward compatibility with this command.

MKDIR or MD (Make directory): (Internal command) Creates a subdirectory.

MODE Commands (Set, Devices): (External command) The MODE command generally configures system devices. Hence, sets the "mode of operation" for the printer(s), the video display, the keyboard, and the Asynchronous Communications Adapter. This command also controls code page switching for the console and printer. The details of the command's functions, however, are so varied that the syntax is complex. Therefore, the following sections cover each of the MODE command's functions separately.

MODE CODEPAGE PREPARE (Set device code pages): (External command) Prepares (chooses) the code pages to be used with a device. This command can be abbreviated as CP PREP.

MODE CODEPAGE REFRESH (Set device code pages): (External command) Reloads and reactivates the code page used with a device. This command can be abbreviated as CP REF.

MODE CODEPAGE SELECT (Set device code pages): (External command) Activates the code page used with a device. This command can be abbreviated as CP SEL.

MODE CODEPAGE/STATUS (Set device code pages): (External command) Displays a device's code-page status. This command can be abbreviated as CP/STA.

MODE COM PORT (Configure serial port): (External command) Controls the protocol characteristics of the Asynchronous Communications Adapter.

MODE DISPLAY (Set display mode): (External command) Switches the active display adapter between the monochrome display and a graphics adapter/array (Color Graphics Adapter, Enhanced Color Graphics Adapter, or Video Graphics Array) on a two-display system, and sets the graphics adapter/array's characteristics.

MODE KEY REPEAT (Set typematic rate): (External command) Adjusts the rate at which the keyboard repeats a character.

MODE PRINTER PORT (Configure printer): (External command) Sets the parallel-printer characteristics.

MODE REDIRECTION (Redirect printing): (External command) Forces MS-DOS to print to a serial printer instead of a parallel printer.

MODE/STATUS (Display device status): (External command) Display the status of a specified device or of all devices that can be set by MODE. This command can be abbreviated as MODE/STA.

MORE (More output filter): (External command) Displays one screen of information from the standard input device, pauses, and then displays the following message: -- More --. When you press any key, MORE displays the next screen if information.

MOVE (Move files): (External command) Moves files from one directory or drive to another directory or drive, optionally renaming the files, and renames directories.

MSAV (Virus scanning software): (External command) Scans your computer's memory and disks for viruses and (optionally) deletes viruses (virus-infected files).

MSBACKUP (Microsoft Backup and Restore): (External command) Backs up and restores one or more files from a hard disk or floppy disk to another disk. (See also BACKUP and RESTORE).

MSCDEX (Microsoft CD-ROM Extensions): (External command) Loads the CD-ROM software extensions in order to access information on CD-ROM discs or drives.

MSD (Examine technical information): (External command) Activates Microsoft Diagnostics, which reports detailed information about your computer hardware, software, and operating environment.

NLSFUNC (National language support): (External command) Supports extended country information (national-language support, or NLS) in MS-DOS and enables you to use the CHCP command. (See also CHCP).

PATH (Set directory search order): (Internal command) Tells MS-DOS to search the specified directories on the specified drives if a program or batch file is not found in the current directory.

POWER (Reduce power consumption): (External command) Helps the program conserve power to the system components when devices (monitors, disk drives, etc.) are idle.

PRINT (Background printing): (External command) Causes the printer to print a list of files while the computer performs other tasks.

PROMPT (Set the System Prompt): (Internal command) Customizes the MS-DOS prompt.

QBASIC (Basic Interpreter): (External command) Loads the BASIC interpreter into memory for BASIC programming.

RECOVER (Recover files or disk directory): (External command) Recovers a file that contains bad sectors or a file from a disk with a damaged directory. MS-DOS 6.0 provides backward compatibility with this command. (See also UNDELETE).

RENAME or REN (Rename file): (Internal command) Changes the name of the disk file(s).

REPLACE (Replace/update file): (External command) Selectively replaces files on one disk with files of the same name from another disk; selectively adds files to a disk by copying the files from another disk.

RESTORE (Restore backed up files): (External command) Restores one or more files created by BACKUP from one disk to another disk (i.e., this command complements the BACKUP command). Additionally, if your backup file was created by MSBACKUP, you need to use MSBACKUP to restore data from that file (i.e., this command has backward compatibility with MS-DOS 6.0). (See also MSBACKUP).

RMDIR or RD (Remove directory): (Internal command) Removes a directory or subdirectory.

SELECT: (External command) In MS-DOS, versions 3 and 4; prepares a disk with the DOS files and configures the CONFIG.SYS and AUTOEXE.BAT files for your country. Note: SELECT is not included (obsolete) in MS-DOS 5.0 and later versions.

SET (Set/show environment): (Internal command) Sets, shows, or removes a system environment variable.

SETVER (Emulate previous DOS versions): (External command) Enables the current DOS version to emulate an older DOS version so that the current version can run a certain program file.

SHARE (Check shared files): (External command) Enables MS-DOS support for file and record locking.

SORT (Sort string filter): (External command) Reads lines from the standard input device, performs and ASCII sort of the lines, and then writes the lines to the standard output device. The sorting may be in ascending or descending order and may start at any column in the line.

SUBST (Substitute path name): (External command) Creates an alias disk drive name for a subdirectory. This command is used principally with programs that do not use path names.

SYS (Place operating system on disk): (External command) Places a copy of MS-DOS (the hidden system files IO.SYS and MSDOS.SYS) on the specified floppy disk or hard disk. Note: To ensure that the disk is bootable (able to load and execute the disk operating system), you must also copy COMMAND.COM to the same disk. If this is done on a floppy diskette, it should be labeled as: "system disk" or "bootable disk".

TIME (Set/show the time): (Internal command) Sets and shows the system time.

TREE (Display all directories): (External command) Displays all the subdirectories on a disk and (optionally) display all the files in each directory.

TYPE (Type file on-screen): (Internal command) Displays a file's contents on the monitor (on-screen).

UNDELETE (Restore deleted files/directories): (External command) Restores (recovers) files and directories that were "erased" with the DEL command.

UNFORMAT (Recover a formatted disk): (External command) Recovers disks that were inadvertently reformatted. Stated in other terms, reconstructs a formatted floppy disk.

VER (Display version number): (Internal command) Shows the MS-DOS version number on the video display unit.

VERIFY (Set/show disk verification): (Internal command) Sets the computer to check the accuracy of data written to the disk(s) to ensure that information is properly recorded, and shows whether the data has been checked.

VOL (Display volume label): (Internal command) Displays the disk's volume label and serial number (if they exist).

VSAFE (Virus protection): (External command) Provides continuous virus protection, monitoring, and detection, and displays a warning when it finds one.

XCOPY (Extended COPY): (External command) Selectively copies groups of files from one or more subdirectories.

MS-DOS Batch Commands[2]

Batch Command: (Internal command) Executes one or more commands contained in an ASCII disk file that has a BAT. extension.

CALL: (Internal command) Runs a second batch file and returns control to the first batch file.

CHOICE: (External command) Suspends or pauses batch file processing and prompts (i.e., displays specific messages) the user to make a "choice" before processing resumes.

ECHO: (Internal command) Displays a message and either permits or inhibits the display of batch commands and messages by other batch subcommands as MS-DOS executes the subcommands.

FOR..IN..DO: (Internal command) Enables iterative (repeated) processing of an MS-DOS command.

GOTO: (Internal command) Jumps (transfers control) to the line following the label in the batch file and continues batch-file execution from that line.

IF: (Internal command) Enables (permits) conditional execution of an MS-DOS command.

PAUSE: (Internal command) Suspends batch-file processing until the user presses a key, and optionally displays a user's message.

REM (Remark): (Internal command) Places a comment (remark) within a batch file or within the CONFIG.SYS file. MS-DOS ignores any lines that begin with REM.

SHIFT: (Internal command) Shifts command-line parameters one position left when a batch file is invoked.

MS-DOS Configuration Commands[3]

BREAK (Ctrl-Break checking): (Internal command) When on, causes MS-DOS to look for a Ctrl+Break or a Ctrl+C to stop a program.

BUFFERS (Set number of disk buffers): (Internal command) Sets the number of disk buffers set aside (allocated) by MS-DOS in memory.

COUNTRY (Set country-dependent information): (Internal command) Instructs MS-DOS to modify the input and display of date, time, and field divider information, the order in which characters are sorted, and which characters can be used in file names to match the formats of different countries.

DEVICE (Set device driver): (Internal command) Instructs MS-DOS to load, link, and use a special device driver.

DEVICEHIGH (Loads device driver into upper memory): (Internal command) Instructs MS-DOS to load, link, and use a special device driver in the reserved (upper) memory of an 80386 or greater computer, which frees conventional memory for programs and other uses.

DOS (Load DOS into high memory): (Internal command) Tells MS-DOS to manage the upper-memory area and/or to load itself into the high-memory area (HMA). The latter procedure frees conventional memory. This command requires an 80286 computer or greater with extended memory.

DRIVPARM (Define block device): (Internal command) Defines or changes the parameters of an existing block device, such as a disk drive when you start MS-DOS.

FCBS (Set Control Blocks): (Internal command) Specifies the number of MS-DOS file-control blocks (FCBs) that can be open simultaneously and how many always are kept open.

FILES (Set maximum open files): (Internal command) Specifies the number of file handles that MS-DOS can open (access) at any given time (generally, one file handle per file).

HIMEM.SYS (Extended memory manager): (External command) Manages the high-memory area (HMA) where device drivers and TSR programs are loaded.

INCLUDE: (Internal command) Tells MS-DOS to execute the contents of a configuration block as though a copy of that block were substituted for the include command.

INSTALL (Load TSR into memory): (Internal command) Starts a memory-resident program from CONFIG.SYS. Valid programs to start with "INSTALL" are FASTOPEN, KEYB, NLSFUNC, SHARE, and other programs that remain in the computer's random-access memory (RAM).

LASTDRIVE (Specify last system drive):

(Internal command) Sets the last valid drive letter acceptable to MS-DOS.

MENUCOLOR: (Internal command) Specifies the text and background colors for the startup menu and is only valid within menu block.

MENUDEFAULT: (Internal command) Specifies the default menu item and timeout for the start-up menu and is valid only within a menu block.

MENUITEM: (Internal command) Defines an item in the start-up menu and is only valid within a menu block.

MULTICONFIG: Designs a multiple configuration selection menu from which you can choose a specific configuration to "boot" your computer.

NUMLOCK: (Internal command) Turns your keyboard NumLock on or off when you start the computer. This command is only valid in a menu block.

RAMDRIVE.SYS (Emulate disk drive in RAM): (External command) Simulates a physical disk drive using random-access memory (RAM).

REM (Remark): (Internal command) Places remarks or "hidden statements" in the CONFIG.SYS file. MS-DOS ignores lines that begin with REM.

SHELL (Specify command processor): (Internal command) Specifies or changes the default MS-DOS command processor (command interpreter) or modifies some command-processor defaults (e.g., the size of the environment).

STACKS (Allocate interrupt storage): (Internal command) Allots memory used to store information when a hardware interrupt occurs.

SUBMENU: (Internal command) Defines an item in the start-up menu that, when selected, displays another menu. This command is only valid in a menu block.

SWITCHES: (Internal command) Defines MS-DOS start-up options.

MS-DOS® Debug (Utilities) Commands[4]

NOTE: All commands in this Reference are "External".

DEBUG: Starts Debug, a program that allows you to test and debug executable files.

DEBUG A (Assemble): Assembles 8086/ 8087/8088 mnemonics directly into memory.

DEBUG C (Compare): Compares two portions of memory.

DEBUG D (Dump): Display the contents of a range of memory addresses.

DEBUG E (Enter): Enters data into memory at the address you specify.

DEBUG F (Fill): Fills addresses in the specified memory area with values you specify.

DEBUG G (Go): Runs the program currently in memory.

DEBUG H (Hex): Performs hexadecimal arithmetic on two parameters you specify.

DEBUG I (Input): Reads and displays one byte value from the port you specify.

DEBUG L (Load): Loads a file or contents of specific disk sectors into memory.

DEBUG M (Move): Copies the contents of a block of memory to another block of memory.

DEBUG N (Name): Specifies the name of an executable file for a Debug L (load) or W (write) command, or specifies parameters for the executable file being debugged.

DEBUG O (Output): Sends the value of a byte to an output port.

DEBUG P (Proceed): Executes a loop, a repeated string instruction, a software interrupt, or a subroutine; or traces through any other instruction.

DEBUG Q (Quit): Stops the Debug session, without saving the file currently being tested.

DEBUG R (Register): Display or alters the contents of one or more central-processing-unit (CPU) registers.

DEBUG S (Search): Searches a range of addresses for a pattern of one or more byte values.

DEBUG T (Trace): Executes one instruction and displays the contents of all registers, the status of all flags, and the decoded form of the instruction executed.

DEBUG U (Unassemble): Disassembles bytes and displays their corresponding

source statements, including addresses and byte values. The disassembled code looks like a listing for an assembled file.

DEBUG W (Write): Writes a file or specific sectors to disk.

DEBUG XA (Allocate Expanded Memory): Allocates a specified number of pages of expanded memory.

DEBUG XD (Deallocate Expanded Memory): Deallocates a handle to expanded memory.

DEBUG XM (Map Expanded Memory Pages): Maps a logical page of expanded memory, belonging to the specified handle, to a physical page of expanded memory.

DEBUG XS (Display Expanded-Memory Status): Displays information about the status of expanded memory.

MS-DOS Editor (Utilities) Commands[5]

EDIT (Full-screen text editor): Starts the MS-DOS Editor, which was introduced in DOS 5.0, is a full-screen text processing editor. Using EDIT is similar to using a word processor (kind of a mini-word processor).

(Using EDIT Commands)

Clear(Edit menu): Removes the highlighted text from the file.

Copy(Edit menu): Copies the highlighted text into temporary memory without removing the highlighted text.

Cut(Edit menu): Removes the highlighted text from the file, but keeps the last text you cut in temporary memory.

Display...(Options menu): Changes the colors of the screen.

Exit(File menu): Exits EDIT and provides you with the option to save the file if it has not been saved.

Find...(Search menu): Locates text in the file.

Help Path(Options menu): Specifies the location of the EDIT help file.

New(File menu): Clears the current file, if any, and enables you to save the old file and then create a new file.

Open...(File menu): Loads a file from disk

into memory for editing.

Paste(Edit menu): Places cut or copied text from the temporary memory int the current file.

Print...(File menu): Prints the current file in memory to the printer.

Save(File menu): Saves the current file to disk by the same name as was retrieved or enables you to select a name if the file is new.

Save as...(File menu): Saves the current file in memory by a different name.

Repeat Last Find(Search menu): Repeats the most recent search.

Replace...(Search menu): Locates text in the file and replaces it with other text.

MS-DOS® Edlin (Utilities) Commands[6]

NOTE: All commands in this Reference are "External".

EDLIN: Starts Edlin, a line-oriented text editor with which you can create and change ASCII files.

EDLIN [line]: Displays the line of text you specify.

EDLIN A (Append): Loads a portion of a file into memory when insufficient memory prevents Edlin from loading the entire file.

EDLIN C (Copy): Copies a block of consecutive lines to one or more locations within the file in memory.

EDLIN D (Delete): Deletes the block of consecutive lines you specify.

EDLIN E (End): Writes the current file from memory to a disk and stops the Edlin session.

EDLIN I (Insert): Inserts lines before the line number you specify in the edited file in memory.

EDLIN L (List): Displays the block of consecutive lines you specify.

EDLIN M (Move): Moves the block of consecutive lines you specify to another location in the file in memory.

EDLIN P (Page): Displays all or part of a file, one page (full screen of text) at a time.

EDLIN Q (Quit): Stops the current Edlin session without writing the edited file

from memory to a disk.

EDLIN R (Replace): Searches a block of consecutive lines for a string of one or more characters you specify, and replaces occurrence of that string with another string you specify.

EDLIN S (Search): Searches for the string of one or more characters that you specify.

EDLIN T (Transfer): Merges the contents of another file from a disk with the contents of the file that is in memory.

EDLIN W (Write): Writes the first portion of the edited file from memory to a disk.

MS-DOS Device Drivers[7]

ANSI.SYS: A device driver that gives MS-DOS additional control of the screen and keyboard devices beyond the control features built into the operating system. In other terms, ANSI.SYS defines functions that change (or enhance) display graphics, control cursor movement, and reassign keys.

DBLSPACE.SYS: Enables disk compression, greatly increasing the amount of data you can store on your hard disk (MS-DOS 6.0 only).

DISPLAY.SYS: Provides support for code-page switching to the screen.

DRIVER.SYS: Sets parameters for physical and logical disk drives.

EGA.SYS: Saves and restores an EGA screen when using DOSSHELL and the Task Swapper.

EMM386.EXE: Uses XMS memory in an 80386 or higher processor to emulate EMS memory and provide upper memory blocks (UMB's).

HIMEM.SYS: Manages the use of extended memory on an 80286 or higher processor.

PRINTER.SYS: Enables code-page switching for your printer if you have one of the supported printers or a compatible.

RAMDRIVE.SYS: Uses a portion of random access memory (RAM) to simulate a hard disk--often called a "RAM disk".

SETVER.EXE: Establishes a version table that lists the version number MS-DOS reports to named programs.

SMARTDRV.EXE: Creates a disk cache in extended or expanded memory.

New Features Of MS-DOS Version 6.0[8]

The following CONFIG.SYS commands are new in DOS 6.0:

[COMMON]: Provides a special block of configuration lines that are processed for all menu blocks.

DBLSPACE.SYS: Provides access to compressed drives.

INCLUDE: Interprets another block of configuration lines as though that block were copied into this place in the CONFIG.SYS file.

INTERLNK.EXE: Enables you to use drives and printers from another PC, connected through a serial or parallel cable.

MENUCOLOR: Enables you to choose color selections for menu display during boot process.

MENUDEFAULT: Defines which menu item is initially highlighted as the default and determines the amount of time that should pass before the default is automatically executed.

MENUITEM: Generates a menu display during boot process.

NUMLOCK: Enables you to specify whether the NumLock key is initially (during startup) in the locked or unlocked state.

POWER.EXE: Provides a device driver to control power-saving features in laptops.

SET: Enables you to create and modify environment variables from CONFIG.SYS

SUBMENU: Generates subsidiary menus during boot process.

SWITCHES: Restricts use of Enhanced Keyboard functions; controls where WINA20.386 file is placed; prevents use of F5 and F8 keys to bypass CONFIG.SYS commands.

Other New Commands

The following commands also are new in DOS 6.0:

CHOICE: Enables a batch file to check for user keystrokes.

DBLSPACE: Customizes drives compressed by DBLSPACE.SYS.

DEFRAG: Rearranges files in a disk partition for improved performance.

DELTREE: Deletes a directory and all the files contained within it.

EXPAND: Copies and decompresses files from original MS-DOS 6.0 disks.

FASTHELP: Displays brief help information about commands; less detailed than HELP.

HELP: Displays the complete reference information for all DOS commands.

INTERLNK: Provides a client-side utility for connecting two PCs via serial or parallel cable.

INTERSVR: Provides a server utility for connecting two PCs via serial or parallel cable.

MEMMAKER: Optimizes use of uppermemory blocks (UMBs) by device drivers and terminate-and-stay-resident (TSR) programs.

MOVE: Moves one or more files from one location to another; can also rename a directory.

MSAV: Tests a disk for viruses and (optionally) removes them.

MSBACKUP: Backs up or restores files; archives files to floppies.

MSD: Displays detailed technical information about computer hardware and resident software.

MWAV: Tests a disk for viruses and (optionally) removes them (Microsoft Windows version of MSAV).

MWAVTSR: Allows messages from the VSAFE program to be visible in Windows.

MWBACKUP: Backs up or restores files; archives files to floppies (Windows version of MSBACKUP).

MWUNDEL: Recovers a deleted file (Windows version of UNDELETE).

POWER: Provides a power-control utility for laptops; used with POWER.EXE device driver.

SMARTMON: Monitors and controls efficiency of SMARTDRV cache (Windows utility).

VSAFE: Provides a TSR for active protection against viruses.

[1]From the books, *Using MS-DOS® 6, & MS-DOS® 6 Quick Reference* by Que Development. Copyright (c) 1993. Published by Que®, a division of Prentice-Hall Computer Publishing. Used by permission of the publisher.

[2]From source No. 1 (Que Development). Used by permission.

[3]From source No. 1 (Que Development). Used by permission.

[4]From the book, *Microsoft® MS-DOS® User's Guide and Reference: for the MS-DOS® Operating System Version 5.0*, by Microsoft Corporation. Copyright (c) 1991. Reprinted with permission from Microsoft Corporation.

[5]From source No. 1 (Que Development). Used by permission.

[6]From the book, *Microsoft® MS-DOS® User's Guide and Reference: for the MS-DOS® Operating System Version 5.0*, by Microsoft Corporation. Copyright (c) 1991. Reprinted with permission from Microsoft Corporation.

[7]From source No. 1 (Que Development). Used by permission.

[8]From source No. 1 (Que Development). Used by permission.

Selected High-Level Languages[1]

The following Table represents a list of "selected" high-level languages in which the author thought was some of the more significant (those most familiar) high-level languages, out of the several hundred high-level implemented languages which have been defined since work in computing started. Dates of the languages' first publication have been included. Where a question mark has been used, it means the author was not certain of the date. Because of lack of knowledge, a specific date has been omitted entirely, in a few cases.

High-Level Languages

Ada (Named after Augusta Ada Byron, not an acronym): (1979)

ADAPT (A computer-aided NC parts programming language similar to APT): (date)?

ALGOL-68 (Algorithmic Language 1968): (1968)

ALGOL (Algorithmic Language): (1960)

APL (A Programming Language): (1962)

APT (Automatically Programmed Tools): (1958)

ATLAS (Abbreviated Test Language for "All" Systems): (1968)

BASIC (Beginner's All Purpose Symbolic Instruction Code): (1964)

BLISS (Basic Language for Implementation of System Software) (1970)

C: (So named because its immediate predecessor was the "B" programming language): (1972)

C++ (An object-oriented version of the "C" programming language): (early 1980s)

COBOL (Common Business-Oriented Language): (1960)

COGO (Coordinate Geometry): (1963)?

COMIT [II]: (1957)

Coursewriter III: (1966)?

CSMP (Continuous System Modeling Program): (1968)

CSSL (Continuous Systems Simulation Language): (1967)

dBASE: (date)?

DYNAMO III: (1959)?

ECAP II (Electronic Circuit Analysis Program 2): (1966)

EXAPT (Extended Subset of APT, a language process developed in Germany): (date)?

EZAPT (An APT-based NC processor language): (date)?

Flow-Matic: (1958)

FORMAC (Formula Manipulation Compiler): (1964)

FORTRAN (Formula Translation): (1956)

FOURTH (Fourth-generation language): (late 1960s)

GPSS (General Purpose Systems Simulator): (1961)

ICES (Integrated Civil Engineering

System): (1967)?

IPL-V (Information Processing Language 5): (1957)

ISPL (Instruction Set Processor Language): (1971)

IT (Internal Translator): (1957)

JOSS (JOHNNIAC [John von Neumann Integrator and Computer] Open Shop System): (1964)

JOVIAL (Jule's Own Version of International Algebraic Language): (1960)

LISP (List Processing): (1960)

LTTP (A simplified parts-programming language for two-axis turning applications): (date)?

MACSYMA (Project MAC's Symbol Manipulation): (1972)

MAD (Michigan Algorithm Decoder): (1960)

MPSX (Mathematical Programming System Extended): (1966)

MUMPS (Massachusetts General Hospital Utility Multi-Programming System (1969)

NELIAC (Navy Electronics Laboratory International Algol Compiler): (1960)

OMNITAB II: (1966)

Pascal (So named for the 17th Century French mathematician and philosopher, Blaise Pascal): (1971)

PDS/MaGen (Problem Descriptor System): (1973)?

PILOT: (1969)?

PL/I (Programming Language One): (1964)

PL/M: (1974)?

PROLOG (Programming Logic): (1973)

Reduce: (1967)

SCEPTRE: (1960s)?

SIMSCRIPT: (date)?

SNOBOL (String-Oriented Symbolic Language): (early 1960s)

Speakeasy: (1968)

SPSS (Statistical Programs for the Social Sciences): (1975)?

TRAC: (1965)

TUTOR: (1971)?

UCC-APT (University Computing Company's version of APT): (date)?

[1]Adapted from the book, *Encyclopedia Of Computer Science And Engineering*, Sec-

ond Edition, Editors: Anthony Ralston and Edwin D. Reilly, Jr. Copyright (c) 1983 by Van Nostrand Reinhold Company, Inc., New York, NY. Used by permission of the publisher.

Abbreviations Commonly used in Modulation, Multiplexing and Demodulation[1]

ACSB: Amplitude-Compandored Single Sideband. A registered trademark of Sideband Technology Inc.

ACSSB: Amplitude-Compandored Single SideBand

ADM: Adaptive Delta Modulation

AFSK: Audio-Frequency-Shift Keying

AM: Amplitude Modulation

ANBFM: Adaptive Narrow-Band Frequency Modulation

APK: Amplitude Phase Keying. (Same as QAM)

APCM: Adaptive Pulse-Code Modulation

ASK: Amplitude-Shift Keying

AWGN: Additive White Gaussian Noise

Bd: Baud

BPSK: Binary Phase-Shift Keying

CDM: Companded Delta Modulation

CDMA: Code-Division Multiple Access

CFSK: Coherent Frequency-Shift Keying

C/N: Carrier-to-Noise ratio

Compandor: A contraction of compressor-expander

CPFSK: Continuous-Phase Frequency-Shift Keying

CPM: Continuous-Phase Modulation

CVSD: Continuously Variable Slope Delta modulation

CW: Continuous Wave (In Amateur Radio [Ham], CW usually means a continuous carrier wave keyed on-and-off by Morse code).

DAV: Data Above Voice

DBPSK: Differentially Binary Phase-Shift Keying

DCPSK: Differentially Coherent Phase-

Shift Keying

DEBPSK: Differentially Encoded Binary Phase-Shift Keying, with carrier recovery

DECPSK: Differentially Encoded Coherent Phase-Shift Keying

DFSK: Double Frequency-Shift Keying

DIV: Data In Voice

DLL: Delay-Locked Loop

DPCM: Differential Phase-Code Modulation

DPMM: Digitally Processed Multimode Modulation

DPSK: Differential Phase-Shift Keying

DS: Direct Sequence (A technique used in spread spectrum).

DSB: Double SideBand

DSBSC: Double-SideBand Suppressed Carrier

DUV: Data Under Voice

FAX: Facsimile

FDM: Frequency-Division Multiplexing

FDMA: Frequency-Division Multiple Access

FFSK: Fast Frequency-Shift Keying. (Same as MSK)

FH: Frequency Hopping (A modulation technique used in spread spectrum).

FM: Frequency Modulation

FSK: Frequency-Shift Keying

FSTV: Fast-Scan Television

GMSK: Gaussian-filtered Minimum-Shift Keying

ICW: Interrupted Continuous Wave

ISB: Independent SideBand

ISI: InterSymbol Interface

LPC: Linear Predictive Coding

LSB: Lower SideBand

MAP: Maximum *A posteriori* Probability (A mathematical estimative technique used in data demodulation. See ML).

M-ary: M is a variable representing the number of states (in modulation)

MCW: Modulated Continuous Wave

MASK: Multiple Amplitude-Shift Keying

MFSK: Multiple Frequency-Shift Keying

ML: Maximum Likelihood. (A mathematical estimative technique used in data demodulation. See MAP)

MPSK: Multiple Phase-Shift Keying

Modem: Modulator-demodulator

MSK: Minimum-Shift Keying (Same as FFSK).

MSTV: Medium-Scan Television

MUX: Multiplex(er)

NBFM: Narrow-Band Frequency Modulation

NBPSK: Narrow-Band Phase-Shift Keying

NCFSK: Noncoherent Frequency-Shift Keying

NLA-QAM: Nonlinear Amplified QAM [Quadrature Amplitude Modulation]

NLF-QPSK: Nonlinearly Filtered QPSK [Quadrature Phase-Shift Keying] (Aslo known as Feher's QPSK)

OOK: On-Off Keying

OQPSK: Offset [or Staggered] Quadrature Phase-Shift Keying

PAM: Pulse-Amplitude Modulation

PCM: Pulse-Code Modulation

PDM: Pulse-Duration Modulation (Same as PWM).

PFM: Pulse-Frequency Modulation

PLL: Phase-Locked Loop

PM: Phase Modulation

PSK: Phase-Shift Keying

PWM: Pulse-Width Modulation (Same as PDM).

QAM: Quadrature Amplitude Modulation (Same as APK).

QASK: Quadrature Amplitude-Shift Keying

QPPM: Quantized Pulse-Position Modulation

QPRS: Quadrature-Partial-Response modulation System

QPSK: Quadrature Phase-Shift Keying (quadraphase)

RC: Raised Cosine; Reduced Carrier

SC: Suppressed Carrier

SCPC: Single Channel Per Carrier

S/N: Signal-to-Noise ratio. (Expressed in dB)

SQAM: Staggered [or Offset] Quadrature Amplitude Modulation

SQPSK: Staggered [or Offset] Quaternary Phase-Shift Keying

SSB: Single Sideband

SSBSC: Single-Sideband Suppressed Carrier

SSMA: Spread-Spectrum Multiple Access

SSTV: Slow-Scan Television

TADI: Time Assignment Digital Interpolation. (A technique for sending bursts of

data during pauses in speech)
TDM: Time-Division Multiplexing
TDMA: Time-Division Multiple Access
TFM: Tamed Frequency Modulation
TH: Time Hopping. (A technique used in spread spectrum)
USB: Upper Sideband
VF: Voice Frequencies
VFCT: Voice-Frequency Carrier Telegraphy
VSB: Vestigial Sideband
VSDM: Variable-Slope Delta Modulation
WBFM: Wideband Frequency Modulation
WGN: White Gaussian Noise
WPM: Words Per Minute (A unit of speed in telegraph systems).
8PSK: Eight-ary [or Octal] Phase-Shift Keying

[1]From the book, *The ARRL Handbook for Radio Amateurs* 1993 (70th ed), The American Radio Relay League. Used by permission of the publisher.

Electrical Characteristics of Logic Families[1]

Bipolar logic families (listed in chronological order of development):

DCTL—Direct-coupled Transistor Logic. First commercial integrated circuits. Poor noise immunity. High current. Not used for new designs. Low cost.

RTL—Resistor-Transistor Logic. Low speed, poor noise immunity. Low fan-out capability. Not used for new designs.

DTL—Diode-Transistor Logic. Low speed. Not used for new designs.

HTL—High-Threshold Logic. Greater noise immunity than DTL.

RCTL—Resistor-Capacitor-Transistor Logic. Similar to RTL, but higher speed.

TTL—(Also T²L) Transistor-Transistor Logic. The most popular logic family at present. Greater speed and noise immu-

nity than RTL or DTL. High fan-out capability. Moderate power consumption.

ECL—Emitter-Coupled Logic. Very high-speed, high input impedance, low output impedance. Popular for new designs of high-speed circuitry.

I²L—Integrated Injection Logic. Increased density and decreased power consumption over TTL.

Metal-Oxide Semiconductor (MOS) Logic Families (listed in chronological order of development):

PMOS—P-channel MOS. Lower power consumption than bibolar logic. Lower speed than bibolar logic. Oldest MOS type. Least popular for new designs.

NMOS—N-channel MOS. Twice the speed of PMOS. Increased density over PMOS. Greatly increased density over bipolar families. Popular for new designs, especially microprocessors.

CMOS—Complementary MOS. High noise immunity. Very low power consumption. Great fan-out capability. Popular for new designs where low power consumption is required, including microprocessor designs.

[1]From the book, *Electronics Data Handbook,* by William Barden, Radio Shack, a Tandy Corp Company, Copyright (c) 1986. Used by permission of the publisher.

Semiconductor Abbreviations[1]

The following table shows abbreviations for semiconductor devices.

α—Alpha (ratio of collector to emitter current)

A, a—Anode

ß—Beta (current gain)

C, c—Collector, cathode

C_{IN}—Input capacitance

C_{OUT}— Output capacitance
C_{PD}—Power dissipation capacity
C_X—Expander output capacitance
D, d—Drain
E, e—Emitter
F_{alpha}—Alpha cut-off frequency
F_{CLOCK}—Input clock frequency
F_O—Output frequency
F_T—Current gain bandwidth product
F_{max}—Maximum operating frequency or clock
G, g—Gate
G_c—Current gain
G_{PB}—Common-base power gain
G_{fs}—Common-source forward transfer conductance
G_v—Voltage gain
I_C—Maximum collector current
I_{CC}—Supply current
I_D—Drain current
I_{DD}—Quiescent device current
$I_{f(av)}$—Maximum average forward current
I_{fm}—Maximum peak forward current
I_{fs}—Maximum peak surge current
I_{FSM}—Maximum peak forward current, surge
I_I—Input current at maximum input voltage
I_{IH}—High-level input current
I_{IL}—Low-level input current
I_{IN}—Input current
I_O—Average rectified current, forward
I_{OH}—High-level output current
I_{OL}—Low-level output current
I_{OS}—Short-circuit output current
I_R—Average rectified current, reverse
I_r—Maximum dc reverse current
I_X—Expander current
k, k—Cathode
NF—Noise figure
P_D—Maximum device power dissipation
P_T—Total power input, all terminals
P_{in}—Input power
P_{out}—Output power
PIV—Peak inverse voltage
Q—True output
R_O—Output impedance
S, s—Source
T—Temperature
T_A—Operating free-air temperature
T_L—Lead temperature
T_{PHL}—Propagation delay time, high-to-low level output

T_{PHZ}—Output disable from high level
T_{PLH}—Propagation delay time, low-to-high level output
T_{PLZ}—Output disable from low level
T_s—Storage temperature range
T_{SU}—Data setup time
T_w—Pulse width
U, u—Bulk (substrate)
V_f—Maximum dc voltage drop
$V_{f(av)}$—Maximum average forward voltage drop
V_{BE}—Base-emitter voltage
V_{CBO}—Maximum collector-base voltage
V_{cc}—Collector supply voltage
V_{CE}—Collector-emitter voltage
V_{CEO}—Maximum collector-emitter voltage
V_{DD}—Dc supply voltage
V_{DS}—Drain-source voltage
V_{EBO}—Maximum emitter-base voltage
V_F—Average forward voltage
V_{GS}—Gate-source voltage
V_{IH}—High-level input voltage
V_{IK}—Input clamp voltage
V_{IL}—Low-level input voltage
V_{IN}—Input voltage
V_{OH}—High-level output voltage
V_{OL}—Low-level output voltage
V_{T+}—Positive-going threshold voltage
V_{T-}—Negative-going threshold voltage

[1]From the book, *Electronics Data Handbook*, by William Barden, Radio Shack, a Tandy Corporation Company. Copyright (c) 1986. Used by permission of the publisher.

Greek Alphabet

Aα	alpha		Nν	nu
Bβ	beta		Ξξ	xi
Γγ	gamma		Οο	omicron
Δδ	delta		Ππ	pi
Εε	epsilon		Ρρ	rho
Ζζ	zeta		Σσ	sigma
Ηη	eta		Ττ	tau
Θθ	theta		Υυ	upsilon
Ιι	iota		Φφ	phi
Κκ	kappa		Χχ	chi
Λλ	lambda		Ψψ	psi
Μμ	mu		Ωω	omega

Greek Symbols Used for Electronics

The following Table shows common uses of Greek symbols for electrical quantities.

α angles, coefficients, attenuation constant, transistor current transfer ratio, cutoff frequency

ß angles, coefficients, phase constant, transistor current amplification factor

γ angles, electrical conductivity, propagation constant

Γ complex propagation constant

Δ increment or decrement, determinant, permittivity

ε dielectric constant, permittivity, electric intensity, base of natural logarithms

ζ coordinates, coefficients

η intrinsic impedance, efficiency, surface charge density hysteresis

θ angular phase displacement, time constant, reluctance, angles

ι unit vector

κ susceptibility, coefficient of coupling, Boltzmann's constant

λ wavelength, attenuation constant

Λ permeance, total inductance

μ permeability, amplification factor, "micro"

ν reluctivity, frequency

ξ coordinates

π 3.14159...

ρ resistivity, volume charge density, coordinates, reflection coefficient

σ surface charge density, complex propagation constant, electrical conductivity, leakage coefficient, deviation

Σ summation

τ time constant, volume resistivity, time-phase displacement, transmission factor, density

φ magnetic flux, angles, phase deviation

Φ scalar potential

χ dielectric flux, phase difference, coordinates, angles

ω angular velocity

Ω ohms, solid angle

Common Mathematical Signs and Symbols

. radix (base) point

· multiplication symbol; logic and function

∞ infinity

+ plus; positive; logic or function

- minus; negative

x times

÷ divided by

/ divided by (expressive of a ratio)

= equal to

≅ approximately equal to

≈ approximately

≠ not equal to

~ similar to

< less than

<< much less than

≤ equal to or less than

≥ equal to or greater than

α proportional to; varies direct as

→ approaches

: ratio sign; is to; proportional to

∴ therefore

@ at the rate of; at cost of

e natural number = 2.71828

π pi ≈ 3.14159...

( ) parentheses (use to enclose a group of terms)

[ ] brackets (use to enclose a group of terms that includes one or more groups in parentheses).

Common Mathematical Signs and Symbols

{ }	braces (use to enclose a group of terms that includes one or more groups in brackets
$\angle$	angle
°	degrees (arc or temperature)
'	minutes; prime
"	seconds; double prime
∥	parallel to
⊥	perpendicular to
...	and beyond
∇	(del or nabla) vector differential operator
$\sqrt{}$	square root of
$^3\sqrt{}$	cube root of
::	equals, as (proportion)
dx	differrential of x
Δ	(delta) difference
Δx	increment of x
x+y	x added to y; x OR y
x-y	y subtracted from x
x÷y	x divided by y

Metric (SI) Prefixes

Prefix	Letter/ Symbol	Factor	Pronunciation
exa	E	10^{18}	ex'a
peta	P	10^{15}	pet'a
tera	T	10^{12}	ter'a
giga	G	10^9	ji'ga
mega	M	10^6	meg'a
kilo	k	10^3	kil'o
hecto	h	10^2	hek'to
deka	da	10	dek'a
deci	d	10^{-1}	des'i
centi	c	10^{-2}	sen'ti
mili	m	10^{-3}	mil'i
micro	i	10^{-6}	mi'kro
nano	n	10^{-9}	nan'o
pico	p	10^{-12}	pe'co
femto	f	10^{-15}	fem'to
atto	a	10^{-18}	at'to

Units of Measure[1]

This list contains abbreviations of units of measure used in scientific and technical communications; these usually appear in their abbreviated form.

General

K 1,000 or 1024 (= 2^{10}); the latter refers mainly to measures of computer storage capacity.

M 1,000,000 or 1,048,576 (= 2^{20}); the latter refers mainly to measures of computer storage capacity.

Time

ms, msec millisecond (10^{-3} sec)
is, isec microsecond (10^{-6} sec)
ns, nsec nanosecond (10^{-9} sec)
ps, psec picosecond (10^{-12} sec)

Speed

Megaflop Million floating-point operations per second.

MIPS Million instructions processed per second.

Electricity

Hz Hertz (cycles/sec)
KHz Kilohertz (10^3 cycles/sec)
MHz Megahertz (10^6 cycles/sec)
Kc Kilocycle (10^3 cycles)
Mc Megacycle (10^6 cycles; sometimes, 10^6 cycles/sec = 1 MHz)
iW Microwatt (10^{-6} watts)
mW Milliwatt (10^{-3} watts)
KW Kilowatt (10^3 watts)
mV Millivolt (10^{-3} volt)
mA Milliamp (10^{-3} amp)

Storage

Kb Kilobit (10^3 bits)
Mb Megabit (10^6 bits)
Gb Gigabit (10^9 bits)
Tb Terabit (10^{12} bits)
KB Kilobyte (10^3 bytes)
MB Megabyte (10^6 bytes)
GB Gigabyte (10^9 bytes)
TB Terabyte (10^{12} bytes)
L(x) Location of x (in main memory)
C(A) Contents of location A (in main memory)

I/O

bps Bits per second
chps Characters per second
chpi Characters per inch
cps Cards per second
cpm Cards per minute
lpm Lines per minute
rpm Revolutions per minute

Miscellaneous

iMicron (10^{-6} meter)
mbar Millibar (10^{-3} bar [cgs unit of pressure])

[1]From the book, *Encyclopedia Of Computer Science And Engineering*, Second Edition, Editor: Anthony Ralston, Associate Editor: Edwin D. Reilly, Jr. Copyright (c) 1983 by Van Nostrand Reinhold Company, Inc., New York, NY. Used by permission of the publisher.

national Telephony & Telegraphy)
ECMA (European Computer Manufacturers Association)
ISO (International Organization for Standardization)
IEC (International Electrotechnical Commission)
ITU (International Telecommunications Union)

DE FACTO STANDARDS

When a vendor's product (practice, device, or configuration) that, by virtue of its widely or universal use, has the 'effect' of a standard (but whose status has not officially been declared by a recognized standard-setting organization, e.g., ANSI), it becomes a "de facto" standard. Apple, Ashton-Tate, Digital, H-P, IBM, Intel, Lotus, Microsoft, Motorola and many other hardware and software vendors have set de facto standards.

Standards Organizations

The following organizations set standards for computers, communications and related products throughout the world:

UNITED STATES

ANSI (American National Standards Institute)
EIA (Electronic Industries Association)
IEEE (Institute of Electrical and Electronics Engineers)
NIST (National Institute of Standards and Technology) Formerly National Bureau of Standards (NBS)

CANADA

CSA (Canadian Standards Association)
Electrical and Electronic Manufacturers Association

INTERNATIONAL

CCIR (Consultative Committee on International Radio)
CCITT (Consultative Committee on Inter-

Selected Trademarks*

*Those trademarks followed by an asterisk (*) are "non-registered" trademarks (i.e., trademarks [®], or salesmarks [SM]), all others are registered trademarks® or pending registration. Because of the incredibly fast-moving-pace of tradenames, mergers, and buy-outs of various companies, it would be impossible to have a completely accurate listing of such properly identified tradenames. The author and the publisher which to apologize for any inaccuracies in this listing which might occur.

Trademarks

1-2-3, Lotus Development Corp.
3FGe*, NEC Technologies Inc.
4FGe*, NEC Technologies Inc.
5FGe*, NEC Technologies Inc.
24 Hour City Hall, International Business Machines Corp.
386*, Intel Corp.
386SLC*, International Business Machines

Corp.

400, International Business Machines Corp.

3090*, International Business Machines Corp.

9076 SP1*, International Business Machines Corp.

Academic LANkit*, International Business Machines Corp.

AccuColor*, NEC Technologies Inc.

Acer, Acer Technologies Corp.

ACF/VTAM*, International Business Machines Corp.

Actionwriter, International Business Machines Corp.

AD/Cycle, International Business Machines Corp.

Ada, U.S. Department of Defense.

ADSTAR*, International Business Machines Corp.

Advanced Application Communication System/2*, International Business Machines Corp.

Advanced Function Presentation*, International Business Machines Corp.

Advanced Function Printing*, International Business Machines Corp.

Advanced Peer-to-Peer Networking*, International Business Machines Corp.

ADVANTIS*, International Business Machines Corp.

AFP/SME, Society of Manufacturing Engineers.

AFP*, International Business Machines Corp.

AIform, International Business Machines Corp.

AIX/6000*, International Business Machines Corp.

AIX, International Business Machines Corp.

AIX/ESA*, International Business Machines Corp.

AIX Visualization Data Explorer/6000*, International Business Machines Corp.

AIXwindows, International Business Machines Corp.

Allways, Funk Software.

AML, International Business Machines Corp.

AML/2*, International Business Machines Corp.

ANSI, American National Standards Institute.

ANSYS, E.I. DuPont de Nemours & Co Inc.

AnyNet/MVS*, International Business Machines Corp.

AnyNet/2*, International Business Machines Corp.

AnyNet*, International Business Machines Corp.

AOEXPERT/MVS*, International Business Machines Corp.

APAS, Westinghouse Electric Corp.

APL, International Business Machines Corp.

APL2, International Business Machines Corp.

APL2/6000, International Business Machines Corp.

Apple, Apple Computer Inc.

Applesoft BASIC, Apple Computer Inc.

Application System/Entry, International Business Machines Corp.

Application System/400, International Business Machines Corp.

APPN*, International Business Machines Corp.

ARISTOTLE 2000*, International Business Machines Corp.

ARPANET, U.S. Department of Defense.

AS/400, International Business Machines Corp.

ASociation/400*, International Business Machines Corp.

ASQC, American Society for Quality Control.

Assistant Series, International Business Machines Corp.

AST, AST Research Inc.

AT, International Business Machines Corp.

AT&T, American Telephone and Telegraph Co.

ATICTS, Data Enterprises.

ATI Training Power, American Training International Inc.

Audio Visual Connection, International Business Machines Corp.

Auto-Inking, International Business Machines Corp.

AutoCAD, Autodesk Inc.

AUTOFACT, Society of Manufacturing Engineers.

BAKUP, Software Integration Inc.

BallPoint*, Toshiba.

Bar Code Object Content Architecture*, International Business Machines Corp.

BASICA, International Business Machines Corp.

Basic Compiler/2*, International Business Machines Corp.

BCOCA*, International Business Machines Corp.

Bernoulli Drive, Iomega Corp.

Beyond COMPUTING*, International Business Machines Corp.

BIOS, Tesco Inc.

BISYNC, International Business Machines Corp.

Boeing Calc, Boeing Computer Services.

BookManager, International Business Machines Corp.

BookMaster, International Business Machines Corp.

C/2*, International Business Machines Corp.

C/400, International Business Machines Corp.

CADAM, CADAM Inc.

CADDS4, Computervision.

CAEDS, International Business Machines Corp.

CallPath, International Business Machines Corp.

CallPath CICS/MVS*, International Business Machines Corp.

CallPath CICS/VSE*, International Business Machines Corp.

CallPath SwitchServer/2*, International Business Machines Corp.

CallUp*, International Business Machines Corp.

CAMkit*, International Business Machines Corp.

CAMSCO, CAMSCO Inc.

CapacityPro*, International Business Machines Corp.

CASA/SME, Society of Manufacturing Engineers.

CatchWord, Logitech Inc.

CATIA, Dassault Systems.

Cell-Mate, Clarity Software Corp.

CFM-Short Cycle*, International Business Machines Corp.

CGA, International Business Machines Corp.

CICS*, International Business Machines Corp.

CICS/400*, International Business Machines Corp.

CICS/6000*, International Business Machines Corp.

CICS/ESA*, International Business Machines Corp.

CICS/VSE*, International Business Machines Corp.

CICS/VM*, International Business Machines Corp.

CICS/MVS*, International Business Machines Corp.

CICS OS/2*, International Business Machines Corp.

CIEDS*, International Business Machines Corp.

CIM Advantage, International Business Machines Corp.

Client Series*, International Business Machines Corp.

Client Series*, International Business Machines Corp.

COBOL/2*, International Business Machines Corp.

COBOL/379*, International Business Machines Corp.

COBOL/400*, International Business Machines Corp.

Colorview*, International Business Machines Corp.

Common User Access*, International Business Machines Corp.

CommonView*, International Business Machines Corp.

Compaq, Compaq Computer Corp.

Compaq DeskPro, Compaq Computer Corp.

Compaq Plus, Compaq Computer Corp.

COMPUDYNE*, CompUSA Inc.

COMPUSA, CompUSA Inc.

CompuServe, CompuServe Inc.

Concurrent CP/M, Digital Research Inc.

CP/M, Digital Research Inc.

CRAY, Cray Computers.

Critique, International Business Machines Corp.

Crosstalk XVI, Microstuf Inc.

CUA*, International Business Machines Corp.

Current*, International Business Machines Corp.

CustomPac*, International Business Machines Corp.

DATABASE 2*, International Business Machines Corp.

DATA COLLECTION EDITION*, International Business Machines Corp.

Dataease, Dataease International.

DataHub*, International Business Machines Corp.

Data Manager, Innovative Software Inc.

DataPerfect, WordPerfect Corp.

Data Propagator*, International Business Machines Corp.

DataStructure Series*, International Business Machines Corp.

DataTrade, International Business Machines Corp.

DB2, International Business Machines Corp.

DB2/2*, International Business Machines Corp.

DB2/6000*, International Business Machines Corp.

dBase II, Ashton-Tate.

dBase III Plus, Ashton-Tate.

DEC, Digital Equipment Corp.

DECNET, Digital Equipment Corp.

DeskJet*, Hewlett-Packard Co.

DESQview, Quarterdeck Office Systems.

DevelopMate, International Business Machines Corp.

DFDSM*, International Business Machines Corp.

DFSMS/MVS*, International Business Machines Corp.

DFSMS/VM*, International Business Machines Corp.

DFSMS*, International Business Machines Corp.

DFSMSdfp*, International Business Machines Corp.

DFSMSdss*, International Business Machines Corp.

DFSMShsm*, International Business Machines Corp.

DFSMSrmm*, International Business Machines Corp.

DirectTalk/2*, International Business Machines Corp.

DirectTalk/6000*, International Business Machines Corp.

DirectTalk*, International Business Machines Corp.

Discover/Education*, International Business Machines Corp.

DisplayWrite, International Business Machines Corp.

DisplayWrite Assistant*, International Business Machines Corp.

Distributed Application Environment*, International Business Machines Corp.

Distributed Automation Edition*, International Business Machines Corp.

DISTRIBUTED DATABASE CONNECTION SERVICES/2*, International Business Machines Corp.

Distributed Relational Database Architecture*, International Business Machines Corp.

DNA, Digital Equipment Corp.

Document Retrieval Assistant*, International Business Machines Corp.

DOMAIN, Apollo Computer.

DOS, International Business Machines Corp.

Dow Jones News/Retrieval, Dow Jones & Company Inc.

DProp*, International Business Machines Corp.

DrawMaster, International Business Machines Corp.

DrawPerfect, WordPerfect Corp.

DRDA*, International Business Machines Corp.

DXT/D1*, International Business Machines Corp.

DXT*, International Business Machines Corp.

EAGLE SCAN*, International Business Machines Corp.

Easystrike, International Business Machines Corp.

EBCDIC, International Business Machines Corp.

ECFORMS, International Business Machines Corp.

ECKD*, International Business Machines Corp.

Education/Express*, International Business Machines Corp.

EduQuest*, International Business Machines Corp.

EGA, International Business Machines Corp.

EIA, Electronics Industries Association.

Electrographic, International Business Machines Corp.

Electronic Marketplace*, International Business Machines Corp.

Enterprise System/3090*, International Business Machines Corp.

Enterprise System/4381*, International Business Machines Corp.

Enterprise System/9000*, International Business Machines Corp.

Enterprise System/9370*, International Business Machines Corp.

Enterprise Systems Architecture/370*, International Business Machines Corp.

Enterprise Systems Architecture/390*, International Business Machines Corp.

Enterprise Systems Connection Architecture*, International Business Machines Corp.

EOCF/2*, International Business Machines Corp.

Epson, Epson America Inc.

ES/3090*, International Business Machines Corp.

ES/4381*, International Business Machines Corp.

ES/9000*, International Business Machines Corp.

ES/9370*, International Business Machines Corp.

ESA/370*, International Business Machines Corp.

ESA/390*, International Business Machines Corp.

ESCON*, International Business Machines Corp.

ESCON XDF*, International Business Machines Corp.

EtherNet, Xerox Corp.

ExecJet, International Business Machines Corp.

expEDIte*, International Business Machines Corp.

Explore/Education*, International Business Machines Corp.

Extended Services*, International Business Machines Corp.

Extended Services for OS/2*, International Business Machines Corp.

FAA*, International Business Machines Corp.

Facsimile Support/400*, International Business Machines Corp.

Fastback, Fifth Generation Systems.

FastRef*, International Business Machines Corp.

FASTService, International Business Machines Corp.

FaxConcentrator*, International Business Machines Corp.

FFST/MVS*, International Business Machines Corp.

FFST/2*, International Business Machines Corp.

FFST/400*, International Business Machines Corp.

FFST*, International Business Machines Corp.

Filepath, SDA Associates.

Filing Assistant, International Business Machines Corp.

Financial Application Architecture*, International Business Machines Corp.

Finesse, Logitech Inc.

First Failure Support Technology*, International Business Machines Corp.

First Failure Support Technology/MVS*, International Business Machines Corp.

First Failure Support Technology/2*, International Business Machines Corp.

First Failure Support Technology/400*, International Business Machines Corp.

First Mouse*, Logitech Inc.

FORTRAN/2*, International Business Machines Corp.

FORTRAN/400*, International Business Machines Corp.

FotoMan*, Logitech Inc.

Framework II, Ashton-Tate.

FunctionPac*, International Business Machines Corp.

GDDM*, International Business Machines Corp.

GEARBOX, International Business Machines Corp.

GEM, Digital Research Inc.

Genifer, Bytel Corp.

geoManager, International Business Machines Corp.

GPSS, International Business Machines Corp.

Grammatik, Reference Software International, a division of WordPerfect Corp.

Graphics Assistant*, International Business Machines Corp.

graPHIGS*, International Business Machines Corp.

GrayTouch*, Logitech Inc.

GW-BASIC, Microsoft Corp.

Hardware Configuration Definition*, International Business Machines Corp.

HDLC, International Business Machines Corp.

Hektowriter, International Business Machines Corp.

HelpBuy*, International Business Machines Corp.

HelpCenter, International Business Machines Corp.

HelpClub*, International Business Machines Corp.

HelpLearn*, International Business Machines Corp.

HelpWare, International Business Machines Corp.

Helvetica, Eltra Corp.

Hercules Graphics Card, Hercules Computer Technology.

Hewlett-Packard, Hewlett-Packard Co.

Hiperbatch*, International Business Machines Corp.

Hipersorting, International Business Machines Corp.

Hiperspace*, International Business Machines Corp.

HPTS*, International Business Machines Corp.

Hyperbus, Network Systems.

Hyperchannel, Network Systems.

HyperHelp, International Business Machines Corp.

IAA*, International Business Machines Corp.

IBM, International Business Machines Corp.

IBMLink*, International Business Machines Corp.

IEEE, Institute of Electrical and Electronics Engineers.

IIN*, International Business Machines Corp.

ILE*, International Business Machines Corp.

Illuminated Books and Manuscripts*, International Business Machines Corp.

ILS/400*, International Business Machines Corp.

ImagePlus, International Business Machines Corp.

Imagination Made Possible, International Business Machines Corp.

Impactwriter, International Business Machines Corp.

IMS/ESA, International Business Machines Corp.

IMS Client Server/2*, International Business Machines Corp.

IMS CS/2*, International Business Machines Corp.

Independence Series, International Business Machines Corp.

Independence Series, International Business Machines Corp.

InfoCrafter, International Business Machines Corp.

InfoExplorer*, International Business Machines Corp.

Information Assistant*, International Business Machines Corp.

Information Retrieval Symbol*, International Business Machines Corp

Information Warehouse*, International Business Machines Corp.

InfoTrainer*, International Business Machines Corp.

InfoWindow, International Business Machines Corp.

InPAc*, International Business Machines Corp.

Insurance Application Architecture*, International Business Machines Corp.

Integrated Language Environment*, International Business Machines Corp.

Integrated Platform*, International Business Machines Corp.

Integrated Systems Solutions*, International Business Machines Corp

Intel, Intel Corp.

Intelligent Printer Data Stream*, International Business Machines Corp.

Interactive EasyFlow, Haventree Software Ltd.

IPDS*, International Business Machines Corp.

ISSC*, International Business Machines Corp.

K-RUN, Micro Data Base Systems Inc.

K-REPORT, Micro Data Base Systems Inc.

K-TEXT, Micro Data Base Systems Inc.

K-GRAPH, Micro Data Base Systems Inc.

K-MOUSE, Micro Data Base Systems Inc.

K-COMM, Micro Data Base Systems Inc.

Kidz Mouse*, Logitech Inc.

Knowledge Director*, International Business Machines Corp.

Knowledgeman 2, Micro Data Base Systems Inc.

KnowledgeTool, International Business Machines Corp.

Language Environment*, International Business Machines Corp.

LANStreamer*, International Business Machines Corp.

LaserJet, Hewlett-Packard Inc.

LetterPerfect, WordPerfect Corp.

Library Reader*, International Business Machines Corp.

LinkWay*, International Business Machines Corp.

LoadLeveler*, International Business Machines Corp.

Logitech*, Logitech Inc.

Lotus, Lotus Development Corp.

LSI 11, Digital Equipment Corp.

M, International Business Machines Corp.

Mace Utilities, Paul Mace Software.

Macintosh, Apple Computer Inc.

Mac Plus, Apple Computer Inc.

Macro Assembler/2*, International Business Machines Corp.

Magic Paper*, International Business Machines Corp.

Mailmerge, WordStar International.

Mainframe Communication Assistant*, International Business Machines Corp.

Making it all make sense, Microsoft Corp.

MAP/1, Pritsker & Associates.

MAPICS, International Business Machines Corp.

MARC, E.I. DuPont de Nemours & Co Inc.

MAST, CMS Research.

MERVA*, International Business Machines Corp.

MICLASS, Netherlands Central Organization for Applied Scientific Research.

Micro Channel, International Business Machines Corp.

Micro PDP-11, Digital Equipment Corp.

Microsoft, Microsoft Corp.

Microsoft Excel, Microsoft Corp.

MicroVax, Digital Equipment Corp.

Midware*, International Business Machines Corp.

Mirror, Central Point Software Inc.

Modern Art*, Logitech Inc.

MouseMan, Logitech Inc.

MouseWare, Logitech Inc.

MQSeries*, International Business Machines Corp.

MS, Microsoft Corp.

MS-DOS, Microsoft Corp.

Multimate Advantage, Multimate International Corp.

Multimedia Presentation Manager/2*, International Business Machines Corp.

Multiscan, Sony Corp of America.

MultiSync, NEC Home Technologies Inc.

MVA/SME, Society of Manufacturing Engineers.

MVS/DFP*, International Business Machines Corp.

MVS/SP*, International Business Machines Corp.

MVS/ESA*, International Business Machines Corp.

MVS/XA*, International Business Machines Corp.

MVSRJS*, International Business Machines Corp.

Mwave*, International Business Machines Corp.

NET/ONE, Ungerman-Bass.

NETCENTER, International Business Machines Corp.

NetView, International Business Machines Corp.

Network Problem and Change Application*, International Business Machines Corp.

Norton Utilities, Peter Norton Computing.

Note-It, Turner Hall Publishing.

NQS/MVS*, International Business Machines Corp.

Office2, Office2.

OfficeVision/MVS*, International Business Machines Corp.

OfficeVision/2*, International Business Machines Corp.

OfficeVision/VM*, International Business Machines Corp.

OfficeVision/400*, International Business Machines Corp.

OfficeVision, International Business Machines Corp.

Office Writer, Office Solutions Inc.

OMNINET, Corvus Systems.

OPC*, International Business Machines Corp.

OpenEdition*, International Business Machines Corp.

Operating System/2, International Business Machines Corp.

Operating System/400, International Business Machines Corp.

Operational Assistant, International Business Machines Corp.

OS/2 Crash Protection*, International Business Machines Corp.

OS/2 32*, International Business Machines Corp.

OS/400, International Business Machines Corp.

OS/2, International Business Machines Corp.

PaintJet, Hewlett-Packard Co.

PAL, International Business Machines Corp.

Palatino, Eltra Corp.

PALS*, International Business Machines Corp.

Paper-Like Interface*, International Business Machines Corp.

Paradox, Borland International Inc.

PASCAL Compiler/2*, International Business Machines Corp.

PC-Kwik, PC-Kwik Corp.

PC, International Business Machines Corp.

PC/XT*, International Business Machines Corp.

PC/FOCUS, Information Builders Inc.

PC DOS, International Business Machines Corp.

PCjr, International Business Machines Corp.

PCjr*, International Business Machines Corp.

PCL, Hewlett-Packard Corp.

PCradio, International Business Machines Corp.

PDP, Digital Equipment Corp.

Pennant*, International Business Machines Corp.

Perfect Circle, The Dana Corp.

Personal CD*, SyQuest Technology

Personal Computer AT, International Business Machines Corp.

Personal Computer XT*, International Business Machines Corp.

Personal Decision Series*, International Business Machines Corp.

Personalized Learning Series*, International Business Machines Corp.

Personal Science Laboratory, International Business Machines Corp.

Personal Security, International Business Machines Corp.

Personal System/2, International Business Machines Corp.

Personal System/1*, International Business Machines Corp.

Person to Person/2, International Business Machines Corp.

Person to Person*, International Business Machines Corp.

PFS:File, Software Publishing Corp.

PFS:Plan, Software Publishing Corp.

PFS:Report, Software Publishing Corp.

PFS:Write, Software Publishing Corp.

PGA, International Business Machines Corp.

Philips, Philips International B.V.

PhoneCommunicator*, International Business Machines Corp.

PhotMotion*, International Business Machines Corp.

Photo Graphic, International Business Machines Corp.

PL/1, International Business Machines Corp.

PlanBuilder*, International Business Machines Corp.

PlanPerfect, WordPerfect Corp.

Plant Floor Series*, International Business Machines Corp.

PlantWorks, International Business Machines Corp.

PLC, Allen-Bradley Corp.

Plug'N'Go*, International Business Machines Corp.

Polaroid Palette, Polaroid Corp.

Port-A-Punch, International Business Machines Corp.

Portmaster, International Business Machines Corp.

PostScript, Adobe Systems Inc.

POWER Gt1*, International Business Machines Corp.

POWER Gt3*, International Business Machines Corp.

POWER Gt3i*, International Business Machines Corp.

POWER Gt4*, International Business Machines Corp.

POWER Gt4e*, International Business Machines Corp.

POWER Gt4x*, International Business Machines Corp.

POWER GTO*, International Business Machines Corp.

PowerOpen*, International Business Machines Corp.

PowerPC*, International Business Machines Corp.

PowerPC Architecture*, International Business Machines Corp.

POWERserver*, International Business Machines Corp.

POWERstation*, International Business Machines Corp.

POWER Team*, International Business Machines Corp.

POWER Visualization Data Explorer*, International Business Machines Corp.

POWER Visualization Server*, International Business Machines Corp.

POWER Visualization System*, International Business Machines Corp.

POWER Visualization Video Controller*, International Business Machines Corp.

PR/SM*, International Business Machines Corp.

Presentation Manager, International Business Machines Corp.

Presentations/DrawPerfect, WordPerfect Corp.

PRIMENET, Prime Computer Inc.

Printer Boss, Connecticut Software Systems Corp.

PrintManager*, International Business Machines Corp.

ProcessMaster, International Business Machines Corp.

Processor Resource/Systems Manager*, International Business Machines Corp.

ProductManager*, International Business Machines Corp.

ProductPac*, International Business Machines Corp.

Professional Editor*, International Business Machines Corp.

Professional Editor*, International Business Machines Corp.

PROFS, International Business Machines Corp.

Project Assistant*, International Business Machines Corp.

ProKey, RoseSoft.

Proprinter, International Business Machines Corp.

PS/1 Club*, International Business Machines Corp.

PS/1, International Business Machines Corp.

PS/ValuePoint*, International Business Machines Corp.

PS/2, International Business Machines Corp.

PS/1*, International Business Machines Corp.

PSF:Graph, Software Publishing Corp.

PSInet*, International Business Machines Corp.

PSL*, International Business Machines Corp.

PSL Explorer*, International Business Machines Corp.

Publisher's PowerPak*, Ventura Software Inc.

Publisher's PowerTools*, Ventura Software Inc.

Q-bus, Digital Equipment Corp.

QBasic*, Microsoft Corp.

QMF*, International Business Machines Corp.

Quickcode, Fox & Geller.

QuickEDI, International Business Machines Corp.

QuickPort*, Toshiba.

Quickwriter, International Business Machines Corp.

Quiet, International Business Machines Corp.

Quietwriter, International Business Machines Corp.

RACF*, International Business Machines Corp.

ReGis, Digital Equipment Corp.

Reporting Assistant*, International Business Machines Corp.

Repository Manager/400*, International Business Machines Corp.

Repository Manager/MVS, International Business Machines Corp.

Repository Manager*, International Business Machines Corp.

RETAIN*, International Business Machines Corp.

Revelation, Cosmos Inc.

RI/SME, Society of Manufacturing Engineers.

RIA, Robotics Industries Association.

RISC System/6000, International Business Machines Corp.

RPG/400, International Business Machines Corp.

RSX-11M, Digital Equipment Corp.

RT, International Business Machines Corp.

RT PC, International Business Machines Corp.

RT Personal Computer, International Business Machines Corp.

Rymer, WordPerfect Corp.

S/390, International Business Machines Corp.

SAA*, International Business Machines Corp.

Samna Word III, Samna Corp.

Scalable POWERparallel Systems*, International Business Machines Corp.

ScanMan, Logitech Inc.

SchoolView*, International Business Machines Corp.

Screen Reader*, International Business Machines Corp.

SD/2*, International Business Machines Corp.

Selectric, International Business Machines Corp.

Selectric Touch, International Business Machines Corp.

Series/1*, International Business Machines Corp.

Series 1/Ring, International Business Machines Corp.

Service Director, International Business Machines Corp.

Service Director/2, International Business Machines Corp.

ServicePac*, International Business Machines Corp.

ServicePlan*, International Business Machines Corp.

Sharp, Sharp Electronics Corp.

Sidekick, Borland International Inc.

Sideways, Funk Software.

SIMAN, Systems Modeling Corp.

Skill Dynamics*, International Business Machines Corp.

SLAM, Pritsker & Associates.

SLAM II, Pritsker & Associates.

SLC*, International Business Machines Corp.

Smart Communications, Innovative Software Inc.

SNA, International Business Machines Corp.

SNAP/SHOT, International Business Machines Corp.

Software Mall*, International Business Machines Corp.

SolutionPac, International Business Machines Corp.

SOS, Goldata Computer Services Inc.

SpeechViewer*, International Business Machines Corp.

SPEED, Horizon Software.

Spreedsheet, Innovative Software Inc.

SQL/DS*, International Business Machines Corp.

SQL/400, International Business Machines Corp.

Storyboard*, International Business Machines Corp.

Streamer*, International Business Machines Corp.

SuperCalc, Computer Associates International Inc.

SuperKey, Borland International Inc.

SwitchServer/2*, International Business Machines Corp.

SwitchServer*, International Business Machines Corp.

SXM*, International Business Machines Corp.

SYBEX, SYBEX Inc.

SyDOS*, SyQuest Technology

Symphony, Lotus Development Corp.

Sysplex Timer, International Business Machines Corp.

System/88, International Business Machines Corp.

System/360*, International Business Machines Corp.

System/370*, International Business Machines Corp.

System/390, International Business Machines Corp.

SystemPac, International Business Machines Corp.

SystemPlan*, International Business Machines Corp.

Systems Application Architecture, International Business Machines Corp.

SystemView, International Business Machines Corp.

SystemXtra*, International Business Machines Corp.

T-A-C, Lotus Development Corp.

TDK, TDK Corp.

TeamFocus, International Business Machines Corp.

Teletype, The Teletype Corp.

The Integrated Reasoning Shell, International Business Machines Corp.

The Source, The Source Information Network.

ThickPad, International Business Machines Corp.

THINK, International Business Machines Corp.

THINKable*, International Business Machines Corp.

ThinkJet, Hewlett-Packard Co.

TI Basic, Texas Instruments Inc.

TIM, Concord Data Systems.

Timation, International Business Machines Corp.

Time Manager, Innovative Software Inc.

TIRS*, International Business Machines Corp.

TMS RMN, Hewlett-Packard Corp.

TopView, International Business Machines Corp.

Toshiba, Kabushiki Kaisha Toshiba

Touch Activity Center*, International Business Machines Corp.

TouchMobile*, International Business Machines Corp.

TouchSelect*, International Business Machines Corp.

TrackMan, Logitech Inc.

Trackpoint*, International Business Machines Corp.

Trackpoint II*, International Business Machines Corp.

TRON, Disney Studios.

True BASIC, Microsoft Corp.

Tulip, Tulip Computers International B.V.

TWX, Teletypewriter Exchange Service.

UL, Underwriter's Laboratories Inc.

Ultimedia, International Business Machines Corp.

Ultrix, Digital Equipment Corp.

Undelete, Central Point Software Inc.

Unformat, Central Point Software Inc.

UNIAPT, United Computing Corp.

Unigraphics, McDonnell-Douglas Corp.

Unimate, Westinghouse Corp.

UNIX, AT&T

USART, U.S. Art Inc.

VALE*, International Business Machines Corp.

VAX, Digital Equipment Corp.

VAXBI, Digital Equipment Corp.

VAXbus, Digital Equipment Corp.

Vectra, Hewlett-Packard Co.

Ventura Publisher, Ventura Software Inc.

Ventura DataBase Publisher, Ventura Software Inc.

Ventura Scan*, Ventura Software Inc.

Ventura Separator*, Ventura Software Inc.

Ventura AdPro*, Ventura Software Inc.

Ventura PicturePro*, Ventura Software Inc.

VGA, International Business Machines Corp.

Virtual Machine/Extended Architecture*, International Business Machines Corp.

Virtual Machine/Enterprise Systems Architecture*, International Business Machines Corp.

Visicalc, Personal Software Inc.

VM/ESA, International Business Machines Corp.

VM/XA*, International Business Machines Corp.

Voice/Phone Assistant*, International Business Machines Corp.

Voice Management Facility/2*, International Business Machines Corp.

VoiceType*, International Business Machines Corp.

Volkswriter Delux, Lifetree Software Inc.

VP Planner, Paperback Software.

VS, International Business Machines Corp.

VSE/ESA*, International Business Machines Corp.

VTAM, International Business Machines Corp.

WANGNET, Wang Inc.

Weitek, Weitek Corp.

Wheelwriter, International Business Machines Corp.

WIN-OS/2*, International Business Machines Corp.

Windows*, Microsoft Corp.

Windows/386*, Microsoft Corp.

WindowTool*, International Business Machines Corp.

WindSurfer*, International Business Machines Corp.

WordPerfect, WordPerfect Corp.

WordPerfect Works, WordPerfect Corp.

Word Processor, Innovative Software Inc.

WordStar 2000, WordStar International Inc.

Working Paper...Not Paper Work, International Business Machines Corp.

WorkPad*, International Business Machines Corp.

Workplace Shell*, International Business Machines Corp.

WorkStation One*, International Business Machines Corp.

Writers' Assistant, International Business Machines Corp.

Writing Assistant*, International Business Machines Corp.

Writing to Read, International Business Machines Corp.

Writing to Write, International Business Machines Corp.

Wyse, Wyse Technology

X25Net*, International Business Machines Corp.

XENIX, Microsoft Corp.

XGA, International Business Machines Corp.

xHLLAPI*, International Business Machines Corp.

Xstation Manager, International Business Machines Corp.

XT*, International Business Machines Corp.

XTree, Executive Systems Inc.

Zenith, Zenith Radio Corp.

Video Standards for IBM and IBM-Compatible Computers[1]

Standard	Horizontal Resolution	Vertical Resolution	Mode	Colors Displayed Simultaneously
CG	640	200	text	16
	160	200	graphics	16
	320	200	graphics	4
	640	200	graphics	2
EGA	640	350	text	16
	720	350	text	4
	640	350	graphics	16
	320	200	graphics	16
	640	200	graphics	16
	640	350	graphics	16
8514/A	1,024	768	graphics	256
HGA	720	348	graphics	1
MCGA	320	400	text	4
	640	200	text	2
	640	400	graphics	2
	320	200	graphics	256
MDA	720	350	text	1
SVGA	800	600	graphics	16
	1,024	768	graphics	256
VGA	720	400	text	4
	360	400	text	2
	640	480	graphics	2
	320	200	graphics	256
XGA	640	480	graphics	65,536
	1,024	768	graphics	256
	1,056	400	text	16

[1]From the book, *Que's Computer User's Dictionary*, Third Edition, by Bryan Pfaffenberger, Ph.D., Copyright (c) 1992 by Que Corporation. Published by Que, a division of Prentice Hall Computer Publishing. Used by permission of the publisher.

Resolutions of Common Video Adapters
for IBM Compatibles and Apple Macintosh

Resolution Adapter	(pixels x lines)
IBM PCs and compatibles:	
Monochrome Display Adapter (MDA)	720 x 350
Color Graphics Adapter (CGA)	640 x 200
Enhanced Graphics Adapter (EGA)	640 x 350
Professional Graphics Adapter (PGA)	640 x 480
MultiColor Graphics Array (MCGA)	640 x 480
Video Graphics Array (VGA) (in text mode)	720 x 400
Video Graphics Array (VGA) (in graphics mode)	640 x 480
Super VGA (extended VGA)	800 x 600
Super VGA (VGA Plus)	1,024 x 768

Apple Macintosh:	
Macintoshes with 9-inch screens	512 x 342
Macintoshes with 12- or 13-inch screens	640 x 480

Acknowledgments, Credits, References & Resources

NOTE: The individuals, publishers, companies, organizations, or institutions listed in this Reference are not responsible for any errors, inaccuracies, or omissions which may have occurred.

References Cited:

1993 Catalog of American National Standards Copyright (c) 1993 by American National Standards Institute. Published by the American National Standards Institute, New York, NY.

3M Corp.

Abbreviations Dictionary, Eighth Edition, by Ralph De Sola, Copyright (c) 1992 by CRC Press, Inc., Boca Raton, FL. Excerpts used by permission of the publisher.

Academic Press, Inc.

Acer Technologies Corp.

Adobe Systems, Inc.

Advanced Materials & Processes®. (Periodical). By ASM International®.

Advanced Micro Devices, Inc.

Advanstar Communications.

Allen-Bradley Corp.

AMACOM. (A division of American Management Association).

Amdahl Corp.

American Telephone and Telegraph Corp. (AT&T). Excerpts used by permission.

American Electronics Association (AEA).

American Federation of Information Processing Societies (AFIPS).

American Management Association.

American Management Systems, Inc.

American National Standards Institute (ANSI).

American Radio Relay League (ARRL).

American Records Management Association (ARMA).

American Society for Quality Control (ASQC).

American Society for Testing and Materials (ASTM).

American Society of Mechanical Engineers (ASME).

American Standards Institute (ASI).

American Training International, Inc. (ATI).

Ameritech Corp.

APCO Bulletin, Published by the Associated Public Safety Communications Officers, Inc., New Smyrna Beach, FL.

Apollo Computer.

Apple Computer, Inc.

Ashton-Tate.

ASM International.

ASM Materials Engineering Dictionary, edited by J.R. Davis. Copyright (c) 1992 by ASM International®, Materials Park, OH.

Associated Business Publications Co., Ltd.

Associated Public Safety Communications Officers, Inc. (APCO).

Association of Research Libraries (ARL).

AST Research, Inc.

AT&T Bell Laboratories

AT&T Network Systems

Autodesk, Inc.

Automation. (Periodical). By Penton Publishing Inc.

Basically Broadband, prepared for AT&T's Network Systems Group by AT&T Bell Laboratories. Copyright (c) 1991 by AT&T. (A pocket glossary of terms....).

Bell Atlantic.

Bell Communications Research (Bellcore).

Bell Laboratories, Inc.

Bell of Canada.

Bell Operating Companies (BOC).

Bell, Pacific.

Bell System (US).

Blackie & Sons. (UK).

Boeing Computer Services.

Borland International.

Bull HN Information Systems, Inc.

Burroughs Corp. Excerpts used by permission.

BYTE. (Periodical). By McGraw-Hill, Inc.

Bytel Corp.

CAD/CAM Dictionary, by Edward J. Preston, George W. Crawford and Mark E. Coticchia. Copyright (c) 1985 by Marcel Dekker, Inc., New York, NY.

CADAM, Inc.

Cahners Publishing Associates, L.P.

Cahners Publishing Co.

Cahners Technical Information Service (CTIS).

Cambridge University Press. (UK).

CAMSCO, Inc.

CCITT, Blue Book, Volume VIII, *V-Series and X-Series Recommendations.*

CCITT, Blue Book, Volume III, *I-Series Recommendations.*

Center for Advanced Studies in Telecommunications (CAST).

Central Point Software, Inc.

Chambers Science and Technology Dictionary, General Editor, Professor Peter M.B. Walker. Copyright (c) 1988 by W & R Chambers Ltd and Cambridge University Press, UK. First published (as Chambers's Technical Dictionary) 1940.

Clarity Software Corp.

CMP Publications, Inc.

CMS Research.

Companies and Their Brands, Eleventh Edition (1993), Edited by Susan L. Stetler. Copyright (c) 1992 by Gale Research, Inc., Detroit, MI.

Compaq Computer Corp.

Comprehensive Dictionary of Measurement and Control, Second Edition, editor, W.H. Cubberly. Copyright (c) 1991 by Instrument Society of America, Research Triangle Park, NC.

CompUSA, Inc.

Computer-Aided Engineering. (Periodical). By Penton Publishing Inc.

Computer and Business Equipment Manufacturers Association (CBEMA).

Computer Associates International, Inc.

Computer Design. (Periodical). By PennWell Publishing Co.

Computer Dictionary: The Comprehensive Standard For Business, School, Library, And Home, by Microsoft Press®. Copyright (c) 1991 by Microsoft Press®, a division of Microsoft Corporation, Redmond, WA. Excerpts reprinted with permission from Microsoft Press.

Computer Publishing Group.

Computer Security Reference Book, by Keith M. Jackson and Jan Hruska. Copyright (c) 1992 by CRC Press, Inc., Boca Raton, FL.

Computervision.

Concord Data Systems.

Connecticut Software Systems Corp.

ConnectPress, Ltd.

Control Data Corp.

Corvus Systems.

Cosmos, Inc.

Cray Computers.

Cray Research Corp.

CRC Handbook of Chemistry and Physics, 73rd Edition (1992-93), Editor, David R. Lide, Ph.D. Copyright (c) 1992 by CRC Press, Inc., Boca Raton, FL.

CRC Handbook of Software Engineering, by Udo W. Pooch. Copyright (c) 1992 by CRC Press, Inc., Boca Raton, FL.

CRC Press, Inc.

Dana, The Corp.

Dassault Systems.

Dataease International.

Data Enterprises.

DEC Professional. (Periodical). By Professional Press, Inc.

Defense Advanced Research Projects Administration (DARPA). U.S. Department of Defense.

Defense Mapping Agency (DMA). U.S. Department of Defense.

Defense Science Board (DSB). U.S. Department of Defense.

De Sola, Ralph. Author/compiler/editor of 18 books about such diverse topics as criminology, free-thought, geography, history, metrication, microfilming, music, and natural history. Mr. De Sola (deceased, 1908-1993)

is the author of *Abbreviations Dictionary*, 8th ed., which is published by CRC Press, Inc.

Dictionary of Computing, General Editor, Valerie Illingworth. Copyright (c) 1983 by Market House Books, Ltd. Published in the United States by Oxford University Press, New York, NY.

Dictionary of Computing, Eighth Edition, by IBM Corp. Copyright (c) 1987 by International Business Machines Corporation.

Dictionary Of Computing & Information Technology, Third Edition, by A.J. Meadows, M. Gordon, A. Singleton and M. Feeney. Copyright (c) 1987 by A.J. Meadows and Kogan Page Ltd. Published by Kogan Page Ltd (UK) and Nichols Publishing Company, New York, NY.

Digital Equipment Corp. (DEC). Excerpts used by permission.

Digital Research.

Digital Review. (Newspaper). By Cahners Publishing Associates, L.P.

Disney Studios.

Dun & Bradstreet.

E.I. DuPont de Nemours & Co., Inc.

Eastman Kodak Co.

EDN®. (Periodical). By Cahners Publishing Co., a division of Reed Publishing (USA).

EE®-Evaluation Engineering. (Periodical). By EE-Evaluation Engineering.

Electronic Data Systems Corp. (EDS).

Electronic Design. (Periodical). By Penton Publishing, Inc.

Electronic Industries Association of Japan (EIAJ).

Electronic Industries Association (EIA).

Electronic Packaging, Microelectronics, and Interconnection Dictionary, by Charles A. Harper and Martin B. Miller. Copyright (c) 1993 by McGraw-Hill, Inc., New York, NY.

Electronic Products. (Periodical). By Hearst Business Communications, Inc./UTP Division.

Electronics. (Periodical). By Penton Publishing, Inc.

Electronics Data Handbook, by William Barden. Copyright (c) 1986 by Radio Shack, a Tandy Corporation Company, Fort Worth, TX. Excerpts used by permission from Tandy Corporation.

Electronics Data Industry Association (EDIA).

Elsevier Communications. (A division of Gordon Publications, Inc.).

Eltra Corp.

Encyclopedia of Associations, Twenty-Seventh Edition (1993), Edited by Deborah M. Burek. Copyright (c) 1992 by Gale Research, Inc., Detroit, MI.

Encyclopedia Of Computer Science And Engi-

neering, Second Edition, Editor: Anthony Ralston, Associate Editor: Edwin D. Reilly, Jr. Copyright (c) 1983 by Van Nostrand Reinhold Company Inc., New York, NY.

Encyclopedia of Telecommunications, editor, Robert A. Meyers. Copyright (c) 1989 by Academic Press, Inc., San Diego, CA. (This work is a derivative from the *Encyclopedia of Physical Science and Technology*, edited by Robert A. Meyers, copyright (c) 1987 by Academic Press, Inc.).

Environmental Protection Agency (EPA). (US).

Epson America, Inc.

European Computer Manufacturers Association (ECMA).

European Space Agency (ESA).

Executive Systems, Inc.

FCC Rules, published by the American Radio Relay League (ARRL).

Federal Aviation Administration (FAA). (US).

Federal Communications Commission (FCC). (US).

Fifth Generation Systems.

Fox & Geller.

Fujitsu Microelectronics, Inc.

Funk Software.

Gale Research, Inc.

General Electric Co.

General Services Administration (GSA). (US).

General Telephone and Electronics (GTE).

Global Engineering Documents.

Goldata Computer Services, Inc.

Gordon Publications, Inc.

Government Management Information Services (GMIS).

Government Printing Office (GPO). (US).

Haventree Software Ltd.

Hayes Microcomputer Products.

Hearst Business Communications, Inc./ UTP Division.

Helmers Publishing, Inc.

Hercules Computer Technology.

Hewlett-Packard Co. (H-P). Excerpts used by permission.

Hitachi Electronics.

Hitchcock Publishing Co.

Honeywell Data Systems.

Horizon Software.

HP Professional. (Periodical). By Professional Press, Inc.

IBM, Partial listing of U.S. trademarks owned by. (Document). Courtesy of, International Business Machines Corporation's Intellectual Property Law Department (IPLD) at Purchase, NY. Excerpts used by permission.

IEEE Standard Dictionary of Electrical and Electronics Terms, Third Edition (1984), Editor-in-Chief, Frank Jay. The Institute of Electrical and Electronic Engineers, with Wiley-Interscience, New York, NY.

Illustrated Encyclopedic Dictionary of Electronics, by John Douglas-Young. Copyright (c) 1981 by Parker Publishing Co, Inc., West Nyack, NY.

Industrial Computing. (Periodical). By ISA Services, Inc.

Industrial Engineering and Management Press. (Institute of Industrial Engineers).

Industrial Engineering Terminology, Revised Edition, by Industrial Engineering and Management Press, Institute of Industrial Engineers, Norcross, GA. Copyright (c) 1991 by Industrial Engineering and Management Press. Published by McGraw-Hill, Inc. (New York, NY) and the Institute of Industrial Engineers.

Industrial Finishing®. (Periodical). A Hitchcock Publication. Hitchcock Publishing Co., a Capitol Cities/ABC Inc, Company.

Industry Week. (Periodical). By Penton Publishing Inc.

Information Builders, Inc.

InfoWorld. (Newspaper). By InfoWorld Publishing, Inc.

Innovative Software, Inc.

Institute of Electrical and Electronics Engineers (IEEE).

Institute of Industrial Engineers (IIE).

Instrument Society of America (ISA).

Intel Corp. Excerpts used by permission.

International Business Machines Corp. (IBM). Excerpts used by permission.

International Communications Association (ICA).

International Electrotechnical Commission (IEC).

International Federation for Information Processing (IFIP).

International Radio Consultative Committee (CCIR).

International Telecommunications Union (ITU).

International Telecommunications Satellite Corp. (INTELSAT).

International, The Telegraph and Telephone Consultative Committee (CCITT)—part of ITU.

Internet. (National Science Foundation).

Iomega Corp.

ISA Services, Inc.

ISDN TALK, prepared for AT&T's Network Systems Group by AT&T Bell Laboratories. Copyright (c) 1988 by Bell Telephone Laboratories, Inc. (A pocket glossary of terms...).

Kabushiki Kaisha Toshiba.

Kogan Page Limited. (UK).

Koren, Johan. Lecturer, Wayne State University, Detroit, MI.

Langley Research Center. (US Department of Defense).

Laser Focus World. (Periodical). A PennWell Publication.

Lewis Publishers, Inc.

Lifetree Software, Inc.

Logitech, Inc.

Los Alamos National Laboratory (LANL). (US Department of Defense).

LOTUS. (Periodical). By Lotus Publishing Corp., a subsidiary of the Lotus Development Corp.

Lotus Development Corp.

Lotus Publishing Corp.

Machine Design. (Periodical). By Penton Publishing Inc.

Madison Heights Public Library. (Madison Hts, MI).

Manufacturing Engineering®. (Periodical). By the Society of Manufacturing Engineers. The official publication of the SME.

Manufacturing Systems. (Periodical). By Hitchcock Publishing Co.

Marcel Dekker, Inc.

Market House Books, Ltd. (UK).

Massachusetts General Hospital.

Massachusetts Institute of Technology (MIT).

Material Handling Engineering. (Periodical). By Penton Publishing Inc.

Materials Engineering. (Periodical). By Penton Publishing Inc.

McDonnell-Douglas Corp.

McGraw-Hill, Inc.

Mechanical Engineering. (Periodical). By the American Society of Mechanical Engineers. The official publication of the ASME.

Memorex Corp.

Memorex Telex.

Micro Data Base Systems, Inc.

Microsoft Corp. Excerpts used by permission.

Microsoft Press. A division of Microsoft Corp. Excerpts used by permission.

Microsoft® MS-DOS® User's Guide and Reference: for the MS-DOS® Operating System Version 5.0, by Microsoft Corporation. Copyright (c) 1991 by Microsoft Corporation, Redmond, WA. Excerpts reprinted with permission from Microsoft Corporation.

MicroStation Manager. (Periodical). By ConnectPress, Ltd.

Microstuf, Inc.

Mitsubishi America.

Modern Dictionary of Electronics, Sixth Edition, by Rudolf F. Graf. Copyright (c) 1984 by Rudolf F. Graf. Formerly published by Howard W. Sams & Co., Inc., now published by Sams, a division of Prentice Hall Computer Publishing, New York, NY.

Modern Materials Handling®. (Periodical). A Cahners Publication. Cahners Publishing Co., a division of Reed Publishing (USA) Inc.

Modern Office Technology. (Periodical). By Penton Publishing Inc.

Motion Control. (Periodical). By Advanstar Communications.

Motorola Inc.

MS-DOS® 6 Quick Reference, by Que Development. Copyright (c) 1993. Published by Que, a division of Prentice Hall Computer Publishing, New York, NY. Excerpts used by permission of the publisher.

Multimate International Corp.

NASA Tech Briefs. (Periodical). By Associated Business Publications Co., Ltd. The official publication of the National Aeronautics and Space Administration.

National Aeronautics and Space Administration (NASA). (US).

National Cash Register Corp. (NCR).

National Computer Graphics Association (NCGA).

National Fire Protection Association (NFPA).

National Information Standards Organization (NISO).

National Research Institute (NRI). (US)

National Science Foundation (NSF). (US).

National Semiconductor Inc.

National Software Testing Laboratory (NSTL). (US).

National Telecommunications and Information Agency (NTIA).

NEC Home Technologies, Inc.

NEC Technologies, Inc.

Netherlands Central Organization for Applied Scientific Research.

Network Systems.

NFPA Journal. (Periodical). By the National Fire Protection Association. The official magazine of the NFPA.

Nichols Publishing Company.

Nippon Electronics Corp. (NEC).

Nippon Telephone and Telegraph (NTT). (Japan).

North American Telecommunications Association (NATA).

Novell, Inc.

Nuclear Regulatory Commission (NRC).

Oak Ridge National Laboratory (ORNL). (US).

Occupational Safety and Health Administration (OSHA). (US).

Office2.

Office Solutions, Inc.

Open Systems Today. (Newspaper). By CMP Publications, Inc.

Optical Fibre Lasers and Amplifiers, by Paul William France, Ph.D. Copyright (c) 1991 by CRC Press, Inc., Boca Raton, FL.

Oxford University Press.

Paperback Software.

Paul Mace Software.

PC/Computing. (Periodical). By Ziff-Davis Publishing Co.

PC-Kwik Corp.

PC Magazine®. (Periodical). By Ziff-Davis Publishing Co., a division of Ziff Communications Co.

PennWell Publishing Co.

Penton Publishing, Inc.

Personal Software, Inc.

Peter Norton Computing.

Pfaffenberger, Bryan, Ph.D. Author of several books on personal computer applications (one of which is *Que's Computer User's Dictionary*, 3rd ed.). Associate Professor in the School of Engineering and Applied Science, University of Virginia.

Philips International B.V.

Plant Engineering®. (Periodical). A Cahners Publication. Cahners Publishing Co., a division of Reed Publishing (USA) Inc.

Polaroid Corp.

Power Transmission Design. (Periodical). By Penton Publishing Inc.

Prentice Hall.

Prentice Hall Computer Publishing.

Prentice Hall Press.

Prime Computer, Inc.

Pritsker & Associates.

Professional Press, Inc.

Purde Library. (Wayne State University, Detroit, MI).

Que's Computer User's Dictionary, Third Edition, by Que Development. Copyright (c) 1992. Published by Que, a division of Prentice Hall Computer Publishing, New York, NY. The author of the book is Bryan Pfaffenberger, Ph.D.

Que Corp. (A division of Prentice Hall Computer Publishing).

Radio Corp. of America (RCA).

Radio Shack. A division of Tandy Corp.

Rand Corp.

Reed Publishing. (USA).

Reference Software International. (A division of WordPerfect Corp).

Reverse Acronyms, Initialisms & Abbreviations Dictionary, Seventeenth Edition (1993), edited by Jennifer Mossman. Copyright (c) 1992 by Gale Research Inc. Detroit, MI. Excerpts reprinted by permission of the publisher.

Robotics Industries Association (RIA).

RoseSoft.

Royal Oak Public Library. (Royal Oak, MI).

Samna Corp.

Sams. (A division of Prentice Hall Computer Publishing).

Scientific and Technical Organizations and Agencies Directory, Second Edition, Edited by Margaret L. Young. Copyright (c) 1987 by Gale Research, Inc., Detroit, MI.

Scientific Computing & Automation®. (Periodical). By Elsevier Communications, a division of Gordon Publications, Inc.

SDA Associates.

Seagate Technology.

Semiconductor Industry Association (SIA).

Sensors™. (Periodical). By Helmers Publishing Inc.

Sharp Electronics Corp.

Shuman, Bruce A. Author of several books. Associate Professor Library Science Program, Wayne State University, Detroit, MI.

Siemens Corp.

Simon & Schuster, Inc.

Society for Computer Simulation (SCS).

Society of Automotive Engineers (SAE).

Society of Manufacturing Engineers (SME).

Software Integration, Inc.

Software Publishing Corp.

Sony Corp.

Source, The Information Network.

Sperry Computer.

Strategic Air Command (SAC). (US Air Force).

SunExpert Magazine. (Periodical). By Computer Publishing Group.

Super Book (summer 93), Retail store products & pricing catalog. Copyright (c) 1993 by CompUSA, Inc., Dallas, TX.

SYBEX, Inc.

SyQuest Technology.

Systems Integration®. (Periodical). A Cahners Publication. By Cahners Publishing Associates, L.P.

Systems Modeling Corp.

TAB BOOKS. (A division of McGraw-Hill, Inc.).

Tandem Computers, Inc.

Tandy Corp.

TDK Corp.

Tektronix, Inc.

Telecommunications and Networking, by Udo W. Pooch, Denis Machuel and John Mccann. Copyright (c) 1991 by CRC Press, Inc., Boca Raton, FL.

Telecommunications Association Council (TAC).

Telecommunications Directory, Fifth Edition (1992-93), Edited by John Krol. Copyright (c) 1991 by Gale Research, Inc., Detroit, MI. (Formerly, *Telecommunications Systems and Services Directory*).

Telecommunications Managers Association (TMA).

Teletype Corp.

Teletypewriter Exchange Service.

Tesco, Inc.

Texas Instruments, Inc. (TI).

The Computer Glossary: The Complete Illustrated Desk Reference, Fifth Edition, by Allan Freedman. Copyright (c) 1991. The Computer Language Company Inc. Published by AMACOM, a division of the American Management Association, New York, NY. Excerpts reprinted with permission of the publisher.

The Computer Language Company, Inc.

The Illustrated Dictionary of Electronics, Fifth Edition, by Rufus P. Turner and Stan Gibilisco. Copyright (c) 1991 by McGraw-Hill, Inc., New York, NY.

The Illustrated Dictionary Of Microcomputers, Third Edition, by Michael F. Hordeski. Copyright (c) 1990 by TAB BOOKS, a division of McGraw-Hill, Inc., Blue Ridge Summit, PA.

The Networking and Communications Desk Reference, by Ken Sochats and Jim Williams. Copyright (c) 1992 by Sams. Sams, a division of Prentice Hall Computer Publishing, New York, NY.

Toshiba Electronics.

Trade Shows Worldwide, Seventh Edition (1993), Edited by Valerie J. Webster. Copyright (c) 1992 by Gale Research, Inc., Detroit, MI. (Formerly, *Trade Shows and Professional Exhibits Directory*).

Tulip Computers International B.V.

Turner Hall Publishing.

U.S. Art, Inc.

U.S. Defense Logistics Agency.

Underwriter's Laboratories, Inc.

Ungerman-Bass.

United Computing Corp.

United Parcel Service, Inc. (UPS).

United States Air Force (USAF).

United States Army.

United States Coast Guard (USCG).

United States Department of Commerce.

United States Department of Defense (DoD, or DOD).

United States Department of Energy (DoE, or DOE).

United States Marine Corps (USMC).

United States Navy.

United States Postal Service (USPS).

University of Waterloo. (Canada).

UNIX Today!. (Newspaper). By CMP Publications, Inc.

Using MS-DOS® 6, by Que Development. Copyright (c) 1993. Published by Que, a division of Prentice Hall Computer Publishing, New York, NY. Excerpts used by permission of the publisher.

US Sprint.

Van Nostrand Reinhold.

Ventura Software, Inc.

Video Electronics Standards Association (VESA).

W & R Chambers Ltd. (UK).

Wang Data Systems, Inc.

Wang, Inc.

Wayne State University (WSU). (Detroit, MI).

Webster's New World Dictionary of Media and Communications, by Richard Weiner. Copyright (c) 1990 by Richard Weiner. Published by Simon & Schuster, Inc., New York, NY.

Weitek Corp.

Western Union Corp. (WU).

Westinghouse Electric Corp.

WordPerfect Corp. (WP).

WordStar International.

World Guide to Abbreviations of Organizations, Ninth Edition (1991), Edited by F.A. Buttress and Henry J. Heaney. Published by Blackie & Sons (UK), distributed in the Americas exclusively by Gale Research, Inc., Detroit, MI.

Wyse Technology.

Xerox Corp.

Zenith Radio Corp.

Ziff-Davis Publishing Co.

Ziff Communications Co.

Zilog, Inc.

Key to Source Codes

For the user's convenience, a "key" to commonly used abbreviations—abbreviations used within the definitions, and used within the parenthetical explanatory notations (source code abbreviations) has been supplied.

Common Source-Code Abbreviations

ACM: Association for Computing Machinery.

AFIPS: American Federation of Information Processing Societies.

ANSI: American National Standards Institute.

ARRL: American Radio Relay League.

AT&T: American Telephone and Telegraph Corp.

BOC: Bell Operating Companies.

CCITT: Consultative Committee on Telephony and Telegraphy.

DARPA: Defense Advanced Research Projects Administration (US Depart-

ment of Defense).
DEC: Digital Equipment Corp.
DOD: United States Department of Defense.
DOE: United States Department of Energy.
EC: European Community.
EDS: Electronic Data Systems Corp.
EIA: Electronics Industries Association.
EPA: Environmental Protection Agency (US).
ESA: European Space Agency.
FAA: Federal Aviation Administration (US).
FCC: Federal Communications Commission (US).
GE: General Electric Co.
GPO: Government Printing Office (US).
GSA: General Services Adminstration (US).
H-P: Hewlett-Packard Co.
IBM: International Business Machines Corp.
IEC: International Electrotechnical Commission.
IEEE: Institute of Electrical and Electronics Engineers.
ISO: International Organization for Standardization.
LANL: Los Alamos National Laboratory (US Department of Defense).
MCI: Microwave Communications Inc.
MIT: Massachusetts Institute of Technology.
NASA: National Aeronautics and Space Administration (US).
NCR: National Cash Register Corp.
NEC: Nippon Electronics Corp. (NEC America).
NIST: National Institute of Standards and Technology.
NSF: National Science Foundation.
ORNL: Oak Ridge National Laboratory.
RCA: Radio Corp. of America.
SI: International System of Units.
TI: Texas Instruments Inc.
UK: United Kingdom.
UPS: United Parcel Service Inc.
US: United States (of America).
USAF: United States Air Force.
USCG: United States Coast Guard.

USMC: United States Marine Corps.
USPS: United States Postal Service.

Common Abbreviations Within Definitions

AC: Alternating Current.
ADA: ADA (Not an acronym).
AND: [circuit or logic gate].
ARPANET: Advanced Research Projects Agency Network.
ASCII: American Standard Code for Information Interchange.
ATE: Automatic Test Equipment.
ATLAS: Automatic Tabulating, Listing and Sorting System.
ATM: Asynchronous Transfer Mode.
AUSINET: Australian Information Network.
Byte: *Byte Magazine* (A McGraw-Hill, Inc. publication).
CAD: Computer-Aided Design.
CAIS: Canadian Association for Information Science.
CEC: Commission of the European Communities.
CERT: Computer Emergency Response Team.
CICS: Customer Information Control System.
CMIP: Common Management Information Protocol.
CMOS: Complementary Metal-Oxide Semiconductor.
COBOL: Common Business-Oriented Language.
CRT: Cathode Ray Tube.
CUG: Closed User Group.
DARPA: Defense Advanced Research Projects Administration.
DASD: Direct Access Storage Device.
DBMS: Data Base Management System.
DC: Direct Current.
DOS: Disk Operating System.
DPPX: Distributed Processing Program Executive.
DSA: Direct Storage Architecture.
ECL: Emitter-Coupled Logic.
EDI: Electronic Data Interchange.
EP: Emulation Program.
EPROM: Eraseable Programmable Read-

Only Memory.

FAA: Federal Aviation Administration (US).

FAX: Facsimile.

FDDI: Fiber Distributed Data Interface.

FET: Field-Effect Transistor.

FIFO: First In, First Out.

FORTRAN: Formula Translator.

I/O: Input/Output.

IBM: International Business Machines Corp.

ILAN: Integrated Local Area Network.

INTELSAT: International Telecommunications Satellite.

ISDN: Integrated Services Digital Network.

LAN: Local Area Network.

Laser: Light Amplification by Stimulation of Emitted Radiation.

LISP: List Processor.

Modem: Modulator Demodulator.

MUMPS: Massachusetts General Hospital Utility Multi-Programming
NASA: National Aeronautics and Space Administration (US).

NCP: Network Control Program.

NOT: [circuit or logic gate].

OR: [circuit or logic gate].

OS/2: Operating System 2.

OSI: Open Systems Interconnection.

PABX: Private Automatic Branch Exchange.

PAD: Packet Assembler/Disassembler.

PBX: Private Branch Exchange.

PC: Personal Computer.

PCs: Personal Computers.

R/W: Read/Write.

Radar: Radio Detection and Ranging.

RAM: Random Access Memory.

RISC: Reduced Instruction Set Computer.

RSCS: Remote Spooling Communications Subsystem.

SCSI: Small Computer Systems Interface.

SGML: Standard Generalized Markup Language.

SMDS: Switched Multi-Megabit Data Service.

SNA: Systems Network Architecture.

TCP/IP: Transmission Control Protocol/ Internet Protocol.

TCP: Transmission Control Protocol.

TTL: Transistor-Transistor Logic.

VAX: Virtual Address Extension.

VHSIC: Very High-Speed Integrated Circuit.

VME: Virtual Memory Extended.

VMS: Virtual Memory System.

VSAM: Virtual Sequential Access Method.

VTAM: Virtual Telecommunications Access Method.

WAN: Wide Area Network.

YIG: Yttrium-Iron-Garnet.